The
Readers' Advisory
Guide *to* Genre Fiction

ALA READERS' ADVISORY SERIES

The Romance Readers' Advisory:
The Librarian's Guide to Love in the Stacks

The Short Story Readers' Advisory:
A Guide to the Best

THE Readers' Advisory Guide TO Genre Fiction

Joyce G. Saricks

AMERICAN LIBRARY
ASSOCIATION
Chicago and London
2001

For Chris, Always

Cover and text design: Dianne M. Rooney; project editor: Eloise L. Kinney; indexer: Janet Russell

Composition by the dotted i in Berkeley and Novarese using QuarkXpress 4.1 on a Macintosh platform

Printed on 50-pound white offset, a pH-neutral stock, and bound in 10-point coated cover stock by Batson Printing

The paper used in this publication meets the minimum requirements of American National Standard for Information Sciences—Permanence of Paper for Printed Library Materials, ANSI Z39.48-1992. ∞

Library of Congress Cataloging-in-Publication Data

Saricks, Joyce G.
    The readers' advisory guide to genre fiction / Joyce G. Saricks.
        p.   cm. — (ALA readers' advisory series)
    Includes bibliographical references and index.
    ISBN 0-8389-0803-9
        1. Fiction in libraries—United States. 2. Readers' advisory services—United States. 3. Reading interests—United States. 4. Fiction genres.
    5. Fiction—Bibliography. I. Title. II. Series.
    Z711.5.S27 2001
    025.5′4—dc21   2001022750

Printed in the United States of America.

05 04   03   5 4 3 2

Contents

Figures List

FIGURES LIST

x

FIGURES LIST

Acknowledgments

Anyone who has ever been involved in a genre study knows it is never finished. Each new book adds insight, another layer, to our understanding of the whole—or opens a new avenue to explore. So it is with this book. Each rereading inspires (and requires) emendations. The deadline has come, however, and the manuscript must be off.

Writing this has been a pleasure, almost an addiction. Never have I, a morning person, burned so much midnight oil, happily chained to my computer. But writing can be a very selfish activity, and both at home and at work, others have filled in for my absences. My deep-felt thanks go to the Downers Grove Public Library and particularly to the excellent staff in my department. They have tolerated my erratic schedule for eighteen months and have supported me mentally, physically, and emotionally. At home I would not have managed without the full support of my husband, Chris, and two teenagers, Bren and Meg, who suffered through late meals (or prepared them themselves), unwashed laundry, and stacks of papers and books, not to mention my frequent lack of attention to matters that deserved more. My heartfelt thanks also to Eloise L. Kinney for shepherding me through the publishing process. She was always available for every question.

Once again I have been fortunate in finding readers willing to devote time and energy to reading—and in some cases rereading—drafts of all the genre chapters and offering their suggestions. I am especially grateful to Sue O'Brien and Lora Bruggeman, fellow Readers' Advisory Librarians at the Downers Grove Public Library, who have spent more hours than I care to consider reading multiple drafts of each chapter and talking with me about genres and authors. Sheila Guenzer, Lynn McCullagh, Marianne Trautvetter, Terri Williams, and Carol Yarmolich, all Readers' Advisors in my department, read faithfully, offered suggestions, and, along with Lora and Sue, supported me as good friends do. Without the genre studies carried out by the Downers Grove Public Library staff and members of the Adult Reading Round Table, I would have lacked much of my background reading and basic understanding of these genres. I am fortunate to be surrounded by such stimulating colleagues. I am fortunate, too, to have administrators who are genre readers. Both Downers Grove Public Library Director Christopher Bowen and Assistant Director Jamie Bukovac read and reacted to drafts of many chapters. My husband, Chris, read and reacted to all chapters, offering astute comments from the point of view of a thoughtful fan of much genre fiction. Marty Charles, my aunt and friend, not only read and commented on all chapters, she researched and typed all the footnote information. I am in her debt. My thanks to other faithful readers: Linda Barnes, Janet Bowen, Rebecca Townsend, Vicky Trupiano, Debbie Walsh, and Deborah Wordinger. Although he also read and reacted to chapters, my profound thanks go to Duncan Smith more for his continuous support and encouragement and for reminding me of the value of *story* in our lives.

1

How to Use This Book

Caveat Lector

Let the reader beware: This is not a book written by a genre specialist but by a generalist, albeit one who enjoys genre fiction, reads widely, and has worked for almost twenty years with genre readers and librarians. This is not intended as a definitive study but as a guide, created to help others who find themselves as I did, at a loss helping readers at my library. This book has been developed to help librarians work with fans of genres, especially those we do not personally read by choice. It is designed to be a springboard for further study—and certainly a training tool.

When we first created a separate Readers' Advisory Department at the Downers Grove Public Library in 1983, we knew we had to learn about popular fiction—quickly. We developed a list of authors, grouped by genres, and used that to familiarize ourselves with the authors and genres our readers already knew and loved. As we read and talked with readers, we learned that there were factors that influenced their choices of one author over another, especially when they were trying to find similar authors, *read-alikes,* ones who wrote "just like" the author they loved. We talked with these readers, and we listened to both the way they described books and their responses to vocabulary we developed to try to help them. We learned early on that the subject of the book was not the most important factor. Readers were not looking for any book with spies; they wanted one that moved with the same fast pacing that Robert Ludlum employs. Or one that delved into motivations and psyches as John le Carré's books do. And, most importantly, they were pleased to find someone to talk with about what they enjoyed, especially because this someone might be able to find them more authors that would satisfy them.

As we progressed, we realized that although the genres differed widely, the way we learned about them did not. When we thought about what we knew about genres in which we did read, how we worked with readers, and how we approached helping them further, we saw that we could use the same techniques with genres in which we were less familiar. We also recognized what we call *appeal elements*. Pacing, characterizations, story line, and frame (physical setting and atmosphere) played important roles in what readers enjoyed about one book over another and helped us recognize others we might suggest. We explored these appeal elements in more depth as we started doing genre studies.

Every book we read and every conversation we had seemed (and, frankly, still does seem) to raise more questions than it answered. What is the audience for a book like Andrea Barrett's *The Voyage of the Narwhal*?[1] Is it only for Historical Fiction readers who might appreciate the details of life and explorations in the 1850s? Would a fan of Literary Fiction also appreciate the layered story with its provocative look at voyages of discovery on physical, emotional, and intellectual levels? What about the Adventure fan? How might I describe the book differently to each reader to let her know that there are elements in this book that might appeal to her?

What about an author like Guy Gavriel Kay? He writes Fantasy, but is there any crossover with the Historical Fiction genre? To answer that question one could either read all of Kay's books or look at reviews and talk with fans. (The answer, by the way, is that some of his later titles, perhaps *The Lions of Al-Rassan*, set in Moorish Spain, or *A Song for Arbonne*, which is set in medieval Provence, might very well work, as they combine a good deal of Historical detail with Fantasy.)[2]

Many of the questions we encountered were—and still are—simply unanswerable. But we talked with readers and among ourselves; we practiced describing books and listened when others talked about books they had enjoyed; and we learned what works—and what does not. Some books seem to sell themselves. Other, equally wonderful books are almost impossible to describe in a way that makes them sound inviting.

Learning to suggest, rather than to recommend, was another major breakthrough. *Recommend* is a word fraught with unintended meaning and emotion. Recommending places us in the role of expert: Take this book; it is good for you. *Suggesting,* on the other hand, makes us partners with readers in exploring the various directions they might want to pursue. Simply altering our vocabulary took some of the pressure off us—and readers—as we shared books.

We learned early on that we could never read enough or remember enough of what we did read. We needed a framework to help us remember. The appeal elements seemed to do that—magically. Thinking about books in terms of their appeal, rather than their subject or the plot, meant that we remembered more. And what we remembered was what we needed to present the book to readers. In the readers' advisory interview, it is appeal—comments about pacing or frame—that readers respond to, not just plot summaries.

It is from this background and experience working with readers that this book evolved. Each separate genre chapter is based on strategies to use to expand our knowledge of the genre and to work with readers, even if we know very little about that particular genre. Everything in this book builds on the premise that to learn about fiction and to satisfy readers we need to be open to a range of possibilities. Most readers appreciate the conversation, the process, more than a quick answer. The readers' advisory interview is a conversation about books. We are not expected to know all the answers. Readers want us to listen and help them explore.

Ever since I first envisioned this book, I have had qualms about writing it, because putting this information down on paper makes the process of helping readers find books so cut and dried. We all know that there is tremendous overlap—*genreblending*—among genres and that it is almost impossible to make firm distinctions between the characteristics of one genre versus another, much less to say with any authority that one writer writes in this genre, not in another. Or that readers of one genre will only like—or never like—another. Even more crucial is the fact that readers may read a book in one way and we in another. (Does Mary Higgins Clark write Mystery or Suspense? Does it matter? It does not matter what we call a genre or a writer's work, but in terms of finding books with similar elements, it makes a difference which mental or physical database we draw on.) The goal of this book is to provide a framework for understanding genre fiction, so we can readily see how to go beyond genre borders.

This book is meant to be provocative. You will disagree with some of my statements and certainly with the choice of some of the authors I have included. Genres are not static; writers are not confined to certain genres or types of books; readers take from books what strikes them, whether it goes counter to common knowledge of a book and expert opinion or not. Again, this book is not meant to be definitive but rather suggestive of possibilities. Your questions, and the answers you discover through your own explorations, will lead you to a deeper understanding of authors, genres, and why readers enjoy them.

Enjoyment is certainly key to using this book and working with readers. That infectious pleasure in discovering interesting books and sharing them with readers is one of the deepest satisfactions of readers' advisory work. My goal with this book is that it might provide enough background in a genre to give a glimpse of what it is about those authors and their books that fans love. Once we understand the pleasure fans take in the books they enjoy, we can relate better to them and share that pleasure. I hope the book encourages every reader to set up a reading plan with some of the titles included. Reading books known to be popular with readers and representative of the genre should provide a basis for understanding and appreciating both authors and genres.

What This Book Is Not

This book is not a comprehensive study of any genre. The expectation is that it provides enough of a sample to indicate the nature of the genre and why fans love it. Examples are meant to be just that: titles in the genre that give an indication of what the genre is like and why fans enjoy the books.

HOW TO USE THIS BOOK

This book is not meant to be prescriptive. My goal has been to create a framework that makes understanding the appeal of genre fiction easier. My experience in providing readers' advisory and training staff indicates that it is important to have such a framework so that we can see how to go beyond it. When we discover an author or hear a patron describe a title or author, we can use the mental framework to see how that author or book might fit in a genre or to see that it does not fit exactly, that it has elements of this genre and that, and that it might appeal to this kind of reader or that one.

One false impression that this kind of book might give is that all authors can be classified, or slotted, within a specific genre. This is not a genre classification guide. It is important to guard against the temptation of overclassifying when we think in terms of genres. Not every author fits into a genre slot, not every book by an author fits in the same genre, and not all readers see an author (or a genre) in the same way. Rather than to create boxes to trap and contain authors so that we can understand them and the way they write, the intent of this book is to break down the walls of classification so we can see beyond genre confines to the way readers really read and writers write.

What This Book Covers

This book is an introduction to fiction genres, but what is a genre? In *Readers' Advisory Service in the Public Library,* we defined *genre* as "any sizable group of fiction authors and/or specific titles that have similar characteristics and appeal; these are books written to a particular, specific pattern."[3] Genres, then, are not limited to the traditional Mysteries, Romances, and so forth, but the idea can be expanded to include any larger group of patterned fiction that shares characteristics and appeal elements.

The following genres are examined in individual chapters: Adventure, Fantasy, Gentle Reads, Historical Fiction, Horror, Literary Fiction, Mysteries, Psychological Suspense, Romance, Romantic Suspense, Science Fiction, Suspense, Thrillers, Westerns, and Women's Lives and Relationships. The omission of two popular "genres" may raise some questions. Although Multi-Cultural and Inspirational authors are mentioned in the chapters, these are not considered on their own. By my definition they are not individual genres; rather, the books understood to constitute each really cut across genres. For example, among Multi-Cultural authors there are writers who fall into all the genres included. That they are African American or Hispanic does not mean that they write a unique type of book. Their Mysteries are far more similar to other Mysteries than they are to Romances or Science Fiction by other Multi-Cultural authors. It is not possible to group their writing and identify characteristics shared by Multi-Cultural authors; their writing does not constitute an individual, separate genre. In the same way, Inspirational authors write across genres. That their stories contain religious elements is not enough to declare them a separate genre. Again, Inspirational Romances are part of the Romance genre, and their only link with Inspirational Mysteries is that they both share a religious flavor.

In the tradition of the genre it explores, each chapter follows the same pattern, discussing each topic described below.

1. *Definition of the Genre* Although these working definitions may be familiar, they are based on how readers perceive the genre: what they expect to find in these books, how they would define it if there were asked. In some cases, there is discussion of what this genre is not—how it differs from related genres.

2. *Characteristics and Appeal* Anyone familiar with my previous book, *Readers' Advisory Service in the Public Library,* will not be surprised to see that these characteristics are based on four elements of appeal found in books: Pacing, Characterization, Story Line, and Frame.[4] The appeal of genres seems to fall out naturally in these four basic categories. Each chapter lists the characteristics of the genre, based on these appeal elements, followed by a descriptive narrative with examples.

One aspect of appeal is not considered separately in every chapter but should be mentioned overall. In all genres there is a range of writing style—from the elegant and poetic writing of some authors to the more pedestrian prose of others. Interestingly, fans of both types of authors praise their work as well written. Many readers see this as the highest form of praise, and any books they enjoy or that have touched them receive this encomium. As a result, I try not to use that phrase to describe any book. My standards for well written may differ widely from yours—and from those of the reader before me. Better to find other words to describe authors whom we feel meet a certain literary standard, as our precision helps other readers decide whether or not they might enjoy the author's style.

3. *Benchmark or Key Authors and Subgenres*   What is a benchmark and does every genre have one? The *benchmark author* is a writer whose work is representative of the genre as a whole. She or he is prolific, currently writing, popular with readers, and typical of the genre. This is the author readers think of if they mention a genre by name. Because of the range of the genres, it is sometimes not possible to identify an author who represents the entire genre in this way. It is often easier to identify benchmark authors for the subgenres, smaller universes, than the genre as a whole. Because of this difficulty, I have often given a number of key authors, rather than identifying a single benchmark.

In many of the fifteen genres described, I have identified appeal-based subgenres, along with characteristics and key authors or benchmarks. Not all genres are diverse enough to warrant the isolation of subgenres, and in these, I have included more key authors to give an idea of the range of the genre.

4. *Preparing to Work with Readers*   This section covers those behind-the-scenes activities that prepare us to work better with readers when we face them at the service desk or in the stacks. I discuss what we know about fans of each genre and what they expect to be given when they ask for a particular genre. There are also strategies, readers' advisory tips, specific to the genre discussed but also often universal, ideas that can be applied across the board in understanding genres and working with readers.

Part of this behind-the-scenes work is gaining familiarity with genres. One of the greatest obstacles to our reading a wide range of genres is the fear that there is nothing in the unfamiliar genre that we will enjoy. To help counteract that, in each genre chapter I have provided a list of authors who write in that genre, but these authors are linked to other genres with which they share appeal elements. The pattern of this list is the same in every chapter; only the name of the genre, and of course the suggested authors, changes. For example,

Adventure fans might be more willing to sample a Science Fiction novel if they knew it also included a large dose of the Adventure elements they enjoy. Thus, in the Adventure category of this list in the Science Fiction chapter, I have suggested Science Fiction authors for fans of Adventure to try. Although the list is designed for librarians to expand their reading interests and familiarity with genres they do not regularly read, it can also be used to tempt fans of one genre to experiment with another.

5. *The Readers' Advisory Interview*   When we ask them to describe books they enjoy, what do readers say they like about an author or genre? And how do we get from that response to book suggestions? These questions are explored in this section of each chapter. I also provide suggestions of how to talk about the genre and genre titles, even those we have not read, because, obviously, we will never read everything that might appeal to readers or that they might ask us about.

As I mentioned earlier in this chapter, there is an extraordinary amount of crossover, of genreblending. Although a book may be called a Mystery, it may also feature Suspense, Adventure, Intrigue, or Romance. Readers understand this subconsciously when they read. We need to learn to look for these crossover elements, so we can suggest a wider range of books readers might enjoy—or be more open to how they have read a book, what elements they respond to. The reader of that blended Mystery might also enjoy titles in the related genres. What do we look for? How do we keep track of these suggestions?

Sure Bets are those titles that appeal consistently to a wide range of readers, from fans of the particular genre to others beyond. As we explore each genre, we need to identify and collect Sure Bets that cover a range of appeal and have been successfully suggested to a variety of readers. Not only are they valuable because mentioning them allows us to let fans know that we have read something in the genre and that we understand its appeal, but also a list of Sure Bets in a genre, or across genres, becomes a lifesaver when our minds go blank, and we cannot remember anything, not even the book we are currently reading. At our service desk, we keep a notebook of Sure Bets, with a page assigned to each genre, and we add titles as we come upon them. Whenever I feel I am having trouble making connections with readers, or the books I put on displays are lingering there far too long, I browse through the Sure Bets notebook and refresh my memory of exceptional suggestions.

"Expanding Readers' Horizons" is another section included in each chapter. In addition to addressing how characteristics of one genre's appeal might lead librarians—and readers—to other genres, there is a list that presents the opposite side of the coin from the list found in the previous section. Although the former leads readers into a particular genre, this list, and the explanatory paragraphs, suggests how readers of the genre under consideration might also find authors to their liking in another genre.

6. *Reference Sources* One point underlined in every chapter is the importance of keeping lists—of Sure Bets, of titles that are "just like" popular authors, and of resources that work well for a particular question or type of reader. These become our Readers' Advisory Reference Resources, often just as valuable as those that are produced commercially, because they reflect our readership and the kinds of questions they ask. Never wait until you find the perfect format; start lists on scraps of paper, so you do not lose the ideas. They can always be "improved" when time and money offer more elegant solutions.

Commercial resources that pertain to a genre are also discussed in each chapter. Because some of the resources cover a number of genres, those are mentioned in the pertinent chapter and described in greater detail in appendix 2. How we use these resources, as well as the kind of information one can expect to find, is covered in each chapter. Although I have tried to choose newer resources that libraries may already have in their collections, the emphasis of this section is on identifying the most useful tools to answer patrons' questions.

There are three appendixes at the end of this book. The first outlines general tips for the Readers' Advisory Interview. Appendix 2 surveys reference books that cover more than one genre. Appendix 3 offers a quick introduction to the genres covered here, with five important authors and titles listed in each genre. I encourage users to use this, along with the authors and titles listed in each chapter, to take author Ann Bouricius's "five-book challenge" (*see* below).

How to Get the Most from This Book

Individual Training

This book was envisioned as a guide for an individual to explore fiction genres. In her excellent study of the Romance genre, *The Romance Readers' Advisory: The Librarian's Guide to Love in the Stacks,* Ann Bouricius extends the "five-book challenge": Read five books a year in a genre you do not already read.[5] She is absolutely right. Although you may want to read quickly through this book to gain an overview of the genres covered, I would certainly say it is better to take time with a genre. Read the chapter, explore the authors and titles, and talk with fans and staff about what they enjoy. Use your newfound knowledge to add that genre to displays, create an annotated booklist, suggest titles to fans, and attract others to the genre.

Staff Training

This book was designed as a tool to train both new and experienced staff, as both an initial training document and a genre refresher. Even if staff members are familiar with a genre, the description, authors, and titles included act as a reminder of aspects they might have forgotten and of links among authors and genres. It opens us up to the way we need to think about books and readers to do the best readers' advisory.

Genre Study

Although this book is really the result of a number of genre studies, with the section "Characteristics and the Genre's Appeal" reflecting the kind of list one would expect to be developed from such a study, it could certainly also be the starting point for your own genre study. Remember, however, that it is not meant to be prescriptive. You will make additional discoveries as you read and talk about a genre among your staff and with fans at your library. What your readers read will not necessarily parallel what users of my library enjoy. Genre study is about making connections, within a genre and beyond. Tips for "Studying a Genre" as well as guidelines for setting up a genre study group are discussed in some detail in *Readers' Advisory Service in the Public Library*.[6] Use those guidelines to embark on your own genre study. This book could be a starting place, but be prepared to revise the findings, based on your group's discoveries.

HOW TO KEEP UP WITH CHANGES IN A GENRE

Studying a genre and reading it extensively provide us with an understanding of the appeal of a genre at a certain point in time. Even if we could explore these genres, one after another, how can we possibly keep up with new developments and new authors when we have gone on to another genre? With new books published every year and authors continually pushing the boundaries of the genres in which they write, the prospect of staying current seems beyond even the most compulsive librarian!

Because we can never read as much as fans of a genre, it is important to develop ways to keep up on developments, trends, and new authors. Reading reviews is probably the easiest, most efficient technique. Library reviewing journals are generally good about reviewing genre fiction. Both *Booklist* and *Library Journal* consistently highlight titles in genres and, to some extent, subgenres. *Booklist* also provides regularly scheduled genre overviews, devoting much of an issue to articles relating to a particular genre and read-alikes for popular authors, as well as booklists. *Library Journal* offers regular columns on genres such as Romance, in addition to their fiction reviews. *Publishers Weekly* also covers genre fiction in the fiction reviews and publishes genre overviews regularly throughout the year.

Fans of the genre, if they are comfortable talking with staff, are an excellent source of information on developments in the genre. Soliciting their comments, as well as observing trends in reserves, can provide us with extensive information.

Consistently including a selection of genres in our broad reading of fiction certainly helps. However, it is important to remember we cannot read everything, and we can never read as much as fans of a genre. It is better to cultivate fans, among patrons or other staff members, to identify useful journals, and to set up a manageable plan for keeping up on genre trends.

Beyond This Guide

A colleague pointed to reviews of new books by Jackie Collins (*Lethal Seduction*) and E. Lynn Harris (*Not a Day Goes By*).[7] Where would you put them? In what genres do they fit? Good questions. Many authors do not fit easily into any specific genre slot, and some authors do not fit at all. That is why we read and study genres: not to learn to slot authors but to be able to think outside the boxes. Collins writes romantic fiction, but not Romances, and "rich-and-famous" elements are foremost. Her books are for readers who like that frame with some romance. These books are soap operas; her fans know that and that is what they like. But if we know about the Romance genre, we know that we do not automatically give her to the Nora Roberts or Debbie Macomber reader. That is the skill studying and thinking about genre fiction teaches us.

Harris shares a surprising number of characteristics with Collins. His books are romantic, but not Romances; "rich-and-famous" elements also play a role in this title. That the protagonist is a bisexual ex-football star complicates the situation and adds other elements to the appeal. However, readers who appreciate this frame, especially the glossy soap-opera stories both Harris and Collins write, may enjoy others who employ the same frame. The point is not that they fit into a genre or do not fit; rather, it is important to recognize that we can identify elements of appeal that cut across genres.

Some authors simply cannot be easily classified. One of my favorites is Dorothy Dunnett, who has written two excellent series set in Renaissance Europe. Is she a writer of Historical Fiction? Adventure, because her books feature large measures of action? Literary, in recognition of the elegance of her language and style? Or even Romance? The answer is that she is an excellent author to suggest to a range of readers who might enjoy this pleasant combination of elements.

Frankly, all this genre classification is really antithetical to readers' advisory work, where we focus on what a reader wants to read and cross genres with abandon as we make suggestions. So why devote years of reading and writing to create a book that defines genres and establishes themes and authors? Because understanding fiction is the backbone of our work, and understanding the genres and conventions and the authors that exemplify them is what allows us to move readers from one to another, to be the knowledgeable resources readers expect and deserve.

Our task as Readers' Advisors, librarians who work with fiction readers, is to show that we value all genres and genre readers. We demonstrate this by becoming familiar with the genres and by making our collections accessible to readers, by acquiring reference sources that allow us to serve readers better (and demonstrate that their queries are "real" reference questions), and by talking with readers, indicating that we understand what they are looking for when they ask for reading suggestions and helping them find what they seek.

We Readers' Advisors are so fortunate. We have a corner on the market of all the best things in the world. We have a collection of books at our fingertips, and, as Readers' Advisors, we know how to find just what we want. We understand, too, that popular fiction meets a variety of needs—that range from pure escapism to paradigms by which we make life's important decisions. We know we can find passion, suspense, adventure, intrigue, mystery, provocative issues, and intellectual stimulation in the pages of books we read and share with our readers.

As readers we know how important it is to be able to have books to suit our mood. Our patrons are readers, too, and their needs are no different from ours. Sometimes we want a *page-turner,* a book that keeps us so engrossed that we race through to the end. Sometimes we prefer a book that pulls us in, and we want to savor every word. Sometimes we seek a book that makes us think about the world in a new way, and at other times we simply want a book we can read without thinking at all. Just as there is a reader for every book, according to Ranganathan, there is a book for every mood and need.[8] We help readers find the books they are in the mood to read.

To serve readers better, we have an obligation to read and talk about what we read. We need to read so that we can appreciate the desperate need many readers feel simply to have a book in hand, a place to escape to. We also need to be enthusiastic sharing books. We must make readers comfortable so that they feel safe asking for suggestions and assistance. This book offers ways to let readers know we value their questions about fiction. And, most importantly, we need to share with readers the permission to enjoy whatever they want to read.

All of us need to give ourselves permission to enjoy reading—of all kinds—and to share that joy with other readers and give them permission to do the same.

Our readers will not value fiction and questions about fiction until we do. Through fiction we offer the world of story to our readers: romance, adventure, intrigue, and much more. These stories feed our spirits, our emotions, and our intellects. They help us understand our own predicament and that of others; they teach us tolerance, amuse us, and inspire us. Sharing stories becomes both our goal and our pleasure as we explore fiction and work with readers in our libraries.

NOTES

1. Andrea Barrett, *The Voyage of the Narwhal* (New York: Norton, 1998).
2. Guy Gavriel Kay, *The Lions of Al-Rassan* (New York: HarperPrism, 1995); ———, *A Song for Arbonne* (New York: Crown, 1993).
3. Joyce G. Saricks and Nancy Brown, *Readers' Advisory Service in the Public Library*, 2d ed. (Chicago: American Library Assn., 1997), 9.
4. Ibid.
5. Ann Bouricius, *The Romance Readers' Advisory: The Librarian's Guide to Love in the Stacks* (Chicago: American Library Assn., 2000).
6. Saricks and Brown, *Readers' Advisory Service*, 100–4.
7. Jackie Collins, *Lethal Seduction* (New York: Simon & Schuster, 2000); E. Lynn Harris, *Not a Day Goes By* (New York: Doubleday, 2000).
8. S. R. Ranganathan, *The Five Laws of Library Science* (1931; reprint, New York: Asia, 1963).

2

Adventure

All of us have come across readers who are also fans of the Indiana Jones and James Bond movies. They like the action and the fast-paced story; the cardboard characters amuse them; and they follow the exploits of the hero from movie to movie. They can hardly wait for the next one! Or they are great fans of all those war movies—the ones that focus on the action, featuring the hero who leads his band of men to outwit and escape the enemy forces, despite the odds against them. Both types allow viewers to become armchair warriors who experience danger and overcome obstacles in exotic locales. And when they have seen all the movies, many come to us, looking for books that offer this same appeal. This is when we turn to the Adventure genre.

A Definition

In his classic discussion of genre fiction, *Adventure, Mystery, and Romance: Formula Stories as Art and Popular Culture*, John G. Cawelti defines Adventure fiction as the story "of the hero—individual or group—overcoming obstacles and dangers and accomplishing some important and moral mission."[1] He also alludes to the archetypical nature of this story pattern, which can be traced back to ancient myths and epics. The traditional Adventure hero passes through an array of frightening perils to reach some goal, as in such classics as *The Odyssey* and *Beowulf.*

In light of this definition, I plan to explore a rather narrow range of books in this chapter. Although books in this genre overlap with Thrillers and Suspense, Adventure novels lack the emphasis on the myriad details of the subgenres—the legal field, medicine, and so forth—that characterize Thrillers and the sustained building of tension found in Suspense. Here, neither details nor possible threats are as important as the action itself. Novels in the Adventure genre are action-packed, feature a hero on a mission, and are often set in exotic locales during times of war or peace. Figure 2.1 summarizes the characteristics of Adventure novels.

FIGURE 2.1

Characteristics of Adventure

1. The story line focuses on action, usually a mission, and the obstacles and dangers met along the way. Survival may be a common theme. Physical adventure and danger are paramount, as the hero is placed in life-and-death situations from which he must rescue himself and others. There is generally a happy ending, with the hero safe and order restored.

2. There is always an identifiable hero, a character readers like and to whom they relate. Through ingenuity and skill, he succeeds in overcoming obstacles and accomplishing a desperate mission.

3. Pacing is generally brisk, as the hero escapes from one dangerous episode to the next. As in Suspense, Adventure novels often take place within a short time span. Even larger books feel as if they are fast-paced; the action creates a sense of movement that suggests quick pacing, although historical detail may slow those with historical settings.

4. Detailed settings are important. These stories are set "elsewhere," and this foreignness underlines the sense of danger and obstacles to be overcome. Maps often accompany these.

Characteristics and the Genre's Appeal

Story Line

If action, striving to succeed at a mission, is the distinguishing feature of this genre, then the story line must emphasize this orientation. In Adventure the plot usually concentrates on the desperate mission on which the hero has embarked. It is always physically dangerous to those involved and usually has serious—life-and-death—ramifications. There is generally one overwhelming obstacle that must be overcome, although there are often lesser difficulties along the way. Take Alistair MacLean's classic novel of Adventure, *The Guns of Navarone.*[2] In this quintessential novel of action-packed Adventure, a commando team is given just forty-eight hours to infiltrate the Greek island of Navarone and destroy the German guns that prevent Allied access to the islands in the eastern Mediterranean. Each member has been picked for his special talents, yet their foray seems dogged by misfortune, too frequently to suggest anything but a traitor in their midst. Although the silencing of the great German guns is their ultimate goal, there are obstacles all along the way, from scaling the seemingly insurmountable cliffs to traversing the rocky terrain safely, not to mention the impediments devised by the traitor. The story moves quickly, from one danger to the next, as we feel—and see, as the time is revealed at each chapter heading—the clock ticking, reinforcing the Suspense elements inherent in the Adventure genre. The plot twists and betrayals, also common elements in Adventure novels, figure prominently.

Story lines may be contemporary or historical, involving civilians or military personnel. There is also a range of violence in Adventure fiction, from the graphic portrayals in Eric Van Lustbader's stories of Nicholas Linnear (*The Ninja* is the first)[3] to the more genteel violence and the suggestion of violence in the works of classic authors Hammond Innes and Nevil Shute.

Other features of the Adventure story line include survival amidst the elements, with physical, human, and animal dangers; escape from difficult situations; and the journey or mission itself. Remember, too, that despite the danger and obstacles, the hero is successful. Others may be lost along the way, but the hero almost always prevails and survives—often to embark on further adventures in later books. Endings may not be the typical "happy ending" of the Romance genre, but they are certainly satisfactory; the mission is carried out, and among the survivors are those we as readers care most about.

Characterization

The nature of the hero is another hallmark of the Adventure genre. He is a strong, moral man, committed to his assigned mission. Although this character is often a stereotype, and secondary characters are more often either good or bad rather than fully developed, the hero and his plight capture the imagination and sympathy of the audience. The Adventure genre often inspires series characters, so that even if the hero is not as fully developed as in Literary Fiction, fans follow his exploits and the changes in his life from book to book and thus gain a sense of knowing the character.

As Cawelti suggests, the hero is a moral man, although, as in the hard-boiled detectives ("Mysteries," chapter 8), the moral code may be one of his own devising. Whether or not these heroes are the appointed leaders of their groups, they are the ones who display the ingenuity and skill that accomplish the mission and save the team from disaster. The hero's natural leadership ability, combined with intuitive skill at interpreting dangers and discovering solutions, sets him apart from the others as the one who lives for the challenges each Adventure offers.

As mentioned above, the characters are usually one-dimensional, good or bad; thus, the villains are almost always drawn in extremes and are very evil. Ian Fleming and his followers specialize in cardboard (but always fascinating) villains to pit against hero James Bond. Having said this, I must add that a more elegant and sophisticated writer such as Jack Higgins shades his characters, making them more gray and adding the depth of characterization that some readers seek. For example, in his classic *The Eagle Has Landed*, his hero, Liam Devlin, is on what most readers would consider the wrong side, an Irishman in the employ of the Germans on a mission to assassinate Churchill.[4] Both the English and German sides are represented by contrasting characters, some admirable and others reprehensible, and Higgins offers the reader the clues necessary to distinguish the good guys from the bad.

The antagonist, on the other hand, is as likely to be a group (Germans or Japanese against American or British military, for example) or a physical obstacle, as an individual. An obvious example, which also speaks to the range of the Adventure genre, is Sheila Every Burnford's *The Incredible Journey,* in which three unlikely heroes (household pets seeking their owners) travel together across the Canadian wilderness to reach their family.[5] Although there are lesser villains in this story (wild animals who make their trip more dangerous), the major obstacles are the terrain and weather, as serious (albeit impartial) a foe as the most obsessed megalomaniac.

Often called a Male Romance because it focuses on male characters and ensures a happy ending, Adventure is singularly devoid of female protagonists or, in fact, of interesting women characters in any role. These are communities of men, and the women, if they appear, are clearly secondary, except in a few cases. One notable exception is Jon Cleary's *High Road to China,* which offers a mission—accomplished by an air journey in the '20s—across Europe to China, a constrained time period, exotic setting, unusual characters (including one of the few heroines in the genre, although she is assisted by two men), and a treasure to be used to ransom her father.[6] American heiress Eve Tozer has just arrived in London when a mysterious Asian gentleman accosts her and announces that her father has been kidnapped by a Chinese warlord. The only way to save him is to take a priceless jade statuette as payment—and she has just eighteen days to present it. Only flight will get her there in time, so she enlists the help of two ex-Royal Air Force pilots. With three planes she, the pilots, and the Chinese guide embark on their quest, meeting adversity and perils at every refueling stop. Tongue-in-cheek humor, the mainstay of much genre fiction, features prominently in this lighthearted Adventure.

Pacing

Pacing, as mentioned above, is generally quite brisk. The books feel as if they move quickly, even if they are longer books. The action moves the story along at a breakneck speed, as the hero and his crew escape danger after danger. As in both *The Guns of Navarone* and *High Road to China,* often the mission must be accomplished within a limited time span, and this fact telescopes and intensifies the action.

Frame

Physical setting plays an important role in Adventure stories. It is vital that the action take place elsewhere, away, outside the normal, everyday world. Heroes must go on a mission to another place, which then must be described in physical and cultural terms, as in James Clavell's *Shogun,* where seventeenth-century feudal Japan provides the backdrop for Adventure.[7] By its nature, this elsewhere is dangerous, without the comforts and safety of home. Heroes are out of their element, and compensating adds to their character and the story. Gary Jennings's stories, for example, would not feel nearly as dangerous if they were not set in such exotic locales with the heroes carrying out hazardous assignments in perilous times. (*Aztec* plants Cortés firmly in Montezuma's Mexico, while *The Journeyer* sends Marco Polo to Kublai Khan, and *The Raptor* places the hero in the bloody court of the king of the Ostrogoths.)[8]

Thus, the prototypical Adventure story features a hero on a mission, and he must face a range of obstacles along the way. The reader gets a firsthand look at the exotic locale in which the story is set. He participates in suspenseful derring-do as the hero extricates himself from multiple dangers along the way and overcomes the physical dangers found in this "elsewhere" to complete his mission successfully. Jack B. Du Brul's *Vulcan's Forge* offers the typical over-the-top scenario with everything one could ask for in an Adventure novel: a power-mad megalomaniac, crazy Russians killing each other and everyone else in their way, mad scientists, and a "white knight" to save the day.[9] This is the first in a projected series featuring engineer–geological consultant Philip Mercermine, who, in this episode, tries to rescue the daughter of a friend, caught up in a Russian scheme involving an underwater volcano and a fuel that will allow the Russians to achieve world domination. Although the plot verges on the Thriller genre, the political machinations are secondary to the Adventure theme in this novel for fans of Clive Cussler.

Style

As in all genres, the Adventure genre exhibits a range of styles, including the poetic, elegant prose of James Dickey in his story of survival during World War II, *To the White Sea,* which mixes violence and beauty in the first-person narration of a downed American pilot trying to escape Japan on his own.[10] At the other end of the spectrum we find Cussler's more prosaic, conversational prose, which creates a different mood and attracts a different audience. Here, too, the tongue-in-cheek humor and exaggerated characters and peril simply add to the fans' enjoyment. These are not dangers—physical or human—that touch us closely. Suffice it to say that here, as elsewhere, there are stylistic differences. However, we should not be surprised to hear a fan laud Cussler for his "well-written" stories, even if we know this comment is counter to literary taste. Any writer whom a reader enjoys writes well, no matter what the style. It is a question of personal definition and a subject best avoided in the readers' advisory interview.

Key Authors and Subgenres

Benchmark

For most readers, one name says it all when it comes to Adventure: Clive Cussler. Since his first book in 1976 *(Raise the Titanic),* Cussler, or really his hero, Dirk Pitt, has set the standard for the Adventure genre.[11] Pitt is the typical Adventure hero: the independent protagonist who is not necessarily the highest ranking among his "community of men," but he is certainly the one turned to when disaster strikes and the one who manages to regroup the men and achieve the mission. He is resourceful and inventive in the way he brings about a solution to whatever problems he faces. He does not necessarily resort to violence, and, in his earlier titles at least, he is often without the expensive gadgetry that accompanies his later escapades. With the most innocuous and prosaic tools, just a little string and wax perhaps, Pitt can fix or rig almost anything. Although Adventure—the mission to be accomplished and the obstacles met along the way—is the focus of each Pitt novel, there is also usually some Suspense and often a treasure to be found. Cussler's books also feature a measure of humor, not only in the outrageous antics of Pitt and his friends, but in other characters and situations as well. Because there is little or no sex and seldom extended and graphic violence, these are often titles requested by and suggested to younger readers, who appreciate the Adventure without the other distractions. Women seldom play a critical role in Cussler's books; his series typifies the prototypical man's world. To get a sense of Cussler's style, try *Atlantis Found* for an example of his action-filled writing.[12]

Subgenres of Adventure

The many genres and subgenres that overlap with Adventure are discussed in other chapters. Here I consider two subgenres of Adventure: Exotic and Military. Figure 2.2 lists the four characteristics of Exotic Adventure.

EXOTIC ADVENTURE

Cussler's novels typify this subgenre. As well as being the overall benchmark for the genre, he also increasingly exemplifies the Exotic Adventure subgenre, especially in recent years, as his stories have verged more and more on the fantastical. (For example, in 1992's *Sahara*, not only does Abraham Lincoln make an appearance, but the weaponry has evolved from the string and sealing wax to futuristic James Bond–like devices.)[13]

FIGURE 2.2

Characteristics of Exotic Adventure

1. Setting is in exotic locales, and the setting and sense of place (often isolated and primitive) emphasize the danger.

2. Characters are stereotypes, and villains are often cartoonish. Secondary characters are seldom of any substance.

3. Plots are usually out of the ordinary and often contain fantastic elements; thus, humor may play a role in the story.

4. At the end of the books, there is a sense that justice has been done; good triumphs over evil.

These are frequently novels of excess. Many feature characters who are more extreme, plots that are more far-fetched, and locales that are often unknown and thus potentially more dangerous. Many also feature situations that may be ludicrously violent and dangerous, although Cussler remains less so. Over-the-top is the key. This is a subgenre that has a strong following, and these readers also often enjoy the superhero Adventures featuring James Bond, written by Ian Fleming and his successors. Although it may be an arbitrary decision, I feel these books fit better here than with Thrillers, as it is the extravagance of plot, characters, and weaponry that appeal to most fans, rather than the Espionage details.

Eric Van Lustbader also fits into this subgenre, with his adventures of Nicholas Linnear (who should certainly be played by Bruce Willis in the movie). Larger-than-life heroes and villains, many women in sexually explicit scenes (but not allowed pivotal roles in the story), and violence add a curious dimension to novels in which the hero also recites haikus. These are for action readers who like the eastern locales and philosophy.

Exotic Adventure may also be set in the past. Dorothy Dunnett's two excellent series of Exotic Adventure with historical settings provide a good example. Her long, captivating novels of Adventure, Intrigue, and Romance, freely laced with literary quotations and allusions, offer pleasant diversion. The first series features Francis Crawford of Lymond, the second son of a sixteenth-century Scots family. This picaresque hero amuses himself with intrigue in the courts of France, the Middle East, Russia, and England and eventually finds his place and his love in six elegant, witty, erudite, adventure-packed novels, beginning with *The Game of Kings*.[14] The second series, set in fifteenth-century Netherlands and Europe, features Nicholas (Niccolo) vander Poele, merchant, banker, and adventurer. The first of the series is *Niccolo Rising*.[15] These intricately plotted Adventures explore Renaissance culture, business, and politics across Europe and as far afield as Africa and Iceland, as Nicholas travels for business and, sometimes, revenge.

Other interesting authors to read to gain an appreciation of the popularity of Exotic Adventure are Robert Lewis Taylor and Lucia St. Clair Robson. Taylor won a Pulitzer Prize for *The Travels of Jamie*

McPheeters, which recounts the adventures of Jamie as he accompanies his father from Kentucky to the California goldfields and explores the West along the way.[16] Another of his novels, however, *A Roaring in the Wind,* a tale of frontier life in Montana, is the one that flies off the display of "Good Books You May Have Missed" in my library. [17] Robson has written historical Adventures set in America, as well as the more unusual *Tokaido Road,* in which Lady Asano poses as a samurai and travels the Tokaido Road to escape her father's killer and bitter enemy.[18] Her mission is to restore her father's honor and name.

Two additional Exotic Adventure writers are worth discovering, even though their style and stories reflect another generation and worldview, not to mention more moderate versions of the subgenre's characteristics. Nevil Shute and Hammond Innes have written stories set primarily on the sea, featuring strong (and serious) moral heroes who fight the odds in exotic locales to accomplish their missions and set the world aright. Their characters are more usually quite ordinary men, who, when faced with a difficult situation, discover they have extraordinary reserves of strength and the required special skills. Written for the most part from the '40s on, these have the feel of a time past, when there was the possibility of a moral universe and right-acting denizens. These authors and their characters see the world as a place that can be made better. There is an underlying morality in these books, a feeling that problems can be fixed. Overall these books are more serious and issue-oriented than Cussler's. These thoughtful, more gentle Adventure novels appeal to fans of old-fashioned stories. For an example of Shute's style, try *Trustee from the Toolroom,* which moves from an exciting but disastrous struggle against the sea in a small ship in which a husband and his wife are lost, to the brother, the chivalrous uncle and trustee, who also fights the sea as he battles to recover and protect his young niece's inheritance.[19] One of Innes's later titles, *Isvik,* features all the familiar elements of Adventure: the perilous search in the waters off Antarctica for a ghost ship and the hero-adventurer who possesses the necessary survival skills to conquer the harsh landscape and complete his mission.[20] Sea stories, including those by Shute and Innes, play an important role in the Adventure genre, as the following discussion of Military Adventure makes clear.

MILITARY ADVENTURE

Military Adventures offer idealistic heroes who adhere rigorously to their moral codes. For most, the military and the concomitant responsibilities are their entire life. There is little time for families. And, in fact, we see most in military situations, on the battlefield or in preparation for battle, involved in military activities. Because it is not standard military practice, there is seldom one man operating alone. Usually there is a group of men, although one emerges as the leader (not necessarily because of rank) when the difficult situation arises. These are men on a mission, and they operate in more realistic situations than do the heroes of Exotic Adventure. Figure 2.3 lists the three characteristics of Military Adventure.

The classic benchmark of this subgenre is Alistair MacLean. Such titles as his *Guns of Navarone* set the standard for Military Adventure for today's readers and writers. The contemporary benchmark is W. E. B. Griffin (fondly called Web by his myriad fans), whose series of novels have taken millions of readers back through the rigors of World War II and beyond with the U.S. Marines. These are blockbuster Adventures, featuring the fast pace, sense of immediacy, and danger that the genre requires, as well as the series characters that fans appreciate and learn to know intimately. In *In Danger's Path*, for example, Admiral Nimitz, General MacArthur, and even President Franklin Delano Roosevelt appear as supporting characters in the ongoing

---

FIGURE 2.3

Characteristics of Military Adventure

1. Although there is an identifiable hero, he is almost always part of a community of men. Strong secondary characters play important supportive roles. These are often series, featuring recurring characters.

2. Characters and plots are more realistic, and plots often feature real people and historical events.

3. Survival is a major theme, as these characters in military situations spend more time in immediate peril of their lives.

---

saga of Brigadier General Fleming Pickering and his colleagues, this time on a mission of rescue in the Gobi Desert.[21]

Jack Higgins is another writer who has explored the military subgenre. His titles involve more building of suspense as the plans to carry out the required mission evolve and are put into place, but as the tension builds, so does the pacing, pulling the reader through the smaller adventures to the finale. Higgins presents more complex characters and layered plots, which add another element to the Military Adventure details.

Another aspect of contemporary Military Adventure is the soldier-of-fortune Adventure, currently popularized by Richard Marcinko. Because their extensive military skills are not needed by their own countries, these mercenaries, including a team of Navy Seals, use their skills and experience to battle a range of villains, from terrorists to the Russian Mob and neo-Nazis. Marcinko's *Rogue Warrior* series features fast-acting, hard-talking mercenaries, as well as the cartoon villains and heroes, exotic locales, and out-of-the-ordinary plotlines.[22] Marcinko's books, however, include more violence than most in this genre. The language is also harder, not only in terms of the professional jargon (luckily, he provides a glossary as well as an index!), but also in the level of obscenities. His books are not for every reader, yet we have fans of both sexes who are not put off by the violence and strong language and who clearly appreciate the Military Adventures in which he and his men are engaged.

Some writers place their novels of Military Adventure in historical settings. Authors such as Bernard Cornwell and Patrick O'Brian appeal both to readers who appreciate the historical detail these novelists emphasize in creating their characters and settings as well as to those who simply like good Adventure stories. O'Brian's series of almost twenty novels, beginning with *Master and Commander*, is set during the Napoleonic wars and features Jack Aubrey, an officer in the British navy, and his unorthodox friend, intelligence officer Dr. Stephen Maturin.[23] O'Brian's novels are all part of an ongoing story, each an episode linked to those before and after. Details of ships, the lives of sailors, and the politics and reality of war aboard ship fill these historical tales of Military Adventure.

Two good examples of Historical Military Adventure are the series by Cornwell. The Sharpe series, set in the Napoleonic War and previously (*Sharpe's Triumph* comes first chronologically), and the Starbuck Chronicles (*Rebel* is the first), set in the U.S. Civil War, feature series characters; and each book leads up to and describes, in detail, a particular battle.[24] Historical notes at the end of each book add an informative and authoritative touch, setting the books firmly in the period they describe.

To support the frame of the stories, authors often include maps or detailed plans of ships. Extensive historical notes, as at the end of each of Cornwell's titles, relate the known historical facts of the fictionalized events and are frequently found in those books that feature Military Adventure with historical settings.

Others, such as Alexander Kent, Philip McCutchan, Richard Woodman, and Douglas Reeman, stress Adventure and the mission to be accomplished more than the historical detail. McCutchan, for example, has several series of Military Adventures, set in different historical periods: the Halfhyde novels are set in the late nineteenth century (*Beware, Beware, the Bight of Benin* is the first), and the Chatto adventures begin then and run through World War I (*Apprentice to the Sea* is the first); the Cameron (beginning with *Cameron Comes Through*) and the Kemp series (*The Convoy Commodore*) are set at sea during World War II; and the Ogilvie series (*Lieutenant of the Line*) takes place in India during the British occupation.[25] Officers on a mission, with full measures of action and adventure, characterize McCutchan's stories.

The Military Adventure subgenre is not currently in vogue—among writers at least. Its heyday was the '70s and '80s, when authors such as Max Hennessy and Douglas Reeman wrote novels of Adventure set in World War I and II, and MacLean appeared with regularity on the best-sellers lists. Somehow Vietnam has not proved an adequate substitute for World Wars I and II, and the novels that have come out of that war seldom emphasize Adventure elements.

Preparing to Work with Readers

Readers of Adventure are a diverse lot who may also read in a number of related genres. There are, however, several general characteristics that describe these fans. First, Adventure readers expect the general template of characteristics mentioned earlier in the chapter: a hero on a mission; detailed, exotic settings "elsewhere"; danger, with action, whether frequent or following a suspenseful buildup; and the ultimate success of the mission with the hero safe. *Cinematic* is a term often applied to Adventure story lines, and it is one readers may also employ as they describe books they enjoy. These are stories made for the big screen, with larger-than-life heroes on seemingly impossible missions, often striving for the ultimate goal of making the world safe, if not actually saving it through their efforts. As in Romance and Suspense, readers expect a happy ending.

Readers revel in the exaggerations of characters and story line, which they find most frequently in Adventure with a contemporary setting. These provide a kind of humor that appeals to many readers. We find these extremes primarily in the Exotic Adventure subgenre, as might be expected from the name. The comments about these authors focus on the character of the villain, the foreignness of the setting, and the details of the gadgetry.

Fans read Adventure not only for the vicarious danger/escape motif, but they also read many of the authors for the details of the times, weaponry, or the additional obscure facts they provide. Clive Cussler fans praise the curious details of treasure hunting, for example, a technique to raise the *Titanic* (before its popularity skyrocketed with the blockbuster movie). Dorothy Dunnett readers prize her characters, stories, and the details of life in another time and place. Military fiction readers devour the details of battle as well as the preparations and forays to discover the special information the missions involve.

And as in all genres, fans read for the formula and for the stories that pull them in—the characters they can relate to and the stories that enthrall them. These are mythic heroes, off to face their dragons, in whatever form, in order to accomplish their missions. They only lack the beautiful princess as reward.

If you are not a reader of Adventure, start with the key authors discussed above. Those are the most popular authors, the ones your readers most likely refer to when they talk about Adventure they have read and loved. Figure 2.4 shows some additional authors, whose Adventure novels may remind you of genres you already read and enjoy.

FIGURE 2.4

An Introduction to the Adventure Genre

Adventure Writers to Try, If You Enjoy . . .

Fantasy	George MacDonald Fraser
Gentle	Hammond Innes
	Nevil Shute
Historical	James Clavell
	Philip McCutchan
Horror	Gary Jennings
Humor	George MacDonald Fraser
Literary	James Dickey
Romance	Dorothy Dunnett
Suspense	Alistair MacLean
Thriller	Clive Cussler
	Jack Higgins
Western	Robert Lewis Taylor

Readers' Advisory Interview

Adventure is one of the genres for which, if you cannot elicit useful information about books readers have enjoyed, you can often success-fully ask about movies. Potential fans may find the movies easier to recall than books, and because many classic Adventure movies were based on books—*Von Ryan's Express, The Bridge on the River Kwai,* and *The Guns of Navarone,* to name a few—it is often easy to convince those who have enjoyed the movie to try these or similar books.

This is also a genre in which we can discover a great deal about books we have not personally read, just by looking for a few signs as we work with patrons. Maps, whether of a large area or with details of a specific terrain, often indicate that there are Adventure elements in the story. Not that maps or detailed drawings are not found else-where in Adventure and in other genres, but in these historical Adventure novels especially, they often give a clue to the story line. A map of the United States, for example, suggests a journey and surely adventures along the way. On the other hand, the detailed drawings of nineteenth-century ships in Patrick O'Brian's Military Adventures also suggest the accuracy of the detail to be included in the novel. An exotic location or the presence of military details, for example, would suggest either of the subgenres discussed. And as they do in the Thriller genre, covers of Adventure novels may also suggest their theme.

When suggesting titles, do not forget the classics. In fact, occasionally a reader will inquire for more books like those he enjoyed in his youth: the great Adventure tales of Robert Lewis Stevenson, Alexandre Dumas, C. S. Forester (the Hornblower series), and Rafael Sabatini. Swashbuckling tales are not as common today, but they do exist. Try the Fantasy Sword and Sorcery tales by authors such as Steven Brust, George MacDonald Fraser's Flashman series, Wilbur Smith's *Birds of Prey* and *Monsoon* (piracy on the high seas),[26] or Westerns by Louis L'Amour.

One last point in the readers' advisory interview. Many unthinkingly consider this a genre read only by men. Those of us who work with readers know this is not true. Although the audience may include more men than women, there is much in this genre—despite the absence of strong female characters—that appeals to readers of both sexes: action, exotic locales, and happy endings among the most important.

Sure Bets

When all else fails—our minds are blank and we can come up with no suggestions for readers—try describing these Sure Bets. L'Amour's *The Walking Drum*, set in twelfth-century Western Europe and the Middle East, is one I have had a lot of success with.[27] It is the story of a young man who seeks revenge for the death of his mother and the destruction of his estate by a neighboring lord. He also seeks his father, a corsair held captive in Turkey, he believes. There is action in almost every chapter; there is either an actual fight or battle scene, or we follow the intense buildup to such a scene in the next chapter. The action drives the pacing, pushing us as readers to read faster and faster. L'Amour is an unexpected find for fans of this genre, as he is a writer who appeals to a wide range of readers across several genres, even though he is probably best known as a writer of Westerns.

Nevil Shute offers a number of titles with solid hooks that make them easy to describe to readers. In *The Pied Piper* our mild-mannered, older hero is caught in France when war is declared.[28] As he begins to make his way back to England, he encounters families of British citizens, caught as he was, who beg him to get their children back to England. Unlike Hameln's piper, John Sidney Howard's efforts are all to the good, but how he makes his way and what happens to the growing group create a touching, albeit low-key, Adventure.

Another Sure Bet is *Blood Tide* by Robert F. Jones.[29] Here, a former Navy officer avenges his daughter against a drug lord in a high-velocity shoot-out in the Philippines. When in doubt and searching for something to suggest, always remember the benchmarks: writers of Contemporary Adventure Clive Cussler and Alistair MacLean or of Historical Adventure Bernard Cornwell and Dorothy Dunnett.

Expanding Readers' Horizons

Adventure is also a genre rife with crossover. Almost every genre offers novels with enough of the characteristics of the Adventure genre to entice fans looking for a change of pace.

Although Adventure may not be the key element, any Fantasy novel involving a quest certainly requires a great deal of action, not to mention exotic locales and possibly military encounters. Suggest Raymond E. Feist, David Eddings, Robert Jordan, or Terry Goodkind to Adventure readers ready for something different.

Historical Fiction offers numerous possibilities in almost all historical periods. Fans should sample a range from Henryk Sienkiewicz's *With Fire and Sword,* first of a massive trilogy set in seventeenth-century Eastern Europe; to the Romantic Adventure novels of Patricia Veryan, which include history, romance, intrigue, and adventure in eighteenth-century Scotland; to the more serious and character-centered *Hannibal* by Ross Leckie, which tells of the Carthaginian general's attack on Rome, as well as the personality of the man who engineered it.[30]

Although many titles in the Romance genre offer Adventure in exotic settings, suggesting this genre to Adventure fans raises other questions. How will readers react to a suggestion to move from a genre that, for the most part, excludes women to one that focuses on women? Readers willing to take this chance will find action-filled plots in the

Historical Romances of Loretta Chase, Veryan, and Susan Wiggs, as well as in Ann Maxwell's contemporary Romances.

In Romantic Suspense we are confronted with the same basic issue as in Romance: The protagonists are women. Still writers such as Sandra Brown and Elizabeth Lowell (who also writes as Maxwell) add strong action and adventure elements to their novels of Romantic Suspense.

The Thriller genre proposes a number of directions for Adventure fans to pursue. Fans of the stories of James Bond's or Dirk Pitt's exploits may also enjoy Tom Clancy's Jack Ryan stories or Patrick Robinson's submarine Techno-Thrillers, in which the technical detail, exotic locales, and increasingly fantastic plots usually compensate for the more conventional characters. Jack Higgins's fans might experiment with the more cerebral Espionage by authors such as John E. Gardner and John le Carré. Fans of Exotic Adventure might enjoy Michael Crichton for the action, fast pace, and location. And readers of Adventure fiction often also enjoy true-life Adventure, such as Sebastian Junger's *The Perfect Storm* or Jon Krakauer's *Into Thin Air*.[31] Figure 2.5 offers additional authors to take readers beyond the Adventure genre.

Reference Sources

Identifying the "best" reference books for the Adventure genre is not an easy task because there are no recent titles devoted solely to this genre.[32] Thus, we must rely on sections devoted to Adventure in books aimed at a wider range of readers and librarians.

Where to Find . . .

INFORMATION ABOUT THE AUTHOR

Contemporary Authors (*see* appendix 2) provides extensive information about many of these authors, from classic Alistair MacLean to more recent authors such as Richard Marcinko. Because of the overlap with Historical Fiction, information about some Adventure authors can also be found in *Twentieth-Century Romance and Historical Writers* (*see* chapter 5 or 10 for details). Both these sources provide biographical and bibliographical information as well as insights into the authors and their works.

FIGURE 2.5

Expanding Readers' Horizons

Authors to Take Readers beyond the Adventure Genre

Fantasy	Raymond E. Feist
	Robert Jordan
Gentle	Dorothy Gilman
Historical	Henryk Sienkiewicz
	Wilbur Smith (*River God*)[33]
Inspirational	Tim F. LaHaye and Jerry B. Jenkins
	(Left Behind series)
Romance	Ann Maxwell
	Patricia Veryan
Romantic Suspense	Sandra Brown
Science Fiction	David Weber
Thriller	Tom Clancy
	Michael Crichton
Western	Louis L'Amour

Although I am not including Web sites and addresses, because of their often transitory nature, I do advocate using a basic search engine to locate an author's Web page for additional information.

PLOT SUMMARIES

Adventure is one of *Fiction Catalog*'s (*see* appendix 2) subject headings, so annotations can be found there for many titles. Plot summaries are also accessible on *NoveList* (*see* appendix 2) through an author or title search or by using Adventure in either of the subject access searches. *Adventure* is a subheading under each genre in *What Do I Read Next?* (*see* appendix 2); searches lead to annotations in the genre sections of the books or to main entries on the Web version. Adventure is also a subject heading used in *Sequels, To Be Continued, American Historical Fiction,* and *World Historical Fiction,* all of which offer title or series annotations. (The first two reference sources are described in detail in appendix 2, the last two in chapter 5.)

SUBGENRES AND THEMES

Genreflecting (*see* appendix 2) defines Adventure more broadly than I do in this chapter, but there are subgenres that relate to the titles covered here ("Male Romance," "Wild Frontiers and Exotic Lands," and "Military and Naval Adventure," with both contemporary and historical settings). Numerous subgenres and themes are also accessible on *NoveList* in the "Browse Subjects" function.

GENRE DESCRIPTION, BACKGROUND, AND HISTORY

None of the other sources currently available provide this information.[34]

Novels in the Adventure genre appeal to our *Wanderlust* and to our desire to test our limits and explore the boundaries of our universes. Adventure takes us from the confines of our small worlds to traverse the known world and beyond. With a select group of companions we embark on our mission, our quest, facing danger and privation, and always succeed in the end, despite the rigors of the trip. Adventure novels are stories of action, heroes, villains, danger, and survival— not to mention ultimate success. They appeal to a deep-seated desire to participate on a quest and to attain the grail. Small wonder that they remain so popular and blend so well with other currently popular genres—Thrillers, Science Fiction, Fantasy, Romance, Romantic Suspense, Suspense, and even Westerns.

NOTES

1. John G. Cawelti, *Adventure, Mystery, and Romance: Formula Stories as Art and Popular Culture* (Chicago and London: Univ. of Chicago Pr., 1976), 39.

2. Alistair MacLean, *The Guns of Navarone* (Garden City, N.Y.: Doubleday, 1957).

3. Eric Van Lustbader, *The Ninja* (New York: M. Evans, 1980).

4. Jack Higgins, *The Eagle Has Landed* (New York: Holt, 1975).

5. Sheila Every Burnford, *The Incredible Journey* (Boston: Little, Brown, 1961).

6. Jon Cleary, *High Road to China* (New York: Morrow, 1977).

7. James Clavell, *Shogun* (New York: Delacorte, 1975).

8. Gary Jennings, *Aztec* (New York: Atheneum, 1980); ———, *The Journeyer* (New York: Atheneum, 1984); ———, *The Raptor* (New York: Doubleday, 1992).

9. Jack B. Du Brul, *Vulcan's Forge* (New York: Forge, 1998).

10. James Dickey, *To the White Sea* (New York: Houghton, 1993).

11. Clive Cussler, *Raise the Titanic* (New York: Viking, 1976).

12. ———, *Atlantis Found* (New York: Putnam, 1999).

13. ———, *Sahara* (New York: Simon & Schuster, 1992).

14. Dorothy Dunnett, *The Game of Kings* (New York: Putnam, 1961).

15. ———, *Niccolo Rising* (New York: Knopf, 1986).

16. Robert Lewis Taylor, *The Travels of Jamie McPheeters* (Garden City, N.Y.: Doubleday, 1958).

17. ———, *A Roaring in the Wind* (New York: Putnam, 1978).

18. Lucia St. Clair Robson, *The Tokaido Road: A Novel of Feudal Japan* (New York: Ballantine, 1991).

19. Nevil Shute, *Trustee from the Toolroom* (New York: Morrow, 1960).

20. Hammond Innes, *Isvik* (New York: St. Martin's, 1992).

21. W. E. B. Griffin, *In Danger's Path* (New York: Putnam, 1998).

22. Richard Marcinko, *Rogue Warrior* (New York: Pocket Books, 1992).

23. Patrick O'Brian, *Master and Commander* (Philadelphia: Lippincott, 1969).

24. Bernard Cornwell, *Sharpe's Triumph* (New York: HarperCollins, 1998); ———, *Rebel* (New York: HarperCollins, 1993).

25. Philip McCutchan, *Beware, Beware, the Bight of Benin* (New York: St. Martin's, 1975, © 1974); ———, *Apprentice to the Sea* (New York: St. Martin's, 1995); ———, *Cameron Comes Through* (New York: St. Martin's, 1986); ———, *The Convoy Commodore* (New York: St. Martin's, 1987); ———, *Lieutenant of the Line* (New York: St. Martin's, 1972).

26. Wilbur Smith, *Birds of Prey* (New York: St. Martin's, 1997); ———, *Monsoon* (New York: Thomas Dunne, 1999).

27. Louis L'Amour, *The Walking Drum* (New York: Bantam, 1984).

28. Shute, *The Pied Piper* (New York: Morrow, 1942).

29. Robert F. Jones, *Blood Tide* (New York: Atlantic Monthly, 1990).

30. Henryk Sienkiewicz, *With Fire and Sword* (1884; in modern translation by W. S. Kuniczak, 1st ed., Fort Washington, Pa.: Copernicus Society of America; New York: Hippocrene Books, © 1991); Ross Leckie, *Hannibal* (Washington, D.C.: Regnery, 1996).

31. Sebastian Junger, *The Perfect Storm: A True Story of Men against the Sea* (New York: Norton, 1997); Jon Krakauer, *Into Thin Air: A Personal Account of the Mount Everest Disaster* (New York: Villard, 1997).

32. Michael Gannon's forthcoming study of Adventure and Suspense, part of Libraries Unlimited's Genreflecting Advisory series, will fill a gap by providing solid reference information on this genre.

33. Smith, *River God* (New York: St. Martin's, 1994).

34. See note 32 above.

3

Fantasy

Fantasy may be the most ubiquitous of the genres, as it is an element of most fiction, almost regardless of how realistic the story is. It is also an ancient form, the genre of myth and legend, as well as of the fairy tales and other stories of our childhood. The world of faerie, magic, sorcery, and enchantment all live on in Fantasy. And Fantasy is a genre that has few age limits, with adults and children often reading and enjoying the same stories. (What else could account for the enormous popularity of Harry Potter as I write this?)

A Definition

Although Fantasy most frequently overlaps with Science Fiction, there are significant links to Horror, Romance, and Adventure as well. Both Fantasy and Horror draw on everyday fears and produce realms and creatures that are larger than life and often not of us or this world. However, while Horror creates a nightmare situation in which characters strive to survive and temporarily defeat the evil, Fantasy is more affirming, giving protagonists a chance to win the battle against the dark. Science Fiction also presents a challenging unknown, but, unlike Fantasy, it offers technical explanations and ways to "know," to discover through science and empirical means.

Horror and Fantasy share an intuitive approach to the world, in contrast to the rational outlook of Science Fiction. Like Romance, Fantasy may have a romantic tone, and some stories certainly project the same emotional appeal, but the magical elements supplant the romantic interest as the most important element. Adventure abounds in many types of Fantasy, but again it is secondary to the magical elements of the story.

Like Science Fiction, Fantasy is not easily defined, or not neatly in a single phrase or two. If Science Fiction emphasizes ideas, then Fantasy delves more into relationships. The stories it tells appeal more to the emotions than to the intellect. As does Science Fiction, Fantasy deals with otherness of time or place; settings may be contemporary or historical but something is different—the train platform in Eva Ibbotson's *The Secret of Platform 13* or the talisman that aids nurse Kitty McCulley in Elizabeth Ann Scarborough's *The Healer's War*.[1] Fantasy, however, exists in a world that never could be, while Science Fiction worlds are possible, even if improbable. Science Fiction generally offers something new and different, but Fantasy frequently takes a familiar story, legend, or myth and adds a twist, bringing it to life again. The key to Fantasy, however, seems to be the presence of magic. If there is not magic, the story may fit in the Horror, Science Fiction, Romance, Historical Fiction, or Adventure genres. When magic dominates, the story must be Fantasy. Figure 3.1 delineates the characteristics of the Fantasy genre.

Characteristics and the Genre's Appeal

Frame

The presence of magic or enchantment is the element that most clearly distinguishes Fantasy from other genres. The amount ranges throughout the genre, but its presence, to some extent at least, ensures that readers understand they are in a Fantasy world. Magic may manifest itself in the existence of a magical sword or magical powers; there may be creatures that we readers know can exist in none but a magical world; or there may be a feeling of otherness, a sense of enchantment that grows throughout the story. Just as Merlin in the myriad

---

FIGURE 3.1

Characteristics of the Fantasy Genre

1. Magic figures prominently in the story.

2. Story lines feature "good" (light) versus "evil" (dark), and protagonists battle and ultimately conquer the dark forces.

3. Characters, clearly defined as good or bad, often attain special magical gifts, and the story lines explore ways to discover one's own potential, magical or otherwise.

4. Characters may include mythical creatures—dragons, unicorns, elves, wizards—as well as more common animals, and the story line may be based on a myth, legend, or other traditional tales.

5. Detailed settings describe another world, often Earth, but out of time.

6. In general, books start slowly as the author sets the scene, often involving a large group of characters in a strange world. Pacing increases later as more adventure elements appear.

7. Books are frequently part of a series. There is often a continuing story, told over several books.

Arthurian fantasies practices magic, so do the elves of Emma Bull's Urban Fantasy stories conjure up this otherworldliness that magic engenders. The presence of magic may be explicit, as in Arthurian stories and Bull, or it may simply be hinted at and perhaps expanded as the story develops. For example in R. A. MacAvoy's *Tea with the Black Dragon*, the story of Mayland Long—his true identity and special powers—unfolds slowly, and as we begin to suspect his true nature and secret, we see more and more of his magic.[2] This enchantment or magic may take unexpected forms, but if it is present, this is Fantasy.

Setting is another important aspect of the frame of Fantasy novels. Detailed settings frame the stories, and the otherness created by writers is vital in preparing the stage. Some authors, referred to as "world builders," create strong settings for their stories, whether single title or series. Among these are classic authors such as Lloyd Alexander (the Chronicles of Prydain, of which *The Book of Three* is the first), Ursula K. LeGuin (Earthsea Trilogy, beginning with *Wizard of Earthsea*), Andre Norton *(Witch World)*, and J. R. R. Tolkien for Middle Earth (*The Fellowship of the Ring* is the first of his trilogy), as well as newer authors like Patricia Wrede (Lyra series, beginning with *Raven Ring*).[3] Others, Elizabeth Scarborough, for example, use contemporary settings, but alter them slightly to create that sense of otherness. Scarborough's Songmaster series begins with the devils arguing about how to get humans to destroy themselves and then returns to a seemingly normal world—but one without the old folk songs. It is through music (or rather, the destruction of music, of the old folk songs) that the devils see the way to get humankind so unhinged that total destruction of the world is the only possible result. Many urban fantasies are set in near-future, near-realistic, but certainly recognizable locales. In Rosemary Edghill's *The Sword of Maiden's Tears,* a library student rescues an elf, caught in this, the lowest of worlds, and mugged in New York City.[4] In this first volume of a trilogy, the final battle against evil (a beast out of our world and time) takes place in the New York City subway, thus intricately blending the real and the fantastic.

The otherness of these settings, although important, is not the only aspect to be considered. Part of the appeal of Fantasy is the detail with which these settings—this otherness—are brought to life. Fantasy novels take us to another place, so intricately described, that we can accept all that happens. And despite all the magic that exists in these other worlds, the sense of reality is so great that we can visualize the action and characters absolutely. Orson Scott Card has remarked that he has received letters praising the detailed world he created for his Alvin Maker series. This is a parallel American West very like its historical antecedent, but it is also a place where very different events have occurred. The reader who wrote to thank Card for clarifying that George Washington had been hanged in this Alternate History of America was caught up in that other, but obviously very realistic, historical past.[5]

Story Line

Fantasy is a genre of contrasts—good and bad, light and dark—but here the light emerges victorious. In Horror a hint of the evil always survives, but in Fantasy there is the expectation of ultimate victory over the dark side, and that is very satisfying for fans. Even in the darker Fantasy series of Stephen Donaldson (The Chronicles of Thomas Covenant, the Unbeliever) or Stephen King (The Dark Tower), the expectation of ultimate victory over the forces of evil keeps readers following the adventures. Donaldson's antihero protagonist Thomas Covenant may be damaged, a leper, but he still combats the dark forces that inflict their evil on the Land.[6] Fantasy is ultimately an optimistic genre, with the forces of good eventually conquering evil (although it may take several long books in a series to accomplish this). The pattern of the genre leads to a hopeful outcome, no matter how grievous the trials along the way.

Beyond this contrast between good and evil, story lines offer a range of possibilities. Much of Fantasy involves a quest of some sort, and it is easy to see how this theme fits into this story pattern. A band of characters embarks on a dangerous mission and, after a series of adventures, succeeds in attaining their goal. Tolkien's Lord of the Rings Trilogy is certainly the modern archetype of this story; however, although the quest appears in many forms, at the heart of the story the fate of the world is always at stake, and the final confrontation involves a pitched battle against evil. Another example, Guy Gavriel Kay's Fionavar Tapestry Trilogy, beginning with The Summer Tree, places five University of Toronto students in another time and place, in the midst of a struggle against the evil Unraveller.[7] They come into their own powers and join with Arthur Pendragon in the battle to save the world, as do Frodo, Bilbo, and their band in Tolkien's stories.

Although quests play a role in many Fantasy stories, they are not the only popular theme. Themes may revolve around the retellings of myths or fairy tales, as in the series edited by Terry Windling and featuring adaptations of fairy tales, some even with modern settings (Sleeping Beauty reimagined in Nazi Germany, for example, in Jane Yolen's Briar Rose).[8] Arthurian legends are always popular, and although many of us catalog them in Fiction, rather than with the Fantasy books, they certainly fit the criteria for Fantasy novels. How else would we classify Merlin, the ultimate magician; the treacherous Morgan le Fay; or the magical sword Excalibur? (Persia Woolley's series, starting with Child of the Northern Spring, relates the familiar story through Guinevere's eyes.)[9] In fact, the Arthurian stories also reflect the Fantasy genre's emphasis on coming-of-age stories, more generally showing youth coming into their own magical powers. That is certainly what happens in many Fantasy novels, from Kay's Fionavar Tapestry and Tolkien's classics to the Urban Fantasy of Bull to J. K. Rowling's Harry Potter. (Because it overlaps with characterization, this theme is discussed in more detail below.)

In addition to Quests and coming-of-age stories, Fantasy also features stories of Alternate or Parallel Worlds. Unlike the Alternative Worlds discussed in chapter 12, "Science Fiction," here magic plays an important role and distinguishes these series from the speculative ones discussed there. Terry Brooks's Magic Kingdom series (*Magic Kingdom for Sale—Sold!*) is the first, and Katherine Kurtz's Deryni saga (beginning with *Deryni Rising*) are popular examples, as are Card's Tales of Alvin Maker series (*Seventh Son*).[10] In these, worlds are created that mirror our own: the historical West in Card's, contemporary Earth in Brooks's, and medieval Europe in Kurtz's. Even though it is not a parallel world, the map of Piers Anthony's Xanth, which bears a startling resemblance to Florida, tends to make us more comfortable with the location, this "other" Florida. To these vaguely familiar settings we bring our own understanding of time and place, and the authors build on that knowledge in creating their magical worlds.

One last theme should be mentioned: political intrigue. This plays an important role in many Fantasy series by the genre's most popular authors: Robert Jordan, Raymond E. Feist, Terry Goodkind, Kurtz, and others. Elements of court intrigue and the machinations of those with power—or desiring it—often serve to increase the pacing of the story.

Fantasy usually tells a continuous story, broken into sections and published as separate books. Science Fiction, on the other hand, is more likely to be episodic. Most Science Fiction novels in series, as in the *Star Trek* series, relate a separate adventure, and these series are not as closely tied together as those in Fantasy. Fantasy often tells a single story, but instead of being published as one unwieldy volume, it is broken into several, often leaving the reader hanging, waiting a year or more to take up the story again. (The end of the second volume of Tolkien's Lord of the Rings Trilogy is a good example; the closing scene of *The Two Towers* is a literal cliff-hanger, with Frodo hanging on for his life.)

Characterization

Just as the story lines focus on the battle between good and evil, so are the characters usually recognizable as one or the other. Clearly defined stereotypical characters are an appeal in many genres and Fantasy is no exception. They are not cardboard; within the confines of their type they are carefully and interestingly drawn, but they are types nonetheless. That is not to say that characters are branded as one or the other, but generally our protagonists can tell—they can feel the good or evil—and even if they do not act on their impressions, they, and we readers, usually have a sense of the true nature of the characters in the stories. For example, in the second title of George R. R. Martin's series, A Clash of Kings, we meet Tyrion, a dwarf and scion of an evil family.[11] Yet we know his blood also contains vestiges of nobility that will win out in the end. Although unappealing physically and apparently of evil stock, Tyrion is recognizable by readers for his innate goodness.

Characters play a more important role in the Fantasy genre than they do in Science Fiction, and the protagonist is particularly important. These often complex characters are frequently on journeys of discovery, whether actual physical journeys or less tangible mental or emotional journeys. They may have special gifts or powers, magical in their deepest nature, that they are just discovering in themselves and are seeking to master. These are books about discovering one's own potential, magical and otherwise, and thus have strong appeal as coming-of-age stories. Harry Potter in Rowling's enormously popular series beginning with *Harry Potter and the Sorcerer's Stone* must go to Hogwarts School of Witchcraft and Wizardry to master his special powers.[12] In another variation, Sparrowhawk, hero of LeGuin's *Wizard of Earthsea*, having accidentally unleashed an evil force into the world, must, as he matures, develop the power to subdue that evil.

Characters in Fantasy novels are seldom what they seem. They may be hiding their true identity, as Aragorn does in Tolkien's classic The Lord of the Rings Trilogy. Aragorn hides behind the identity of a Ranger named Strider until he is prepared, and the time is right, to reveal his true nature. Sometimes the character does not realize that he is hiding his identity, as in Robert Silverberg's Majipoor series, in which Lord Valentine's own body has been taken over by the son of the king of the dreams (who now rules cruelly in Valentine's stead), and Valentine finds himself in a very different body. Once he discovers his true identity, he must work to resolve the political crisis that besets his land. *Sorcerers of Majipoor* is the first chronologically in this series.[13]

One last point about characters of Fantasy novels: They are not always human. As in Science Fiction, where aliens may dominate a story, here nonhumans are often protagonists. These characters have very human characteristics and are individuals we readily relate to and see as human, although perhaps a little different. Tolkien's hobbits, Richard Adams's rabbits, and Brian Jacques's peace-loving creatures (mice, moles, shrews, and squirrels) pitted against the vicious rats, weasels, stoats, and foxes all speak to us with human voices and attributes.[14] No matter what species or magical creatures they are, we readers relate to and care about them.

Pacing

Pacing in Fantasy is more closely related to that in Historical Fiction. Although the books almost always start slowly, setting the stage with the intricately developed location and multiple characters, they usually move more quickly later, as Adventure elements often play an important role. Readers who are expecting stories that take off from page 1 may need to be warned.

Key Authors and Subgenres

Benchmark

Many of us came to the Fantasy genre through J. R. R. Tolkien. As Diana Tixier Herald writes in her excellent study of the genre, *Fluent in Fantasy: A Guide to Reading Interests,* he is the "father of modern fantasy."[15] As such he has numerous imitators, but his writing has also set the standard of what is expected by fans of the genre. His are stories of epic quests, with unexpected heroes and their companions battling the forces of evil to save the world from ultimate darkness. And succeeding. Originally written for children in the '50s, Tolkien's series found a mass audience in the '70s when his popularity mushroomed. Newer, and often younger, Fantasy fans, however, remind us that there is much more to the genre than just Tolkien. They may deign to read him, but many are interested in other stories and styles.

Today's benchmark stands out without question: J. K. Rowling. Her Harry Potter series has taken the reading public by storm. The fact that her titles dominated the *New York Times* Best Sellers List forced that venerable publication to create a Children's List. How can I call a children's author the benchmark, you might ask? Rowling is a perfect example of the ageless appeal of the genre. More than any other genre, Fantasy really knows no age limits. Younger readers appreciate some stories written for adults, and we adults can hardly resist much of what appears for children, from the classic authors (L. Frank Baum's Oz series, beginning with *The Wonderful Wizard of Oz,* and C. S. Lewis's Narnia series, starting with *The Lion, The Witch, and the Wardrobe*) to more recent series by Susan Cooper (The Dark Is Rising sequence, beginning with *Over Sea, Under Stone*) and Philip Pullman's trilogy, His Dark Materials, the first of which is *The Golden Compass.*[16] However, Rowling herself says that she is writing not simply for children, but rather the story she needs to tell. Those of us who promote reading for children should be grateful, but that the series is enjoyed by children should not detract from its universal appeal and the layers of meaning that characterize the best Fantasy—or the best in any genre.

When he turns eleven, the orphaned Harry Potter learns that he is to go to Hogwarts School of Witchcraft and Wizardry to become a wizard in the tradition of his parents before him. What happens then—how he battles evil in each book, leading up to the expected final confrontation in the final volume—has entranced literally millions of readers around the world. And Harry has become a publishing phenomenon. Popularity as well as themes that represent the characteristics of the Fantasy genre make Rowling an apt benchmark.

Subgenres of Fantasy

Reference books identified below discuss myriad subgenres and themes, from Faerie to Urban Fantasy. Thus, if we find readers desiring a particular type, these are easily retrievable. On the other hand, more and more readers describe Fantasy by the mood the books evoke, from the darker, brooding stories of Stephen Donaldson and Stephen King to the boisterous humor of Terry Pratchett and Piers Anthony. Because the differences are in tone rather than any of the other characteristics, I will discuss them from that point of view.

Pratchett is the name to remember for the humorous end of the Fantasy genre. His Discworld series, now more than twenty volumes, sets the standard for laugh-out-loud adventures, enjoyed on many levels by a wide range of readers, even those who also appreciate darker, more literary stories. Satirical, lampooning every available target, these novels set the stage with their titles and never let up. Try *Carpe Jugulum* as a recent example.[17] The title, which means "Seize the Throat," promises vampires; and readers are not disappointed by the Magpyrs who, like *The Man Who Came to Dinner,* come to a christening and stay to try to take over the kingdom. Eccentric characters populate Pratchett's stories, and the wordplay, both in the text and his special explanatory notes, verbal and visual gags, and over-the-top plots make them vastly entertaining reading.

Two other long-running series deserve mention: Anthony's Xanth novels and Robert Lynn Asprin's M.Y.T.H. books. Anthony's feature endless puns and wordplays, and the first, *A Spell for Chameleon,* won the August Derleth Award, the British Fantasy award.[18] In Xanth, a land of magic and wizards, only Bink has no magic. Thus, he embarks on a quest to discover it. Eccentric characters, outrageous puns, and improbable stories characterize Anthony's popular series.

Asprin's series, notable for the puns even in the titles (*Myth Conceptions,* for example), are more slapstick.[19] These novels relate the exploits and adventures of a hapless pair: a magician who has lost his powers and the inept apprentice with whom he travels as he tries to regain them.

Humor abounds in the Fantasy genre. Note, however, that just because titles include a strong vein of humor does not mean they are fluff. As in all genre books, they can be read at many levels, and the humorous stories simply handle important issues differently. Also noteworthy are Stephen Brust (the Vlad Taltos series with a wisecracking P.I.–assassin), Orson Scott Card (Alvin Maker), and Fritz Leiber (Fafhrd and the Gray Mouser).

As he does in the Science Fiction genre, the prolific Roger Zelazny tends to write both humorous and darker Fantasy. On the humorous end are the punning titles that indicate fairy tale or myth retellings. Or they are that ostensibly. In reality they offer a range of literary and media allusions that leave the reader gasping. Although some readers may find the sophomoric humor exasperating, others will enjoy the wordplay. My personal favorite is *If at Faust You Don't Succeed*, written with Robert Scheckley.[20] In the ongoing battles for supremacy during the millennium, Archangel Michael and his nemesis Mephistopheles choose Johann Faust as their pawn. Unfortunately, they kidnap a burglar by mistake, and Faust spends his time trying to catch up so he can play his destined role. Zelazny's other major series, the Amber books, follow the adventures of Prince Corwin and his son, Merlin. Elegantly written with less humor but complex, darker worlds and details, these appeal to readers who like their humor in more moderate doses.

On the other end of the spectrum are Fantasy novels that are significantly darker in tone. These are not Horror, but they are stories filtered through a bleaker worldview, where the stakes are seen as too high for the levity of puns and wordplay. Generally these are more atmospheric, more densely written, and directed toward weightier themes than their opposites. King's Dark Tower series is a good example. (First of these titles is *The Gunslinger.*)[21] All elements combine to underline the mood of the book: short sentences, terse dialogue, desert landscape, and a haunted hero on an obscure mission (an antiquest perhaps). As the hero explains, parodying Tolkien's words and theme, "There are quests and roads that lead ever onward, and all of them end in the same place—upon the killing ground."[22]

Even Donaldson's leper antihero Thomas Covenant can hardly compete with King's hero for dark mood. In contrast to King's sparse language, Donaldson employs more elegant, denser prose in describing Covenant's fate. In a story that harkens back to Samuel Taylor Coleridge's "The Rime of the Ancient Mariner" in tone and plot, Covenant, too, proves a reluctant hero. A man who does not understand his role and does not want to accept it, he is nevertheless sent on a mission to save the Land.

Fantasy series by Robert Jordan and Raymond E. Feist, clearly influenced by the characters, story line, and melancholy tone of Tolkien, also reflect this bleaker outlook. Jordan's Wheel of Time series (*The Eye of the World* is the first) is a character-centered series that follows the adventures of three companions on a quest to reach the Eye of the World before the evil one escapes.[23] Magic and special powers enhance this tale of adventure, suspense, and romance, not to mention the obligatory battle against evil. Nine titles are expected to comprise this popular series.

Feist joins elements of Science Fiction with Fantasy in his Riftwar saga. (First is *The Magician,* revised and greatly improved in 1992 and now only available in two volumes, *Magician: Apprentice* and *Magician: Master.*)[24] When the magical kingdom of Crydee is invaded by forces from another dimension, Pug and Tomas, apprentices who come into their own powers, begin the fight to regain supremacy. Politics, moral questions on the nature of power and treatment of captives, military strategy, and swashbuckling adventure combine with magical powers in this dark, action-oriented Fantasy. The presence of more extensive technology also provides a link to Science Fiction, and this makes a good crossover series for fans of that genre.

Terry Goodkind and George R. R. Martin warrant mention here as well. Also influenced by Tolkien, both are in the midst of very popular ongoing series. Goodkind's series, The Sword of Truth, features the adventures of Richard Cypher and Kahlen and includes wizards, magic swords, political intrigue, and the reversal of expected gender roles, as Richard supplies the magic while Kahlen oversees the troops. *Wizard's First Rule* is the first.[25] Martin's Song of Fire and Ice saga, beginning with *A Game of Thrones,* promises to be a vast tapestry of power struggles and intrigue in a land where magic has almost disappeared, seasons last for decades, and the long winter has only brought infighting and a battle for the throne.[26]

Urban Fantasy offers a range of elements that appeal to readers, but it also tends to be darker still. The emphasis on societal issues, power or its absence, and general urban blight make these bleaker stories. An excellent example is Neil Gaiman's *Neverwhere.*[27] When Londoner Richard Mayhew deserts his fiancée to rescue an injured young woman they pass on the street, his life changes forever. He becomes part of her quest in London Below, a historic underground city populated by people who have fallen through the cracks. Bleak, atmospheric, graphically rendered (as expected by someone whose greatest fame stems from his illustrated novels), this haunting story can be appreciated on many levels.

Although not overwhelmingly dark, much Fantasy is pervaded by an elegiac tone, leavened by humorous touches. Writers such as Zelazny and Mercedes Lackey write series that represent both ends of the spectrum (for example, Zelazny's Amber series mentioned earlier and Lackey's Bardic Voices series, with its mix of music, magic, and mystery. The first is *The Lark and the Wren*).[28] Others sit more firmly in the middle, veering in one direction or the other. This middle ground constitutes the bulk of the genre, with popular writers such as David Eddings (his multi-volume series, the Belgariad—*Belgarath the Sorcerer* is the first—followed by the Mallorean, have kept readers turning the pages and provide a good introduction to the genre), Barbara Hambly (dragons and mages in her series beginning with *Dragonsbane*), Stephen Lawhead (Fantasy with a Christian emphasis, but his popular Pendragon series—*Taliesin* is the first—features Arthurian myths), and Melanie Rawn (subsequent titles in her Mageborn series—*The Ruins of Ambrai* is the first—are always eagerly awaited) drawing on both ends to produce satisfying Fantasy.[29]

Preparing to Work with Readers

Readers who particularly ask for Fantasy—and I have frequently had readers come to me to say they are interested in starting to read in this genre—are usually looking generally for stories with magical elements. They appreciate the fact that goodness triumphs over evil in these stories, and they expect a well-developed setting, populated by interesting characters. Beyond that there are any number of directions to pursue. From retellings of fairy tales and Arthurian legends, Celtic and Asian Fantasy, to stories of wizards, elves, and uncommon animals or other beasts, Fantasy celebrates the victory of good over evil, while exploring a variety of themes. A general understanding of the range of the genre, lists carefully crafted to reflect themes readers frequently request, and good reference sources are all invaluable.

Fans of Fantasy represent the widest age range of any genre. We need to be prepared to assist adults as well as much younger readers interested in exploring this genre. This is a good crossover genre for grade-school children who are good readers; in Fantasy and Science Fiction they often discover the treasures that await them in the adult collections of our libraries. We lure younger readers with Katherine Kurtz, Terry Brooks, Andre Norton, Anne McCaffrey, and Patricia A. McKillip and continue to enchant adults with Susan Cooper (The Dark Is Rising series), Brian Jacques, and J. K. Rowling. Currently teens at my library especially enjoy Mercedes Lackey, Robert Jordan, and Terry Goodkind. Fantasy can be read and appreciated on many levels and reread for a new understanding of the deeper meaning of stories enjoyed in the past. One word of warning, however. Fantasy novels may also contain themes that parents are not keen on their children exploring. There may be sexual situations, sometimes homosexual, in some of the authors who seem appropriate for teens and younger. I always encourage the parents to read the books first if they have any concerns.

Readers tend to be series-oriented, and, as do all series readers, they want to read the titles in order, and they certainly expect the library to have copies of every title in a series they love. Because many, if not most, Fantasy series start out as paperbacks, this can be a considerable problem. We need to be aggressive in ordering these series early on and then pursuing every avenue to fill in titles in popular series when the paperbacks are out of print. Like fans of other genres, these readers never see interlibrary loan as a good alternative to actually having the desired titles in our collections.

The Fantasy genre has also produced a large number of shared worlds, in which more than one writer places adventures in a world created by another author, as well as joint titles. For example, stories of Conan the Barbarian were first written by Robert E. Howard, but several popular authors have also tried their hand at these Sword and Sorcery stories, from L. Sprague de Camp to Jordan. Other series are based on computer or role-playing games. The most popular examples are the myriad Dragonlance books, a spin-off of Dungeons and Dragons, a role-playing game. Owned and published originally by TSR, Dragonlance features multiple, closely interconnected series that fans continually request and that remain difficult to sort out, not to mention purchase. Among the most requested are the Dragonlance series by Margaret Weis and Tracy Hickman (*Dragons of Autumn Twilight* is an early title), and the Forgotten Realms series by R. A. Salvatore (*The Crystal Shard* opens his Icewind Dale Trilogy).[30] Fans appreciate being made aware of these series by multiple authors and consisting of shared worlds. They are often good suggestions for a fan of one of these authors currently at loose ends. At my library we Cutter these titles under the series name, as that seems more useful for browsers or readers of the series than the names of the individual authors.

Fantasy offers big books and often long series, and these readers are not daunted by size. Whether the story is complete in one large volume or several, readers seem to devour the series they enjoy and then demand the next volume before it is even written. Alternative suggestions of similar authors or series are always a good idea. We are not above quizzing fans for further reading suggestions and then sharing them with other interested readers.

Fantasy readers seem not quite so aloof as many Science Fiction fans. We have found them interested in discovering new authors that may have the same appeal as others they have enjoyed and willing to try our suggestions. That being the case, we need to be prepared for fans, armed with suggestions to tide them over while they wait for their favorites to publish another entry in their favorite series—and because they usually have to wait at least a year for the next volume, they are often receptive. It is important to identify the authors and series popular at our own libraries, talk with fans, and read the books and about them to discover why they are so popular, to try to discover authors that are similar. For example, readers of Jordan's Wheel of Time series may like similar quest novels, such as George R. R. Martin's *A Game of Thrones* and L. E. Modesitt Jr.'s Recluce series (*The Magic of Recluce* is the first).[31] Fans of J. R. R. Tolkien may enjoy these, as well as Raymond E. Feist's Riftwar series (*The Magician* starts the adventures of the orphaned Pug and his motley band), Brooks's somewhat less intense Shannara series (*The Sword of Shannara* is the first), or Guy Gavriel Kay's Fionavar Tapestry Trilogy, beginning with *The Summer Tree*.[32]

Short stories provide an excellent introduction to the genre, for readers and librarians alike. In addition to the ongoing collections of award-winning Fantasy, a particularly useful recent publication is *Legends*, which collects short stories based on the series of some of the most popular Fantasy authors writing today: Stephen King, Terry Pratchett, Orson Scott Card, Martin, Jordan, and more.[33] Short stories allow readers to experiment, to sample an author's style and subject matter before pursuing an author or series. In this case, especially, they also provide readers with a taste of the series they might read.

The Fantasy genre also boasts authors who have made their name and reputation in other genres. King comes immediately to mind. In addition to his reputation as a Horror writer, King has established himself in the Fantasy genre, with his classic *The Stand* and the Dark Tower series.[34] Science Fiction writers who also write popular Fantasy series include Piers Anthony, Roger Zelazny, Elizabeth Moon, and Card. Readers who know their Fantasy writing may also be interested in pursuing the work of these writers in other genres.

One last issue to consider in preparing to work with Fantasy fans is a controversy among writers, a certain snobbishness it seems, about the superiority of one genre over another. There seems to be a feeling among some writers that Science Fiction is the genre designation of choice, and that it is better to be considered a writer of Science Fiction than a writer of Fantasy. This affects a pair of very popular authors: Anne McCaffrey and Marion Zimmer Bradley. Both state emphatically that they write Science Fiction, but their books are beloved by Fantasy fans, probably cherished more by them than by readers of Science Fiction. Yes, there may be a scientific basis for these stories set in other worlds, but the feel of the stories and characters appeal far more readily to Fantasy fans than to Science Fiction readers. Thus, we successfully offer McCaffrey's Dragonriders of Pern series and Bradley's tales of Darkover to Fantasy readers, rather than to Science Fiction fans. Figure 3.2 offers additional authors for fans of other genres to try to discover something similar in the Fantasy genre.

Readers' Advisory Interview

Faced with a reader of a genre I am less comfortable discussing, I rely on what that reader says about what he enjoys in a genre or a particular type of story. Does he talk about a type of character? Or a story based on myth or legend? Or perhaps a setting that appeals?

FIGURE 3.2

An Introduction to Fantasy

Fantasy Writers to Try, If You Enjoy . . .

Adventure	Raymond E. Feist
	Robert Jordan
Gentle	C. S. Lewis
Historical	Mary Stewart (The Merlin Quartet)
Horror	Terry Brooks (*Running with the Demon*)[35]
Humor	Piers Anthony (Xanth series)
	Orson Scott Card (Chronicles of Alvin Maker)
	Terry Pratchett
Inspirational	C. S. Lewis (Narnia)
	Stephen Lawhead
Literary	Mervyn Peake
Mystery	Stephen Brust (Vlad Taltos series)
Psychological	Stephen R. Donaldson
Romance	Rosemary Edghill
	Melanie Rawn
	Patricia Wrede (*The Magician's Ward*)[36]
Science Fiction	Raymond E. Feist
Thriller	Roger Zelazny (Amber series)
	George R. R. Martin
Western	Stephen King (The Dark Tower series)

If this is a reader new to the genre, and he wants to explore Fantasy, I need information about other authors or titles he has enjoyed, no matter what the genre. If he talks about characters, I might explore further with questions about whether humans or animals are preferred. How much overt magic would be interesting? Does he want a familiar story, a fairy tale, or Arthurian retelling? Or something completely new?

If readers ask for stories of parallel worlds, we turn to the reference books, unless, of course, we really are knowledgeable fans of the genre. (Even then, we might appreciate the backup authority, and certainly readers enjoy discovering reference books to explore on their own, especially those with many lists.) In fact, many of these questions can be answered by the reference tools discussed below. Types of characters and thematic groupings lend themselves well to these tools.

On the other hand, readers who describe books by tone require us to probe further and sort by other factors, such as the amount of humor. More humorous Fantasy novels are easily identified by the titles themselves. Puns in the title are likely to indicate a less serious bent. Time period may be another factor. Readers who want a medieval feel or a contemporary world can be helped by cover drawings or descriptions on book jackets (I always like to verify the period by reading the book jacket).

I have occasionally had readers, especially younger readers, seeking books with more Adventure elements. Here, as in Historical Fiction, maps may indicate Adventure elements, and I discover these as I flip through the pages with the reader. Reference books can help, too, as I know that Sword and Sorcery titles as well as Quests are likely to contain Adventure.

Sure Bets

Although I have mentioned Guy Gavriel Kay's Fionavar Tapestry, another of his titles, *Tigana,* appeals to a wide range of readers.[37] With its setting similar to medieval Italy, this story reveals a rich interweaving of political intrigue, rich cultural detail, and memorable characters.

An unusual Fantasy novel is Jeanne Larsen's *The Silk Road.*[38] Set in eighth-century China, this novel takes a historical world, filled with accurate cultural and historical details, adds an element of magic to enhance the story, and thus plays on the idea of how stories are retold and transmuted through their retellings down through the centuries. The heroine is the daughter of a lord who is abducted by Tibetan traders. What happens, and what we learn about the Silk Road and life along it, ranges from historical truth to magical Fantasy and much in between.

Another author to be familiar with is Patricia Wrede. She writes humorous Fantasy, filled with Adventure and Romance, for a range of readers. From her classic Alternate World Regency Romance, *Sorcery and Cecelia,* to her series for younger readers (and older), the Enchanted Forest Chronicles (beginning with the humorous *Dealing with Dragons,* which lampoons any number of Fantasy, fairy tale, and sexual conventions), Wrede continues to delight readers.[39]

Not all Fantasy deals with the fantastic and the unreal. Jane Yolen transmutes the fairy tale Briar Rose, or Sleeping Beauty, into a twentieth-century story of the Holocaust. Rebecca always remembered her grandmother's telling of the Sleeping Beauty story and her claim to be Briar Rose, but when the old woman dies, Becca, now a journalist, decides to investigate in an attempt to discover any truth behind the tale. In the telling and retelling, Yolen underlines the universal nature of stories, and in particular of fairy tales, as Becca uncovers the truth of her grandmother's past.

Expanding Readers' Horizons

Fantasy readers find much that appeals in other genres; if they find books of similar feel and tone, they seem not to mind the lack of magic too much. Historical Fiction has a wealth of material for Fantasy readers who appreciate the "historical" settings of much Fantasy. The connection is probably the intricately detailed setting; the feel of another, earlier time (these are not for fans of Urban Fantasy, with its contemporary settings); and big books. Good choices are Jennifer Roberson and Lucia St. Clair Robson and Arthurian Fantasy by authors such as Persia Woolley.

The Romance genre also offers a number of authors who are read and loved by Fantasy fans. Any of the authors described in chapter 10, "Romance," in the section on "Alternative Reality Romances" might appeal to Fantasy readers, as these Romances offer paranormal elements. Susan Carroll's *The Bride Finder* might be of particular interest, as it centers on a family gifted with unusual powers and the "Bride Finder," who magically discovers the proper wife for each heir in the family.[40] Other Romances may have characters that are fairy tale archetypes, like Cupid, or fairy godmothers, as in Cathie Linz's Marriage Makers series, beginning with *Too Sexy for Marriage*.[41]

Fantasy readers may find satisfaction in the Horror genre, in the evil creatures that are created, but they have to be resigned to the fact that evil is not conquered but is left to menace future generations. Crossover authors Stephen King and Raymond E. Feist (*Faerie Tale* is Horror with strong Fantasy elements)[42] are good suggestions, as well as stories of enchanted creatures, witches, warlocks, vampires, werewolves, and monsters, such as Laurell K. Hamilton's Anita Blake, Vampire Hunter, series. H. P. Lovecraft's weird tales of the Cthulhu Mythos may also appeal to fans of Dark Fantasy.

Adventure pervades much Fantasy, and Fantasy fans, for whom the Adventure element is important, find titles that appeal in that genre. As his work becomes less founded in reality, Clive Cussler becomes a better bet for these readers. Quest fans may discover Adventure titles that they enjoy, but most titles lack the elegiac, melancholy tone of Fantasy Quests. And they certainly lack the magic. Katherine Neville's *The Eight* features the fate of the world hanging on the acquisition of a chess set, once owned by Charlemagne.[43] In addition to some similar plot elements, the book, at 550 pages, should be long enough to satisfy Fantasy fans. Another interesting possibility is *Invisible World* by Stuart Cohen, which explores the worlds of ancient tapestries and maps and a quest, directed by a dead man, to Inner Mongolia.[44]

Science Fiction attracts some Fantasy fans as well, in part because many authors write in both genres, and their fans read across the genre borders with abandon. Anne McCaffrey and Marion Zimmer Bradley, who claim to write Science Fiction, not Fantasy, are certainly reasonable choices. The key is that the Science Fiction should not contain too much technical detail or space travel and not be set in a world that depends on these. Science Fiction stories of alternate and parallel worlds, like Philip K. Dick's *The Man in the High Castle*, may also appeal.[45]

Among possibilities in the Mystery genre might be Eric Garcia's *Anonymous Rex*.[46] What humorous Fantasy fan could resist this hard-boiled detective who just happens to be a dinosaur? Or perhaps consider Richard Brautigan's *Dreaming of Babylon*, which relates the tale

---

FIGURE 3.3

Expanding Readers' Horizons

Authors to Take Readers beyond the Fantasy Genre

Adventure	Clive Cussler
	Katherine Neville
Historical	Lucia St. Clair Robson
	Persia Woolley
Horror	Stephen King
	Raymond E. Feist
Literary	Isabel Allende
Mystery	Eric Garcia
Romance	Susan Carroll
Science Fiction	Anne McCaffrey
	Marion Zimmer Bradley

---

of the incompetent P.I., dreaming of another time, with both humor and some of the bleaker tone some Fantasy readers seek.[47] Figure 3.3 offers authors, from other genres, who might appeal to Fantasy fans.

Reference Sources

There are a number of helpful reference sources aimed specifically at the Fantasy genre. Diana Tixier Herald's *Fluent in Fantasy: A Guide to Reading Interests* offers an exceptional overview of the genre, including core lists, award winners, subgenres and themes, history, and numerous titles to suggest to readers.[48] If you can only afford one title for this genre, this is the one to buy.

Also useful are *St. James Guide to Fantasy Writers* and Neil Barron's *Fantasy and Horror: A Critical and Historical Guide to Literature, Illustration, Film, TV, Radio, and the Internet.*[49] The former provides inviting, detailed author biographies, a complete bibliography of the author's works, and some useful comments on individual titles, while the latter offers a detailed historical perspective of the genre, excellent core lists, annotated titles, and the related film, television, radio, and Internet resources. Both are useful tools for librarians and excellent browsing for fans or others interested in the genre.

Where to Find . . .

INFORMATION ABOUT THE AUTHOR

St. James Guide to Fantasy Writers provides this information and covers a wide range of authors. Unfortunately, because this series will probably be discontinued, the information will be dated within a few years. *Contemporary Authors* (*see* appendix 2) offers similar information for a growing number of Fantasy authors.

PLOT SUMMARIES

Turn to Barron's *Fantasy and Horror* for excellent plot summaries. Herald's *Fluent in Fantasy* also offers numerous pithy annotations. General resources described in appendix 2—*Sequels, Genreflecting, Fiction Catalog, What Do I Read Next? NoveList*, and *To Be Continued*— also provide annotations for many titles.

SUBGENRES AND THEMES

Fluent in Fantasy is the primary source for this information, but *Genreflecting* contains much of the same information, and thus it is also available on *NoveList*.

In addition to the information from *Genreflecting, NoveList* provides access to subgenres through both its subject search features. By searching "Describe a Plot" under Fantasy, we discover more than 3,000 titles with some form of that subject heading. Under "Browse Subjects," subdivisions of that heading are listed, ranging from Fantasy Fiction divided by country to Humorous Fantasy and Urban Fantasy.

What Do I Read Next? offers similar searching capabilities. Subgenres and themes are listed in a separate index under "Fantasy" in the book version, and in the "Genre Search" function of the Web version, one can select from among a list of subheadings from the pull-down menu.

GENRE DESCRIPTION, BACKGROUND, AND HISTORY

Barron's *Fantasy and Horror* is the most comprehensive source for this type of information. Herald provides a more concise history in her *Fluent in Fantasy,* and both that title and *Genreflecting* list other useful reference tools that can provide this and other information. In addition, the annual volume of *What Do I Read Next?* gives a summary of trends in the genre over the previous year. Feature articles in *NoveList* also explore aspects of the genre.

CORE LISTS AND BEST BOOKS

Barron and Herald provide this information consistently, and Herald's lists also appear on *NoveList.*

Fantasy is a genre that inspires lifelong fans. They may read other genres at certain periods in their lives, but they come back to Fantasy, rereading their favorites and discovering new authors and new directions. When we read Fantasy authors like Robert Jordan, we get a taste of this long-lived appeal. These are often elegantly written stories with a haunting quality. We sense there is something just behind the story, something bigger than the story itself, that hints at a larger meaning. These are the stories of legends come to life, and the popularity of the genre attests to the continuing importance of this kind of story in our lives.

NOTES

1. Eva Ibbotson, *The Secret of Platform 13* (New York: Dutton Children's Books, 1998); Elizabeth Ann Scarborough, *The Healer's War* (New York: Doubleday, 1988).
2. R. A. MacAvoy, *Tea with the Black Dragon* (New York: Bantam, 1983).
3. Lloyd Alexander, *The Book of Three* (New York: Holt, 1964); Ursula K. LeGuin, *Wizard of Earthsea* (Berkeley, Calif.: Parnassus, 1968); Andre Norton, *Witch World* (New York: Ace Books, 1963); J. R. R. Tolkien, *The Fellowship of the Ring: Being the First Part of the Lord of the Rings* (Boston: Houghton, 1965); Patricia Wrede, *Raven Ring* (New York: Tor, 1994).
4. Rosemary Edghill, *The Sword of Maiden's Tears* (New York: Daw Books, 1994).
5. Orson Scott Card, untitled luncheon speech at Public Library Association Pre-Conference, March 28, 2000.
6. Stephen Donaldson, *Lord Foul's Bane* (New York: Holt, 1977).

7. Guy Gavriel Kay, *The Summer Tree* (New York: Arbor House, 1985, © 1984).

8. Jane Yolen, *Briar Rose* (New York: T. Doherty Associates, 1992).

9. Persia Woolley, *Child of the Northern Spring* (New York: Poseidon Press, 1987).

10. Terry Brooks, *Magic Kingdom for Sale—Sold!* (New York: Ballantine, 1986); Katherine Kurtz, *Deryni Rising* (New York: Ballantine, 1970); Orson Scott Card, *Seventh Son* (New York: T. Doherty Associates, 1987).

11. George R. R. Martin, *A Clash of Kings* (New York: Bantam, 2000). Note: book 1—*A Game of Thrones* (New York: Bantam, 1996); book 2—*A Song of Fire and Ice* (New York: Bantam, 1999).

12. J. K. Rowling, *Harry Potter and the Sorcerer's Stone* (New York: Arthur A. Levine Books, 1998, © 1997).

13. Robert Silverberg, *Sorcerers of Majipoor* (New York: HarperPrism, 1996).

14. Richard Adams, *Watership Down* (New York: Macmillan, 1974); Brian Jacques, *Redwall* (New York: Philomel, 1986).

15. Diana Tixier Herald, *Fluent in Fantasy: A Guide to Reading Interests* (Englewood, Colo.: Libraries Unlimited, 1999), p. 28.

16. L. Frank Baum, *The Wonderful Wizard of Oz* (Chicago: G. M. Hill, 1900); C. S. Lewis, *The Lion, the Witch, and the Wardrobe* (New York: Macmillan, 1950); Susan Cooper, *Over Sea, Under Stone* (New York: Harcourt Brace, 1966); Philip Pullman, *The Golden Compass* (New York: Knopf, 1996).

17. Terry Pratchett, *Carpe Jugulum* (New York: HarperPrism, 1999).

18. Piers Anthony, *A Spell for Chameleon* (New York: Ballantine, 1977).

19. Robert Lynn Asprin, *Myth Conceptions* (New York: Ace Books, 1985).

20. Roger Zelazny and Robert Sheckley, *If at Faust You Don't Succeed* (New York: Bantam, 1993).

21. Stephen King, *The Gunslinger* (New York: Signet, 1982).

22. Ibid., 158–59.

23. Robert Jordan, *The Eye of the World* (New York: T. Doherty Associates, 1990).

24. Raymond E. Feist, *The Magician*, rev. ed. (New York: Doubleday, 1992).

25. Terry Goodkind, *Wizard's First Rule* (New York: Tor, 1994).

26. Martin, *A Game of Thrones* (New York: Bantam, 1996).

27. Neil Gaiman, *Neverwhere* (New York: Avon, 1997).

28. Mercedes Lackey, *The Lark and the Wren* (Riverdale, N.Y.: Baen, 1992).

29. David Eddings, *Belgarath the Sorcerer* (New York: Ballantine, 1995); Barbara Hambly, *Dragonsbane* (New York: Ballantine, 1985); Stephen Lawhead, *Taliesin* (Westchester, Ill.: Crossway, 1987); Melanie Rawn, *The Ruins of Ambrai* (New York: Daw Books, 1994).

30. Margaret Weis and Tracy Hickman, *Dragons of Autumn Twilight* (Renton, Wash.: TSR, 1984); R. A. Salvatore, *The Crystal Shard* (Lake Geneva, Wis.: TSR, 1988).

31. L. E. Modesitt Jr., *The Magic of Recluce* (New York: Tor, 1991).

32. Feist, *The Magician,* rev. ed (New York: Doubleday, 1992); Brooks, *The Sword of Shannara* (New York: Ballantine, 1977).

33. *Legends, vol. 1: Short Novels by the Masters of Modern Fantasy* (New York: Tor, 1999).

34. King, *The Stand* (Garden City, N.Y.: Doubleday, 1978).

35. Brooks, *Running with the Demon* (New York: Del Ray/Ballantine, 1997).

36. Wrede, *The Magician's Ward* (New York: Tor, 1997).

37. Kay, *Tigana* (New York: Penguin, 1990).

38. Jeanne Larsen, *The Silk Road* (New York: Holt, 1989).

39. Wrede, *Sorcery and Cecelia* (New York: Ace Books, 1988); ———, *Dealing with Dragons* (New York: Harcourt Brace, 1990).

40. Susan Carroll, *The Bride Finder* (New York: Ballantine, 1998).

41. Cathie Linz, *Too Sexy for Marriage* (Toronto; New York: Harlequin, 1998).

42. Feist, *Faerie Tale* (Garden City, N.Y.: Doubleday, 1988).

43. Katherine Neville, *The Eight* (New York: Ballantine, 1989, © 1988).

44. Stuart Cohen, *Invisible World* (New York: ReganBooks, 1998).

45. Philip K. Dick, *The Man in the High Castle* (New York: Putnam, 1962).

46. Eric Garcia, *Anonymous Rex: A Detective Story* (New York: Villard, 2000).

47. Richard Brautigan, *Dreaming of Babylon: A Private Eye Novel, 1942* (New York: Delacorte/S. Lawrence, 1977).

48. Herald, *Fluent in Fantasy.*

49. David Pringle, ed., *St. James Guide to Fantasy Writers* (Detroit: St. James, 1996); Neil Barron, *Fantasy and Horror: A Critical and Historical Guide to Literature, Illustration, Film, TV, Radio, and the Internet* (Lanham, Md.: Scarecrow, 1999).

4

Gentle Reads

"I want a *nice* story."

"They don't write books like they used to!"

If readers have said this to you, you understand the real need we in libraries feel to find Gentle Reads for those who want something other than the often violent and sexually explicit books on the bestsellers lists. But how do we know what is gentle enough—or too gentle? And which readers are good candidates for these authors?

This is probably the most difficult genre for librarians and readers—even if we are fans. Helping someone select books that are gentle enough is one part of the problem; trying to remember if there is anything in a book that might offend is the other part of the problem (and then discovering what we considered innocuous is the one aspect that makes the book too much for a reader). What offends one reader is often what another reader enjoys in a book. And because readers usually do not know what it is they do not want to read about until they come across it in a book we have suggested, our credibility suffers. This can appear to be a no-win situation! However, we have discovered that this category acts as a catchall, a funnel for gentle stories across the genres. The key for readers is that gentle quality, and although some books mentioned here may also fit in other genres elsewhere, we desperate librarians gather them here—so we have a range of books to suggest to readers who seek that quality.

A Definition

When we first recognized the need for books of this type at my library, we called the genre Warm Milk. The term came from a conversation a colleague had with a reader. She was looking for books that gave her the same satisfaction and feeling of well-being she felt after drinking warm milk. Charming though that label may be, it is not quite as descriptive as we need in working with the wide range of readers who seek books in this genre. Thus, we transformed it to Gentle Reads, although the feeling these books create remains true to the original description.

Before discussing what Gentle Reads are, it is important to point out what they are not. The Gentle Reads genre does not equal Inspirational or Christian Fiction. Although there are certainly authors of Inspirational Fiction who fit within this category, Gentle Reads are much more. To have a list comprised of only titles with a religious bent is to do an injustice to, and quite possibly offend, many of the readers of this genre. Although such lists are useful and may supplement our lists of Gentle Reads, they should not be given out interchangeably or discussed as synonymous. Many books within this genre are simply gentle stories with no religious connotation at all.

Gentle Reads are "feel-good" books. Strictly speaking, they should contain no strong language and no explicit sex or violence, reflect conventional values, and end happily. Beyond that, they are evocative, and, whether they boast contemporary or historical settings, they take the reader back to a gentler, less hurried time. They are cheerful, hopeful stories, told from a peaceful, soothing perspective. Like Horror they appeal primarily to the emotions, but rather than evoking a feeling of fear, they project a comfortable sense of well-being. These are lovely, satisfying books that reflect an uncomplicated, although not necessarily unsophisticated, lifestyle. Figure 4.1 lists the characteristics of Gentle Reads.

FIGURE 4.1

Characteristics of Gentle Reads

1. Evocative stories take readers back to a comfortable time and place, which may have a contemporary or historical setting, usually in a small town or rural area. These novels should contain no explicit sex, violence, or strong language.
2. Gentle pacing takes the reader on a leisurely story filled with comfortable characters and no unsettling surprises.
3. Story lines emphasize relationships among characters, rather than suspense or even social issues. Genial humor often underlines these stories.
4. Although characters are certainly comfortable companions, they are also often the source of the humor that lightens the tone of these books.

Characteristics and the Genre's Appeal

Frame

The setting, the environment in which the story takes place, is one of the keys to the satisfaction these stories bring. Frames are suggestive and frequently have a timeless quality. These books are often set in small towns, but even if they take place in urban areas, they reflect a close-knit community. Humor may play an important role as well, but even those books without outright humor display a lighter, more genial touch, as does Linda Nichols's *Handyman*, a lighthearted, romantic story about a troubled young woman who mistakes a handyman for a famous self-help psychologist and finds her life greatly improved.[1]

Books may have historical settings, or these may be contemporary, but in either case a timeless quality pervades the story. Vita Sackville-West's *All Passion Spent* reflects this tone.[2] In this gentle, elegiac, elegantly written tale, Lady Slane finds herself at loose ends after the death of her domineering husband, until she realizes that she can finally make her own decisions and follow her own interests. This is a book about reminiscences, and although a novel bounded by death, it is by no means depressing. Instead, it is a quiet, thoughtful, and thought-provoking story about life and the choices we make. The time period in which the story is set is not important; that the story itself and the issues are timeless is clear in the telling.

In all Gentle Reads the absence of explicit sex, violence, and strong language is key. These are "safe" books, and readers do not want to be surprised. Unfortunately, it is increasingly difficult for us as librarians to identify these titles and be able to offer guarantees. On the other hand, just because readers appreciate the security of this genre does not mean that they are not willing sometimes to venture further afield. Suggestions of types of books that go slightly beyond the strict confines of this genre are given in the "Expanding Readers' Horizons" section of the "Readers' Advisory Interview," below.

Pacing

These comfortable, often meandering stories wash over the reader with their gentle tone and unhurried pace. Eudora Welty, a classic author of the genre, brings her southern charm to bear in all her stories. *Delta Wedding,* for example, evocatively relates the story of the Fairchild family, living on a plantation in the Mississippi Delta in the early '20s and all involved in the preparations for Dabney's wedding.[3] The story is much more than that, however; it is an intimate examination of the personalities and emotions of all gathered there for this occasion, woven together as only such an inimitable southern storyteller can.

Story Line

Another key to the Gentle Read genre is that these are leisurely paced stories, filled with comfortable, sympathetic characters. In Jennifer Chiaverini's *The Quilter's Apprentice,* domestic pleasures (specifically quilting) provide the impetus for a crotchety old woman to divulge her long-held secrets through the stories she tells her young apprentice.[4] Realization and acceptance accompany these tales, and slowly but surely Sylvia Compson gives up the pain of the past and reconciles herself with what is left of her family, reentering the community and bringing her exquisite skills as an award-winning quilter. Home truths are at the core of many of these stories, and, as in this tale that revolves around quilting, they emphasize homey skills and satisfactions. After all, the only necessities that quilting requires are time, space, and friends. These are not characters involved in solitary quests; they are friends and companions who help one another, whatever the time or place.

Not a lot happens in most of these novels. The story lines are straightforward and easy to follow, without the complexities inherent in some other genres. However, we must be careful not to conclude that simply because these are nice, less complicated stories, they are poorly written. Many of the authors write with a poetic elegance that matches that of much Literary Fiction. Less complicated does not equal lower quality. Kaye Gibbons's lyrical explorations of rural life in the South employ sensitivity and power in describing strong female characters caught up in difficult, sometimes tragic situations. Although she certainly qualifies for inclusion in both the Literary Fiction and Women's Lives and Relationships genres, she also offers a voice that fans of Gentle Reads respond to and respect. Try *Charms for the Easy Life* as an introduction to her work.[5] Here, through the lives of three generations of women, Gibbons evokes the rural South in the first half of the twentieth century in a heartwarming, old-fashioned story.

Characterization

These are often ordinary characters in ordinary situations, but the extraordinary can also play a role, as long as the gentle nature of the story remains. For example, Dorothy Gilman's *Caravan* adds an exotic setting—the Sahara—and characters—desert nomads and a kidnapped young woman—to a story that still holds enough of the Gentle Read aura to appeal to fans.[6] Clearly, situations need not always be sweetness and light. Sandra Dallas's books reflect hardships in the lives of the characters, and even death plays a role, as in books by Sackville-West and the novels of Richard Paul Evans. However, because these tragedies are not sudden or violent, only part of the natural events, they still fit within the boundaries of this genre. *Heartwarming* and *poignant* are both terms used to describe novels in this genre, and the latter, at least, reflects the range of emotion involved.

Characters drive the stories and are more important than the actual events. It is the endearing characters that readers remember and seek in similar titles, as well as the comfortable situations. No matter what the setting, the reader feels at home with the characters and the situations in which they find themselves. That is not to say, however, that these characters are lacking in the wit and sometimes eccentricities that endear them to readers and add humor, or at least a lighter touch, to the stories. Paul Gallico's Mrs. 'Arris, the charming charwoman with her Dior gown, takes readers on adventures to Paris and beyond. (*Mrs. 'Arris Goes to Paris* is the first of this lighthearted series.)[7] And Angela Thirkell's series set in Anthony Trollope's fictional Barsetshire brims with endearing, but quite eccentric, characters. (*High Rising* is the first of this delightful series.)[8] Although characters may be familiar and comfortable, they may also be whimsical and endearing in less conventional ways.

Key Authors

Currently the most popular writers in this genre are Jan Karon and Rosamunde Pilcher. In my library at least, Karon's series of books set in Mitford, North Carolina, are almost never on the shelf, no matter how many copies I buy. These heartwarming tales of Timothy Kavanaugh, an Episcopal priest, have touched the hearts of millions, with their simple stories of faith amidst hardships and the joys and sorrows of everyday life. Humor (whenever he quotes Scripture, his dog, Barnabas, stops misbehaving and listens attentively) adds to these gentle stories, and even though tragedy sometimes accompanies them, there is always the sense that "all's right in the world." *At Home in Mitford* is the first in this popular series.[9] Although certainly extraordinarily popular with many readers, Karon does not have a universal appeal. Some find the religious emphasis too intrusive, while others complain of "saccharine" characters and plots. This is, of course, one of the dangers with Gentle Reads. For each reader there is a level of gentleness beyond which they do not want to go, and as in all genres, authors appeal to readers for a variety of expected and unforeseen reasons.

Pilcher is an author who might be considered a benchmark in Women's Lives and Relationships as well as here. Although she was already the author of several more romantic novels, her popularity soared with *The Shell Seekers,* published in the United States in 1988.[10] Her leisurely paced novels feature strong, interesting women discovering themselves and sorting out their family and marital relationships. Although she raises difficult issues, she broaches them safely, not portraying nasty scenes but simply raising questions and then resolving them. Her Englishness distinguishes her from her American counterparts as well; there is something in the style, tone, and emphases of English representatives of this genre that set them slightly apart, for readers as well, although certainly there are readers who read both American and English writers with equal enthusiasm.

Another author to know is Dorothy Gilman, mentioned earlier in this chapter, as well as in the chapters on Thrillers and Mysteries, because her generally upbeat and descriptive stories, which fit neatly in other genres, also have enormous appeal to fans of Gentle Reads. Gilman is a versatile writer with a range of titles. Her Mrs. Pollifax stories, which feature an elderly female spy, appeal primarily to readers of Cozies, the gentle Mysteries. Even though there may be some violent episodes, the overall tone assures readers of the happy outcome. Single titles appeal across the board to readers of well-crafted, and generally gentle, stories. Among these are some that are a little darker, such as *Incident at Badamya,* a more suspenseful and harsh tale of postwar Burma, a kidnapping, and dangerous characters who are not what they appear.[11] (This is one I would suggest only to Gilman's fans or to readers who like to explore beyond the genre, not simply across the board to Gentle Reads fans.) On the other hand, *Thale's Folly* gives us poor Andrew Thale, battling writer's block and an overpowering father.[12] Sent to investigate an inheritance, his aunt's Massachusetts estate, Andrew finds a group of eccentric squatters, a new purpose in life, and, eventually, even love.

Of course, the classic benchmark of the genre is Miss Read. Thrush Green, the quintessential English village, provides the setting for Miss Read's most famous series, more than a dozen novels since 1959 (*Thrush Green* is the first) that explore village life—the satisfactions and intrigues that provide the daily grist for the mill of gossip.[13] The stories center on schoolteachers Miss Watson and Miss Fogerty, Dr. Lovell, and Rev. Henstock but include the loves and lives of all the villagers. With its close-knit community, emphasis on friendships and relationships, and gentle, upbeat stories, Miss Read's books contain all the hallmarks of the genre and consistently fulfill her readers' expectations. Unfortunately for her fans, Miss Read seems to have retired herself with the publication of her latest book, *A Peaceful Retirement*.[14]

Other "classic" authors still read by the genre's fans include D. E. Stevenson, Elizabeth Goudge, and Elizabeth Cadell. Stevenson's Mrs. Tim, whose antics enliven British military life before and after World War II, still has a satisfied following of readers who read and reread the series, which begins with *Mrs. Tim Christie*.[15] Although she is best remembered for this series, Stevenson has also written other popular nonseries titles. Goudge wrote both contemporary and historical stories set in the British Isles and Commonwealth. They feature romantic entanglements and family stories that touch the heart. *Green Dolphin Street,* the story of sisters, the man they love, and the directions fate moves lives, is a book reread and treasured by fans, a book to be shared with others.[16] Cadell is one of the authors fans of this genre remember fondly. Many readers have told me how her books transported them to other times and places. Try *The Corner Shop* as an example of her romantic stories; here, there is also an element of Mystery, as the story plays out.[17]

Contemporary American writers of the genre are Sandra Dallas, Clyde Edgerton, Terry Kay, and Nicholas Sparks. Dallas writes Gentle Reads with historical settings, close friendships among strong women characters, and hard times, but these difficult situations are enfolded in upbeat stories. In *The Persian Pickle Club,* quilting again plays an important role, as a group of women in rural Harveyville, Kansas, during the depression meet to quilt and socialize.[18] There is trouble here as well, however, and when a long-buried secret is uncovered, the group bands together to protect each other and their families.

Edgerton, another southerner like Eudora Welty, adds a large dose of humor to his tales of small-town life in the South and West, often adding a touch of Mystery as well. Characters reign supreme and the story rambles along, with nothing much happening, but an enjoyable trip is had by all. *Walking across Egypt* is a classic.[19] Mattie Rigsbee, even at seventy-eight, remains independent and only wishes she had grandchildren. When runaway Wesley Benfield enters her life, she does what she has to, even if it means breaking the law, to give him the break he needs.

GENTLE READS

Kay joins many other authors of Gentle Reads in setting his stories in the past, but again, the nostalgic stories have a timeless quality. Memories play an important role in many of his novels; looking back to other times—good and bad—creates detailed, resonant stories that remind readers of other, better days. *To Dance with the White Dog* is one of his most beloved.[20] Here Sam Peek, mourning his wife of fifty-seven years who has recently died, returns to his roots to attend his sixtieth class reunion. The dog of the title, perhaps only a figment of his imagination, helps him to reconcile his memories and come to terms with his grief, with death, and with life.

Sparks writes serious, often sentimental, sometimes tragic, stories of love. Like Kay's these are not Romances, although there may be Romance readers who appreciate them. Instead they are timeless stories of love, lost and found, and of how people survive its loss. Try *A Walk to Remember* to sample his style.[21] This ultimately upbeat story, told from the perspective of forty years later, recounts the unexpected love that blossoms between a high school football hero and the minister's daughter.

The appeal of English villages means that British authors are often successful, as was Miss Read, Pilcher, Stevenson, and Cadell, at attracting an American audience for their Gentle Reads novels. Two popular English writers today are Ann Purser and Rebecca Shaw. Purser patterns her stories after Miss Read's example and presents the quiet village, with the undercurrent of gossip and relationships propelling the story. (*Pastures New* is a good introduction.)[22] Shaw's cozy English village stories focus on colorful characters and safe surroundings, even though some of the problems of the late twentieth century appear. Try *The New Rector* to sample her style.[23]

Sometimes one or two titles of an author's work fit within the genre, but the author may write in other genres as well. It is always worth keeping track of good examples of the genre, even if the author only has one. Coral Lansbury is an example of this phenomenon. A professor of English at Rutgers, she also wrote several novels over the years, but one, *Sweet Alice,* is a good Gentle Read suggestion for fans at the less gentle end of the genre.[24] Nothing terrible happens, nor are there explicit sexual scenes, but the heroine is less conventional, and there is a hint of sexuality. This is a charming story of an Englishwoman, raised in genteel poverty; her son Alaric, who would have been more comfortable in his namesake's century; and their inheritance. One day it would be all theirs, if it were not for the three murderous aunts who stand in their way. This is a sophisticated but lighthearted farce, filled with unbelievable yet endearing characters and situations. (Imagine a cross between Barbara Pym and Donald Westlake.) Although it is not for every reader of the genre, many will be pleased by this character-centered story, filled with classical references that add to the readers' amusement.

Preparing to Work with Readers

Who reads Gentle Reads? When we started trying to identify this audience, we were surprised at the range of readers in all age groups. For many readers, these are the books for those times we all know when we simply have to have a book in hand and a safe world to escape to. There have been years when, between Thanksgiving and Christmas, we have not been able to find any of Miss Read's books on the shelf! Other readers select them along with a wide range of other genres, while still others may read them exclusively. We do need to be aware, however, that these are not necessarily the books for that proverbial "little old lady." We all know many, many older readers who prefer—and request—something very different: a racy Romance or novels of Hard-Edged Suspense. And although Christian Fiction is certainly not synonymous with Gentle Reads, we know many readers, fans of Gentle Reads and other genres, who appreciate Janette Oke's historical prairie novels and others by Christian publishers. Fans of Miss Read and Dorothy Gilman include some of our most sophisticated readers, which confirms the literary standards of fans of this genre and of many of the books that fall within this classification.

We should keep in mind that readers of this genre may read a variety of types and styles of books. Some prefer a more sophisticated story, others something less complicated. Or they are looking for one type today, but they may be seeking something quite different next time. As in every genre, there is a range of writing styles and tone, and we, as Readers' Advisors, need to be aware of the range in offering possibilities to readers.

When readers describe books that fit within this genre, they usually talk about character-centered books. However, unlike readers of the character-centered novels of Literary Fiction, which often focus on social and moral issues, these readers, when they choose Gentle Reads, are generally not requesting such provocative books. Rather, they describe heartwarming, or perhaps nostalgic, stories that portray smaller, even domestic, pleasures. Gentle Reads generally reflect a smaller cast of characters and a narrower focus. These readers seek a more circumscribed story, a community of characters with an emphasis on the personal relationships. They describe evocative stories, and often mention humor, or at least a lighter touch.

Interestingly, although it is often high on their list of likes and dislikes, they are less likely actually to mention the fact that they do not enjoy explicit sex, violence, or language. Just as in the Romance genre it is often difficult to ascertain how much sex readers will tolerate in a book, here, too, they seem reluctant to bring up a matter very dear to their hearts. They often talk in euphemisms: "They don't write books like they used to." Or, "I miss those old-fashioned stories." Both of these generally refer to their dismay at the amount of what they consider objectionable that they discover in much modern fiction. We need to listen for these clues that help us direct them to books they will find more satisfying.

As will be clear below in the "Reference Sources" section, there are not convenient lists of these books for our readers. We need to keep a list of authors we come across in reviews, discover in our own reading, or hear about from fans of this genre. The best authors for this list are those who write just in this genre, as we can safely suggest any of their books to fans. However, we should also keep track of authors of only one book or the one title by an author who also writes in other genres. In the case of the latter authors, readers may enjoy the author enough to experiment with the rest of his or her work. I am surely not alone in encountering a request for authors in this genre almost every day. This is also the type of book I always look for to include on general displays or to offer readers whenever it seems appropriate. Keeping a list is the only way to find authors in this genre when we need them. Figure 4.2 offers additional authors to acquaint fans of other genres with Gentle Reads.

FIGURE 4.2

An Introduction to Gentle Reads

Gentle Reads Writers to Try, If You Enjoy . . .

Adventure	Gilbert Morris
Fantasy	George MacDonald
Historical	Van Reid
	Jessamyn West
Humor	Coral Lansbury (*Sweet Alice*)
	Angela Thirkell
	Paul Gallico
Inspirational	Janette Oke
	Joseph Girzone
	Thyra Bjorn
Literary	Eudora Welty
Romance	Jane Peart
	Eva Ibbotson
Romantic Suspense	Dorothy Gilman (*Thale's Folly*)
Western	Brock and Bodie Thoene (Saga of the Sierras)
Women's Lives	Rosamunde Pilcher
	Lillian Beckwith
	J. Lynne Hinton (*Friendship Cake*)[25]

Readers' Advisory Interview

We know what readers expect when they ask for Gentle Reads, and we have some ideas of authors that fit within the genre. But how do we offer them to other readers we think may also enjoy them? As readers talk about what they enjoy in the books they read, we listen for the clues that lead us to this genre: Do they talk about character-centered books that focus on the relationships among characters, rather than on a single protagonist? Upbeat stories? Books that unfold at a leisurely

pace? Ordinary characters? A timeless quality? Old-fashioned stories? All of these are clues that Gentle Reads may be a good choice for
these readers. As we describe these authors and their books, offering
suggestions to the readers, we need to be careful to use the same
terms in return, to focus on the aspects they mention, to expand to
other characteristics as the books demand, but to make suggestions
within the range that the readers have requested.

Patrons who want "guarantees" when we suggest Gentle Reads are
one of the most difficult problems we face working in this genre. Can
we assure them that there is nothing in a particular book that will offend them? How could we possibly know? I think there are two issues
involved here. One is that readers simply want to be reassured that it
is okay to take the book. They seem to have a fear that someone at the
circulation desk will laugh at them, or think less of them, for reading
this book—whatever it is. This is a fear experienced by readers of all
genres, but it is an easy problem to solve. Just as when they ask us if
we have read the book they want to take, we either answer that we have
read it or that someone has, or that it got good reviews, and thus assure the reader that it is "safe" to check it out.

The other "safe" issue, whether this book is safe to read or whether
it might contain something offensive, is another problem altogether.
Although I get this question from adults who have concerns that
there not be anything distasteful in what they read, I am even more
likely to encounter the question from a parent, seeking a book for his
or her teen. We never offer guarantees. If parents have doubts or concerns, we encourage them to read the book first, before giving it to
their children. If readers have concerns for themselves, we offer them
reviews and tell them to bring it back if it is not to their liking. What
offends me in books may not bother another reader at all, and I may
skim over something that another reader finds abhorrent. In my experience, no book can be guaranteed "safe." When we work with readers
of all ages, we offer suggestions, a range of possibilities. We encourage readers to try these and to come back for other suggestions if
these do not satisfy them. We remind them they do not need to finish
every book they start, and we generally fall back on solid readers' advisory techniques as we build a relationship with these readers.

Because Gentle Reads is not a traditional genre, lists of useful
titles are hard to find. We need to keep lists of authors and titles that

have worked for our readers. This is the time to rely on the collaborative nature of readers' advisory and ask other librarians to suggest titles in the genre. That this query has appeared on the readers' advisory maillist Fiction_L more than once suggests that many of us face readers daily who request the kinds of titles included in the Gentle Reads genre.[26]

Sure Bets

It will not come as a surprise that there are Gentle Reads authors who appeal beyond the confines of the genre. These authors tell satisfying, heartwarming, old-fashioned stories with memorable characters. What is there not to like?

A personal favorite who is also consistently appreciated by a range of fans is Eva Ibbotson. She writes graceful, enchanting stories, generally set in Austria in the first part of the twentieth century. Her characters are always slightly unconventional, and their stories touch our hearts. In *Song for Summer,* Ellen, raised by suffragette aunts in Bloomsbury, wants nothing more than to run a household, rather than to march for women's rights.[27] She secures a position as housemother in a private boarding school in Austria. It is 1937, just as the war is changing lives and countries forever, but Ellen creates an ocean of calm and tranquility in the school. Still, when danger arises and the mysterious Marek needs her help, she comes to his assistance and helps rescue a famous violinist from the Nazis.

Dori Sanders is another author to know and share with readers. Suggest *Her Own Place,* another novel of nostalgia and memories, as elderly Mae Lee Barnes looks back on her life, lived in rural South Carolina and filled with joys and sorrows.[28] Although unlucky in marriage, she is lucky in life and passes on her fortitude and spirit to her five children.

No list of Gentle Reads would be complete without Fannie Flagg. Her *Fried Green Tomatoes at the Whistle Stop Cafe* is a contemporary classic.[29] Contemporary and historical story lines chart life in a small Alabama town from the late '20s, with the joys and sorrows, secrets and dreams of the characters set firmly on center stage. Family stories and gossip abound in this story that reveals much about the nature of the characters then and now.

Expanding Readers' Horizons

As should be clear from the previous discussion, Gentle Reads are few and far between; sometimes a single book by an author qualifies; sometimes an author can be counted on to produce a number of novels within the genre. There is also extensive overlap between Gentle Reads and a number of other genres, particularly Romance, Mystery, Literary Fiction, and Women's Lives and Relationships. Just as we watch for books in the Gentle Read genre, we need to be aware—when we read, when we read reviews, and when we talk with readers—about books from other genres that may please these fans.

For fans of Gentle Reads the Romance genre offers a number of gentler authors, those who do not generally include explicit sexual encounters, who might appeal. Debbie Macomber, with her gentle romances and small-town (or at least enclosed community) life, is a good suggestion, as is Marion Chesney, for fans who like a historical setting and madcap humor. Annie Kimberlin's humorous, small-town stories (*Romeo and Julia*) and Ruth Wind's moving family stories (*Meant to Be Married*) make good suggestions, even if they also address difficult issues.[30]

From the Mystery genre we might consider authors such as M. C. Beaton (both her Hamish Macbeth and Agatha Raisin series might appeal), and other authors of Cozy Mysteries (with the body and any violence well offstage) might work. Try Jane Langton, as the relationship between Homer and Mary Kelly may enhance the appeal of this series for these readers. (*The Memorial Hall Murder* is a classic title.)[31] Joan Hess's Claire Malloy mysteries, featuring a bookseller and her daughter (*Strangled Prose* is the first); Dorothy Cannell's zany Ellie Haskell Mysteries, beginning with *The Thin Woman*; Nancy Atherton's Aunt Dimity series, if your reader does not mind that a ghost is one of the central characters (*Aunt Dimity's Death* is the first); and, of course, Charlotte MacLeod, whose Mystery series run the gamut from romantic (the Sarah Kelling series, beginning with *Family Vault*) to outlandish (the Grub-and-Stakers gardening club adventures, written under pseudonym Alisa Craig and beginning with *The Grub-and-Stakers Move a Mountain*) and the Professor Peter Shandy series (*Rest Ye Merry*) falling somewhere in between.[32]

Women's Lives and Relationships offers a number of authors who have strong appeal for fans of Gentle Reads. Maeve Binchy and Barbara

Whitnell write stories of women that are usually gentle enough for these readers. Others—Joanna Trollope, Jean Stubbs, Mary Sheepshanks, and Elizabeth Berg—may also work, but some of their story lines contain issues (divorce or abuse, for example) beyond what Gentle Read fans want to read. The style and tone match what they find in Gentle Reads, but the subject matter may be too controversial. Still, these authors are good suggestions with that proviso.

Old-fashioned is a phrase to pursue when readers use it in a readers' advisory interview. They, and many of us, think of it in a very positive sense: books that reflect conventional values and mores but tell a good story. Many older authors from a number of genres fit into that category and may make good suggestions for fans of Gentle Reads. From the Adventure genre, both Hammond Innes and Nevil Shute write this type of book, and their stories have many qualities that appeal to fans of this genre. Classic authors of Romantic Suspense—Victoria Holt, Phyllis Whitney, Barbara Michaels, and Mary Stewart—all make good suggestions. Their stories, for the most part not dated, tell of romantic adventures, but they lack the violence and sex that characterize many of the stories in the same genre written today. Espionage Thrillers by Helen MacInnes and Evelyn Anthony also make good suggestions for these readers. Even some of the Suspense novels of Mary Higgins Clark may be gentle enough for fans of this genre, although we need to exercise care in suggesting them, allowing readers to see that there may be elements beyond what they enjoy and offering other titles in case Clark does not appeal. Figure 4.3 offers authors from other genres who might appeal to fans of Gentle Reads.

Reference Sources

Because Gentle Reads is not a genre acknowledged by any compiler of reference sources, we must pull information from any source we find. Primarily, our lists of Gentle Reads, compiled through our own reading, reviews, and suggestions from readers, comprise the mainstay of our "reference" library.

FIGURE 4.3

Expanding Readers' Horizons

Authors to Take Readers beyond the Gentle Reads Genre

Adventure	Hammond Innes
	Nevil Shute
Fantasy	Anne McCaffrey (Dragonriders of Pern series)
Historical	Jeanne Williams
Humor	Charlotte MacLeod (Mystery series)
	Dorothy Cannell (Mystery series)
Literary	Kaye Gibbons
	Barbara Kingsolver
Mystery	Charlotte MacLeod
	Rhys Bowen
	M. C. Beaton
Romance	Ruth Wind
	Debbie Macomber
	Susan Haley (*Getting Married in Buffalo Jump*)[33]
Romantic Suspense	Barbara Michaels
	Mary Stewart
	Victoria Holt
	Phyllis Whitney
Science Fiction	C. S. Lewis
Suspense	Mary Higgins Clark
Thriller	Helen MacInnes
	Evelyn Anthony
Western	Molly Gloss
	Judy Alter
Women's Lives	Maeve Binchy
	Barbara Whitnell
	Joanna Trollope

Where to Find . . .

INFORMATION ABOUT THE AUTHOR

Contemporary Authors (*see* appendix 2) includes useful information on many of the authors who write in this genre. Because these authors may write in other genres, there may also be information in the St. James Press series (*Twentieth-Century Romance and Historical Writers* is described in chapters 5 and 10 and *St. James Guide to Crime and Mystery Writers* is described in chapter 8).

PLOT SUMMARIES

NoveList (*see* appendix 2) uses "Gentle Reads" as a subject heading, so there is access to summaries of the books they include in their database. As it is listed as a genre heading in *To Be Continued* (*see* appendix 2), annotated entries for series in this genre can be identified there. *Fiction Catalog* (*see* appendix 2) lists similar books under the heading "Cheerful Stories."

One last observation about fans of this genre: They are among the most passionate sharers of the books they have loved. They pass treasured titles from one reader to the next among a group they know can be trusted to cherish that author in return. These books have a distinctive emotional element; when readers offer these titles, they are careful to expose themselves only to others whom they believe will also respect the emotions involved. If they share books with us as well, we know we have earned their trust and respect.

NOTES

1. Linda Nichols, *Handyman* (New York: Delacorte, 2000).
2. Vita Sackville-West, *All Passion Spent* (Garden City, N.Y.: Sun Dial Press, 1931).
3. Eudora Welty, *Delta Wedding* (New York: Harcourt Brace, 1946).
4. Jennifer Chiaverini, *The Quilter's Apprentice* (New York: Simon & Schuster, 1999).
5. Kaye Gibbons, *Charms for the Easy Life* (New York: Putnam, 1993).
6. Dorothy Gilman, *Caravan* (New York: Doubleday, 1992).
7. Paul Gallico, *Mrs. 'Arris Goes to Paris* (Garden City, N.Y.: Doubleday, 1958).
8. Angela Thirkell, *High Rising* (New York: Carroll & Graf, 1933).

9. Jan Karon, *At Home in Mitford* (Elgin, Ill.: Lion Pub., 1994).

10. Rosamunde Pilcher, *The Shell Seekers* (New York: St. Martin's, 1988).

11. Gilman, *Incident at Badamya* (New York: Doubleday, 1989).

12. ———, *Thale's Folly* (New York: Ballantine, 1999).

13. Miss Read, *Thrush Green* (Boston: Houghton, 1960, © 1959).

14. ———, *A Peaceful Retirement* (Boston: Houghton, 1997).

15. D. E. Stevenson, *Mrs. Tim Christie* (New York: Holt, 1973).

16. Elizabeth Goudge, *Green Dolphin Street* (New York: Coward-McCann, 1944).

17. Elizabeth Cadell, *The Corner Shop* (New York: Morrow, 1967).

18. Sandra Dallas, *The Persian Pickle Club* (New York: St. Martin's, 1995).

19. Clyde Edgerton, *Walking across Egypt* (Boston: Hall, 1988).

20. Terry Kay, *To Dance with the White Dog* (Atlanta: Peachtree Publishers, 1990).

21. Nicholas Sparks, *A Walk to Remember* (New York: Warner Books, 1999).

22. Ann Purser, *Pastures New* (London: Orion, 1994).

23. Rebecca Shaw, *The New Rector* (London: Orion, 1994).

24. Coral Lansbury, *Sweet Alice* (New York: E. P. Dutton, 1989).

25. J. Lynne Hinton, *Friendship Cake* (New York: HarperCollins, 2000).

26. Readers' advisory maillist, available at Fiction_L@maillist.webrary.org.

27. Eva Ibbotson, *Song for Summer* (New York: St. Martin's, 1998).

28. Dori Sanders, *Her Own Place* (Chapel Hill, N.C.: Algonquin Books, 1993).

29. Fannie Flagg, *Fried Green Tomatoes at the Whistle Stop Cafe* (New York: Random House, 1987).

30. Annie Kimberlin, *Romeo and Julia* (New York: Love Spell Books, 1999); Ruth Wind, *Meant to Be Married* (New York: Silhouette Books, 1998).

31. Jane Langton, *The Memorial Hall Murder* (New York: Harper & Row, 1978).

32. Joan Hess, *Strangled Prose* (New York: St. Martin's, 1986); Dorothy Cannell, *The Thin Woman: An Epicurean Mystery* (New York: St. Martin's, 1984); Nancy Atherton, *Aunt Dimity's Death* (New York: Viking, 1992); Charlotte MacLeod, *Family Vault* (Garden City, N.Y.: Doubleday, 1979); Alisa Craig, *The Grub-and-Stakers Move a Mountain* (New York: Doubleday, 1981); MacLeod, *Rest Ye Merry* (Garden City, N.Y.: Doubleday, 1978).

33. Susan Haley, *Getting Married in Buffalo Jump* (New York: E. P. Dutton, 1987).

5

Historical Fiction

"I need to read a fiction book for my history class, and I need to be certain it's accurate. We're studying the Civil War."

"I've always wanted to know more about Queen Elizabeth and Renaissance England, but those biographies are just too dry. Is there anything else I can read?"

"We're going to France for our vacation. I'd like some Historical Fiction set there, especially in Lyon."

If these queries sound similar to ones asked in your library, you know how popular Historical Fiction can be with readers, as well as the wide range of interests and reading tastes to which the genre appeals. Readers of Historical Fiction share a secret. They have discovered a painless method of learning history—through the fictionalized accounts of historical periods, people, and events presented by novels in this genre. When they read Historical Fiction that features real people or stories that explore a particular time or event, they may have uncovered as much historical fact as many students of history. They have learned to explore history on the magic carpet of Historical Fiction.

Even for fans the Historical Fiction genre can seem daunting. Historical novels are, for the most part, *big* books, which require a major investment of time to read. Nevertheless, it sometimes appears to harried Readers' Advisors that fans devote themselves to the genre, devouring Historical Fiction and always looking for more of the type they enjoy. It seems impossible to keep up with fans of this genre! However, understanding the characteristics of the genre and why readers love it helps us work with readers, no matter how much Historical Fiction we have read.

A Definition

Formulating a definition that encompasses all aspects of a diverse genre is always difficult. And, as we all know, each fan of Historical Fiction will have his own definition of the genre and books that are included. (Of course, once we discover how this reader defines the genre and what he is looking for that day, we know how to proceed. A request for Historical Fiction similar to Catherine Coulter's racy Historical Romances or Anne Perry's somber Historical Mysteries will likely lead us in different directions from a request for more novels like Charles Frazier's Pulitzer Prize–winning *Cold Mountain*.)[1]

For purposes of this discussion, I define Historical Fiction as a novel set in the past, before the author's lifetime and experience. (Thus, novels about World War II might be considered Historical Fiction if the author were born after 1945, but Jane Austen's comedies of manners are not Historical Fiction, as she writes about the times in which she lived.) Through its serious respect for historical accuracy and detail, Historical Fiction enhances the reader's knowledge of past events, lives, and customs. The goal of authors of Historical Fiction is to bring history to life in novel form. Figure 5.1 lists characteristics of Historical Fiction based on this definition.

Although they rely heavily on historical facts and details, Historical Romances, Mysteries, or Adventure are not considered in this chapter. Instead, they are covered in the respective genre chapters. This is a judgment call; I firmly believe that Elizabeth Peters fills her novels of turn-of-the-century Egypt with as much historical detail as many Historical novels, but the primary emphasis of the series is Mystery, not History. In the section "Expanding Readers' Horizons,"

FIGURE 5.1

Characteristics of Historical Fiction

1. There is a wealth of accurate historical detail relating to set-ting (geography, customs, beliefs, culture, society, habits) as well as to characters and events.

2. Characters may be real or fictional, but they are portrayed in such a way that they fit the times. Their lives and actions are shaped by the historical times and details, not vice versa.

3. Story lines may focus on a particular historical event or time period or they may follow the life of a character (real or fic-tional). Novels may raise difficult social or moral issues through the plot.

4. Historical novels are usually big books, with stories that un-fold at a leisurely pace. Even shorter Historical Novels are usually so densely written that they must be read slowly.

---

below, there are a number of suggestions of authors in other genres who are careful about their historical detail and are thus good sug-gestions for Historical Fiction fans (*see also* Figure 5.3).

Characteristics and the Genre's Appeal

Frame

First, in Historical Fiction, there is a wealth of accurate historical detail relating to the setting (geography, customs, beliefs, culture, society, habits, etc.) as well as to characters and events. Most readers would agree that the frame, constituted of these details, along with the tone of the novel, is the first element they respond to as they read Histor-ical Fiction. In fact, in many of the novels of James A. Michener, this frame is almost a character in its own right. *Chesapeake,* for example, tells the story of an area of the Maryland shore and the generations of people that inhabit it.[2] The place, the land itself, is the dominant in-fluence on human characters and events. Other novels present a combination of these elements. Fans read to discover the details of life in a particular period or to follow a famous person's life. They expect a good story and interesting, believable characters, but readers want to be immersed in the times, to experience a particular period in history or a detailed description of the life and times of a famous historical figure.

Some authors are more skilled at integrating the historical information into the story than others. More sophisticated authors deftly blend the details without overwhelming the story and without placing large sections of "history" in the midst of the plot. The best make the historical details an integral part of the story. For example, Sharon Kay Penman illustrates the life and times of Richard III in *The Sunne in Splendour* by presenting the politics, personalities, and power struggles in fifteenth-century England.[3] As the reader follows Richard from his childhood to Bosworth Field, Penman weaves the historical events and details of the period into the character's life experiences. It makes a wonderfully rich story.

It is not simply the wealth of details but also the accuracy that is so important to fans of the genre. Many readers, myself included, trace a great deal of our knowledge of history to Historical Fiction. We may not respond to the often dry style of straight history texts or biographies, with their interminable footnotes and caveats. We turn to Historical Fiction to understand history from the inside, from the perspectives of individuals caught up in events from the past. Even though we know we are not consulting primary sources and understand that the authors have, by necessity, taken some liberties with characters and events in telling their stories, we trust the novelists— and their editors—to have the integrity to keep to the facts as they are generally known. Hence, fans and librarians look for presentations consistent with the times and facts.

Characterization

The second element relates to the characterizations. Readers expect accuracy in the presentation of characters as well. Even if they are not real historical personages, they must fit within the novel and the times. Glaring anachronisms of language, behavior, or straightforward fact distract and sometimes cause readers to distrust the author's research.

For example, discovering twentieth-century colloquialisms in a novel set in the fourteenth century wreaks havoc in the context of a Historical novel and can, in fact, add unintentional humor.

Historical figures need to act in ways that are consistent with known facts, and fictional characters must act in a believable fashion for the times and places. All should fit within the story and times and act in ways that could have actually happened. Most importantly for readers is that they *feel* real. Although James Goldman presents a rather disquieting look at the last four years of King John of England's life in *Myself as Witness*, he nevertheless creates a believable, complex, well-rounded portrait of a man remembered mostly for his alleged tyranny but whose life and actions were not totally despicable.[4] John comes alive in this novel, as readers are forced to consider events behind the known story. Classic author of Historical Fiction Zoe Oldenbourg accomplishes the same feat in her novels of medieval France. In *The World Is Not Enough*, she focuses on what life was like for young wife Alix, forced to run the castle and fief while her husband, and many of the men from the estate, are fighting in Jerusalem.[5] Her subdued, unromanticized characterization adds a measure of verisimilitude to the story.

Story Line

The third characteristic applies to the story lines in Historical Fiction, which emphasize either a particular time or event or follow the lives of characters in a time. Ann Baer's *Down the Common* illustrates this plot emphasis in a straightforward, unemotional, and rather bleak account of a year among the peasants and rural nobility in medieval England.[6] One sees their existence with its everyday drudgery, even among the supposed better-off aristocracy, in a completely unromanticized account. The characters themselves are not important except in the way they reveal the kind of life people actually led.

Wilbur A. Smith's novel of ancient Egypt, *River God*, provides extensive details of clothing, customs, manners and mores, as well as crucial information about the times, 1780 B.C., when Egypt was politically divided.[7] History comes alive in this story of political machinations, random and ritual violence, and the lives of the fictional characters close to the throne of the pharaoh. Like Ken Follett's *Pillars of the*

Earth, which recounts the building of a medieval English cathedral, this story, too, focuses on the outcome, and the actions that lead to that outcome, more than on the characters.[8]

Other Historical novels place greater importance on the characters and less on plot. Characters take priority, and the lives of the protagonists are more important than events during the time. For example, Max Byrd's Historical novels of Thomas Jefferson (*Jefferson*), Andrew Jackson (*Jackson*), and Ulysses S. Grant (*Grant*) offer a kind of warts-and-all Historical Fiction, presenting real people without idealizing them and exploring events in their lives without the constraints imposed by strict biography.[9] Gore Vidal takes this approach a step further with his provocative reinterpretations of the lives of his characters and his extensive social criticism, as in *1876*, a novel that skewers politicians and social climbers in that centennial election year.[10]

In the Historical novels of some authors, the distinction is harder to make. These may combine characters and settings with particular events to create a viable story. Michael Shaara's Pulitzer Prize–winning *Killer Angels* examines the Battle of Gettysburg through the eyes of the men who fought there, both generals and common soldiers, and places the decisive battle on a much more intimate, personal plane.[11] He thus explores this chosen historical event in considerable depth and with a great deal of emotion. Steven Pressfield evokes a similar feeling in his novel *Gates of Fire.*[12] The Battle of Thermopylae in 480 B.C. is the ostensible topic, but, in fact, this novel, told through the eyes of a Spartan survivor, explores the nature of the Spartan warriors, their training as well as their psychological and emotional motivations, their families, and their philosophy toward war and the state. Descriptions of the battle take very little space by comparison, and the reader comes away with a more complete sense of the battle, those who fought, and the implications of their defeat. Readers may choose and appreciate these books for either the emphasis on character or on events—or for both.

Pacing

The final element relates to pacing in Historical Fiction. Historical novels are usually longer books (almost always more than 300 pages), and they are not generally referred to as "fast-paced," even if they include Adventure elements. A phrase such as "leisurely unfolding" perhaps better describes the pacing of most novels in this genre. In many, however, there is an immediacy to the pacing that pulls the reader quickly into the story, even though most of these may not be defined as fast-paced in the same manner as books in other genres, such as Suspense or Adventure. Historical novels may be densely written, but the story envelops the reader, drawing him in and keeping him enthralled. In addition, the necessity of creating the atmosphere and details of the past often makes these slow-starting books, although the pacing often picks up midway. In *Hannibal*, by Ross Leckie, early details of the Carthaginian general's life unfold slowly, but the intimate, first-person narration pulls readers quickly into the story.[13] As we are expected to do, we empathize with the young Hannibal and sense his tragic end from the tone of the first chapter, but the pacing of the story picks up as action increases later in the book.

Key Authors

To understand the popularity of the genre and work well with readers, it is important to read typical authors. In some genres there is a clear-cut benchmark, a writer whose work characterizes the genre, who is prolific, popular, and typical. Unfortunately, in Historical Fiction, there is currently no author who fits this role. Howard Fast might once have been the benchmark, but his writing is no longer as popular as it was even twenty years ago. James Michener is the name many readers would immediately have associated with Historical Fiction ten years ago. His novels, which feature the history of a place even more than of an individual, were known for their vast scope, immense size, and interesting details of a place in time and the people who populated it. (Today, Edward Rutherford's novels—*Sarum*, *Russka*, and *London*—come closest to these and their appeal.)[14] Jean Auel and Diana Gabaldon are certainly popular, but their work is not typical of the entire genre. With almost twenty books to his credit, Patrick O'Brian is prolific, but again his popularity is limited to readers who enjoy detailed Historical Military Adventure, and he is considered in chapter 2, "Adventure." Cecilia Holland writes novels of Historical Fiction that cut across the genre, but she has never gained the popularity that would ensure her position as benchmark.

Certainly, in addition to Michener and Fast, there are classic authors who are still read and appreciated by fans of the genre, even though they are not as popular as they once were. It behooves us to be aware of Mary Renault and Nigel Tranter. Renault has brought ancient Rome and Greece to life for readers since she began her career in the late '50s. Try *The King Must Die* to sample her work.[15] This, and its companion, *The Bull from the Sea,* retell the Theseus legend and offer insight into both Greek custom and story, while *The Last of the Wine* explores the life and times of Alexander the Great.[16] Tranter's recent death put his name in the news and his books back in the hands of readers. He has almost single-handedly recounted the history of Scotland and brought it and things Scottish to the attention of fans of the genre in more than 100 books. The trilogy of books chronicling the life of Robert the Bruce (Robert I of Scotland) are among his most famous. *Robert the Bruce: The Steps to the Empty Throne* is the first.[17]

Other authors requested by readers include Judith Merkle Riley and John Jakes. Although Riley has obviously mastered the details of the historical periods about which she writes, it is her characters that bring readers back to her stories. The fascinating women who populate her novels recognize the sometimes-subtle role of women in history in a way that history texts often ignore. *The Serpent Garden* offers romance, intrigue, and adventure as Flemish artist Susanna Dallet travels to London and the court of Henry VIII.[18]

Although Jakes will never be one of the great stylists of the Historical Fiction genre, none of us in libraries can doubt his enormous popularity. From his initial success with the Kent Family Chronicles, detailing the story of the American Revolution (*The Bastard* is the first), he has maintained his reputation for providing popular accounts of events in American history, and he continues to attract readers.[19] A more recent series, beginning with *Homeland*, follows the Crown family of Chicago from World War I.[20]

Preparing to Work with Readers

As important as understanding the characteristics of Historical Fiction is knowing something about the fans of the genre and how to work with them, especially if we are not fans ourselves. What do we know about fans of this genre?

First, fans read to learn about historical events, or characters, or the life and customs in another time. They are not just interested in dry facts and dates; they expect history to come alive through the stories these writers fashion. Historical Fiction allows them to explore characters and facts in story form, to place people and events in a larger perspective in ways that are more entertaining, involving, and expansive than straight history.

In Historical Fiction they find a range of books that provide this detail. On the one hand, there are the action-packed Historical novels that feature many of the elements of the Adventure genre. An especially good example is Louis L'Amour's *The Walking Drum*.[21] In this story of a young boy seeking his father, a corsair captured and kept from returning to his French estates, the action starts in the first chapters, and the action and adventure sequences fill almost every subsequent chapter, keeping the pace unusually brisk for novels in this genre. In addition to the action emphasis, this novel offers a fascinating picture of life and thought in twelfth-century Europe and the Middle East.

These action-oriented Historical novels also feature appealing and interesting characters. Nobel Prize–winner Henryk Sienkiewicz produces a large cast of characters involved in the battles between Poles and Cossacks in Eastern Europe of the 1640s in a trilogy that begins with *With Fire and Sword*.[22] Yet the focus is on the battles, the adventure, and the political intrigue, with the characters as the means to enliven these historical events.

An author who relies less on physical action is Jean Auel, whose prehistory series opens with *Clan of the Cave Bear*.[23] Although characters are important, they are a focus only inasmuch as they explore the possibilities of what people at the time and in that environment might do. We follow their lives, but through them, we learn about the times, not necessarily the individual personalities.

On the other hand, there are also Historical novels that feature characters and their lives, and through that examination, they offer the historical detail fans desire. These character-centered novels provide glimpses into the lives of fictional and real people through the description of actual events and an interpretation of the characters' reactions to them. They often provide a very intimate portrayal of the protagonist, who is frequently a person from history. For example, Jacqueline Park, in *The Secret Book of Grazia dei Rossi*, provides a fascinating view of the lives of Jews in Italy in the late fifteenth century.[24] Grazia's memoir, a diary kept for her son, reveals details of the culture, politics, and personalities of the time.

Many of these Historical novels that focus on characters are more elegantly written and have a definite intellectual appeal. Charles Frazier's Pulitzer Prize–winning *Cold Mountain* probably surprised many readers who expected a novel of Civil War battles but found, instead, a nineteenth-century American *Odyssey,* as the hero makes his lonely way home from the war. These literary, character-centered Historical novels may feature more elegant language, as well as the darker, sometimes elegiac, tone found in novels such as Michael Shaara's *Killer Angels,* with its heartfelt story of the Battle of Gettysburg as seen through the eyes of the participants, and Ross Leckie's *Hannibal,* the intimate first-person account of the great Carthaginian soldier who braved the Alps in winter to attack Rome and fulfill his father's promise to defeat it. Like Shaara's, this is a novel of military strategy, but it also reveals political machinations and provides a surprisingly intimate glimpse into Hannibal's private life.

Secondly, many fans prefer to read about a particular country and time, or they have particular countries and times they will not, by choice, read about. We have all met readers who will only read about the American West or nothing set in England. I even know one reader who will not read anything in which Oliver Cromwell appears! As in every other genre, readers may not be interested in exploring beyond these boundaries, no matter how similar another book may seem. We librarians should not be surprised by these restrictions.

On the other hand, if a reader is interested in a particular period or historical figure, he or she may tolerate a wide range of quality in the writing style and be willing to read across the genre and beyond to related genres—Mystery, Adventure, and Romance—to find books about that person or event. Someone interested in reading everything about England's King Henry VIII and his six wives will want to see *everything*, from Bertrice Small's steamy Historical Romance, *Love, Remember Me*, to Margaret George's journal-based novel, *The Autobiography of Henry VIII.*[25]

While some fans read about particular characters or times, others look for a particular style of writing. These readers may read about a wide range of countries and historical periods, just to enjoy that style. For example, readers who love Literary Fiction may read a wide range of elegantly written or award-winning Historical Fiction, simply because they appreciate the quality of the writing. Others may prefer novels in diary form and read all, no matter the main character, country, or time period. We need to be open to these possibilities when we listen to readers talk about what they enjoy.

Fourth, most, if not all, Historical Fiction readers do not consider time travel or Alternative History part of the genre, and many disdain novels that include it. Time travel involves too much unreality and often Romance to attract many fans from this genre. This is not to say that some readers of Historical Fiction, especially fans of more romantic Historical Fiction, may not appreciate a writer such as Diana Gabaldon. Because of the way her novels flow, time travel is less obtrusive and less frequent than in some, and she also adds a tremendous amount of historical detail. Others may find some of the Time Travel Science Fiction very satisfying as well. (Connie Willis is a good suggestion for readers who want to explore further; if one can get beyond the basic premise—going back in time from the twenty-first century—readers find all the historical detail they could desire.) Alternative History, on the other hand, is anathema to fans of Historical Fiction, because the hypothesis is that history did not happen quite as we know it.

Fifth, fans of Historical Fiction are also good candidates for suggestions of narrative nonfiction. Readers of a particular period appreciate seeing the accompanying nonfiction about the time, including materials about dress, customs, and culture. Those who are exploring a particular character in Historical Fiction also enjoy the Biographies that relate to the same person or others during that time. Nonfiction readers can also be enticed to explore the fiction collection if we show them the links between the history books they currently enjoy and fiction that is similar. A number of authors of Historical Fiction—especially George Garrett, Jeanne Mackin, Sharon Kay Penman, and George—are also excellent suggestions for readers of Biography. These authors expect their readers to have a certain basic knowledge of the period, or at least a historical perspective, and thus they move quickly into the specifics of a situation and characters, rather than providing extensive background information. For example, Mackin's *The Queen's War* provides basic facts about the rift between the aging King Henry II and Queen Eleanor of Aquitaine, but a fuller appreciation of the novel requires some understanding of the characters of the two antagonists, their history, as well as a general understanding of the times, including Eleanor's Courts of Love and the chivalric tradition.[26]

Finally, Historical Fiction readers like big books in which they can immerse themselves. Many appreciate a broad scope of history, a large cast of characters, and a wealth of historical, social, and cultural detail. Others may prefer a smaller scope, but they are no less adamant on the necessity of the detail.

In exploring a new genre, it is often difficult to find a starting point, a book that appeals because it is similar to the type we already read and enjoy. Figure 5.2 lists Historical Fiction authors who provide a good introduction to this genre but whose writing also has similarities to another genre.

Readers' Advisory Interview

In the readers' advisory interview, I have found it very useful to encourage readers to talk about Historical Fiction they have enjoyed, rather than asking first about a preference for country or time period. Even if they begin to describe an author or title I have read, I listen to what they tell me they have enjoyed about the book. (Too often I have found what they enjoy far different from what I have liked about a book, so I am more careful now!)

FIGURE 5.2

An Introduction to Historical Fiction

Historical Fiction Writers to Try, If You Enjoy . . .

Adventure	Henryk Sienkiewicz
Fantasy	Jennifer Roberson
Gentle	Eugenia Price
	Jeanne Williams
Inspirational	Thomas B. Costain
Literary	Michael Shaara
	George Garrett
	Hella A. Haasse
Romance	Rosalind Laker
Thriller	Margaret Birkhead
Western	Don Coldsmith
Women's Lives	Gillian Bradshaw
	Molly Gloss
	Claire Cooperstein (*Johanna*)[27]

- Do they talk about adventure or action, or do they mention evocative descriptions and interior, psychological views of characters?
- How do they describe the main characters? Are they real or fictional? Do real historical characters mingle with fictional ones?
- Does the story cover a long span of time or just a few days or weeks?
- Do they talk about the historical details, events, or political and social issues?

All these details give us clues as to the type of Historical Fiction they have enjoyed in the past and what they might be looking for today. For example, if a reader says she has just read M. M. Kaye's *The*

Far Pavilions, I listen to how she describes this Romantic Adventure set in nineteenth-century India.[28] If she talks about the wonderful love story and the Adventure, I might suggest another Historical novel with strong Adventure and Romance elements, whether it is set in India or not. (For example, one of the series by Patricia Veryan—the Golden Chronicles, of which *Practice to Deceive* is the first, or the Tales of the Jewelled Men, beginning with *Time's Fool*.[29] Both feature Adventure, Intrigue, and Romance against a backdrop of Jacobean England and Scotland, not to mention Bonnie Prince Charlie.) If she talks about how much she learned about the history and culture of India, I might suggest Paul Scott's Raj Quartet, a series of Historical novels also set in India and beginning with *The Jewel in the Crown*.[30] These explore historical events as well as Indian culture and the role of the English in India.

References to real characters as protagonists, rather than simply as background in the novels, would send me to authors such as Max Byrd (mentioned earlier) and George Garrett, who is known for his fascinating portraits of historical figures, primarily Elizabethan. In *The Death of the Fox,* for example, he examines the life, and death, of Sir Walter Raleigh.[31] These readers might enjoy other Historical novels that focus on the lives of fictional protagonists, as it may simply be the character focus they desire. I would also certainly consult Historical Fiction reference books (described below) that index specific characters, real and fictional.

Readers who talk about stories that span longer periods of time may be interested in series that cover many years and events in the life of a character. Depending on the time period favored and the amount of action versus introspection or character focus, I might suggest a Family Saga (Elswyth Thane's Williamsburg series, which opens with *Dawn's Early Light* and chronicles two families from before the American Revolution through World War II), a novel of the North American westward expansion (perhaps Don Coldsmith's *Tallgrass* and *South Wind,* tales of the settlement of Kansas Territory from the sixteenth through mid–nineteenth centuries), or a novel that portrays the history of a country or an area or relates the life of a historical figure (Edward Rutherford's *London* perhaps, with its story of the great metropolis).[32] Mention by the reader of books that cover a

HISTORICAL FICTION

shorter time period might send me to a reference book that indexes specific historical events, such as a single battle.

Many of the titles already discussed would be good suggestions for readers seeking historical details, but other authors also emphasize political and social issues. For fans of these, I might suggest *A Private Renaissance,* an elegantly written, dense, demanding, fascinating first-person account of the life of Isabella d'Este.[33] Maria Bellonci depicts an exceptional woman who lived during extraordinary times and raises interesting issues concerning the role of women in politics, questions that transcend the sixteenth century in which the story is set. Or I might suggest Karleen Koen's *Through a Glass Darkly,* which lays a number of political and social issues (the role of women, the dissipation of French court society, the South Sea Bubble) on a more romantic story.[34]

Increasingly, stories of the West, often written by women and featuring strong women characters, are gaining popularity with readers of both Westerns and Historical Fiction. Less likely to be Traditional Westerns, these stories are set on the emerging frontier, and although they may exhibit the trappings of the Western—cowboys, frontier justice, showdowns in cattle towns—they reflect more the strength of Historical Fiction in the abundance of details and a real sense of a particular time and place. Jane Smiley's Spur Award–winning novel, *The All-True Travels and Adventures of Liddie Newton,* exemplifies this element.[35] Liddie travels from Illinois to pre–Civil War Kansas with her abolitionist husband. There she finds life on the frontier, even the more civilized frontier, to be harder than she imagined and fraught with danger, from both humans and the environment. Details of the abolitionist movement, the Jayhawkers and the Bushwackers, Lawrence and the state of Kansas at the time, and the perils of life for both men and women on the plains extend this beyond the strict confines of the Western genre.

Generally more realistically developed than their Western counterparts, these Historical novels of the West often present a horrifyingly authentic glimpse of life on the frontier. They delve deeper into the realities of life on the edge, and treat the issues realistically rather than mythically. Glendon Fred Swarthout's *The Homesman* depicts the fate of unfortunate women, faced with the torments of life on the frontier: the isolation, the cruel weather, the death of family members (especially children).[36] Dementia was the destiny of many women, no matter how strong they might be.

Having ascertained what a reader enjoys, the next task is to begin suggesting books without playing "Twenty Questions" or panicking and admitting our total ignorance. There are several ways to proceed without being caught in either trap. The general suggestions in "Tips for the Readers' Advisory Interview," appendix 1, are a good place to start, but there are also some specific suggestions relating to Historical Fiction.

When looking at books with readers, check for maps and genealogies. These are a bonus for fans, and they add to the authenticity of the novel. Sometimes the maps may be of an area, suggesting that the book covers a wider geographic region and includes more action and perhaps Adventure elements. Or they may be on a much smaller scale. An example is the house plan in Pamela Belle's *Wintercombe,* which suggests a smaller, more intimate scale, and perhaps a more domestic emphasis.[37] A genealogy or family tree, on the other hand, is a clear indication that Family Saga elements figure prominently in this novel.

Flipping through a book gives a sense of how densely written it is. More white space suggests more dialogue, likely less description, and perhaps more involvement of the reader in the story. More description and more historical detail, and thus less white space, may imply that the reader is placed more in the role of observer. Based on a reader's comments of what he or she enjoys, one may be a better suggestion than the other. It is useful to involve readers in this process of looking at the book. Flipping through a book, I might say, "This looks as if it has more description and may include more details of the time," for example, and then, if they take the book, I also ask them to come back and confirm the premise.

Books that include historical notes at the end are particularly good suggestions for students who may be required to read Historical Fiction as a supplement to a history class or for any of us who like to learn our history through Historical Fiction. Bernard Cornwell, who writes Historical Adventure set primarily in the nineteenth century, does this consistently, as do other writers. Readers particularly concerned about historical accuracy prize these titles.

Sure Bets

For those times when our minds go blank and we need to start describing books to jump-start them, it is always a good idea to have Sure Bets to call upon. A good suggestion in this genre is Pulitzer Prize–winner Andrea Barrett's *The Voyage of the Narwhal.*[38] Set in the mid–nineteenth century, this is a novel, rich in detail, of voyages of discovery on many levels—physical, as the action of the story centers on a voyage to the Arctic to rescue a previous expedition and to discover whether there is an open sea at the top of the world; emotional, as both male and female characters explore their relationships and options; and intellectual, as Barrett examines the nature of these voyages and their results. It is a story that appeals to a wide range of readers, both men and women.

Edith Pargeter, who also wrote under the pseudonym Ellis Peters, has a range of titles that appeal to many readers. As Pargeter she writes densely detailed, character-centered English Historical Fiction; and as Peters her Brother Cadfael Historical Mystery series, mentioned in chapter 8, "Mysteries," appeals to readers who enjoy both the character she has created as well as the details and insight into a time. The Heaven Tree Trilogy, which includes *The Heaven Tree, The Green Branch,* and *The Scarlet Seed,* chronicles the Talvace family, stone carvers building a thirteenth-century English cathedral.[39] It is an excellent example of her exceptional storytelling, memorable characters, and eye for historical detail.

Jeanne Williams writes evocatively of both the American West and Scotland. Her stories are characterized by a romantic tone that permeates the historical setting and details, as well as the relationships of the characters. Still there are the requisite historical details and strong sense of time and place. *Lady of No Man's Land* chronicles the civilizing of the plains, focusing on the development of the Oklahoma Panhandle in the 1880s, while Oklahoma is still Indian territory.[40] Kristin, an immigrant who earns her livelihood as a sewing lady, traverses the area, facing natural and human enemies, visiting ranches, and sewing for the women there. Maps and historical details (the general lawlessness of the Cherokee Strip, the development of barbed wire, the arduous labor of cattle ranching) underscore Williams's research and the authenticity of the story. Yet the novel is romantic as well, especially in tone, complete with happy ending.

Expanding Readers' Horizons

The crossover from Historical Fiction to the Mystery, Adventure, and Romance genres is extensive, and finding authors in related genres that satisfy Historical Fiction fans may be more straightforward than in any other genre. Basically fans are seeking other fiction with extensive historical details and an emphasis on the other elements they enjoy.

Readers who prefer plot-centered Historical Fiction will find a wealth of authors in these related genres. Patrick O'Brian and Dorothy Dunnett, both described in detail in chapter 2, "Adventure," are excellent suggestions. O'Brian's series follows the adventures of Naval officer Jack Aubrey and his friend, Stephen Maturin, a doctor and spy, during the Napoleonic Wars. Detailed drawings of the ships of the times, as well as extensive details of life in the navy and of the battles fought, add the historical background fans require.

Dunnett's two series range further afield and feature dashing Renaissance heroes, adventurers and merchants, who explore a wide range of countries and cultures. Her first series features Scots adventurer Francis Crawford of Lymond, a picaresque hero who travels the known world, from the British Isles to France, the Middle East, and even Russia, looking for his heritage. *Game of Kings* is the first.[41] The second series, beginning with *Niccolo Rising*, features fifteenth-century merchant banker-adventurer Niccolo vander Poele of Brugges.[42] Dunnett writes in the romantic historical tradition popularized by Dumas (*fils* and *pere*), emphasizing swashbuckling adventure, romantic entanglements, intrigue on many levels, and precise historical details.

Actual events and real people figure in the work of some authors of Historical Romances, and these may appeal to Historical Fiction readers who appreciate this element. Rosalind Laker, who writes in both the Historical Fiction and Romance genres, consistently explores specific time periods and the fictional and real characters who lived then. For example, *The Golden Tulip* features seventeenth-century Dutch painting and Vermeer.[43] Anya Seton's classic, *Katherine*, depicts the life of Katherine Swynford, mistress of John of Gaunt, in a compelling love story brimming with historical detail.[44]

In her Romantic Historical novel, *Circle of Gold*, Karen Harper recreates a particular time and the customs of a people.[45] The place is Appalachia; the time, the 1820s. Shaker life and culture come alive in this detailed evocation of time and place, seen through the eyes of poor Kentucky hill girl Rebecca, who is taken to live with the Shakers when her mother dies. Catherine Cookson creates much the same atmosphere and feel on the other side of the Atlantic in her provocative descriptions of problems in the poor communities dependent on mines and mills for their sustenance. (For example, see *The Girl,* the story of Hannah, whose hard life in the nineteenth-century Lancashire mining towns is accentuated by her illegitimacy.)[46]

Adventure and Romance combine in the works of several authors of Historical Romances. Diana Gabaldon adds time travel to her series, which begins in Scotland in 1945 and quickly goes back to 1743, the time of the Battle of Culloden. After the first title, *Outlander,* the series entries move, in subsequent installments, from France to America.[47] Readers appreciate the historical detail as well as the love interest between the protagonists.

Veryan is known by many for her humorous Georgian romps, which fit clearly in the Romance genre. Her Golden Chronicles and Jewelled Men series, mentioned above, add elements of Intrigue and Adventure, with spies and funds for the restoration of Bonnie Prince Charlie, not to mention the fate of the English Crown, at stake. Their historical detail and feel for the times make them popular reading for fans of Historical Fiction.

Adding the Adventure and Intrigue elements and tying them to particular battles, wars, or other events allow authors to create a real sense of the times while still producing a satisfying romantic story. Julie Tetel is a good example. Her Historical Romances, set in seventeenth- and eighteenth-century United States, provide a solid historical background to an elegantly written Romance. *Sweet Seduction,* for example, involves extensive historical details of the War of 1812 from the perspective of Jane Shaw, a female spy, determined to protect her father's Maryland plantation, currently the headquarters for General Ross and his redcoats.[48]

Historical Fiction readers who emphasize plot over characters may also appreciate the puzzles of Mysteries with strong historical settings. Anne Perry writes two series, both set in Victorian England. The longest running features Inspector Pitt and his well-born wife, Charlotte, in a series of adventures that explore the serious social and class issues in Victorian England. (In the first, *The Cater Street Hangman*, Charlotte and Thomas meet and fall in love, amidst the investigation of her sister's murder.)[49] Humorous secondary characters give these a lighter feel than her other series, which features William Monk, a policeman who has lost his memory in an accident. As he struggles to regain his memory and his career, he is assisted by, among others, Hester Latterly, a nurse who trained with Florence Nightingale in the Crimean War and who has her own forthright ideas of the role of nurses and women in general in Victorian society. This series, which opens with *The Face of a Stranger*, features bleak, evocative, atmospheric Mysteries that also delve into the underside of Victorian society.[50]

On the other side of the Atlantic, Margaret Lawrence writes an equally detailed, descriptive series featuring Hannah Trevor, a midwife in Maine. (First in that series is *Hearts and Bones*.)[51] Set immediately after the Revolutionary War, these novels vividly, and rather bleakly, re-create the hardships of the times and the choices faced by the inhabitants of the newly created United States.

Historical Mysteries provide an excellent, often shorter introduction to a particular historical period, and that may be one of the reasons for their popularity. Readers interested in ancient Rome, for example, might be more willing to pursue the Mystery series by either Steven Saylor (*Roman Blood*) or Lindsey Davis (*The Silver Pigs*) before embarking on Colleen McCullough's more daunting volumes that present Rome's history.[52] (*The First Man in Rome* is the first.)[53]

Many authors in sundry genres employ detailed historical settings, center their stories around real events, or feature characters from history. These can generally be found in the reference titles highlighted in Figure 5.3, and they offer fans of the Historical Fiction genre endless directions to pursue.

Reference Sources

After a long dry spell in the production of useful readers' advisory materials on Historical Fiction, suddenly, in the late '90s, several were published. Of particular interest are Lynda Adamson's *American Historical Fiction: An Annotated Guide to Novels for Adults and Young*

FIGURE 5.3

Expanding Readers' Horizons

Authors to Take Readers beyond the Historical Fiction *Genre*

Adventure	Patrick O'Brian
	Dorothy Dunnett
Gentle	Jessamyn West
Inspirational	Linda Chaikin
Literary	Gore Vidal
	Thomas Pynchon (*Mason and Dixon*)[54]
Mystery	Elizabeth Peters
	Anne Perry
Psychological	Caleb Carr
Romance	Patricia Veryan
Thriller	Alan Furst
Western	Norman Zollinger
	Will Henry
Women's Lives	Cindy Bonner

Adults and *World Historical Fiction: An Annotated Guide to Novels for Adults and Young Adults.*[55] Together the books, which update classic reference titles, annotate almost 10,000 Historical Fiction titles and survey American and world history from prehistory to the late twentieth century. The books are organized chronologically, with indexes for subjects, authors, titles, geographic locations, and genres. Appendixes indicate award winners and books suitable for young adult readers. Entries also comment on historical accuracy, a key point for many of our readers. Because an attempt was made to include only titles that are in print or generally available, this title is very useful for libraries and collection development.

Another title worth noting is Daniel Burt's *What Historical Novel Do I Read Next?*[56] The main volume includes almost 7,000 Historical Fiction titles; entries give author, title, series information, story type, names of major characters, time period, locale, and plot summary. Indexes appear in a separate volume and include "Time Period," "Geographic," "Subject," "Fiction Character Name," "Historical Character Name," "Character Descriptor," "Author," and "Title." The "Historical Accuracy" note with each entry increases the usefulness of this source. The main drawback of this source is that an attempt has been made to include everything, and many titles are long out of print and unavailable, even in large library systems. Working with students can become very frustrating when every title we check is unavailable.

Where to Find . . .

INFORMATION ABOUT THE AUTHOR

Twentieth-Century Romance and Historical Writers remains the best source, although it is sadly out of date, and, according to the publisher, it will not be revised and reprinted.[57] Author entries include complete bibliographies and signed critical essays that characterize the author's style and tone and analyze several titles. These essays are valuable, because they are written in a way that helps us draw comparisons to other authors and to characterize the genre.

Many of these authors are also profiled in *Contemporary Authors.* (*See* appendix 2.)

PLOT SUMMARIES

In addition to Adamson's titles and Burt's book, annotations are available in *NoveList, What Do I Read Next? Fiction Catalog, To Be Continued,* and *Sequels.* (*See* appendix 2.) In the first two, index access is available by country or time period. *Fiction Catalog* provides index access only by geographic area (usually country or city and then by broad time period, often centuries). Lee Gordon and Cheryl Tanaka's *World Historical Fiction Guide for Young Adults* is another useful source that includes annotations, but coverage does not include the United States.[58]

SUBGENRES AND THEMES

It is important to discover sources that index particular historical and fictional figures and events, as well as time periods (although these are not exactly subgenres or themes). All titles described above provide this access, as does Donald K. Hartman and Gregg Sapp's *Historical Figures in Fiction*.[59] This book covers more than 4,000 novels published after 1940 in which almost 1,500 historical figures appear as significant characters. Although there are references to book reviews, titles are not annotated.

GENRE DESCRIPTION, BACKGROUND, AND HISTORY

Both *Genreflecting* (*see* appendix 2) and *Twentieth-Century Romance and Historical Writers* provide genre background and history.

CORE LISTS AND BEST BOOKS

What Historical Novel Do I Read Next? provides numerous excellent lists of books—a recommended list by time period and country and area, as well as lists of the most popular time periods, settings, subjects, and historical figures. *Genreflecting* includes a list of classics that are still available.

Because Web sources change almost daily, it is best to search and find sources that match your individual library's needs. One site of long-standing is Soon's Historical Fiction.[60] This is a place to pose questions as well as a resource with archives of information on Historical Fiction. *Genreflecting* also lists other Web sites for Historical Fiction.

The Historical Fiction genre covers a wide range of novels, from the more serious and literary to those with elements of Romance, Adventure, and Mystery. Some are intimate and psychological portraits of those who people a particular time; others are more exterior and action oriented. Setting or atmosphere, the frame, is the most important element.

Through fiction, much of a country's culture and story is preserved for future generations. Historical Fiction is part of a long tradition of retelling and preserving past events. Look at Homer and his stories of the Trojan War, sung for generations to keep the history and the story alive. Interestingly, in German the word *Geschichte* means both story and history. The best Historical Fiction combines both those elements, story and history, in a way that helps readers understand and remember the past. Although readers appreciate a wide variety of Historical Fiction and fiction with historical settings in other genres, they share the same expectations: a well-researched and memorable story, rooted in a time past, peopled with characters long dead, brought alive again through an author's imagination.

NOTES

1. Charles Frazier, *Cold Mountain* (New York: Atlantic Monthly, 1997).

2. James A. Michener, *Chesapeake* (New York: Random House, 1978).

3. Sharon Kay Penman, *The Sunne in Splendour* (New York: Holt, 1982).

4. James Goldman, *Myself as Witness* (New York: Random House, 1979).

5. Zoe Oldenbourg, *The World Is Not Enough* (New York: Carroll & Graf, 1998).

6. Ann Baer, *Down the Common* (New York: M. Evans, 1997).

7. Wilbur A. Smith, *River God* (New York: St. Martin's, 1994).

8. Ken Follett, *Pillars of the Earth* (New York: Morrow, 1989).

9. Max Byrd, *Jefferson* (New York: Bantam, 1993); ———, *Jackson* (New York: Bantam, 1997); ———, *Grant* (New York: Bantam, 2000).

10. Gore Vidal, *1876* (New York: Random House, 1976).

11. Michael Shaara, *The Killer Angels* (New York: McKay, 1974).

12. Steven Pressfield, *Gates of Fire* (New York: Doubleday, 1998).

13. Ross Leckie, *Hannibal* (Washington, D.C.: Regnery, 1996).

14. Edward Rutherford, *Sarum* (New York: Crown, 1987); ———, *Russka* (New York, Crown, 1991); ———, *London* (New York: Crown, 1997).

15. Mary Renault, *The King Must Die* (New York: Pantheon, 1958).

16. ———, *The Bull from the Sea* (New York: Pantheon, 1962); ———, *The Last of the Wine* (New York: Pantheon, 1956).

17. Nigel Tranter, *Robert the Bruce: The Steps to the Empty Throne* (New York: St. Martin's, 1969).

18. Judith Merkle Riley, *The Serpent Garden* (New York: Viking, 1996).

19. John Jakes, *The Bastard* (New York: Pyramid Books, 1974).

20. ———, *Homeland* (New York: Doubleday, 1993).

21. Louis L'Amour, *The Walking Drum* (New York: Bantam, 1984).

22. Henryk Sienkiewicz, *With Fire and Sword* (1884; in modern translation by W. S. Kuniczak, 1st ed., Fort Washington, Pa.: Copernicus Society of America; New York: Hippocrene Books, © 1991).

23. Jean Auel, *Clan of the Cave Bear* (New York: Crown, 1980).

24. Jacqueline Park, *The Secret Book of Grazia dei Rossi* (New York: Simon & Schuster, 1997).

25. Bertrice Small, *Love, Remember Me* (New York: Ballantine, 1994); Margaret George, *The Autobiography of Henry VIII* (New York: St. Martin's, 1986).

26. Jeanne Mackin, *The Queen's War* (New York: St. Martin's, 1991).

27. Claire Cooperstein, *Johanna* (New York: Scribner, 1995).

28. M. M. Kaye, *The Far Pavilions* (New York: St. Martin's, 1978).

29. Patricia Veryan, *Practice to Deceive* (New York: St. Martin's, 1985); ———, *Time's Fool* (New York: St. Martin's, 1991).

30. Paul Scott, *The Jewel in the Crown* (New York: Morrow, 1966).

31. George Garrett, *The Death of the Fox* (Garden City, N.Y.: Doubleday, 1971).

32. Elswyth Thane, *Dawn's Early Light* (Mattituck, N.Y.: Aeonian Press, 1943); Don Coldsmith, *Tallgrass* (New York: Bantam, 1997); ———, *South Wind* (New York: Bantam, 1998).

33. Maria Bellonci, *A Private Renaissance* (New York: Morrow, 1989).

34. Karleen Koen, *Through a Glass Darkly* (New York: Random House, 1986).

35. Jane Smiley, *The All-True Travels and Adventures of Liddie Newton* (New York: Knopf, 1998).

36. Glendon Fred Swarthout, *The Homesman* (New York: Weidenfeld & Nicolson, 1988).

37. Pamela Belle, *Wintercombe* (New York: St. Martin's, 1988).

38. Andrea Barrett, *The Voyage of the Narwhal* (New York: Norton, 1998).

39. Edith Pargeter, *The Heaven Tree Trilogy* (1960–63; reprint, New York: Warner Books, 1993).

40. Jeanne Williams, *Lady of No Man's Land* (New York: St. Martin's, 1988), also published in paperback as *Prairie Bouquet* (New York: St. Martin's, 1988).

41. Dorothy Dunnett, *Game of Kings* (New York: Putnam, 1961).

42. ———, *Niccolo Rising* (New York: Knopf, 1986).

43. Rosalind Laker, *The Golden Tulip* (New York: Doubleday, 1991).

44. Anya Seton, *Katherine* (Boston: Houghton, 1954).

45. Karen Harper, *Circle of Gold* (New York: E. P. Dutton, 1992).

46. Catherine Cookson, *The Girl* (New York: Morrow, 1977).

47. Diana Gabaldon, *Outlander* (New York: Delacorte, 1991).

48. Julie Tetel, *Sweet Seduction* (Toronto, New York: Harlequin, 1993).

49. Anne Perry, *The Cater Street Hangman* (New York: St. Martin's, 1979).

50. ———, *The Face of a Stranger* (New York: Fawcett Columbine, 1990).

51. Margaret Lawrence, *Hearts and Bones* (New York: Avon, 1996).

105

HISTORICAL FICTION

52. Steven Saylor, *Roman Blood* (New York: St. Martin's, 1991); Lindsey Davis, *The Silver Pigs* (New York: Crown, 1989).

53. Colleen McCullough, *The First Man in Rome* (New York: Morrow, 1990).

54. Thomas Pynchon, *Mason and Dixon* (New York: Holt, 1997).

55. Lynda Adamson, *American Historical Fiction: An Annotated Guide to Novels for Adults and Young Adults* (Phoenix: Oryx, 1998); ———, *World Historical Fiction: An Annotated Guide to Novels for Adults and Young Adults* (Phoenix: Oryx, 1998).

56. Daniel Burt, *What Historical Novel Do I Read Next?* (Detroit: Gale, 1997).

57. Aruna Vasudevan and Lesley Henderson, eds., *Twentieth-Century Romance and Historical Writers,* 3d ed. (Detroit: St. James, 1994).

58. Lee Gordon and Cheryl Tanaka, *World Historical Fiction Guide for Young Adults* (Fort Atkinson, Wis.: Highsmith Press, 1995).

59. Donald K. Hartman and Gregg Sapp, *Historical Figures in Fiction* (Phoenix: Oryx, 1994).

60. Soon's Historical Fiction [Online], (Austin, Texas, 1995) [cited March 28, 2001]); available at <http://uts.cc.utexas.edu/~soon/histfiction>.

6

Horror

From classic ghost and vampire stories to hauntings and supernatural visitations, Horror stories, and the thrill they produce, fill our waking and sleeping hours. From ancient times with stories of Lilith and the ghosts of the dead, Horror has always held its own among fiction genres, although the popularity of these stories has waxed and waned throughout the centuries. Horror in literature has been termed mankind's effort to invoke and subdue the demonic. There is a certain pleasure to be derived from the chill that Horror creates, as well as from the relief at being able to close a book to escape its thrall—temporarily at least, as the best of the genre tends to stay with its fans.

A Definition

Many of us recognize Horror from television and movies, even if we are less familiar with the books. Baby boomers grew up on *The Twilight Zone,* with its mix of spooky stories and a supernatural twist, while *The X-Files* has spurred today's surge of interest in this genre (and Science Fiction, too). Teenagers flock to showings of *Scream* and its sequels, as well as to every reincarnation of Jason in the various *Friday the Thirteenth* screenings.

But what constitutes a Horror story? Horror, despite the numerous themes that propel its stories, is one of the most straightforward genres to define and understand on a very basic level. Horror fiction has as its goal producing fear in readers. It contains a monster of some type, and supernatural elements figure prominently. Thus, Horror certainly includes stories of ghosts, ghouls, and vampires of wide variety. The genre runs the gamut from Anne Rice's tales of vampires and other ghouls, related in her characteristic provocatively erotic voice, to Bram Stoker's classic, *Dracula,* which creates the loathsome Dracula, hunted by those who fear him.[1] What is important is the feeling of foreboding that permeates the novels, the sense of unease, as we await the unexpected. Horror novels, then, are stories of nightmares come to life, complete with monsters of various descriptions; and as in all our nightmares, surprise is a crucial element. We never know exactly when the terror will invade our lives. Figure 6.1 lists the characteristics of the Horror genre.

FIGURE 6.1

Characteristics of the Horror Genre

1. The atmosphere creates a sense of menace and evokes an emotional response from the reader. The story is characterized by a dark tone and a sense of foreboding.

2. The story line employs monsters of some kind, usually supernatural. Graphic violence, strong language, and explicit sex are often aspects of Horror, used to enhance the effect of the supernatural and the impact of the story.

3. Endings are generally unresolved. Although it may be beaten down temporarily, the Horror lives on.

4. Unexpected incidents, designed to jolt the reader, accelerate the pacing and keep the story moving quickly.

5. Protagonists are often haunted, shattered individuals. Antagonists are always sinister, monsters in some form, whether real or imaginary.

Characteristics and the Genre's Appeal

Frame

The atmosphere in Horror novels must, the fans tell us, evoke an emotional response, a chill, a sense of menace, a feeling of supernatural terror. This special atmosphere or setting must permeate the novel. It is what readers are expecting and looking for when they ask us for Horror fiction. Unlike Science Fiction, which appeals to the intellect, Horror appeals first and foremost to the emotions. The point of a good Horror story is to evoke an emotional and spiritual response in the reader: true fright.

In Horror all elements (story line, characterization, pacing) help create this sense of menace and contribute to this emotional impact. This special frame permeates the novel. Readers never escape this feeling, at least not for long. In fact, many Horror novels highlight the horrific or supernatural element by employing different typefaces, such as bold type, or capitals, or italics. (This is a technique Stephen King frequently uses to emphasize and underline the horrific, for example in *Bag of Bones*.)[2] There may also be a prologue that establishes this horrific atmosphere right from the beginning. For example, the introductory pages of Douglas J. Preston and Lincoln Child's *Relic* set the stage by revealing to readers that something very nasty has already taken place in the Amazon jungle to destroy all members of the expedition, and the "treasure" being returned to New York is bound to create even more devastation.[3] Our interest is piqued and we simply wait, anxiously, to see what will happen next.

Because the setting and atmosphere are so important, they are often very detailed. If there is a haunted house, you will know where all the windows are, what wall and floor coverings are there, how it smells, sounds—and, especially, how it feels. If you have read any of Clive Barker's Horror novels, you know what intimate details you get of the world of the dead, for example, in his short novel *Cabal*.[4] In fact, the setting and atmosphere may be described more completely and vividly than the characters. You can feel and sense the evil, sometimes even before you see it. There is no question that Hill House, from Shirley Jackson's classic psychological ghost story, *The Haunting of Hill House*, embodies the appropriate sense of dread and disquiet long before the actual horrific incidents occur.[5] Its very description reflects the menace the house contains. A reader coming upon such descriptions, and influenced by the mood they create, would have no doubt about what lay ahead for the protagonist—and himself as a reader.

It goes without saying that the bleak and disturbing tone of much Horror fiction also reflects and enhances this dark atmosphere. Even though Horror novels are decidedly dark, readers find in them a surprising amount of humor, albeit grim. There are often puns and plays on words that amuse the fans, and some authors are noted for their macabre humor. Greg Kihn, in his series of off-the-wall reworkings of Ed Wood Horror films from the '50s, spoofs those Grade B movies but also adds visceral Horror to the black comedy. First in the series is *Horror Show*.[6]

Story Line

The presence of the supernatural pervades these stories and sets Horror apart from other genres. Not only does it affect the mood and tone of the story, it influences the story line as well. In fact, story lines in the Horror genre do not necessarily flow in a logical order, because of the influence of the supernatural. This does not bother fans, as it is part of what they expect to find in Horror. However, this is one of the reasons why Horror may not be as satisfying to fans of other genres, such as those who enjoy Mysteries, for example, where loose ends are tied up and justice triumphs. In Horror, the supernatural leads to the unexpected. H. P. Lovecraft was among the first authors in the genre to suggest that there is a parallel universe of unimaginable horrors that occasionally finds ways to break through into our own. (Try *The Dunwich Horror* and subsequent stories featuring the dreaded *Necronomicon* by the mad Arab Abdul Alhazred.)[7] Classic contemporary authors, including King ("The Mist") and Dean R. Koontz (*The Bad Place*), have also used this theme.[8]

In addition, it is important to recognize that Horror novels usually contain graphic violence and themes of sensuality and sexuality that seem to go hand in hand with creating this menacing atmosphere. These elements may be offensive to readers new to Horror, who are not expecting them. For fans, this heightened level of gore and sex simply add to the visceral quality they expect. For a taste of this style, explore Poppy Z. Brite's gory tales of "goth" vampires (*Lost Souls*) and other creatures of the night.[9]

The ending of a Horror novel is crucial to its appeal and also sets these novels apart from those in other genres. In Horror novels readers do not know how the story will end, and this is a direct contrast to many other genres, especially Mystery and Romance, in which readers can often predict the ending after the first few pages. (Readers do not know the details of each novel's conclusion, but in Romance, they understand that the couple in question will resolve the issues that keep them apart; and in Mysteries, justice will be done, with the murderer apprehended.) In Horror novels the endings themselves are often vague, sustaining the menacing atmosphere rather than tying loose ends together. The horror has been beaten down for now, but it is not dead. The evil is still lurking. Although the monster may have been killed, an egg remains, left unseen. *Talons*, by Anthony Mancini, includes strong elements from the Suspense and Thriller genres, but the ending is pure Horror.[10] The novel tells of a golden eagle, genetically altered by the Chernobyl disaster, that terrorizes New York City. And although the eagle is trapped and killed at the end, a literal egg does survive, as does the possibility of the horror living on.

Curiously, there are rarely sequels in Horror fiction, even though most of the novels end as if the author is planning one. (One of the few examples of a sequel is *The Reliquary*, by Preston and Child, which follows the enormously popular *Relic*.[11] Even though this sequel would probably appeal more to fans of Medical/Scientific Thrillers, it does end with the possibility that some of the horror has survived.) On the other hand, there are occasionally traditional series. An extraordinarily popular example is Laurell K. Hamilton's vampire hunter, Anita Blake (*Guilty Pleasures* is the first), and her human and supernatural companions in stories set in St. Louis in a near-future time when even the Undead have rights.[12] Each novel constitutes an adventure and follows the general characteristics of the genre, although the ongoing characters are more fully developed than in most single-title Horror novels. This interesting series has introduced many non-Horror readers to the genre. The strong female protagonist reminds readers of an older Buffy the Vampire Slayer, and her ongoing relationship with the master vampire Jean-Claude, in addition to the less bleak tone, has attracted many Romance fans.

Pacing

The pacing helps create and sustain Horror's unique atmosphere. Pacing in Horror novels is often erratic, with scenes of calm followed, without warning, by more intense scenes. This unexpected quality, these sudden changes, add to the menacing nature. Readers expect to get a jolt at irregular, unpredictable intervals in Horror novels. These differ from those we find in a genre such as Suspense, where readers know more than the protagonists and thus anticipate these episodes. But because in Horror these interludes occur erratically and unexpectedly, thus capturing the essence of living in a nightmare, there is a very real sense that the pacing is out of control, and, by inference, so are characters and plot.

Characterization

What about characters in Horror novels? They are usually haunted, shattered individuals or in some way susceptible, vulnerable; these are people out of control. There are not many happy-go-lucky characters in Horror fiction. (And if they do appear, they are unlikely to survive the first fifty pages!) The character of the villain or evil force is always sinister; these are monsters in some form. In fact, the villains do not need to be realistic, just plausible, unlike other genre fiction that insists on realistic characters, even among the bad guys.

One of the most interesting features of characterization in Horror is how point of view can help Readers' Advisors separate Horror from Hard-Edged Suspense, which generally has a different readership. In serial killer novels like Thomas Harris's *Silence of the Lambs,* the readers find the point of view of both the killer and the detective, and they know what each is thinking and doing.[13] Although there can still be grisly moments, they are not unexpected, because we know the killer and his plans. This knowledge makes all the difference in how readers react to the story. There are exceptions, but generally speaking, Horror fans do not often find serial killer novels satisfying in exactly the same way; in Hard-Edged Suspense, they know too much and lose the desired element of total surprise. Also, endings in Suspense tie things up, with the good guys in control, while Horror offers open, unresolved endings. In Suspense, as opposed to Horror, the characters are generally more in control. In Horror, they seem to have little control, and, as the evil is generally unknown, its appearances are jarring and unexpected. (Even if the evil has been identified, its appearance is unpredictable and can precipitate an electric moment of adrenaline rush.)

Within Horror novels, point of view can create very different types of novels, depending on whether it is the innocent's point of view or the evil's point of view that the reader follows. An example of a novel told from the evil's point of view is Anne Rice's *Interview with the Vampire*.[14] Here we see the action from the vampire's point of view, and that intensifies the atmosphere and the reader's relationship to the story and characters. Horror novels in which the reader sees the action from the evil's point of view often have a very different, more disturbing, feel. By contrast, the characterization in Horror novels by King allows the reader to identify with the protagonists—often ordinary people caught up in an extraordinary situation—and to empathize with them and their plight. We are pulled in by the sympathetic characters, rather than distanced by the sinister protagonist when we are placed in the viewpoint of the evil. Both have the intended effect of books in this genre, but that effect is achieved quite differently in each case.

Key Authors and Subgenres

Benchmark

Although I examine two distinct subgenres of Horror separately below, I also want to acknowledge that Horror is unique among fiction genres in that there is a clear benchmark for the entire genre: Stephen King. Few would question King's preeminent popularity and productivity. His first Horror novel, *Carrie,* was published in 1974, and he continues to make his mark on the Horror genre and on publishing in general.[15] (He turned the budding e-book industry on its head when he published his first e-book, *Riding the Bullet,* in spring 2000.)[16] Under his real name as well as his pseudonym, Richard Bachman,

King has written almost forty Horror novels, as well as a few dark Fantasy novels, and even a few mainstream novels (for example, *The Girl Who Loved Tom Gordon,* although even this contains the suggestion of the supernatural).[17] King's books are generally characterized by sympathetic, although certainly haunted, protagonists; a "normal" environment into which the horror intrudes; and a long buildup to the horrific situation. He has written Horror novels in both subgenres—Storyteller and Visceral—although most of his writing falls within Storyteller. Visceral Horror is represented by his books published as Bachman, most notably *The Regulators;* these more often feature graphic violence early on, and it escalates quickly.[18]

Subgenres of Horror

To understand the range and appeal of the Horror genre, it is best to break it down into subgenres and consider typical authors under each type. Most reference books create subject distinctions to discuss the range of the genre. Anthony J. Fonseca and June Michele Pulliam's excellent study of the genre, *Hooked on Horror,* devotes individual chapters to common thematic devices: "Ghosts and Haunted Houses," "Vampires and Werewolves: Children of the Night," and "Splatterpunk: The Gross-Out," to name a few.[19] I would argue that the real difference in the way Horror books appeal to fans is whether the books are violent from the beginning and throughout or whether the author starts in a more normal world and builds the horrific element to a climax at the end. The important point to consider in identifying subgenres is when the violence occurs and to what extent the tone that this style creates pervades the book. With these thoughts in mind, I suggest two subgenres of Horror: Storyteller and Visceral.

Storyteller and Visceral Horror represent opposite ends of the range of Horror novels, with books that combine aspects of the two scattered across the spectrum. Thus, a list of special characteristics that distinguish the two is not necessary, although it should be noted that the two types engender totally different moods to which readers respond—or do not. The distinctions between Storyteller and Visceral Horror lie in the timing of the violence, when the supernatural elements and the gore are introduced, and in the kinds of universes the authors create.

STORYTELLER HORROR

This subgenre is distinguished by the slow building of Horror; neither the reader nor the protagonist suspects the terrible danger until quite late in the story, as opposed to Visceral Horror in which the violence appears early and throughout the novel. In his classic Horror novel, *The Shining,* King, the quintessential Storyteller Horror writer, typifies this pattern.[20] By the way, if you only know this tale from the movie, read the book, which is certainly one of his very best. In case you are not familiar with the story, it is about a dysfunctional family. Danny, the son, has a *Shine,* a familiar who speaks to him and warns him of the future. His father, Jack, is an alcoholic, who becomes abusive when he drinks. In a last-ditch attempt to hold the family together, Jack takes a job as a winter caretaker in a mountaintop hotel. We readers feel a strong sense of foreboding from the very first. At the hotel circumstances are gradually revealed to be not just a little strange, but very strange, and the horror that lives there starts taking Jack over. After that, there is nonstop action as Danny and his mother try to escape.

That point, however, is literally 300 pages into this 450-page novel. King spends most of the novel building the atmosphere, the sense of foreboding and menace, and creating characters to whom we respond. When the horrific elements occur, they affect us differently than they would have if we had been introduced to them in the first chapter. In my experience, both as a reader and in working with others, Storyteller Horror appeals to a wider range of readers, outside the Horror genre, who simply like a good story and can tolerate the horrific elements because King and others who write this type have prepared us with hints along the way.

The second distinction between these two subgenres is in the kind of universe the authors create. Writers such as King and Dean R. Koontz start out in normal worlds, which are subsequently invaded by horrific elements, and the stories then build to the terrifying climax. In Orson Scott Card's *Homebody,* builder Don Lark has survived the tragedy of the deaths of his wife and daughter in an automobile accident and now spends his time rebuilding his life by renovating houses.[21] However, in one old mansion he buys, he has met his match. As his repairs progress, the house becomes stronger and stronger, and the supernatural intrudes more and more into the story until the final confrontation at the end. Charles Grant often uses the same technique in his Horror novels, normally set in small towns. Bizarre events multiply until the horror threatens to overwhelm hero and reader alike, as in *Symphony,* the first in his Millennium Quartet, featuring the Four Horsemen of the Apocalypse and the evils of war each represents.[22]

King, the overall benchmark for the genre, also stands as the benchmark for the Storyteller subgenre. His books, primarily noted for the building of menace and the creation of Horror out of ordinary worlds, people, and events, demonstrate the technique and appeal of books of this type. Other Storyteller Horror writers popular among fans include Koontz *(Watchers)*, Dan Simmons *(Summer of Night)*, John Saul *(Right Hand of Evil)*, Peter Straub *(Ghost Story)*, and Bentley Little *(The House)*.[23]

VISCERAL HORROR

In contrast to Storyteller Horror, Visceral Horror introduces violence at the beginning of the novel and the intensity never flags. We meet the evil early on in the story; explicit sex and violence, as well as strong language, pervade these novels. Clive Barker's republished *Books of Blood* illustrates the grisly appeal of this Horror subgenre.[24] (This is, by the way, a collection of short stories, a form that many Horror readers and writers relish.) In "Dread," one of these stories, his protagonist sets out to prove that fear is the basic motivating force in human behavior, and he does this by exploring the dark side of the psyche through graphic and violent scenes of physical torture that mirror the victim's inner torment. Intense, gory, explicit, and, for fans, very satisfying, these stories exhibit Barker's bleak worldview and his morbid sense of humor.

Unlike the Storyteller Horror, in which writers start out with fairly normal worlds, authors writing in this subgenre disorient readers early on. They place us in worlds and situations unlike our own, and, removed from what we know, we feel the Horror more intensely. Anne Rice, for example, takes us into the world of the vampire. She alters our perspective, and we see events from the inside out, participating in the horror rather than observing it. This technique is disorienting and can be quite disturbing.

Rice sets the standard in this subgenre. Although her books may not contain as much graphic violence as some other authors, the impact on the reader of her stories is the same. Much of the effect of Rice's stories rises from their explicit sexual nature. Erotic, sometimes sadistic and perverse, her seductive stories pull readers into a carefully constructed web. Although she is best known for her two vampire series, she has explored a wide variety of ghouls and witches in great detail and with enormous success. Her ability to pull the reader into the consciousness of the horrific character creates a chilling sense of unease that readers relish. This skill means that her stories need not be intensely graphic to produce the same effect. Fans relish her sensual language and the perverse, arcane, and weird characters and situations she presents.

Poppy Z. Brite, whose first novel, *Lost Souls,* was published in 1992, is another author to read to understand this subgenre. An elegant style, steamy decadence, explicit sex, and graphic violence characterize her novels and short stories, which feature vampires and ghouls of many descriptions. *Splatterpunk* is the term often applied to her writing, although not necessarily by fans, and the name certainly leaves no doubt about the nature of the stories. Despite the violence a great part of Brite's appeal seems to be the teenage "goth" characters, and she is a writer often sought by teen readers.

Other practitioners of this subgenre are Richard Laymon (*The Stake*), Brian Lumley (*Necroscope* series), Brian Stableford (*The Werewolves of London*), and S. P. Somtow (*Vampire Junction* and sequels).[25] We might call these examples of "videogame" Horror, because they emulate the explicit gore of many of the intensely graphic games so popular today.

Preparing to Work with Readers

What do we know, and need to know, about fans of the Horror genre? We know that they expect the unexpected. They demand characters, events, and situations that surprise them. They read Horror because they enjoy being frightened. Atmospheric stories appeal to them; authors need not necessarily be literary stylists, but they must tell a story infused with a creepiness, a growing dread of the outcome. How much "blood and guts" they request varies, as discussed below. However, fans of the Horror genre read to be frightened, to confront their personal nightmares, or to experience the terror they had not even imagined before. Their favorite writers are those who meet these expectations.

The best way to help readers is to gain an understanding of the range of the genre ourselves. More frequently than with any other genre, I have encountered librarians with a genuine reluctance to read Horror. This should not surprise us in light of what we have discovered about the gory descriptions demanded by the genre and the emotional response Horror evokes. Because I believe it is important to sample each genre so that we can relate better to fans, I think it is necessary to discover strategies to explore even those genres that we find distasteful. These are techniques that work, no matter what the genre

If staff are reluctant to read or even skim the book, they need to learn about it by reading about both the book and author in reference sources and reviews. This gives them an idea of what to expect, and they are less likely to come upon something really disturbing if they then skim a few pages here and there to get a feel for the book.

In familiarizing themselves with the book, they should look for atmosphere. Does the horror start early on or later? They should also talk with fans to discover what it is they love about the author and book. What makes the book so scary?

Short story collections are another good way to become familiar with important authors, past and present. From these we get an introduction to an author's style and the kind of Horror that author writes, just as we do from novels. However, short stories are not necessarily easier to read if we are uncomfortable with the genre. The atmosphere is often even more intense because it is distilled into the shorter format.

Another problem that we encounter with the Horror genre is that, like Romances, these titles are not always reviewed in the library literature, in part, perhaps because they are often published by small presses. In addition, some of the most popular titles among readers have been passed by word of mouth; they are cult books, titles we may not have heard about. If we make an effort to solicit suggestions from fans of the genre, we can often keep up-to-date on the most recent titles, as well as authors whose work we should collect.

FIGURE 6.2

An Introduction to the Horror Genre

Horror Writers to Try, If You Enjoy . . .

Fantasy	H. P. Lovecraft
	Stephen King (Dark Tower series)
Historical	Chelsea Quinn Yarbro
	Barbara Hambly (*Those Who Hunt the Night*)[26]
Humor	Greg Kihn
Literary	M. R. James
	Michael Cadnum (*Nightlight*)[27]
Mystery	Tanya Huff
Psychological	Shirley Jackson
Romance	Laurell K. Hamilton
Science Fiction	John Farris (*The Fury*)[28]
Suspense	Stephen King (*The Shining* or *Bag of Bones*)
Thriller	Douglas Preston and Lincoln Child
	John Saul
Western	Stephen King (Dark Tower series)

Figure 6.2 lists Horror writers you might want to try if you enjoy one of these other genres. Going from a genre we already read and appreciate to an author of Horror who writes similarly may help us understand and better appreciate the Horror genre.

Readers' Advisory Interview

The most important question to consider in working with readers is not how graphic and violent the Horror is, but how early it appears in the book. Those Horror readers who really do not like a lot of gore can tolerate much more if it occurs later in the novel, once they know and care about the characters. (This is the same phenomenon that occurs with the amount of sex in Romances; sex too soon or too graphic early may be off-putting to some readers. If it occurs later in the novel and between a couple who care about each other, it is less likely to offend, no matter how graphic.) The more intense examples in the genre are often those that are grisly right away.

Intensity is another issue to consider. Many in the Storyteller subgenre build intensity slowly, while examples of the Visceral are often more intense early on. Each reader has a comfort level, and the easiest way to discover it is to offer a range of suggestions that reflect the diversity of the Horror genre. This is a genre that relies on an emotional impact, and although readers may not have a firm grasp of what they are looking for, they are generally able to reveal their preferences as they react to possibilities. Each of us has a level of creepiness beyond which we do not want to go, and to work successfully with readers, we need an idea of the range of possibilities the genre offers so we can present them to readers.

Remember, too, that some Horror readers have particular subject interests. They may say they like anything with vampires or witches or whatever. For these, we use the reference tools described below to identify titles. However, even though readers may come first with subject requests, they often discover, as they read more, that they really prefer a particular mood, the special atmosphere that evokes that emotional chill from a certain type, not subject, of a book.

Now, how can we best help readers find what they are looking for? In a slight twist on the general readers' advisory technique, I ask readers to tell me the scariest parts of books they have enjoyed. Armed with this information, I can make suggestions that are more likely to fit within the level of scariness they enjoy. In offering suggestions, I try to contrast these types of Horror and let the reader choose. Do they like those that start out fairly normally but then things start to go awry? Or do they prefer to be thrown right in the middle of a horrific situation?

We keep mental (or physical) lists of authors and titles to follow up on these questions. For example, John Saul, Charles L. Grant, Stephen King, and Dean R. Koontz build the horror and atmosphere more slowly, while authors such as Clive Barker and Brian Lumley, as well as S. P. Somtow and Brian Stableford, tend to present the horrific elements much earlier.

If the readers are not certain which they might enjoy, I describe several and offer possibilities. Collections of short stories, especially ones that run the gamut of appeal, are also a good bet to suggest to readers. Just as they can help staff become better acquainted with the genre, they offer readers a chance to sample the genre. In my experience, most genre readers do not necessarily like short stories, but this is not true in Horror. Because the genre depends so heavily on atmosphere, Horror lends itself well to this format.

We should also remember the classic Horror writers, as they often make good suggestions, especially for readers who want to experiment. Readers new to the genre may not have discovered Shirley Jackson, H. P. Lovecraft, M. R. James, and Daphne du Maurier, and they might be pleased to see that stories by these classic authors are still accessible—and chilling.

When we talk with readers, we describe books in terms of that atmosphere, how it makes the reader feel, how it pulls readers into the horror (either immediately or more slowly), how readers relate to characters and share their plight or observe them from a distance. We offer authors and titles based on their responses to these descriptions.

Teenagers comprise a very large section of Horror fans. I am not certain why Horror has such a strong appeal for this age group. It may be because there are often teen protagonists. Certainly, there is a suspension of societal rules; kids are often in charge, solving problems and fighting evil, without assistance from adults. Teens, like the rest of us, enjoy Horror for the chill it evokes. They read everyone from Christopher Pike and R. L. Stine to V. C. Andrews, King, and Anne Rice.

We do need to exercise caution, however. Just because Horror is popular with young adults, we should not automatically assume it is the genre to suggest to someone who simply wants a good read. We need to be aware of the amount of sex in some Horror novels, especially in those that start out with violence, but even in others. Sometimes titles that feature teen protagonists also have strong sexual themes.

Sure Bets

Because a number of readers have preconceived notions about the Horror genre, it is not as easy to identify Sure Bets here. They simply do not have the universal appeal of some books in other genres. This does not prevent us from putting examples of the best on displays and in readers' hands, but the appeal is not always so obvious.

Koontz's *Watchers* is a title we have successfully suggested to a wide range of readers. The Horror element seems less intense, and, because it is part of the Storyteller subgenre, it builds more, preparing readers along the way. The dog with near-human intelligence—he eventually communicates with his family via computer—is a great hook!

King, of course, as an author whose books always reach the bestsellers lists, is the mainstay of our short list of Sure Bets. I like to give unfamiliar readers *The Shining*, which I still consider one of his best. The size is not so daunting, and the Horror builds delightfully.

Expanding Readers' Horizons

Suggesting other Horror writers to a fan of the genre is one thing, but we should also remember that almost none of us reads exclusively in a particular genre and that readers are always excited at the prospect of discovering other writers that might meet their needs and interests. Thinking in terms of crossing genres is important for us as Readers' Advisors, too. Just because someone mentions one genre does not mean that is the only possibility for us to pursue.

Horror offers several directions for crossover. This crossover works in terms of both the themes explored in Horror, as well as the appeal and tone of Horror novels. For example, fans of stories of vampires, werewolves, and other beasts of the night will find, perhaps unexpectedly, series in the Romance genre that may interest them. Lori Herter's dark vampire romances (*Obsession* is the first) or Susan Krinard's lyrical werewolf and vampire novels (*Prince of Wolves* et al.) make good suggestions for fans.[29]

There is significant thematic overlap with Medical/Scientific Thrillers, described in chapter 14, "Thrillers." Writers such as Michael Palmer, Robin Cook, and Tess Gerritsen offer much that appeals to fans of Horror. Several writers of Horror also write dark Fantasy. Fans of the Horror novels of King, Koontz, and Dan Simmons, to name a few of these authors who write in more than one genre, might also enjoy the Fantasy these authors write.

Some crossover is less obvious and is based on appeal rather than theme. Horror readers appreciate darkly atmospheric tales and do not always require the presence of the supernatural. Although, as I mentioned earlier, fans are unlikely to enjoy serial killer novels for the same reasons they like Horror, there may be novels of Hard-Edged Suspense or Mystery that appeal to them. Writers such as David Lindsey and T. Jefferson Parker, with their dark atmosphere and bleak tone, not to mention the explicit violence, may work. Or an author like Andrew Klavan, who has written both Softer- and Hard-Edged Suspense as well as Psychological Suspense (*The Animal Hour*),[30] might be a good suggestion. Robert Bloch's *Psycho,* more Suspense than Horror by my definition, certainly has elements that would appeal to Horror readers. [31] Other possibilities come to mind as we consider what it is that Horror readers enjoy—and more specifically what the reader standing in front of us mentions—and think about what we know about the characteristics of other genres and what they have to offer. Figure 6.3 lists additional authors to take readers beyond Horror.

FIGURE 6.3

Expanding Readers' Horizons

Authors to Take Readers beyond the Horror Genre

Fantasy	Dean R. Koontz
	Stephen King
Mystery	T. Jefferson Parker
Psychological	Stephen King (*Misery*)
Romance	Susan Krinard
Suspense	David Lindsey
Thriller	Robin Cook
	Tess Gerritsen
	Michael Palmer

Reference Sources

The Horror genre has also benefited from the increased interest in producing genre reference tools. Several useful titles have been published within the last few years. If I had to choose just one, however, it would be *Hooked on Horror*, another in Libraries Unlimited's Genreflecting Advisory series.[32] Anthony J. Fonseca and June Michele Pulliam have created a valuable resource that covers the history, subgenres, and themes, as well as core lists, award winners, and references to other genres with which Horror crosses over.

Where to Find . . .

INFORMATION ABOUT THE AUTHOR

St. James Guide to Horror, Ghost, and Gothic Writers, one of the last in this excellent series created by St. James Press, provides useful biographical information, as well as a complete bibliography and analysis of some titles.[33]

Contemporary Authors (*see* appendix 2) also provides useful author biographies.

PLOT SUMMARIES

Fiction Catalog, NoveList, and *What Do I Read Next?* all provide plot summaries for Horror fiction. (*See* appendix 2 for details of these titles.) Another useful source is Neil Barron's *Fantasy and Horror: A Critical and Historical Guide to Literature, Illustration, Film, TV, Radio, and the Internet*, which also provides annotations for the titles included.[34]

SUBGENRES AND THEMES

Barron's *Fantasy and Horror* indexes themes, as does Fonseca and Pulliam's *Hooked on Horror. NoveList* and *What Do I Read Next?* also provide access to subgenres and themes through their subject search functions.

GENRE DESCRIPTION, BACKGROUND, AND HISTORY

Barron's *Fantasy and Horror* and *St. James Guide to Horror, Ghost, and Gothic Writers* provide genre background and history. *Hooked on Horror* is another place to look for this kind of information, as is *Genreflecting*, to a lesser extent.

CORE LISTS AND BEST BOOKS

Both Barron's and Fonseca and Pulliam's titles include core lists of titles for readers and collection development. *Genreflecting* lists award winners, as well as a valuable list of short story collections.

Horror is another genre, like Romance, that has yet to achieve legitimacy among critics. Its growing popularity in the mass media, however, bespeaks the place it holds among fans. Horror is also a genre that attracts extreme opinions. Fans love it, or types of it, while others look at it with distaste and pride themselves in never having sampled it—and never wanting to! (This latter reaction is unfortunate, as some of our best storytellers have specialized in this genre and have written Horror that transcends the reservations of the most intransigent anti-Horror group.)

According to Fonseca and Pulliam, "Horror allows us to experience the emotion of fear in a controlled setting."[35] Reading Horror stories and viewing Horror films provide us with an opportunity to face down monsters vicariously, to confront the evil and walk away unharmed. We can always close the book if the story becomes too frightening.

NOTES

1. Bram Stoker, *Dracula* (London: Constable, 1897; New York: Doubleday and McClure, 1899).
2. Stephen King, *Bag of Bones* (New York: Scribner, 1998).
3. Douglas J. Preston and Lincoln Child, *Relic* (New York: Forge, 1995).
4. Clive Barker, *Cabal* (New York: Poseidon Press, 1988).
5. Shirley Jackson, *The Haunting of Hill House* (New York: Viking, 1959).
6. Greg Kihn, *Horror Show* (New York: Tor, 1996).
7. H. P. Lovecraft, *The Dunwich Horror* (New York: Bart House, 1945).
8. King, "The Mist," in *Skeleton Crew* (New York: Viking, 1985); Dean R. Koontz, *The Bad Place* (New York: Putnam, 1990).
9. Poppy Z. Brite, *Lost Souls* (New York: Delacorte, 1992).
10. Anthony Mancini, *Talons* (New York: D. I. Fine, 1991).
11. Preston and Child, *The Reliquary* (New York: Forge, 1997).
12. Laurell K. Hamilton, *Guilty Pleasures* (New York: Ace Books, 1993).

13. Thomas Harris, *The Silence of the Lambs* (New York: St. Martin's, 1988).

14. Anne Rice, *Interview with the Vampire* (New York: Knopf, 1976).

15. King, *Carrie* (Garden City, N.Y.: Doubleday, 1974).

16. ———, *Riding the Bullet* (e-book, 2000).

17. ———, *The Girl Who Loved Tom Gordon* (New York: Scribner, 1999).

18. Richard Bachman, *The Regulators* (New York: E. P. Dutton, 1996).

19. Anthony J. Fonseca and June Michele Pulliam, *Hooked on Horror: A Guide to Reading Interests in Horror Fiction* (Englewood, Colo.: Libraries Unlimited, 1999).

20. King, *The Shining* (Garden City, N.Y.: Doubleday, 1977).

21. Orson Scott Card, *Homebody* (New York: HarperCollins, 1998).

22. Charles Grant, *Symphony* (New York: Forge, 1997).

23. Koontz, *Watchers* (New York: Putnam, 1987); Dan Simmons, *Summer of Night* (New York: Putnam, 1991); John Saul, *Right Hand of Evil* (New York: Ballantine, 1999); Peter Straub, *Ghost Story* (New York: Coward, McCann & Geoghegan, 1979); Bentley Little, *The House* (New York: Signet, 1999).

24. Barker, *The Books of Blood* (New York: Putnam, 1988).

25. Richard Laymon, *The Stake* (New York: St. Martin's, 1991); Brian Stableford, *The Werewolves of London* (New York: Carroll & Graf, 1992); S. P. Somtow, *Vampire Junction* (New York: Tor, 1991).

26. Barbara Hambly, *Those Who Hunt the Night* (New York: Ballantine, 1988).

27. Michael Cadnum, *Nightlight* (New York: St. Martin's, 1990).

28. John Farris, *The Fury* (Chicago: Playboy Press, 1976).

29. Lori Herter, *Obsession* (New York: Berkley Books, 1991); Susan Krinard, *Prince of Wolves* (New York: Bantam, 1994).

30. Andrew Klavan, *The Animal Hour* (New York: Pocket Books, 1993).

31. Robert Bloch, *Psycho* (Mattituck, N.Y.: Rivercity Press, 1976).

32. Fonseca and Pulliam, *Hooked on Horror*.

33. David Pringle, ed., *St. James Guide to Horror, Ghost, and Gothic Writers* (Detroit: St. James, 1998).

34. Neil Barron, *Fantasy and Horror: A Critical and Historical Guide to Literature, Illustration, Film, TV, Radio, and the Internet* (Lanham, Md.: Scarecrow, 1999).

35. Fonseca and Pulliam, *Hooked on Horror*, p. xv.

7

Literary Fiction

Many readers and librarians may be surprised to see Literary Fiction categorized as a type of genre fiction. Surely such an act is a form of blasphemy! Literary Fiction readers, a group that includes many librarians, tend to see their favorite authors as the epitome of literary standards and style. The authors who write Literary Fiction win the highest accolades available to writers (except, perhaps, bestseller status). It hardly seems fair to link them with genre fiction.

Although readers may not recognize this as a genre, even if they read Literary Fiction, it helps librarians to do so. As with all genres, certain elements characterize the books that these readers seek. When we consider this as a genre, with identifiable characteristics and a particular pattern of writing, it is far easier to help those readers seeking more books that attain the literary standards they desire.

A Definition

If Literary Fiction is a genre, how do we define it? All genres have a Literary dimension, novels that are better written, that are acknowledged for their style and elegance, even though they still fit within that particular genre. The implications of this are useful for us as Readers' Advisors, as we quickly learn that readers who appreciate more literary titles may enjoy them whether they are classified as Mysteries, Science Fiction, or any other genre.

Literary Fiction is critically acclaimed, often award-winning, fiction. These books are more often character centered rather than plot oriented. They are provocative and often address more serious issues. These are not page-turners, per se, although their fans certainly find them engrossing and compelling reading. As we defined the genre in *Readers' Advisory Service in the Public Library,* these are "complex, literate, multilayered novels that wrestle with universal dilemmas."[1] Figure 7.1 lists the characteristics of Literary Fiction.

FIGURE 7.1

Characteristics of Literary Fiction

1. Literary style is important. Attention is paid by authors and readers to words and how they are woven together. Elegant, often poetic language is employed. The structure of the novel itself may be more complex, even experimental.

2. Characters emerge as more important than story lines, and the philosophical questions central to these books are often explored more through character than through story. Characters, even secondary characters, are multi-dimensional and often act in ways that are unpredictable.

3. Story lines are provocative. Literary Fiction operates in the realm of ideas as well as practicalities, and these novels often consider universal dilemmas. Endings are often open or ambiguous.

4. Pacing is slower, as these are usually densely written books. Complex characters and story lines, as well as obscure language or style, force readers to read more slowly to understand the layers of embedded meaning. There is generally more description than dialogue.

5. The tone of Literary Fiction may be bleaker, darker, because of the seriousness of the issues considered.

Characteristics and the Genre's Appeal

Language

Language and writing style are primary keys to the appeal of books and authors in this genre. When talking with fans of Literary Fiction, it becomes almost impossible for us as librarians not to describe books as "well written," because by any literary standards, they are. Still, it is better to discover other words to describe these novels: "elegantly written," "lyrical," and perhaps "layered" are terms that provide the same information about the use of language and style without the chance of misunderstanding by readers.

Fans of Literary Fiction prize complex language and interesting style. Words are important in their own right; how an author says something is almost as important as what is said. Knowing this, we understand better the range of books that might appeal to fans of this genre and, more importantly, what will not. Language runs the gamut from the spare, unadorned prose of Kent Haruf in *Plainsong* and the slangy jargon of Roddy Doyle's *Paddy Clarke Ha, Ha, Ha* to the lyrical, evocative, yet sometimes brutal language of Cormac McCarthy in his Border Trilogy (*All the Pretty Horses* is the first).[2] Although it varies greatly in terms of tone, language must also be appropriate to the topic and sense of the novel.

This is also a genre that allows greater leeway in terms of style, and prose styles are often more complex and experimental. Stories may be told through stream of consciousness, letters, diaries, or alternating points of view among the characters, to mention but a few possibilities. Because style and use of language are so important to fans, authors are more comfortable experimenting with forms in this genre in which the understanding that there is no set pattern *is* the pattern. Examples of these varying styles include the stream of consciousness of William Faulkner (*The Sound and the Fury*), the magical realism of Nobel Prize–winner Gabriel Garcia Marquez (*One Hundred Years of Solitude*) or Isabel Allende (*The House of the Spirits*), or simply the unconventional style of Thomas Pynchon, with its picaresque story, wordplay and puns, and encyclopedic knowledge (*Gravity's Rainbow* won the National Book Award).[3]

Characterization

Readers who love character-centered stories turn frequently to Literary Fiction. Here, intimate, introspective glimpses of characters allow readers to watch them develop. Relationships among characters are important, too, as they are in genres such as Women's Lives and Relationships and Romances. Anne Tyler's quirky characters are a familiar example. No matter how outlandish the characters seem, we find that if we analyze them, they are also surprisingly familiar. She allows us to see something of ourselves and those we know in even the quirkiest of these. Throughout her accessible, satisfying stories, she offers insights into her characters—and thus into our own lives. The award-winning *The Accidental Tourist,* in which the solitary Macon is forced to create a new life after his marriage of twenty years fails, and *Breathing Lessons,* in which a journey to a funeral brings resolution and a rebirth of affection to the lives of Maggie and Ira Moran, are good examples of her style and characterizations.[4]

Story Line

In the story lines of Literary Fiction, authors probe a range of themes. Like its counterparts in Science Fiction and Thrillers, for example, Literary Fiction tends to deal with serious, provocative topics. J. M. Coetzee, twice named winner of the prestigious Booker Award, writes of his native South Africa, but the local issues he addresses have universal implications. Violence pervades the lives and worlds of his characters in these often allegorical tales, for example *Disgrace,* in which the protagonist must consider his own sexual proclivities—and future—in light of the gang rape of his daughter.[5]

The lighthearted, however, also has its place in this genre. From the imaginative playfulness of John Barth (*The Sot-Weed Factor*) and Robertson Davies (*Murther and Walking Spirits*), with his frequent literary and cinematic references, to the outrageous, slapstick writing of Kurt Vonnegut, among others, humor, although often ironic, abounds in this genre, and it is frequently used as a device to explore the problems.[6]

These are novels that explore universal dilemmas, and the truths they expose lift the story from the bounds of the subject classification. For example, Nicholas Shakespeare's *The Dancer Upstairs* is one of the most interesting books I have read in the last few years, but, based on subject headings (and thus, the subject of the story) and my reading interests, it seems an unhappy match.[7] A book about guerillas (terrorists) in South America would not be high on my list. Yet this intricately plotted, elegantly written story haunts me still, more than three years after I read it. A journalist wants one last story before his bureau closes, and he would like to interview the mystery man responsible for the arrest of the rebel leader. In his attempts to get this interview, he encounters the man truly responsible for this arrest. And it is the story of police officer Augustin Rejas, now living in obscurity, that we, along with our journalist, hear. This fascinating story raises interesting questions about the nature of revolution, the disparity between cultures, and corruption in the government. Shakespeare points out, as his models John le Carré and Graham Greene did before him, that there are no easy choices, no easy ways to create a life in a world in which there are no clear-cut good and evil. In Literary Fiction the story line almost always takes the reader beyond the basic plot into the world of larger issues and broader implications.

Endings in Literary Fiction are often inconclusive. Authors tantalize the readers with options but do not always indicate which eventuality occurs. Our understanding of the characters allows us to make our own choices. In Peter Hoeg's *Smilla's Sense of Snow* we leave Smilla off Greenland, walking on the frozen ocean.[8] To what future? Readers loved or hated the ending, and I was engaged in more than a few discussions about it at the readers' advisory desk. Generally speaking, fans of Literary Fiction appreciate an author's skill at creating such an open-ended—and certainly discussable—conclusion.

Although I have suggested that the story line of Literary Fiction is not the genre's greatest strength, there is no denying that many of its practitioners are, above all, storytellers. Wallace Stegner is an excellent example. Whatever else his novels and short stories say about the human condition, they tell a good story. The Pulitzer Prize–winning *Angle of Repose* remains my favorite, a novel that touches the reader with its very human story of a wheelchair-bound history professor who tries to escape the traumas of his own life by researching his grandmother's.[9] Her story—she was an Eastern lady, who married a mining engineer and thus explored the West from Montana and

Colorado to Mexico—is one of hardships and the loss of love, and the two story lines, set in different times, parallel each other in surprising ways. This is a great "story," but it is also one filled with provocative layers of meaning.

Pacing

Whether longer books or shorter, Literary Fiction is almost never deemed "fast-paced." Authors pride themselves on the layers of meaning in their works, and as the words themselves are important, readers read more slowly to savor the language and discover the author's message. The novels of Richard Powers exemplify this. Although they tell interesting stories that move right along, it is impossible to read them quickly. We are held back by the pleasure of the language, the speculations provoked by the layered plot, the quirkiness of the characters. In *The Gold Bug Variations,* for example, we pursue scientist Stuart Ressler, in the past and present, through intellectually fascinating examinations of music, language, and genetic code.[10] A tribute to and play on both Johann Sebastian Bach's "Goldberg Variations" and Edgar Allan Poe's short story, "The Gold Bug," this stimulating, erudite novel fascinates and holds the reader spellbound. A quick read of a novel so rich is likely physically, and certainly mentally, impossible.

Tone

The tone of Literary Fiction is often darker, as befits the serious themes with which much of it is concerned. Patricia Anthony's *Flanders,* set in Europe during World War I, stars American volunteer and Texas sharpshooter Travis Lee Stanhope, who describes his adventures in letters home to his brother.[11] With his thoughts colored by the constant presence of death and his increasingly heavy drinking, these letters reflect his growing understanding of the life he left. Thus, the tone is melancholy, elegiac. His dreams, in which he follows those who have died before him, add a surreal, haunting element to this atmospheric story.

However, the more serious tone of much Literary Fiction does not mean that the genre is without humor. Some is more subtle, as is Joanne Harris's *Chocolat,* a slyly humorous look at a small French town, "invaded"—during Lent, no less—by chocolatier Vianne; her small, wild child; and her voluptuous, seductive chocolates.[12] The magical stories of Alice Hoffman, especially *Practical Magic,* with its three generations of sisters and their magical sensitivities, exemplify this as well.[13] Other authors write a more raucous, sometimes biting, humor. Michael Malone (*Handling Sin,* which probes everyday absurdities through both characters and plot), John Barth (*The Sot-Weed Factor*), erudite and irrepressible, and William Gaddis (*J R*), the premiere contemporary American satirist, are examples.[14]

Key Authors

The recent lists of the century's best books have been topped by James Joyce, and particularly his masterpiece *Ulysses.*[15] Unfortunately, those votes from scholars are not enough to qualify him as benchmark for this genre. He would certainly be the most unread benchmark mentioned in this book! Challenging and fascinating though his writing may be, it is not much read and appreciated by the readers we assist in our libraries.

In this genre no single author currently dominates the scene. Some authors, however, are important for us to be familiar with. Oprah has done a great deal to promote fine writing in the authors she has chosen for her on-air Book Club. Toni Morrison, long appreciated by fans of the genre, has been given a much broader exposure, and rightfully so. In her award-winning *Song of Solomon* and *Beloved,* as well as in her other novels, Morrison charts the lives of African American women, past and present.[16] However, her books resonate with readers of all races, and her literary style and technique reinforce her insightful stories.

Another Oprah author, Anita Shreve, has long been a favorite among readers who appreciate interesting characters and a provocative story. Each novel seems quite different from the others, a stylistic attribute that Literary Fiction readers appreciate. (For many of them, *same* does not mean what it means to readers of other genres. They prize Shreve for her ability to create a completely different story and type of novel. When they ask for someone similar, they do not want the same story or characters; they want a similarly original and satisfying work.) Perhaps her best to date is *The Weight of Water,* in which a photographer accepts an assignment to document a murder/suicide case from the late 1800s.[17] As she is drawn into that story and even begins to investigate the facts in local accounts, her own life is about to fall apart in a fashion frighteningly similar to that case. Parallel story lines, layers of meaning embedded in actions in both centuries, and secrets hidden and revealed all add to the satisfactions of this work.

Certainly John Updike and Saul Bellow deserve mention here with accessible Literary authors. With his quartet of novels plotting the state of America as seen through the life of Harry Angstrom (*Rabbit, Run* is the first of this series of four titles, each published a decade apart), Updike has secured his reputation as one of the premiere writers of this genre.[18] However, it is his extensive oeuvre that continues to amaze, challenge, and satisfy readers. From his early myth-based *The Centaur,* which fuses fantasy and reality, to his sweeping novel of American history and society, *In the Beauty of the Lilies,* Updike remains both popular and stimulating.[19]

Bellow, Nobel laureate and multiple award winner, writes provocative novels (as well as novellas and short stories) that reflect universal dilemmas. From the picaresque *The Adventures of Augie March* to the more recent, more thoughtful *Ravelstein,* Bellow chooses urban academic settings primarily to reveal his view of contemporary culture.[20]

Preparing to Work with Readers

What do we know about fans of this genre? We know that they often read reviews. They look not for which authors are on the best-sellers lists but which ones are well reviewed in prestigious newspapers and magazines. They want to see the *New York Times'* "Bear in Mind" list, because these are among the titles they would more frequently like to look at. (It should be noted, however, that at least one Literary Fiction title reaches the best-sellers lists every year. Examples include Michael Ondaatje's *The English Patient,* Arundhati Roy's *The God of Small Things,* E. Annie Proulx's *The Shipping News,* and Kazuo Ishiguro's *The Remains of the Day.*)[21]

Within the boundaries of style these readers may read a surprising variety. They consider themselves adventurous readers, and, in fact, they may be interested in exploring books from other genres, as long as they are up to their literary standards. If they see us as readers of Literary Fiction, they may want to know what we have read recently and enjoyed. And unlike most readers, who, when they ask if we have read a book, simply want to know if it is okay for them to take it, these readers truly want to hear what we thought of books we have read and liked or disliked.

It is for these readers that we keep lists of award-winning titles and authors. They like to evaluate the books that have won awards for themselves. Is it really good enough by their standards? Reference sources that keep us up-to-date on these winners are particularly useful with this audience. We also keep track of interesting lists of "Best" authors for these readers, as they like to sample the best and see how these authors fare according to their personal standards. Be prepared for the fact that these readers keep their own lists, both of new titles and classics they may have missed. They always welcome new titles to add to these lists.

Literary Fiction readers prefer books that demand more from them. The style, the language, and the issues considered may all require an intelligent reader willing to invest some time and effort in unraveling the puzzle these books often present. Basically, fans of this genre are looking for other elegantly written, acclaimed novels that they can discuss with their circle of friends who share similar reading tastes.

These are readers who will want to read all of an author they have enjoyed, but they do not want to read the same book over and over. Again, the pattern of this genre is that there is not a concrete pattern. In fact, some authors write different kinds of books with almost everything they publish. Timothy Findley, Jane Smiley, Margaret Atwood, and Anita Shreve do this consistently; almost every title explores new literary dimensions or presents the story in a different way. It should also be noted that these authors are not particularly prolific. Unlike writers in other genres, whom one can count on for at least a book a year, these authors do not publish every year, and every new title is anticipated by their fans.

These are also readers who choose books more frequently for style and literary quality and are thus more likely to read across genres than many other readers, who choose more by other appeal elements. They enjoy a range of books of high literary quality even if they are on widely different topics from a range of genres. Martin Cruz Smith, with his bleak and layered Mysteries, may be as appealing as Ruth Rendell's psychological explorations or Robertson Davies's evocative character studies, told with expansive imagination and verve. Figure 7.2 lists additional Literary Fiction writers to try if you are a fan of these other genres.

FIGURE 7.2

An Introduction to Literary Fiction

Literary Fiction Writers to Try, If You Enjoy . . .

Adventure	Andrea Barrett (The Voyage of the Narwhal)[22]
Fantasy	Isabel Allende
	Gabriel Garcia Marquez
Gentle	Eudora Welty
Historical	Gore Vidal
Horror	Jonathan Carroll
Humor	Richard Russo
	Michael Malone
Inspirational	Charles Williams
Mystery	Arturo Perez-Reverte
Science Fiction	Anthony Burgess
Thriller	Nicholas Shakespeare (The Dancer Upstairs)
	Peter Hoeg (Smilla's Sense of Snow)
Western	Cormac McCarthy
Women's Lives	Toni Morrison
	Margaret Atwood

Readers' Advisory Interview

When these readers ask for assistance and tell us authors they have read and appreciated, they are not necessarily looking for another author "just like" the authors they have read. They are usually looking for another acclaimed author with an interesting, or perhaps similar, style. They like to experiment. They also like to discuss why they did or did not like a book, what the author should have done, or why the book did not work for them. Although we generally discourage staff from giving personal recommendations to readers, we might make an exception with this group. If we do make personal recommendations, however, we can expect these readers to come back and discuss the books with us. They are almost never embarrassed to tell us they did not like a book—and why. Unlike most fiction readers, they do not have to like the book to find it satisfying. Furthermore, they see this discussion with other readers about how the book affected them as an integral part of their enjoyment of Literary Fiction.

Like other genre fans, Literary Fiction readers want to read everything a favorite author has written. When they are ready to go on to someone new, they may want a current title by another provocative author or they may want to fill in with classic authors. Lists of classic titles everyone should have read are good suggestions to use in working with these readers. Readers of this genre also appreciate short stories, and prizewinning collections offer numerous examples of authors whose novels—or collections of stories—they might explore.

Like readers of other genres, fans of Literary Fiction recognize the attraction of thematic links among books. Witness the unexpected popularity of a group of recent novels centered around Jan Vermeer, the seventeenth-century Dutch painter, and his paintings. All published within a two-year span, these must have been inspired by the recent exhibition of Vermeer's paintings. Katharine Weber's *Music Lesson* places an art historian in an Irish Republican Army plot to steal the famous painting; John Bayley's *The Red Hat* offers a trio of curious friends and a Mossad agent in a tale of ambiguous sexuality and reality; Tracy Chevalier's *Girl with a Pearl Earring* returns to Vermeer's own household and speculates on the identity of the model and how this young peasant woman finds herself in such a position;

and Susan Vreeland, in *Girl in Hyacinth Blue,* traces the provenance of the purported Vermeer, revealing the painting's origins and the social history of the country through the lives of its owners.[23] Thematically and stylistically quite different novels, all have been sought by readers who appreciate the disparate views of the artist and his work.

International and Multi-Cultural authors often have a particular appeal for fans of Literary Fiction. For International authors to be published in the United States, they must have attained a certain literary standard, and that guarantees some interest from these readers. Among these writers some of the most interesting literary experiments are carried out, and that, too, is a draw for fans of this genre. Unique, challenging, and thoughtful titles from these authors should be noted and shared with fans of Literary Fiction. Although best known for her series starting with *Women of Brewster Place,* Gloria Naylor's haunting *Bailey's Cafe* is perhaps a better choice for this audience.[24] Here, in this mystical meeting place, souls come when there is nowhere else to go and relate their heartfelt, disturbing stories. Difficult but ultimately optimistic, this book touches readers on many levels. Chinese-American Gish Jen and Cuban-American Oscar Hijuelos explore the clash of cultures, often humorously. Salman Rushdie, Kazuo Ishiguro, Michael Ondaatje, Rosario Ferre, Ruth Prawer Jhabvala, and Nadine Gordimer explore their native countries and cultures and beyond.

Sure Bets

Discovering Sure Bets is both easier and more difficult in this genre. Although there are perhaps fewer authors with a wide-ranging popular appeal, readers who appreciate one author in this genre will likely enjoy others, as well as literary stylists in other genres. Those authors who have appeared on the best-sellers lists are good suggestions—David Guterson's *Snow Falling on Cedars,* titles by Margaret Atwood, as well as by Pat Conroy, Anne Tyler, and Alice Hoffman.[25] Authors who have been chosen for Oprah's Book Club also make good suggestions, although the emphasis is often more on women's than universal issues.

Jane Smiley is an author whose writing typifies Literary Fiction, and she is a popular choice for a wide range of readers. At my library at least, it was with the publication of two novellas, *Ordinary Love and Good Will,* in 1989, that she gained a real following among readers who appreciate her skill at language and exploring difficult topics.[26] Even now we give these haunting, psychological stories to readers, and they come back hungry for more. Readers may love or hate her work, but they always want to read and discuss her books—another indication of both her popularity and her status as a writer of provocative material.

John Irving, whose success was firmly established with *The World according to Garp*, in 1978, has also benefited from interesting movie versions of his books.[27] Irving's distinctive style attracts readers, and although there are always darker moments in his novels, the upbeat, optimistic tone is another draw.

Spanish author Arturo Perez-Reverte works as a Sure Bet in my library. Readers enjoy the elegant prose (although that surely has something to do with the translator as well); the intricate, often literary puzzles; the intriguing characters; and the layered stories. *The Flanders Panel* makes a good starting place.[28] His description of the painting that forms the crux of the story is so vivid that I had to pull both hard- and softcover copies to prove to a patron, who had read and appreciated the book, that the painting was not on the cover.

Expanding Readers' Horizons

We can turn to almost any genre and find titles that fans of Literary Fiction will enjoy (*see* Figure 7.3 for a list of authors that might appeal to readers of Literary Fiction). Historical Fiction has a great deal to offer Literary Fiction readers who are not put off by the historical settings. Dorothy Dunnett, with her Historical Adventures (set in Renaissance Europe), classical quotations, and generally pleasing literary references, is a good choice. Another author to suggest is Sharon Kay Penman. Her detailed examinations of the people and the times (both her Mystery series beginning with *The Queen's Man* and set in the court of Eleanor of Aquitaine and her historical novels set primarily in thirteenth- through fifteenth-century England and Wales) satisfy and fascinate readers.[29] Other suggestions include Michael Shaara's intimate and evocative account of the Civil War (*The Killer Angels*), Margaret George's compelling biographical portraits (*The Memoirs of Cleopatra*), and Steven Pressfield's character-centered exploration of ancient Greece (*Gates of Fire* is the first).[30]

FIGURE 7.3

Expanding Readers' Horizons

Authors to Take Readers beyond the Literary Fiction Genre

Adventure	Dorothy Dunnett
Gentle	Eudora Welty
Historical	Steven Pressfield
	Margaret George
	Sharon Kay Penman
Horror	Michael Cadnum
	M. R. James
Mystery	P. D. James
	Martin Cruz Smith
Psychological	Minette Walters
	Ruth Rendell
Science Fiction	John Varley
	Ursula LeGuin
Suspense	Thomas Harris
Thriller	John le Carré
	Martin Cruz Smith
Western	Larry McMurtry
Women's Lives	Kaye Gibbons
	Barbara Kingsolver

In Science Fiction Ursula LeGuin and Neal Stephenson are both good choices. LeGuin consistently explores philosophical and intellectual issues, while Stephenson's virtuoso blend of language and ideas attracts readers from many genres. Mary Doria Russell and Gene Wolfe must also be included here as well. Certainly Russell's *The Sparrow* offers readers the ideas and characters fans of Literary Fiction demand, and Wolfe's series (especially the Book of the New Sun, which begins with *The Shadow of the Torturer*) challenge and fascinate readers.[31]

Adventure offers, in addition to Dunnett, mentioned with Historical Fiction above, James Dickey and classics by Alexandre Dumas (*per* and *fil*) and Homer. Although he is the author of only a few novels, Dickey's work tends to push the boundaries of what is expected in everything he writes. From the layered and stylistically complex *Alnilam* to *To the White Sea*, Dickey interposes difficult issues in elegantly written novels.[32] As I mentioned briefly above, readers of Literary Fiction often enjoy discovering or rereading classics. Dumas father and son offer a wealth of stories, as does Sir Walter Scott. We have high school students required to read Homer's *Odyssey*, and this is one title that I particularly recommend listening to on tape. It was, after all, meant to be heard, not read, and the language and repetition suit the oral tradition.

Literary Fiction readers might also appreciate two authors from the Horror genre: classic author M. R. James (*Ghost Stories of an Antiquary*) and Michael Cadnum (*The Judas Glass*), a poet whose elegant prose heightens the effects of the Horror.[33] The Thriller genre offers, among others, Scott Turow's densely written Legal Thrillers and John le Carré's elegant Espionage Thrillers. In Psychological Suspense, Minette Walters and Ruth Rendell are both excellent crossover suggestions. The Mystery genre, too, has many authors that appeal to readers who like well-written stories: Martin Cruz Smith's ironic Mysteries featuring Russian Inspector Renko and his intriguing Gypsy duet (*Gypsy in Amber* and *Canto for a Gypsy*),[34] P. D. James's series featuring Adam Dalgleish, and James Lee Burke's haunting, atmospheric detective stories set in the South.

Another genre with extensive crossover is Women's Lives and Relationships. Many strong female writers tell stories of women, and those authors might fit easily in either genre. Toni Morrison, Anita Shreve, Jane Hamilton, and others from chapter 16 would be good suggestions for fans of Literary Fiction.

Reference Sources

Where does one find reference material on a genre that is not an established genre? In this instance, luckily, in many established and familiar readers' advisory tools. The best single volume source is another of the Genreflecting series: Nancy Pearl's *Now Read This: A Guide to Mainstream Fiction, 1978–1998*.[35] The focus of the book is on "mainstream fiction," which Pearl defines as "novels set in the twentieth century that realistically explore aspects of human experience: love, fear, despair, hatred, aging, and death, as well as the moral and ethical decisions and choices people make throughout a lifetime."[36] Many of these are also prizewinners. Each entry, organized alphabetically in chapters divided by primary appeal ("Setting," "Story," "Characters," and "Language"), provides publishing information, a one-sentence annotation, secondary appeal, subject headings under which it is indexed, and a section called "Now try," which lists similar authors and the reason for suggesting them, a technique that is a real breakthrough in providing read-alikes. An appendix identifies award winners, and access is provided through title, subject, and author indexes. Books that make good book discussion choices are indicated in the entry, although they are not indexed.

Where to Find . . .

INFORMATION ABOUT THE AUTHOR

Contemporary Authors (*see* appendix 2) should cover any authors in this genre, except perhaps classic authors from earlier centuries. Biographical material is not difficult to discover on these critically acclaimed authors.

PLOT SUMMARIES

The general sources described in appendix 2—*Fiction Catalog*, *NoveList*, and *To Be Continued*—offer this information. Although it began as a genre-only source, *What Do I Read Next?* has expanded its coverage to include some books in this category. "Literary Fiction" is not an accepted subject heading in any of these sources. However, in NoveList's Browse Subjects function, one can type in Literary and find related headings, including award winners. The Best Fiction function provides access to award winners in all genres, and there is a separate section for Literary awards. These lists link to full entries in the database.

SUBGENRES AND THEMES

Themes are accessible in Pearl's *Now Read This,* as well as through the subject access provided by related headings in *NoveList.*

GENRE DESCRIPTION, BACKGROUND, AND HISTORY

This material does not seem to be readily available, although one could explore it through the history of a country's literature in standard literature reference sources.

CORE LISTS AND BEST BOOKS

Lists of award-winning fiction meet this need to some extent. Easy sources are Pearl's book and *NoveList;* however, many nongenre sources, not covered in this book, will also provide this information.

For decades Literary Fiction comprised the core of our libraries' fiction collections. It was the collection readers felt comfortable asking for—and the one librarians could safely "recommend" to any reader. Although no longer *the* most popular genre, Literary Fiction has lost none of its appeal for fans, who continue to challenge us librarians to find them books that offer elegantly written, provocative explorations of universal themes.

NOTES

1. Joyce G. Saricks and Nancy Brown, *Readers' Advisory Service in the Public Library,* 2d ed. (Chicago: American Library Assn., 1997), 26–27.

2. Kent Haruf, *Plainsong* (New York: Knopf, 1999); Roddy Doyle, *Paddy Clarke Ha, Ha, Ha* (New York: Viking, 1993); Cormac McCarthy, *All the Pretty Horses* (New York: Knopf, 1992).

3. William Faulkner, *The Sound and the Fury* (New York: Jonathan Cape and Harrison Smith, 1929); Gabriel Garcia Marquez, *One Hundred Years of Solitude* (New York: Harper & Row, 1970); Isabel Allende, *The House of the Spirits* (New York: Knopf, 1985); Thomas Pynchon, *Gravity's Rainbow* (New York: Viking, 1973).

4. Anne Tyler, *The Accidental Tourist* (New York: Knopf, 1985); ———, *Breathing Lessons* (New York: Knopf, 1988).

5. J. M. Coetzee, *Disgrace* (New York: Viking, 1999).

6. John Barth, *The Sot-Weed Factor* (Garden City, N.Y.: Doubleday, 1960); Robertson Davies, *Murther and Walking Spirits* (New York: Viking, 1991).

143

7. Nicholas Shakespeare, *The Dancer Upstairs* (New York: Nan A. Talese, 1997).

8. Peter Hoeg, *Smilla's Sense of Snow* (New York: Farrar, Straus & Giroux, 1993).

9. Wallace Stegner, *Angle of Repose* (Garden City, N.Y.: Doubleday, 1971).

10. Richard Powers, *The Gold Bug Variations* (New York: Morrow, 1991).

11. Patricia Anthony, *Flanders* (New York: Ace Books, 1998).

12. Joanne Harris, *Chocolat* (New York: Viking, 1999).

13. Alice Hoffman, *Practical Magic* (New York: Putnam, 1995).

14. Michael Malone, *Handling Sin* (Boston: Little, Brown, 1986); William Gaddis, *J R* (New York: Knopf, 1975).

15. James Joyce, *Ulysses* (New York: Random House, 1946).

16. Toni Morrison, *Song of Solomon* (New York: Knopf, 1977); ———, *Beloved* (New York: Knopf, 1987).

17. Anita Shreve, *The Weight of Water* (Boston: Little, Brown, 1997).

18. John Updike, *Rabbit, Run* (New York: Knopf, 1960).

19. ———, *The Centaur* (New York: Knopf, 1963); ———, *In the Beauty of the Lilies* (New York: Knopf, 1996).

20. Saul Bellow, *The Adventures of Augie March* (New York: Viking, 1953); ———, *Ravelstein* (New York: Viking, 2000).

21. Michael Ondaatje, *The English Patient* (New York: Knopf, 1992); Arundhati Roy, *The God of Small Things* (New York: Random House, 1997); E. Annie Proulx, *The Shipping News* (New York: Scribner, 1993); Kazuo Ishiguro, *The Remains of the Day* (New York: Knopf, 1989).

22. Andrea Barrett, *The Voyage of the Narwhal* (New York: Norton, 1998).

23. Katharine Weber, *Music Lesson* (New York: Crown, 1998); John Bayley, *The Red Hat* (New York: St. Martin's, 1998); Tracy Chevalier, *Girl with a Pearl Earring* (New York: E. P. Dutton, 2000); Susan Vreeland, *Girl in Hyacinth Blue* (Denver, Colo.: MacMurray & Beck, 1999).

24. Gloria Naylor, *Women of Brewster Place* (New York: Viking, 1982); ———, *Bailey's Cafe* (New York: Harcourt Brace, 1992).

25. David Guterson, *Snow Falling on Cedars* (San Diego: Harcourt Brace, 1994).

26. Jane Smiley, *Ordinary Love and Good Will* (New York: Knopf, 1989).

27. John Irving, *The World according to Garp* (New York: E. P. Dutton, 1978).

28. Arturo Perez-Reverte, *The Flanders Panel* (New York: Harcourt Brace, 1990).

29. Sharon Kay Penman, *The Queen's Man* (New York: Holt, 1996).

30. Michael Shaara, *The Killer Angels* (New York: McKay, 1974); Margaret George, *The Memoirs of Cleopatra* (New York: St. Martin's, 1997); Steven Pressfield, *Gates of Fire: An Epic Novel of the Battle of Thermopylae* (New York: Doubleday, 1998).

31. Mary Doria Russell, *The Sparrow* (New York: Villard, 1996); Gene Wolfe, *The Shadow of the Torturer* (New York: Simon & Schuster, 1980).

32. James Dickey, *Alnilam* (Garden City, N.Y.: Doubleday, 1987); ———, *To the White Sea* (Boston: Houghton, 1993).

33. M. R. James, *Ghost Stories of an Antiquary* (Freeport, N.Y.: Books for Libraries Press, 1969); Michael Cadnum, *The Judas Glass* (New York: Carroll & Graf, 1996).

34. Martin Cruz Smith, *Gypsy in Amber* (New York: Putnam, 1971); ———, *Canto for a Gypsy* (New York: Putnam, 1972).

35. Nancy Pearl, *Now Read This: A Guide to Mainstream Fiction, 1978–1998* (Englewood, Colo.: Libraries Unlimited, 1999).

36. Ibid., p. xiii.

8

Mysteries

For many of us in libraries, Mysteries are the most popular genre
among readers. (It would not surprise me if a poll of public librarians
found this their favorite as well.) Mystery bookstores, Web sites, and
reference books abound. Although the puzzles of Agatha Christie and
other writers of the Golden Age continue to be popular—especially
in school curricula—it is the character- and series-centered Mysteries
that now reign supreme. Exploring the characters' lives—their past
and present, relationships, and friendships—has become, for many
readers, as important as solving the Mystery. Series dominate all aspects of the genre, from hard-boiled Private Investigators (P.I.s) to
Cozies, in contemporary as well as historical Mysteries. Although the
Mystery remains the key, fascination with the characters' lives attracts
more and more readers.

A Definition

Mysteries consist of a puzzle; the author provides clues to the solution but attempts to obscure some information so that the puzzle cannot be solved too easily. We, along with the detective, are drawn into
the puzzle in an attempt to solve it. This puzzle involves a crime, usually murder, and the resulting body. There is an investigator (or a

team of investigators), amateur or professional, who solves the question of "who-dun-it." The Mystery tracks this investigation, with its concomitant exploration of victim's, murderer's, and detective's lives.

As with all genres currently, however, there is an enormous amount of crossover in the Mystery genre. Many libraries, mine included, have a separate section for Mysteries and thus a working definition, however vague, so our catalogers can decide whether to put a book in Mystery or Fiction. At least, that is the expectation. In fact, Mysteries have become increasingly difficult to define. At my library we have Lawrence Sanders in Fiction, along with Ridley Pearson, Michael Connelly, and Stephen White. Yet there is a body in each of these and an investigation that reveals the identity of the killer as well as the motive for the crime. Why do we not catalog them as Mysteries?

Here again, I like to recall the "Good Old Days" when Mysteries were under 300 pages, and you could tell at a glance that this (or the Western or other genre book) fit in the genre collection, rather than in Fiction. Now that Mysteries are as long as or longer than many novels, the distinction becomes more difficult. The answer to what belongs in the Mystery collection is that there is no definitive answer; there is often no clear-cut distinction between Mysteries (and most other genre fiction) and Fiction. We make our best guess, based on how a book is reviewed, whether we have others by that author or in that series, and, most importantly, where we believe readers expect to find the book. We make mistakes, sometimes putting part of a series in Mystery and part in Fiction; we recatalog whole series (luckily my library has the best technical services department in the whole world, and they have never balked at this); we explain to readers regularly that the authors they seek are in one collection or another. Patrons may be opinionated about what should go where, but they are usually gracious and accept our explanations.

Characteristics and the Genre's Appeal

As in the Romance genre, novels that fall within the Mystery genre follow a particular pattern: A crime is committed. An investigator pursues the clues, interviewing suspects and drawing conclusions.

The crime is solved and the culprit brought to justice. And as it does in the Romance genre, this bare-bones plot outline can become so much more. *See* Figure 8.1.

Story Line

The crime and subsequent investigation form the heart of the story line in this genre. Because the crime is almost always murder, I use that term in this discussion. There should be a murder and an investigation, not to mention a body, for a title to qualify as a Mystery.

The point of Mysteries is to examine the clues and solve the puzzle. This brings in the character of the investigator, and these two appeal elements—characterization and story line—mesh intricately as the crime is solved. For some readers, solving the puzzle before the investigator is the goal. They want the writer to play fair, present the clues, and allow them a chance to solve the Mystery. (Do not offer these readers Agatha Christie's classic puzzle, *The Murder of Roger*

FIGURE 8.1

Characteristics of the Mystery Genre

1. A crime, usually a murder, has been committed, and there is a body.

2. An investigator (or investigative team) attempts to discover "who-dun-it." Mysteries are often written as a series, following the investigator through several cases.

3. Secondary characters, whether suspects or supporting characters in the investigation, play an important role in the appeal of the Mystery. They may also be series characters.

4. The investigator follows clues, working to solve the puzzle. Readers know "who-dun-it" and usually why at the end. Order is restored, but justice "by the book" does not always result.

5. The frame in which the Mystery is set—whether physical location, additional details, or tone—plays a crucial role in the appeal of the Mystery.

Ackroyd.[1] Christie tricks the reader with a totally unexpected twist at the end, and those who expect authors to play fair will not be pleased.) Others read Mysteries to participate in the investigation and in the lives of the investigators. In fact, the character of the investigator often determines the appeal of the Mystery to the reader. With the increased popularity of series, these readers find much to their liking. Many tell us they read as much to see what is happening in the characters' lives as to appreciate the clever Mystery plot. Fans of Elizabeth Peters's Amelia Peabody Mysteries, set in Egypt at the turn of the twentieth century, clamored for *He Shall Thunder in the Sky* as much to discover what would happen with Ramses and Nefret as to test wits with Amelia in uncovering the latest Mystery.[2] No wonder authors occasionally despair and do nasty things to their characters if they feel they are not appreciated for their intricate plots! Dana Stabenow, for example, kills protagonist Kate Shugat's lover Jack in *Hunter's Moon,* not a positive move judging from readers' reactions, although the book was well reviewed by critics.[3] The quintessential example is, of course, Sir Arthur Conan Doyle's attempt to do in Sherlock Holmes at Reichenback Falls, in *The Memoirs of Sherlock Holmes.*[4] He was then forced to "resurrect" him in *The Return of Sherlock Holmes.*[5]

Within this puzzle and the investigation to discover the solution to "who-dun-it," authors offer an enormous variety. Some focus on the intricacies of the puzzle. Robert Barnard, an Agatha Christie scholar and emulator, typically presents an intricate puzzle to be untangled by both reader and detective. Try *The Corpse at the Haworth Tandoori* for an example of his wickedly funny and complex style.[6] Others add strong elements of Suspense and Intrigue, with the characters often faced with considerable danger throughout the investigation. *The Red Scream,* by Mary Willis Walker, is a good example of this technique; here, journalist Molly Cates reinvestigates the case of a serial murderer on death row, and as the suspense builds, she finds her own life in jeopardy.[7] Still others focus on particular social issues and weave them into their stories, as does Barbara D'Amato in the stories of investigative reporter Cat Marsala. (*Hard Case,* a report on Chicago's trauma centers that exposes murder, is the first.)[8]

Above all, it should be clear that many Mysteries are more than straightforward puzzles written to a pattern. Most involve layers of information about the plot and characters; these must be peeled away, with secrets revealed one by one, until the solution is unveiled. P. D. James's complex, layered novels of detection, following the exploits of Scotland Yard Commander Adam Dalgleish, are read by fans of Mysteries as well as those who appreciate character-driven Literary Fiction.

The issue of "justice" is one that is considered throughout this genre, because the administration of justice is at the heart of the solution of the Mystery. "Legal justice" is not always an option, however, and when it is not, investigators have been known to take the law into their own hands, to see that justice is effected, even if it means operating outside the law. An example is the mercurial Kathleen Mallory in Carol O'Connell's series. (*Mallory's Oracle* is the first.)[9] Unorthodox, but very successful, methods are the hallmark of the investigative style of this New York Police Department detective.

Characterization

Although the investigation is surely the touchstone of the Mystery, the character and appeal of the investigator are becoming more and more important to fans, who read series and want other characters just like the ones whose adventures they have already read and enjoyed. Although investigators—whether professional or amateur—are types and behave in specific ways, the characterizations are not flat. In the myriad series that dominate the Mystery genre, we follow the characters over years, learning more and more as the author embellishes their lives and offers insights from their past into their current actions. Many readers crave these glimpses into their private lives almost as much as they want to follow the investigation; the two go hand in hand in the appeal of these stories.

Whether in a Mystery with a series character or one that stands alone, characterizations in Mystery are treated differently than they are in other genres. In Adventure, for example, we do not necessarily want to follow Dirk Pitt's life; we simply want to know what will happen next in this Adventure, and he is our guide. In Horror we respond to what the protagonist experiences—we share the same emotions—but we do not necessarily want more details of his life. In Romances we only follow the characters until they tie the knot, so to speak; then we expect new characters and a new Romance, in part because series characters as such do not exist in the genre. In Mystery, however, fans want to know far more about the characters than authors seem willing to tell and expect their adventures to continue long after authors tire of a particular character. Most authors do not resort to Doyle's solution of killing off his detective, only to have to bring Sherlock Holmes back from the dead at the insistence of irate readers. The more likely solution today is that the author embarks on another series and lets a character rest for a time—or permanently. Other authors of long-running series allow us slowly to see the background and past lives of their characters. For example, in *Listen to the Silence,* Marcia Muller explores P.I. Sharon McCone's family history, while in *"O" Is for Outlaw,* Sue Grafton finally reveals details of Kinsey Millhone's youthful marriage, and we meet her ex-husband, now himself in trouble and fighting for his life.[10]

Although the protagonist is certainly an important draw for fans, even secondary characters are more important here than in many other genres. The sidekick, who also appears from book to book, often plays a key role in solving the Mystery and in attracting readers. A classic example is Archie Goodwin, general factotum and dogsbody for the reclusive Nero Wolfe. Although there may be no doubt that it is through Wolfe's superior brain power that the Mysteries are solved, there is also no denying that it is Goodwin's hard work gathering and presenting clues that sets up the solution. (Try *Too Many Cooks* to sample Rex Stout's style and the relationship between the humorous Goodwin and the often crotchety Wolfe.[11] Here Wolfe, accompanied by Archie, attends a convention of great chefs of the world, and, in return for a recipe, he solves a murder and clears a famous chef's name.) Fans would certainly feel the loss of recurring secondary characters Grandma Mazur and Lula in Janet Evanovich's enormously popular series featuring bounty hunter Stephanie Plum. (*One for the Money* is the first.)[12] Much of the series' characteristic humor and charm derives from the interaction with the secondary characters.

Frame

Frames flourish in the Mystery genre. Easiest to identify is the setting, either a specific geographical place or a time period in a particular place. Ellis Peters's Brother Cadfael series sets the standard. Peters provides extensive information about twelfth-century England, from politics to daily life; about life in a Monastery in Shrewsbury; about life in England during that time, with fairs and religious ceremonies mixed with the routine of eking out an existence. Although fascinating, these extensive details are not crucial to the Mystery. Yet they provide the kind of frame readers love and seek. *A Morbid Taste for Bones* is the first in this series.[13] American Mystery writer Tony Hillerman offers similar satisfaction with his Mysteries, although in these the frame is Native Americans of the contemporary American Southwest, their culture and customs. Try *Thief of Time* for a taste of his work.[14]

Some authors set contemporary Mysteries in specific locales and attract readers who enjoy the geographic details and feel of a place, along with their Mystery. In Sara Paretsky's V. I. Warshawski novels, set in Chicago and the surrounding suburbs, we locals can plot her course as V. I. pursues clues. Los Angeles comes alive in the hands of Michael Connelly, as Police Detective Harry Bosch uncovers murders; and Cynthia Harrod-Eagles's Bill Slider traverses London and surrounding counties, offering detailed information about the geography as well as the people.

Other authors focus on the occupations or hobbies of the sleuths, and the details add interest and variety to the plots. First Virginia Rich, with *The Cooking School Murders,* and then Diane Mott Davidson, with her series featuring caterer Goldy Bear (*Catering to Nobody* starts the series), put gourmet cooking and Mysteries with recipes on the map.[15] Among Amateur Detectives we have herbalists, historical and contemporary (Peters's Brother Cadfael series and Susan Wittig Albert's China Bayles), actors (Simon Brett's Charles Paris), journalists (Edna Buchanan's Britt Montero and Walker's Molly Cates), antique and rare book dealers (Jonathan Gash's Lovejoy and John Dunning's Cliff Janeway), gardeners (Ann Ripley's Louise Eldridge and John Sherwood's Celia Grant), teachers (Gillian Robert's Amanda Pepper), clergy (Harry Kemelman's Rabbi Small and Margaret Coel's Father John O'Malley), and almost any profession imaginable. In the course of the Mystery, readers learn almost as much about the profession or hobby of the detective as they do about the investigation, and for many readers, this is the chief satisfaction.

Still other writers frame their Mysteries with a particularly evocative tone. Premiere of these is Sharyn McCrumb, whose Ballad

Novels, set in Appalachia and combining a true historical past with a fictional present, offer as much mood as Mystery. These haunting, elegiac stories feature a cast of recurring characters—often Vietnam vet police chief Spencer Arrowood and elderly, clairvoyant Nora Bonesteel—and deftly link past history with the present in stories that evocatively explore psychology as well as murder. *If Ever I Return, Pretty Peggy-O* is the first in the series.[16]

Pacing

Pacing is the hallmark of many genres (especially Thriller and Suspense), but the importance of a particular pacing is less of an issue in Mysteries. Although there is considerable difference in the pacing of the actual books, from the detailed, involved, literary Mystery novels of James to the flying farces of Joan Hess and much in between, readers do not frequently mention pacing as a reason for reading Mysteries in general or a particular author, although it may be one of the subconscious reasons they prefer one over another at a particular time. Pacing is less likely to be a factor they consider, although they may want to know where a book falls on the pacing range. The bigger books are generally more involved and slower paced, although Elizabeth George's Mysteries, for example, were slower moving even before the page count trebled. The nature of the story, the investigation and concern with details, must slow the story, make it move at a pace slower than a book filled primarily with Adventure, Suspense, or humor, but the fascination with the characters draws readers on and makes the pacing less noticeable. Mystery readers accept that books in this genre are not necessarily fast paced, although they certainly are compelling, because we want to discover who committed the crime and how the solution will be reached.

Key Authors and Subgenres

Benchmark

The Mystery genre offers no clear benchmark, no current author who typifies the genre and stands out as the most representative and popular. Perhaps the genre has always been too vast and diverse for such an exemplar, although Agatha Christie certainly stood for many years as the representative of the most popular aspects of the genre and its appeal. Her puzzles set the standard that was emulated—or used as a springboard to expand the genre's boundaries.

Key Authors

Among the most popular of the current Mystery writers are Janet Evanovich, Sue Grafton, Michael Connelly, Robert B. Parker, Elizabeth George, P. D. James, and Dick Francis. Always on the best-sellers lists, these writers represent various subgenres but also possess those qualities that entice fans who might generally read another type of Mystery or a different book altogether. Evanovich, the most recent entrant in the popularity stakes, sets her humorous Mysteries in New Jersey, where bounty-hunter-in-training Stephanie Plum, often assisted by her eccentric grandmother, brings bail-bond jumpers to justice—and frequently finds herself involved in a more serious Mystery. Evanovich is unique in that she is hard to place in any of the subgenres, and, in fact, she combines aspects of all in her Mysteries: the whimsy of the Cozy Amateur (although there is certainly more violence), the authority of the police (because, as a bounty hunter, she is a representative of the court), and the investigative style of a rather inept P.I.

Grafton, the author of the "Alphabet Mysteries," expects to put her P.I., Kinsey Millhone, through at least twenty-six investigations. The California setting and the "soft-boiled" investigator have attracted a vast reading audience comprised of both men and women.

Connelly's writing focuses primarily on series police detective Harry Bosch, although he also has excellent single titles. Bleak, atmospheric, violent scenes characterize his stories, as well as damaged heroes, suspenseful story lines, and often elegant prose. However, this series, with Harry Bosch essentially investigating on his own, appeals as much to fans of the Private Investigator Mysteries as of the Police Detectives, where he technically fits.

Parker has one of the longest-running series, still popular with a wide range of readers who return every year to devour the exploits of P.I. Spenser, his associate Hawk, and his longtime love, Susan Silverman. Descriptive scenes of Boston and the Northeast, witty dialogue, strong and sympathetic characters, action and building tension, stories that pull readers into the characters and the problems they face all characterize his books.

American George sets her popular Mystery series, which features Scotland Yard investigators Thomas Lynley and Barbara Havers, in England. Englishwoman James also employs a Scotland Yard investigator, Adam Dalgleish, in her primary series, although P.I. Cordelia Grey also stars in a series of books, with and without Dalgleish. James and George both appeal to readers seeking literate, character-centered stories.

Finally, Francis, an author who has written far more single title Mysteries than series, links all his stories to horse racing, as is certainly understandable for the retired steeplechase jockey, whose titles also appeal to Thriller fans and others who appreciate the Adventure elements and details. Each of these is discussed in further detail in the appropriate subgenre.

Subgenres of Mysteries

The key to the way readers select Mysteries is the character and specific type of investigator, the detective. The story line may control how the characters act, but the personality of characters directs the book and its appeal to readers. Thus, the most straightforward way to examine the Mystery genre is to focus on these investigator types. As discussed below, however, there is also a particular feel that cuts across these types and may draw readers from one type to another. The types of investigator described here are the Private Investigator, Police Detective, and Amateur Detective.

PRIVATE INVESTIGATORS

Today's P.I.s grew out of the tradition established by classic authors Raymond Chandler and Dashiell Hammett in the '30s and '40s, when Philip Marlowe, Sam Spade, and the Continental Op employed their no-nonsense investigative techniques to solve crimes. Some of today's most popular characters are direct descendants of this hard-boiled tradition, while others are more soft-boiled. Figure 8.2 lists additional characteristics of P.I.s.

FIGURE 8.2

Characteristics of Private Investigators

1. Investigations are carried out step-by-step and are usually narrated first-person by the protagonist.

2. Investigators operate under a personal moral code that may not follow the rule of law.

3. Settings are usually urban. The tone is often darker, and many novels highlight serious social issues.

4. Books often have a harder edge and deal with more violent situations, sometimes in explicit detail.

5. Protagonists may be men or women, and their adventures are usually part of an ongoing series.

Because the character of the investigator is the distinguishing feature among these subdivisions, this is the place to start. P.I.s explore cases that, even if they do not start out as murder, usually lead to murder. Characters in these stories are often series characters, and we build a relationship with them and their associates over time through the series. P.I.s are traditionally self-reliant loners who operate independently (although some of today's most popular P.I.s have sidekicks). They differ from Amateur Detectives in that they are hired to perform the investigation and paid for work; in addition, they usually have some training, skills, and a license they may lose if they cross the police too often.

Another characteristic these protagonists share is a personal moral code under which all operate. Like medieval knights or Western heroes, they are on the side of "truth" and "justice"—although they understand that truth may not always be discovered (and proven) or justice meted out if one stays within the confines of the law. None of these is likely to let a little thing like the law stop them, and although they are licensed and generally work within the law, they are not above bending the law discreetly (or otherwise) to solve a case.

Because they have no actual authority to interview suspects, they sometimes pose as members of the official police to question suspects, and if they believe legal justice may fail to be effective, they are not above devising a method of their own to mete it out, as Spenser frequently demonstrates in Parker's series. This ability to take justice into their own hands, to administer it more effectively than even officers of the law often can, makes them very appealing characters. Who would not want to be part of the team that knows what is right and is able to bring it about?

P.I.s usually work on only one case at a time. If there are more cases in the story, they are usually linked in some fashion by the end. Social questions are often highlighted in these stories. Parker frequently raises concerns about women and children; Sara Paretsky is known for tackling corporate and government issues and industries, from waste disposal and big medicine to insurance; Linda Barnes, like fellow-Bostonian Parker, pits Carlotta Carlyle against social evils and gives her a Little Sister, a disadvantaged young girl with whom Carlotta spends time and whose welfare she works to ensure. Operating outside of the law, with techniques unavailable to the police, these P.I.s make good use of their social consciences in working to right social injustice.

The tone of these Mysteries is usually darker, less likely to be humorous, even though the dialogue may be witty. Considering that many P.I.s are not only burned-out policemen, but also recovering alcoholics—for example, Ed McBain's Matthew Hope, Lawrence Block's Matt Scudder, and James Lee Burke's Dave Robicheaux—the bleaker tone should not be a surprise. On the other end, Robert Crais (Elvis Cole) and Parker (Spenser) are known for their one-liners that often lighten a tough situation, but P.I.s do not match the Amateur Detective subgenre for humor and generally present a darker tone.

These Mysteries are almost always narrated first-person. This technique affects our perception of and feeling for the characters as well as the tone of the book. We are intimate to the protagonist's thoughts as well as actions; it is as if the character is talking to us, and thus the feel is more personal. This approach reinforces the manner in which we follow the investigation step-by-step, because we are literally walking in our detective's shoes. However, the first-person voice also affects the tone. If the character is a recovering alcoholic, the book reflects the problems he has seen and his bleaker worldview.

As in all Mysteries, geographical setting is an important part of the frame. P.I.s tend to operate in an urban environment. Even though Burke's Cajun detective Robicheaux tries to isolate himself in rural Louisiana, he is always found by those who seek his skills, and the action generally takes place in town or certainly deals with urban rather than rural crime. (*The Neon Rain* is the first in this series.)[17]

Not only are the settings urban, they are also generally quite detailed. These authors pride themselves on the accuracy of both the geographical details and the feel of the place—the customs and people—as well. Rudolfo Anaya provides both geographic and cultural detail in his Sonny Baca Mysteries set in Albuquerque. In the first, *Zia Summer*, he elegantly combines the history and traditions of Albuquerque with the contemporary problems of the modern city.[18] Dreams and mysticism cohabit with ritual murder and a very modern cult in this evocative, complex Mystery.

KEY AUTHORS

One of the best-known and most popular of current Mystery writers, Sue Grafton is an author librarians ignore at their peril. Although some fans may only know her as the author who writes that alphabet series, they request every book as soon as they think it is time she published another. Kinsey Millhone, originally an investigator for an insurance agency and later a P.I., captured the attention of Mystery fans and rode the wave of women Mystery writers to fame and fortune. *"A" Is for Alibi* was published in 1982, and fans are already worrying what she will do after she reaches Z.[19] Kinsey is a loner, although, over the years, she has collected a group of friends who serve as family. She is ready for anything—she even keeps a little black dress crumpled up in the trunk of her compact car, just in case she needs to dress more professionally on a case. Clever plotting, gritty stories, a sassy heroine, and strong settings set Grafton apart. Kinsey introduces herself in the first few paragraphs of each book, so the reader can start almost anywhere in the series and feel connected to the story and character. Try *"K" Is for Killer, "N" Is for Noose,* or *"O" Is for Outlaw* for typical examples of her style and range.[20]

Another of today's most popular writers is Parker, also mentioned above as one of the genre's key authors. His ongoing series of more than two-dozen Mysteries features the updated hard-boiled P.I. Spenser (no first name), Hawk, and lover Susan Silverman. As Spenser, a Korean War veteran, ages, the books display a decreasing amount of explicitly described violence, but the tension and his and Hawk's investigative skills remain undiminished. Spenser is a curious mix of the hard-boiled detective and the caring '90s man, who has a long-term relationship with his girlfriend, and the Mysteries that feature adolescent children are among his best. Try *Double Deuce* as an example of his style.[21] Here, Hawk has been hired to clean up a Boston housing project and confronts a younger version of himself in its leader. Although Spenser plays backup to Hawk in this outing, we see the relationships that make up Spenser's private life—the strong friendship with Hawk as well as the romantic relationship with Susan. By no means start a reader new to the series with Parker's first, *The Godwulf Manuscript*.[22] I guarantee you will turn off more readers than you will hook, because in this first of his long-running series, Parker had not yet captured the essence of his characters or perfected his style.

Other important American authors of P.I. Mysteries include Dennis Lehane, Robert Crais, and Marcia Muller. Award-winner Lehane explores the lives and cases of detective team Patrick Kenzie and Angie Gennaro in Boston in Mysteries that probe deeply into the psychological underpinnings of crime and detection. This series is becoming increasingly popular with fans of bleak, elegant P.I. novels, as well as those who generally read page-turners. Lehane is extraordinarily skilled at creating multi-layered stories with building suspense, and his appeal reaches beyond the confines of the genre. *Darkness, Take My Hand* is one of his best, a haunting, chilling story in which the team must confront true evil.[23]

Crais offers lighter fare for fans of the subgenre, and his Los Angeles–based Elvis Cole is a good bet for fans of Parker's Spenser series. Both feature witty dialogue, caring detectives, difficult issues, and strong, silent sidekicks. *Voodoo River* is one of his best and a good introduction to the series.[24]

Sharon McCone, the first female P.I., remains one of the genre's best examples in Muller's long-running, popular series. Based in San

Francisco, the tough yet vulnerable McCone investigates cases from Nob Hill to the underbelly of San Francisco society. Try *Till the Butchers Cut Him Down* as a typical example of her style.[25]

Although England does not have as strong a tradition in Private Investigator Mysteries, there are several authors worth knowing. Award-winner Liza Cody writes two well-reviewed and popular P.I. series, one featuring ex-cop Anna Lee and the other wrestler Eva Wylie. Although both are rather violent, harder-edged than many American P.I. Mysteries featuring women, the Wylie series has an even bleaker, cynical tone. Sarah Dunant writes issue-oriented, deftly plotted, elegant Mysteries featuring P.I. Hannah Wolfe. These are good suggestions for fans of Muller and Grafton.

The P.I. as Detective, as described here, is a fairly recent phenomenon; however, there are a number of Mysteries with historical settings that would certainly appeal to fans of this type. One of Anne Perry's series set in Victorian England features William Monk, a policeman who has lost his memory in an accident. As he struggles to regain his memory and his career, he works as a P.I. of sorts, assisted by, among others, Hester Latterly, a nurse who trained with Florence Nightingale in the Crimean War and who has her own forthright ideas of the role of nurses and women in general in Victorian society. This series opens with *The Face of a Stranger*.[26] These Historical Mysteries feature bleak, evocative, atmospheric mysteries that also delve into the underside of Victorian society, as many contemporary P.I.s probe today's society.

A pair of authors have brought new life to ancient Rome with their series of Mysteries featuring P.I.s. Both Lindsey Davis and Steven Saylor probe issues in Roman society through the characters and investigations of their detectives. In Davis's series Marcus Didius Falco is a P.I. in the time of Vespasian (A.D. 69–79); his investigations lead him to the far reaches of the Roman Empire (Germany, Spain, and beyond). Described as "Columbo in a toga," Falco adds an element of humor to the history in these stories.[27] The series begins with *The Silver Pigs*.[28] Saylor, on the other hand, offers Gordianus the Finder, in a series set more than 100 years earlier during the Roman Republic. Suspense, intrigue, and detailed historical setting characterize this series, of which *Roman Blood* is the first.[29]

Numerous authors have continued the adventures of Sherlock Holmes, but one of the most intriguing is Laurie R. King, who has married Holmes to a young feminist, Mary Russell. *The Beekeeper's Apprentice; or, On the Segregation of the Queen* is the first in this series.[30]

POLICE DETECTIVES

Although the most famous of the classic detectives may never have been Police Detectives, the subgenre certainly has had its day, in books, radio (those of us lucky enough to have grown up listening to *Dragnet* know how effective a medium radio can be), television (from *Dragnet* to *Hill Street Blues, Prime Suspect,* and *NYPD Blue*), and the movies (*Lethal Weapon* and *Beverly Hills Cop*, for example, not to mention *L.A. Confidential*, with its noir outlook and feel), the police story has always been popular (*see* Figure 8.3 for characteristics of Police Detective Mysteries).

That the protagonists are members of police departments clearly distinguishes this subgenre from the P.I.s and Amateur Detectives. As policemen (and -women) they have the force of the law on their side—to investigate cases, to question witnesses, to incarcerate possible felons. But also as part of a police department, they are likely

---

FIGURE 8.3

Characteristics of Police Detective Mysteries

1. Either the department as a whole or particular members (almost always detectives) provide the focus for these Mysteries, which are generally series.

2. Details of police departments and police work figure prominently, and the details of the investigative procedures enhance the story.

3. Settings may be urban, suburban, or small town. Details of the setting, a strong sense of place, are often important.

4. The police team or department is generally engaged in working on multiple cases, usually unrelated to each other, and these are not necessarily all solved.

---

overwhelmed by office politics and a heavy caseload. In Police Detective Mysteries we get the details of the investigation, as well as the inner workings of the department, from the police perspective.

Police Detective Mysteries generally involve more than one case. There may be a principal case that is being investigated, but there will be other cases as well, and these may be related to the principal case, or not, and they may be solved, or not. While P.I.s and Amateur Detectives can devote all their time to a single case, Police Detectives must juggle their cases in ways that provide interesting opportunities for writers. On the other hand, Police Detectives work as part of a team, never alone. Detectives are paired with a partner, with whom they share the details of the investigation. These stories are related by a third-person narrator, so we readers have the benefit of more information from a variety of characters to use in solving the cases.

In their investigations, Police Detectives should play by the rules. They have the authority to question suspects but only within strict guidelines. They have all the department's resources at their fingertips—if they can only call in enough favors to have those resources devoted to the case they are working on. Evidence must be handled in a prescribed manner to be admissible in court. All hinges on the precision of the investigation, with little room for ingenuity or alternative approaches. Having said that, I would add that there are always exceptions, authors who push the borders of the genre beyond the traditional confines. Here Connelly's Harry (really, Hieronymous) Bosch of the Los Angeles Police Department, a Vietnam vet who has little respect for the rules of law and less for authority, stands out. Complex, suspenseful plots, a bleak atmosphere, and a knight-errant hero, who prefers to work alone, characterize these award-winning Mysteries. (*Concrete Blonde* is a good example.)[31]

Even more than P.I.s, Police Detectives are likely to be placed in perilous situations, such as armed encounters with dangerous criminals. There seems to be a difference in the amount of violence in American Police Detective Mysteries versus those set in England. The American stories have more violence and more gunplay than their British counterparts. The British stories are certainly often bleak but not necessarily violent. They also display a serious concern for social issues, as in Alan Scholefield's series featuring partners George

Macrae and Leopold Silver of the London Police. (*Dirty Weekend* is the first.)[32] In Edinburgh Ian Rankin's John Rebus Mysteries grow increasingly bleak and problematical. (Try *Black and Blue,* which combines true crime with Rebus's current case.)[33] The complicated relationship between Detective Chief Inspector Lloyd and Inspector Judy Hall, sorted out in the midst of the cases, provides some respite from the weight of the cases in this series by Jill McGown, begun in the early '80s. Try *Picture of Innocence* as a good introduction.[34]

On the American side, violence and gunplay may replace or figure alongside the frequently bleak mood of the Police Detective Mysteries. In Seattle, Detective Lou Boldt always seems to find himself in a violent interchange with the felons he seeks in Ridley Pearson's series. His adventures are fairly typical, especially for a police detective in a large city, faced with a heavy caseload and increasing problems from internal politics, drugs, organized crime, and deranged felons. *Undercurrents* is the first in this gripping series that provides both extensive forensic detail and psychological insights into the perpetrators.[35]

Not all Police Mysteries are bleak and violent, however. Series from both continents reflect a large measure of humor—in dialogue and situation—as well as an upbeat, or at least lighter, tone. For example, England offers Colin Dexter's Inspector Morse series, set in Oxford and popularized by the television renditions, with his uncanny intuition, irascible personality, and dogged investigating, as well as M. C. Beaton's Hamish Macbeth, a constable in the Scottish Highlands, whose unorthodox techniques, intuition, and rather eccentric personality likely appeal more to fans of Cozy Amateur Detective Mysteries than of police stories. American Joan Hess gives us another small-town series with its unique feel—Police Chief Arly Hanks and Maggody, Arkansas—about as far from the mean streets of Connelly or Pearson as one can get. Tony Hillerman's series, set in the American Southwest on Native American reservations, also qualifies as a Police Detective Mystery, although there is less interaction within the department, and because of the lack of staff, officers are often out on their own. Although his books do not offer much humor, they do display a more human touch. Violence is not absent, but it does not dominate these thoughtful mysteries, rich in character, geography, culture, and Native American tradition. It is interesting to note that these lighter Police Detective Mysteries seem almost closer to Amateur Detectives in feel and appeal, and as many readers of Amateur are as likely to read them as are fans of Police Detectives.

This mood-tone distinction seems to reflect geography: Urban police stories are more likely bleak and more violent; those set in small towns are generally lighter, with the details of the crime filtered through the cozy feel of the town and its personalities. One exception is Archer Mayor's series set in Vermont. One might expect these to reflect a more rural environment and thus project a gentler mood. In fact, they deal with serious issues of narcotics and drug trafficking, spousal abuse, and violence. This is not the small-town life one would expect in such a bucolic setting. *The Ragman's Memory* is a good example of Mayor's excellent character development, complex mystery, strong sense of place, and menacing villains.[36]

KEY AUTHORS

Within the Police Detective Mysteries there are those that focus on the department as a team and those that feature a single investigator and assistant, and the authors that best exemplify this distinction are also key authors in the subgenre. McBain's 87th Precinct Mysteries typify the former. Set against the background of a bustling big-city police department (not unlike New York City's), these Mysteries play out with an ongoing cast of characters. We know them from the first paragraph, thanks to McBain's skill in providing thumbnail sketches of the players and their roles. Although Steve Carella emerges as a "hero" of sorts, it is in fact the interplay of the whole department that makes the series. Try *The Big Bad City* to sample McBain's style and story.[37]

On the other hand, in James's Scotland Yard, we know few of the characters more than superficially. These are the stories of Commander Adam Dalgleish; other characters figure peripherally, but the stories are his and thus have a feel quite different from that produced by McBain's. Here, elegant prose, descriptions, deeper psychological analysis of the suspects, and insights into Dalgleish's own nature and investigation make these Mysteries slower paced, stories to savor as we do more Literary novels.

The distinction between an emphasis on the department as a whole and the investigations of one or two detectives makes an enormous difference in the feel of the story. The story of the busy inner workings and juggling of cases in a police department contrasts with a single character, perhaps with an assistant, who has the backing and credentials of the police but is essentially investigating on his or her own. The latter type crosses over with both P.I.s and Amateurs in terms of feel and appeal. For example, Perry's long-running series featuring Inspector Thomas Pitt and his aristocratic wife, Charlotte, in a series of Mysteries that explore the serious social and class issues in Victorian England combines Police with Amateur Detective. Although Thomas is part of London's police force, that organization plays a very small role, and the Mysteries are solved as much by Charlotte, accompanied by an eccentric cast of secondary characters, and her snooping as by actual police investigation. (In the first, *The Cater Street Hangman,* Charlotte and Thomas meet and fall in love, amidst the investigation of her sister's murder.)[38]

Even now with increasing numbers of women writing Mysteries, including Police Detective Mysteries, the majority of protagonists are still male. (Julie Smith's New Orleans Police Detective Skip Langdon is one of a handful of exceptions—both as a woman and for her involvement in the gritty underside of the Big Easy.) Women are certainly featured more prominently and their intuitive skills are often prized by their colleagues, or at least by their partners, but they are less likely to be in the forefront. Barbara Havers backs up Thomas Lynley in George's series; Gemma James assists Duncan Kincaid in Deborah Crombie's Mysteries; psychologist Daphne Matthews's insights aid Lou Boldt in Pearson's Seattle-based series. Strong, well-developed characters though they are, the women seem still to be playing second fiddle to the men in this subgenre. Yet it is often the women characters who, through intuition and skilled, although not necessarily standard, interviewing techniques, open the cracks in the case that lead to solution. For example, in Crombie's *Dreaming of the Bones,* when Kincaid is clearly too close to a case (the murder of his ex-wife), which is not even his, it is Gemma who quietly makes headway, asking the questions that eventually open up the investigation.[39] As Kincaid admits, she has the ability to make emotional leaps with strangers, a quality many of these women seem to possess.

Police Detectives in Historical Mysteries also appear less frequently. The Perry series is one example. Bruce Alexander covers London a century earlier (late 1800s) in a series that features famous London jurist Sir John Fielding, who created the Bow Street Runners, London's first police force. *Blind Justice* is the first.[40] Robert van Gulik and Laura Joh Rowland take readers further afield—to the Far East—with series set in ancient China and medieval Japan. Although Gulik's Judge Dee is not exactly a police detective, he represents the law, such as it was, solves cases, and administers justice with the authority of a modern police department. (Try *The Haunted Monastery* to explore his style.)[41] Rowland's series, featuring Sano Ichiro and set in seventeenth-century Japan, is full of interesting details of the samurai period. *Shinju* is the first.[42]

AMATEUR DETECTIVES

Amateur Detectives tend to view their cases as "puzzles" (*see* Figure 8.4). They become intrigued with something that does not quite fit in the details of a murder, and they go off on their own to investigate, outside the official investigation but sometimes paralleling it. Or they

---

FIGURE 8.4

Characteristics of the Amateur Detective

1. These "detectives" are not professionals who have been specially trained in detecting techniques; they are more likely to "fall into" a case (often involving someone they know) than to be asked to investigate, and they are usually engaged in only one case at a time.

2. Amateur Detectives have another job or a hobby that occupies their time and the details of which supplement the Mystery. This frame enhances the geographical or temporal setting.

3. Mysteries featuring Amateur Detectives are usually gentler, although there is a range of violence, as well as tone.

---

may themselves be suspects in a case and they investigate to clear their names. They often have a contact in the police force, as did Lord Peter Wimsey in Dorothy Sayers's successful series of Mysteries, which spanned the '20s and '30s. Peter's own brother-in-law, along with other connections in Scotland Yard, supported his investigations and profited from his findings. Successful Amateur Detectives, as Lord Peter certainly was, build a reputation and are often sought for assistance in investigating a case, just as P.I.s are. The difference, of course, is that the Amateur Detectives are not licensed nor do they charge a fee for their efforts. (However, both Amateurs Detectives and P.I.s are looked down upon by the Police Detectives.)

Although they have never been formally trained in police-type investigations, Amateur Detectives tend to be skilled at turning up clues the police manage to miss. (This may be one of the reasons the police dislike them so!) In Cozies (a gentle type of Amateur discussed below), these Amateur Detectives tend to rely more on intuition and their knowledge of human nature, rather than any structured investigation, to discover the true nature of the crime and the criminal. Dorothy Cannell's romps, featuring the inimitable Ellie Haskell, provide a heroine detective who happens on murders in the best Cozy tradition and solves them just as expeditiously. *The Thin Woman* starts the series, in which overweight Ellie Simons falls into murder—and love—attending a family reunion.[43]

Frames, often focused on the profession or hobbies of the investigators, are important in these stories. Jonathan Gash's Lovejoy is an antiques dealer who, as a "divvy," also possesses skills to determine accurately whether something is authentic or a fake. Lovejoy's extensive knowledge of antiques, not to mention his slightly off-color opinions, have made him a popular Amateur Detective, who is not above carrying out a good scam himself. *The Grail Tree* is the first of this long-running series, which has also been imported from British television.[44]

Methods of detection vary widely in this subgenre. Some take their cases and investigations more seriously, following clues with the precision of the best of P.I.s, as does Harry Kemelman in his series of Rabbi Small Mysteries. Here, Talmudic logic parallels and enhances the investigative techniques, as the Rabbi manages to solve the Mysteries intellectually. *Friday the Rabbi Slept Late* is the first.[45] Others casually fall into a puzzle, into trouble, and into a solution, as does Sharyn McCrumb's forensic anthropologist Elizabeth MacPherson. *Missing Susan* is a good example of her sly humor and eccentric characters.[46]

KEY AUTHORS

One of the most popular writers in this subgenre today is relative newcomer Evanovich, who burst on the Mystery scene in 1994 with *One for the Money* and the ongoing tales of bumbling bounty hunter Stephanie Plum, her family and lover, in the wilds of urban (Trenton) New Jersey. Often accompanied by outrageous Grandmother Mazur and cop-lover Joe Morelli, Stephanie shuns conventional tactics and wisdom as she succeeds, despite the odds, in nabbing her man. More than a month before her newest title will be published, we find our shelves empty of her books. Evanovich writes what we, in my library, fondly call "smart-mouth woman books." Her stories are witty, edgy, and humorous (sometimes over the top), with an incredible range of secondary characters and truly ridiculous situations. Her conversational style and slightly romantic tone attract readers from other genres as well.

Other writers of Amateur Detective Mysteries we should become familiar with are Dick Francis, Jonathan Kellerman, Edna Buchanan, Randy Wayne White, and Harlan Coben. The frame of Francis's Mysteries, always something to do with horses and races, pervades the story but does not infringe on the investigation and solution of the Mystery. For example, his recent *10 lb. Penalty* combines a young man's dreams of a racing career with his father's political aspirations in a complex story of Suspense and father-son relationships.[47] Although he does have one series character, Sid Halley, who has appeared in three Mysteries to date, for the most part Francis writes single-title Mysteries, an unusual approach in this series-oriented environment. Because they contain so many other elements and are not part of a series, his titles make good crossovers for readers from the Suspense genre especially.

Kellerman's popular series features child psychologist Alex Delaware and his friend Milo Sturgis, a policeman on the Los Angeles force. Narrated first-person, these stories give a real feel for the medical and psychological background that Delaware brings to play in discovering the villain. Complex plots, building tension, and interesting characters combine to make these, like Francis's, suspenseful reading. The recent *Monster,* although more violent than many of his Mysteries, is a good example. [48]

Buchanan represents another kind of Amateur Detective: the investigator. Not really a detective, Britt Montero, and others like her, come upon murder through their job of investigating a news story or incident. Buchanan, a Pulitzer Prize–winning reporter, gives her own heroine extensive reporting skills, as Britt goes for the story but often comes up with murder. *Contents under Pressure* is the first of this Miami-based series. [49]

White's Doc Ford series is also set in Florida and features engaging characters and humorous dialogue. (These are a good bet for fans of the even wackier Carl Hiaasen Crime Thrillers.) Doc Ford is a government agent turned marine biologist, although detection seems to take up more and more of his spare time, as he solves Mysteries for himself and friends. The series opens with *Sanibel Flats.* [50]

Finally, Coben presents a slightly different Amateur Detective in sports agent Myron Bolitar. You do not need to be a sports fan to appreciate this wisecracking hero and his eccentric assistants, but if you are, you have found a treasure. Bolitar's clients run the gamut of professional sports—golf, tennis, football, and so forth—providing him with a variety of details to amuse and satisfy fans. *Deal Breaker* is the first. [51]

The Cozy, referred to several times throughout this chapter, represents a particular, and currently very popular, type of Amateur Detective Mystery. In these the body is traditionally offstage, and neither death nor any other violent episode is explicitly described. The protagonist, often a woman, solves the Mystery through intuition and her knowledge of human nature. These are often small-town settings, and gossip, as well as casually talking with suspects who are friends and neighbors, plays an important role in providing the information necessary to solve the crime. Fingerprints, markings on the bullet, and autopsy reports (even if they did have access to them) are seldom as crucial in an environment in which one can learn, with a few carefully considered and well-placed questions, just who was leaving the victim's house on the evening in question. Generally speaking, Cozies feature quirky characters; a sense of community (generally small-town or at least enclosed); and an upbeat, often quite humorous tone, which emphasizes humorous dialogue and human foibles. In addition, all Amateur Detectives in Cozies must have some connection with the police; in many cases, the protagonist's boyfriend or husband is on the force. Because they usually contain more dialogue than other Mysteries, Cozies are usually faster paced and shorter.

As already stated, protagonists in Cozies are generally women, although there are certainly exceptions. Two popular series are by Jeff Abbott and Lawrence Block. Abbott's first Jordan Poteet Mystery, *Do Unto Others*, features a librarian-sleuth in a small Texas town.[52] Block's Bernie Rhodenbarr series, in contrast, takes place in Manhattan, where burglar and secondhand book dealer Bernie seems always to get caught with a body in a home he only meant to rob, and thus, he is forced to investigate to save his own skin. The series opens with *Burglars Can't Be Choosers*.[53]

Although suspension of disbelief is certainly a necessary qualification to enjoy Cozies, these are neither simple nor for the simpleminded. Kemelman's mysteries, with their insight into Jewish customs and religion, are Cozies, as are Gillian Roberts's seriocomic adventures of a Philadelphia schoolteacher and her policeman boyfriend. Even the lightest of Cozies offer a wry look at human nature and either an interesting frame or an exploration of social issues on some level.

Mysteries featuring Amateur Detectives, and particularly Cozies, have come into their own in the last decade. Although they may not dominate the best-sellers lists, they support the growing habit of readers who like the "English Village Mystery" or a "nice" Mystery, with a puzzle, interesting characters, and the body well offstage. Certainly, there seem to be more writers who fall into this subgenre than either of the other two.

For many of us, Elizabeth Peters is the benchmark Cozy Mystery writer. Her Mysteries have entertained and educated millions of readers since *The Jackal's Head* appeared in 1968.[54] She has written more than thirty mysteries (nonseries and in three series) and nearly thirty novels of Romantic Suspense under the pseudonym Barbara Michaels. Named a Grandmaster by the Mystery Writers of America in 1998, her reputation is ensured.

Peters's Mysteries feature a variety of themes and frames, but because the author herself is an Egyptologist, things Egyptian remain a prominent feature. She writes a series set in turn-of-the-century Egypt, featuring Amelia Peabody Emerson and her Egyptologist husband, Radcliffe. These are basically humorous Cozy Mysteries, with little explicit violence, sex, or strong language, but Peters takes justified pride in the accuracy of the historical setting and details of the excavations of the tombs, as Victorian Egyptologists unearth the treasures of the pharaohs. Each entry in the series is set in a specific time and reflects actual historical events. The first, *Crocodile on the Sandbank,* is set in the 1880s.[55]

Although critics do not seem to give as much credence to Amateur Detectives, especially Cozies, fans, at my library at least, devour them. Among their favorite Cozy authors are Beaton, Diane Mott Davidson, and Lilian Jackson Braun. Beaton, in addition to the Hamish Macbeth Police Detectives, mentioned above, writes a wickedly funny series featuring the inimitable Agatha Raisin, an abrasive but very human refugee from London who finds murder and mayhem in the English village of Carsley. *Agatha Raisin and the Quiche of Death,* in which Agatha tries to find her place in village society, is the first.[56] Davidson is the current queen of the cooking Mysteries. *Catering to Nobody* introduces gourmet cook-sleuth Goldy Bear, whose subsequent adventures involve murder, motherhood, mayhem, and, always, good food, with recipes included. Braun, author of *The Cat Who* Mysteries, continues to delight fans of both sexes with the antics of two Siamese cats, Koko and Yum Yum and their owner, journalist and later philanthropist Jim Qwilleran, as he solves cases in the rural North Country. *The Cat Who Could Read Backwards* is the first in the long-running series.[57]

As are all Mysteries, those featuring Amateur Detectives tend to be descriptive of time and place, whether contemporary or historical. Mysteries in this subgenre lend themselves to historical topics to a greater extent than either of the other two subgenres, because neither police departments nor true P.I.s play much of a role in history before the middle of the eighteenth century, when the Bow Street Runners preceded the establishment of organized police departments. Ellis Peters deserves credit for much of the current interest in Historical Mysteries and certainly in medieval mysteries. Her series, featuring Benedictine lay brother Cadfael, an Amateur Detective who leans very much toward the Cozy school, takes place in twelfth-century England, in and around Shrewsbury. Historical details, current politics, contemporary medicine (he is an herbalist), and religious and social issues abound, as Cadfael, a returning foot soldier from the Crusades, makes his niche in the religious community as a healer of bodies as well as souls. Peters immerses her readers in the times and sets the standard for Historical Mysteries with her intricate puzzles set securely in a well-detailed historical period. Followers in her footsteps with Medieval and Elizabethan settings are a plethora of writers including Sharan Newman, Margaret Frazer, Edward Marston, Elizabeth Eyre, and Fiona Buckley.

On the other side of the Atlantic, Margaret K. Lawrence has written an evocative, detailed trilogy featuring Hannah Trevor, a midwife in Maine. (First in that series is *Hearts and Bones*.)[58] Set immediately after the Revolutionary War, these novels vividly, and rather bleakly, re-create the hardships of the times and the choices faced by the inhabitants of the newly created United States. Miriam Grace Monfredo brings another era of American history to life in her series featuring feminist librarian Glynis Tryon, of Seneca Falls, New York. Opening in 1848 with the first Women's Rights convention (*Seneca Falls Inheritance*), Monfredo explores the issues of the time, from feminism to those that led to the Civil War.[59]

The Mysteries of Caroline Roe, set in medieval Spain, provide an unusual setting. These elegant, provocative Mysteries feature fourteenth-century Girona physician and Jew, Isaac the Physician, his daughter and assistant, Raquel, and apprentice Yusef. Here political machinations often combine with accurate details of time and place, among more than one level of society, to create a stage on which the Mystery is played out. *Remedy for Treason* is the first.[60]

Preparing to Work with Readers

I personally despair of ever reading enough Mysteries to work with the range of fans who come to our desk asking for suggestions. Although fans of some genres are elusive and must be sought out and roped in before they will talk with us, many Mystery fans, or so it seems, are comfortable with their genre of choice and believe everyone else reads and enjoys Mysteries and should be able to suggest more just like their favorite authors. No small task considering the breadth of this genre. Lists, displays, reviews, and the comments of other readers (staff and patrons) are all invaluable in preparing us to work with readers and helping us when we have actual readers in tow.

What do we know about Mystery fans? Aside from the fact that they tend to be voluble, Mystery readers like series. They follow series characters from case to case and are always on the lookout for the next book in that series and other series that have the same appeal. Keeping lists of suggestions for popular authors is always a good idea. Identifying what makes the author popular, and then discovering other authors who share those characteristics, is the place to start.

Many readers follow a series because they like the detective. This means that fans of a Cozy series might also be interested in a P.I. if the characters are similar. Other readers want a type—they may like Police Detectives and will read all we can give them, or they may be interested in P.I.s set in a particular location, or they may want Mysteries of any kind that have a particular frame—art or gardening, for example. Reference books tend to be much more helpful in identifying authors to satisfy these readers.

The issue of series brings up another problem: paperbacks. Many series begin as paperbacks and then continue in hardcover if the author is successful. Luckily, more and more review journals consider paperbacks along with hardcovers, because if we miss purchasing the early titles in a series, we may never be able to fill them in. Treat paperbacks carefully, cataloging them so that they stay in the collection, available to fans who discover the series later.

Some readers read to discover the answer to "who-dun-it," preferably before the detective reaches his own conclusions. Others read for the frame or the characters. It helps if we have thought about these different appeals, so that we are ready when readers come to us for assistance. Unfortunately, because different readers may read the same book in different ways, we cannot readily sort authors this way. We can, however, be aware of these appeal differences when we listen to what readers say they enjoy in the readers' advisory interview.

As Mystery fans know, more and more Mysteries are set in specific locations and may be popular in that area, even if they are not as popular elsewhere. Although the benchmark in your community may be Robert B. Parker or Janet Evanovich, there may be other "local" authors of whose books you must consistently purchase multiple copies. Because we cannot buy everything, we need to listen to what readers enjoy and request and gear our collections as much as possible to their interests.

One last point to think about as we prepare to work with readers is where to start a reader in a series or with a new author. Some readers insist on reading the first book in a series; if I know that is not the author's best and am unable to dissuade them, I simply tell them that even if they are not enamored of it, they should try another, the one I believe best represents the author's style and story line. As I mentioned with Parker, above, the first in a series is not always the best, and if we are offering an unfamiliar author to a reader, we should make every effort to suggest a representative title. If a reader enjoys a series, he will read all the titles; the key is to hook him with that first book. We watch for good examples of an author as we read, read reviews, and talk with patrons. When we find a reference source that makes such recommendations, we should cherish it and share that information with colleagues and readers. If you are not a mystery reader, you might try some of the suggestions in Figure 8.5.

Readers' Advisory Interview

One problem we always face in working with readers who want to explore such a large and diverse genre is how to zero in on good suggestions. When fans ask for Mysteries, we verify first that they are asking for books with a puzzle: a crime, an investigation, and a solution. Then, depending on whether they are in the mood for a P.I., Police Detective, or Amateur Detective, we might offer a variety of types and characters.

A very useful strategy is to ask the Mystery fan to describe the kind of detective she enjoys. The response is usually very revealing, and the question is far easier to pose and to answer than to query if

---

FIGURE 8.5

An Introduction to the Mystery Genre

Mystery Writers to Try, If You Enjoy . . .

Fantasy	Helen Chappell
Gentle	M. C. Beaton
	Charlotte MacLeod
Historical	Margaret K. Lawrence
	Anne Perry
Humor	Lawrence Block (Burglar)
	Janet Evanovich
Inspirational	G. K. Chesterton
Literary	P. D. James
	Miriam Grace Monfredo
Psychological	Frances Fyfield
Romance	Elizabeth Peters
Romantic Suspense	April Henry
	Elizabeth Peters
Science Fiction	Sharyn McCrumb (*Bimbos of the Death Sun*)[61]
Suspense	Mary Willis Walker
	T. Jefferson Parker
	William Kent Krueger
Thriller	Paul Levine
	Patricia Cornwell
	Thomas Swann
	Douglas Skeggs
	Loren D. Estleman
Western	Michael McGarrity
Women's Lives	Gail Bowen
	Marianne Macdonald

they like Police Procedurals or Amateur Detectives, terms they may not even clearly understand or use themselves. Readers may talk about the loner working on a case, or the extensive police investigation, or the little old lady who stumbles into cases. The description we receive gives us valuable clues as to the type and tone of Mystery we might suggest.

Tone is an important aspect to keep in mind, because it affects the appeal of the Mystery. We listen to the way readers describe the books they enjoy. If they emphasize the lighter tone, they may enjoy a range of Mysteries, from the breezy Cozies of Tamar Myers's Pennsylvania Dutch Mysteries (*Too Many Crooks Spoil the Broth*)[62] to Janet Evanovich's rather incompetent bounty hunter and even Marcia Muller's Sharon McCone series, or the humorous Police Mysteries of Rhys Bowen. Fans of a bleaker tone might also cut across the subgenres with Edna Buchanan (Amateur Detective), James Lee Burke (P.I.), and Michael Connelly (Police Detective). Fans of elegantly written, more literary Mysteries should be made aware of P. D. James, certainly, but they may also enjoy authors such as Elizabeth George and Sharyn McCrumb (her elegiac Ballad series). Readers looking for books that match a particular mood and tone are often willing to read outside the boundaries of the familiar, and thoughtful suggestions are always appreciated.

We can also draw conclusions from the way readers talk about the story line and style of the Mystery. Readers who talk about investigative details are more likely to appreciate Police Detectives and P.I.s. On the other hand, readers who hint more at intuition and extensive frame will likely prefer Amateur Detectives, perhaps even Cozies.

As should be obvious from the preceding discussion, setting and frame are increasingly important. Readers who mention local details and urban environments should be steered first toward urban Police Detective and P.I. Mysteries, while those who talk about villages and enclosed communities will surely want to consider Cozies. Listening to how readers talk about Mysteries they have enjoyed in the past and using the framework of the genre and subgenres discussed earlier allow us to offer suggestions that help readers more readily discover the kinds of Mysteries they are in the mood to read.

Another very important point to acknowledge is that although there are certainly increasing numbers of ethnic writers in every genre, Mystery is one in which this trend has been well established for a number of years, and there are sleuths of almost every conceivable background. Interested readers will find gay and lesbian investigators (Joseph Hansen's David Brandstetter, an insurance investigator, was one of the first to achieve widespread popularity), Hispanic (Rudolfo Anaya's Sonny Baca), Native American (Jean Hager's Mitch Bushy-head and Molly Bearpaw as well as Dana Stabenow's Kate Shugak), and Asian (from Laura Joh Rowland's seventh-samurai Sano Ichiro to Leslie Glass's April Woo, in New York). Black writers and characters are particularly prominent and range the gamut from Walter Mosley's Easy Rawlings to Barbara Neely's cleaning woman–detective Blanche White.

Sure Bets

It is always helpful to have in mind—or even better, written down—the names of those authors who work consistently for a large number of readers who enjoy Mysteries and related titles. If you do not keep a list now, you should start. Every library's clientele is different; your readers will enjoy authors mine may not appreciate as much. Watch for the authors readers talk about and reserve.

One of my standby authors is Canadian Gail Bowen, who needs to be writing more! Set in Regina, Saskatchewan, where her protagonist, Joanne Kilbourn, is a fortysomething professor and mother, these feature intricate Mysteries with a strong social consciousness as well as close-knit family relationships. Readers relate to the characters and story on several levels—the books are filled with intelligent conversation, literary references, far-reaching social and political implications, and an unerring maternal instinct that runs through the series. She explores the nature and emotions of her characters as well as the social issues and crimes that propel the plot. These deal with issues too complex and often nasty to qualify as Cozies, but they exemplify the best of the Amateur Detectives. Readers who used to enjoy Amanda Cross have been very satisfied with Bowen. Be fore-warned that this is another series that is best not begun with the first book. Choose the second, *Love and Murder,* instead, as it provides a better introduction to the characters and relationships.[63]

Another author with a wide-ranging appeal is Nevada Barr, whose National Park Service Ranger protagonist Anna Pigeon is appreciated by both male and female readers. Because Pigeon is posted to different parks around the country, Barr is able to give readers an insider's look into the parks, their history and geography, as well as the particular issues relevant to that locale. In addition to braving natural dangers inherent in her job and solving a murder in each book, Anna must also fight her own personal demons. Barr has created a very human, down-to-earth Amateur Detective, who will appeal especially to readers of female P.I. Mysteries by Sue Grafton and Muller. In *Liberty Falling* Anna returns to New York City to nurse her sister and becomes involved with mysterious occurrences, and then murder, on Ellis Island.[64]

All the authors previously mentioned in this chapter have been popular with readers at my library, and all are good candidates for displays, lists, and other promotion. Aaron J. Elkins has not been mentioned, however, and he is another with broad appeal and more than one series. *Fellowship of Fear* is the first in the series featuring forensic anthropologist Gideon Oliver, whose books have crossover appeal with Patricia Cornwell and others who concentrate on the forensic details of a police investigation.[65] *A Deceptive Clarity* introduces curator and art expert Chris Norgren, whose cases frequently take him abroad from his Seattle base; and, in collaboration with his wife, Charlotte, there is a series featuring female professional golfer, Lee Ofsted (*A Wicked Slice* is the first).[66] His recent *Loot* explores art treasure stolen by the Nazis and includes fascinating historical details. [67] Familiarity with such a versatile author allows us to offer suggestions to a number of fans of different types of Amateur Detectives and others.

Expanding Readers' Horizons

Because none of us can accurately identify all the Mysteries in our collection and then carefully catalog them in a separate collection, we need to be aware of the range of books outside the genre that appeal to Mystery readers. So many genres overlap with Mysteries, in terms of all the appeal elements, that the possibilities are almost infinite—if we open up our own minds and those of readers to see these possibilities.

As I write about these genres, I see an investigative thread that runs through several genres and includes books far beyond the Mystery genre. (Or, rather, these are books that would only be classified as Mysteries in the broadest sense.) Legal Thrillers feature the same investigative techniques, although the outcome may not be the arrest of a murderer. In fact, almost any of the authors in the Thriller genre might appeal to Mystery readers looking for particular elements. Investigators appear in many genres in addition to Mystery, and readers who enjoy that type of character may enjoy reading outside the genre to find the same satisfaction. Romance offers J. D. Robb's Eve Dallas series and Joan Overfield's time travel series, with a London detective going back to Regency England to solve a murder. Iris Johansen's Eve Duncan series, with the forensic details, might appeal, as might John Sandford's series and nonseries Suspense titles.

We place authors in genres where we think the readers are most likely to discover them, but the blurring of the borders of the genres is becoming more frequent. Fans of the P.I. subgenre who are not put off by a vampire partner should try Tanya Huff's series featuring ex-policewoman Vicki Nelson and her unusual partner Henry Fitzroy or Laurell K. Hamilton's Anita Blake, Vampire Hunter, series. Or, in the Fantasy genre, there is Steven Brust's Vlad Taltos series (*Jhereg* is the first).[68]

There is also a group of books that features police departments, and perhaps even detectives, but does not feel like Mysteries to readers. Authors like William Caunitz (*One Police Plaza*), Michael Grant (*Line of Duty*), W. E. B. Griffin (Badge of Honor series, beginning with *Men in Blue*), and Joseph Wambaugh (*The Golden Orange*) have written books, even series, that have more Suspense and Thriller elements than do straightforward Mysteries.[69] This distinction causes us to put their books, perhaps really a subgenre called Police Thrillers, in Fiction, rather than in Mystery. Although crimes are committed and investigations take place, the feel and pattern of the stories are not the same as Mysteries dealing with the same issues: The puzzle and its solution are not necessarily the point of these stories. Still, this group might appeal to readers interested in police investigative techniques and details.

Both the number and popularity of Historical Mysteries have grown dramatically over the last few years. As I mentioned above, they are generally Amateur Detective Mysteries and often feature series characters, with each book an episode in an ongoing story that explores particular places and historical events. Both Historical Fiction and Mystery readers choose these authors and their books for the details of a particular historical period, as well as for the puzzle, and the characters. As in all Historical Fiction, details should be well researched and correct. If real people appear, they should be portrayed according to historical fact. If social and moral questions arise in the progress of the plot, as they often do in Historical Mysteries, they should accurately reflect issues of concern at the time. See Figure 8.6.

FIGURE 8.6

Expanding Readers' Horizons

Authors to Take Readers beyond the Mystery Genre

Fantasy	Steven Brust
Gentle	Dorothy Gilman
Horror	Laurel K. Hamilton
	Tanya Huff
Literary	Martin Cruz Smith
Psychological	Patricia Highsmith
Romance	J. D. Robb
	Joan Overfield (*The Door Ajar*)[70]
Romantic Suspense	Iris Johansen (Eve Duncan)
Science Fiction	Isaac Asimov (Robot series)
Suspense	John Sandford
Thriller	David Ramus
	Stuart Woods
	John Grisham
Western	Loren D. Estleman (Page Murdock)

Reference Sources

As I mentioned earlier, there is an abundance of Mystery Reference books, something for almost every need and taste. Because there are so many, I try to identify the best. If you wish to expand your collection of Mystery reference sources, you will find many to choose from. Among my favorites are *By a Woman's Hand: A Guide to Mystery Fiction Written by Women, Killer Books: A Reader's Guide to Exploring the Popular World of Mystery and Suspense,* and the classic *St. James Guide to Crime and Mystery Writers.*[71]

The first two are written by Jean Swanson and Dean James, and although I appreciate their extensive coverage and interesting indexes, I especially like the way they describe authors and books. Their suggestions of read-alikes are also worth pursuing. *By a Woman's Hand* covers more than 260 women authors of mysteries. They characterize the authors and discuss their style, series characters, and other important or interesting facts, including an author's appeal to readers. Indexes access series characters, geographical location, and type of detective.

Killer Books offers a broader scope but the same wonderful descriptions. Coverage includes traditional Mystery subgenres (Police, Historical, P.I., and Amateur Detectives), but it also goes further afield with chapters on "Suspense/Psychological Mysteries," "Legal Thrillers," "Romantic Suspense," "Capers and Criminals," "Reporters, Writers, and Filmmakers," and "Sci Fi/Horror/Fantasy Mysteries." Descriptions of the authors highlight their appeal. There are indexes to characters, geography, and awards, but there are also interesting unindexed lists within the text (e.g., "Sports," "Gardening").

St. James Guide to Crime and Mystery Writers offers signed articles about each author and includes a complete bibliography as well as analysis of several titles. Its coverage beyond the strict definition of Mystery increases its usefulness. Authors in related genres, such as Thrillers (Eric Ambler, William F. Buckley Jr., and John le Carré) and Suspense (Mary Higgins Clark and Thomas Harris), are discussed. Unfortunately, it is already sadly out of date, and St. James Press has indicated that they have no plans to produce new editions in this series.

We can also look forward to a Mystery genre title in Libraries Unlimited's Genreflecting Advisory series.[72]

Where to Find . . .

INFORMATION ABOUT THE AUTHOR

All three of the titles described above provide useful author information, as does *Contemporary Authors* (*see* appendix 2). *Mystery and Suspense Writers: The Literature of Crime, Detection, and Espionage* is another excellent source of biographical information on the seventy major authors profiled there in signed articles.[73]

PLOT SUMMARIES

In addition to the three titles mentioned above, plot summaries can be found in a number of sources described in appendix 2: *Fiction Catalog, Sequels, NoveList,* and *What Do I Read Next?*

SUBGENRES AND THEMES

A number of resources provide excellent index access to subgenres, themes, characters, and more. Worth noting are two titles by Willetta L. Heising: *Detecting Men: A Reader's Guide and Checklist for Mystery Series Written by Men* and *Detecting Women 3: A Reader's Guide and Checklist for Series Written by Women.*[74] The former covers series, written by men, featuring male and female sleuths. There are indexes by mystery types ("Private Investigators," "Police"), listing first case and author; background (art and antiques, animals); series character (alphabetical by first name!), settings; chronology; title; pseudonyms; and awards. In the main entry, Heising characterizes the series detective with an informative phrase. For example, James Patterson's Alex Cross is described as a "black psychiatrist and homicide cop in Washington, D.C."[75] The latter provides similar information for almost 700 series, written by women, featuring male and female sleuths.

The classic Mystery index is Allen J. Hubin's *Crime Fiction II: A Comprehensive Bibliography, 1749–1990.*[76] Comprehensive it is. Arranged by author, with pseudonyms, it provides author dates; a list of works, with publisher and date; series characters; and references to author entries in selected reference books. Indexes access titles, settings, series, series character chronology (identifies character as Adventurer, Amateur, Criminal, Police, Private, Spy), film versions, screenwriters, and directors.

Swanson and James's books provide access to subgenres and themes, too, as do many of the titles described in appendix 2: *Fiction Catalog* ("Detectives" in the subject index links detective names to their creators); *Sequels* (subject index includes character types, such as Amateur Detectives); *NoveList* (access to specific themes or subgenres through both subject search types, as well as *Genreflecting's* access to subgenres and themes); and *What Do I Read Next?* (themes and subgenres can be selected in the subject searches).

GENRE DESCRIPTION, BACKGROUND, AND HISTORY

Mystery and Suspense Writers offers an excellent overview of the genre, both through the articles on writers, from classic to contemporary, and also in the long essays on aspects of the genre in the second volume. Fourteen essays explore the Mystery genre ("The Armchair Detective," "Black Detective Fiction," "Crime Noir," "The Ethnic Detective," "The Female Detective," "Gay and Lesbian Mystery Fiction," "The Historical Mystery," "The Police Procedural," "Regionalization of the Mystery and Crime Novel," "Religious Mysteries," and "Women of Mystery") and beyond ("The Legal Crime Novel," "The Romantic Suspense Mystery," and "The Spy Thriller").

It should come as no surprise that a Mystery writer excels at summing up the genre. In *Blood Work* writer Michael Connelly describes Mysteries as follows: "Everything is ordered, good and bad clearly defined, the bad guy always gets what he deserves, the hero shines, no loose ends. It's a refreshing antidote to the real world." [77] This is what readers look for, the pattern they seek when they request Mysteries.

NOTES

1. Agatha Christie, *The Murder of Roger Ackroyd* (New York: Dodd, Mead, 1926).
2. Elizabeth Peters, *He Shall Thunder in the Sky* (New York: Morrow, 2000).
3. Dana Stabenow, *Hunter's Moon* (New York: Putnam, 1999).
4. Sir Arthur Conan Doyle, *The Memoirs of Sherlock Holmes* (1893; reprint, New York: Ballantine, 1975).
5. ———, *The Return of Sherlock Holmes* (New York: A. Wessels Company, 1907).
6. Robert Barnard, *The Corpse at the Haworth Tandoori* (New York: Scribner, 1999).

7. Mary Willis Walker, *The Red Scream* (New York: Doubleday, 1994).

8. Barbara D'Amato, *Hard Case* (New York: Scribner, 1994).

9. Carol O'Connell, *Mallory's Oracle* (New York: Putnam, 1994).

10. Marcia Muller, *Listen to the Silence* (New York: Mysterious Press, 2000); Sue Grafton, *"O" Is for Outlaw* (New York: Holt, 1999).

11. Rex Stout, *Too Many Cooks* (New York, Toronto: Farrar & Rinehart, 1938).

12. Janet Evanovich, *One for the Money* (New York: Scribner, 1994).

13. Ellis Peters, *A Morbid Taste for Bones* (New York: Morrow, 1977).

14. Tony Hillerman, *Thief of Time* (New York: Harper & Row, 1988).

15. Virginia Rich, *The Cooking School Murders* (New York: E. P. Dutton, 1982); Diane Mott Davidson, *Catering to Nobody* (New York: St. Martin's, 1990).

16. Sharyn McCrumb, *If Ever I Return, Pretty Peggy-O* (New York: Scribner, 1990).

17. James Lee Burke, *The Neon Rain* (New York: Holt, 1987).

10. Rudolfo Anaya, *Zia Summer* (New York: Warner Books, 1995).

19. Grafton, *"A" Is for Alibi* (New York: Holt, 1982).

20. ———, *"K" Is for Killer* (New York: Holt, 1994); ———, *"N" Is for Noose* (New York: Holt, 1998).

21. Robert B. Parker, *Double Deuce* (New York: Putnam, 1992).

22. ———, *The Godwulf Manuscript* (Boston: Houghton, 1973).

23. Dennis Lehane, *Darkness, Take My Hand* (New York: Morrow, 1996).

24. Robert Crais, *Voodoo River* (New York: Hyperion, 1995).

25. Muller, *Till the Butchers Cut Him Down* (New York: Mysterious Press, 1994).

26. Anne Perry, *The Face of a Stranger* (New York: Fawcett, 1990).

27. Emily Melton, review of *Last Act in Palmyra,* by Lindsey Davis, *Booklist* 92 (March 15, 1996): 1242.

28. Lindsey Davis, *The Silver Pigs* (New York: Crown, 1989).

29. Steven W. Saylor, *Roman Blood* (New York: St. Martin's, 1991).

30. Laurie R. King, *The Beekeeper's Apprentice; or, On the Segregation of the Queen* (New York: St. Martin's, 1994).

31. Michael Connelly, *Concrete Blonde* (Boston: Little, Brown, 1994).

32. Alan Scholefield, *Dirty Weekend* (New York: St. Martin's, 1991).

33. Ian Rankin, *Black and Blue* (New York: St. Martin's, 1997).

34. Jill McGown, *Picture of Innocence* (New York: Ballantine, 1998).

35. Ridley Pearson, *Undercurrents* (New York: St. Martin's, 1988).

36. Archer Mayor, *The Ragman's Memory* (New York: Mysterious Press, 1996).

37. Ed McBain, *The Big Bad City* (New York: Simon & Schuster, 1999).

38. Perry, *The Cater Street Hangman* (New York: Simon & Schuster, 1999).
39. Deborah Crombie, *Dreaming of the Bones* (New York: Scribner, 1997).
40. Bruce Alexander, *Blind Justice* (New York: Putnam, 1994).
41. Robert van Gulik, *The Haunted Monastery* (New York: Scribner, 1969).
42. Laura Joh Rowland, *Shinju* (New York: HarperPaperbacks, 1996).
43. Dorothy Cannell, *The Thin Woman* (New York: St. Martin's, 1984).
44. Jonathan Gash, *The Grail Tree* (New York: Harper & Row, 1979).
45. Harry Kemelman, *Friday the Rabbi Slept Late* (New York: Crown, 1964).
46. McCrumb, *Missing Susan* (New York: Ballantine, 1991).
47. Dick Francis, *10 lb. Penalty* (New York: Putnam, 1997).
48. Jonathan Kellerman, *Monster* (New York: Random House, 1999).
49. Edna Buchanan, *Contents under Pressure* (New York: Hyperion, 1992).
50. Randy Wayne White, *Sanibel Flats* (New York: St. Martin's, 1990).
51. Harlan Coben, *Deal Breaker* (New York: Dell, 1995).
52. Jeff Abbott, *Do Unto Others* (New York: Ballantine, 1994).
53. Lawrence Block, *Burglars Can't Be Choosers* (New York: Random House, 1977).
54. Peters, *The Jackal's Head* (New York: Meredith Press, 1968).
55. ———, *Crocodile on the Sandbank* (New York: Dodd, Mead, 1975).
56. M. C. Beaton, *Agatha Raisin and the Quiche of Death* (New York: St. Martin's, 1992).
57. Lilian Jackson Braun, *The Cat Who Could Read Backwards* (New York: E. P. Dutton, 1966).
58. Margaret K. Lawrence, *Hearts and Bones* (New York: Avon, 1996).
59. Miriam Grace Monfredo, *Seneca Falls Inheritance* (New York: St. Martin's, 1992).
60. Caroline Roe, *Remedy for Treason* (New York: Berkley Books, 1998).
61. McCrumb, *Bimbos of the Death Sun* (Lake Geneva, Wis.: TSR, 1987).
62. Tamar Myers, *Too Many Crooks Spoil the Broth* (New York: Doubleday, 1994).
63. Gail Bowen, *Love and Murder* (New York: St. Martin's, 1993). Originally published as *Murder at the Mendel*, 1991.
64. Nevada Barr, *Liberty Falling* (New York: Putnam, 1999).
65. Aaron J. Elkins, *Fellowship of Fear* (New York: Walker, 1982).
66. ———, *A Deceptive Clarity* (New York: Walker, 1987); Charlotte Elkins and Aaron J. Elkins, *A Wicked Slice* (New York: St. Martin's, 1989).
67. Aaron J. Elkins, *Loot* (New York: Morrow, 1999).
68. Steven Brust, *Jhereg* (New York: Ace Fantasy Books, 1983).

69. William Caunitz, *One Police Plaza* (New York: Crown, 1984); Michael Grant, *Line of Duty* (New York: Doubleday, 1991); W. E. B. Griffin, *Men in Blue* (New York: Jove, 1991); Joseph Wambaugh, *The Golden Orange* (New York: Morrow, 1990).

70. Joan Overfield, *The Door Ajar* (New York: Kensington, 1995).

71. Jean Swanson and Dean James, *By a Woman's Hand: A Guide to Mystery Fiction Written by Women*, 2d ed. (New York: Berkley Books, 1996); ———, *Killer Books: A Reader's Guide to Exploring the Popular World of Mystery and Suspense* (New York: Berkley Books, 1998); Jay P. Pederson, ed., *St. James Guide to Crime and Mystery Writers*, 4th ed. (Detroit: St. James, 1996).

72. Gary Warren Niebuhr's *Make Mine a Mystery* is expected out in 2002 from Libraries Unlimited.

73. *Mystery and Suspense Writers: The Literature of Crime, Detection, and Espionage* (New York: Scribner, 1998).

74. Willetta L. Heising, *Detecting Men: A Reader's Guide and Checklist for Mystery Series Written by Men* (Dearborn, Mich.: Purple Moon Press, 1998); ———, *Detecting Women 3. A Reader's Guide and Checklist for Series Written by Women* (Dearborn, Mich.: Purple Moon Press, 1999).

75. ———, *Detecting Men*, 200.

76. Allen J. Hubin, *Crime Fiction II: A Comprehensive Bibliography, 1749–1990* (New York: Garland, 1994).

77. Connelly, *Blood Work* (Boston: Little, Brown, 1998), 131.

9

Psychological Suspense

Imagine almost any Alfred Hitchcock film that you have enjoyed, and you understand the pull of Psychological Suspense. These are books that play with our minds, that create a frisson of unease, that blend the creepiness generated by the Horror genre with the tension inherent in Suspense. These are stories that attract a range of readers—and filmmakers—and fit uneasily in any related genre into which we try to slot them.

Many genres lend themselves to comparisons between book and film representations, and Psychological Suspense is no exception. Hitchcock is the film master of this genre, but many examples of film noir—those dark, atmospheric, artistic explorations of madness and corruption—please fans of these books as well. Like the movie versions, novels of Psychological Suspense cast the reader in the role of fascinated observer, almost of a voyeur in fact, as we compulsively watch these tales of elegantly twisted plots and minds, of obsession and sometimes revenge, of characters trapped in their own personal nightmares, unfold.

A Definition

If ever there were a group of books that is neither fish nor fowl, this is surely it. Called Suspense, Thrillers, Horror, Mystery, and sometimes just Psychological Fiction, these are genre orphans. I have arbitrarily chosen *Suspense* as the operative noun, because that word implies the building excitement these books produce, even though they are not Suspense in the sense that genre is defined in chapter 13.

These are novels that produce a chill. They play with our minds in very disturbing ways and leave us wondering—about characters, as well as the resolution of the plot. In many ways, these are closer to Horror and to that genre's effect on readers, rather than to Suspense or Thrillers. Because they often portray the characters beset by guilt for imagined or accomplished acts, these stories inexorably draw readers into that nightmare of guilt. The internal, psychological monsters created by authors engender a sense of uneasiness that can be just as disquieting as that produced by the monsters of the Horror genre. These nightmare stories, by writers such as Ruth Rendell/Barbara Vine, evoke a very chilling terror that is more interior but no less harrowing than that produced by Horror.

These books are not clinical studies of particular psychoses. Diagnosis is not the issue in these stories, nor is treatment. Thus, some authors who deal with psychological motivations, such as Jonathan Kellerman in his popular Mystery series, really do not fit within this genre. Although their books are certainly psychological, they are far more clinical than the titles that exemplify Psychological Suspense. Kellerman deals with identification of neuroses and the crimes that often relate to affected victims. Novels of Psychological Suspense deal with the psyche, and there is a sense that there is no cure for or solution to the psychological difficulties. The fact that these neuroses may not even be recognized or acknowledged pervades these stories and drives both characters and plot.

Much fiction, especially Literary Fiction, draws on psychological theories and motivations to propel the story and define the characters. In this genre that tradition is clearly evident, but these stories center on the psychological impact. Although not truly *Suspense*, that term emphasizes the impact of these books, with their building tension and claustrophobic feel. Novels of Psychological Suspense create worlds of unease and potential disaster in which characters explore their options and their obsessions, while the reader observes from the outside. *See* Figure 9.1 for a list of the genre's characteristics.

FIGURE 9.1

Characteristics of Psychological Suspense

1. Elaborately constructed plots create stories characterized by frequent mental twists, surprises, and layers of meaning. Endings may be unresolved. Madness, acknowledged or discovered, often features in these stories. Key to the impact on the reader is the atmosphere, the nightmare quality created.

2. The pacing is more measured and the physical action less intense than in related genres. These are often densely written novels with more description than dialogue.

3. Protagonists are often misfits, who may or may not be sympathetic characters. Readers observe the characters rather than participate in their dilemmas.

4. Writing style is important, and these are often elegantly written.

Characteristics and the Genre's Appeal

Story Line

These are novels that play with our minds. They depict the slow but sure discovery that something is dreadfully wrong in this seemingly normal world and that the demons that haunt the protagonist (and disturb us as observers) are surely psychological. Henry James's "The Turn of the Screw," with its haunting tale of a young governess's tenuous grip on reality, exemplifies this tradition.[1] Sometimes it is not until the very end that we, and the protagonist, recognize that this unsettling feeling that has plagued us throughout is really something more, and certainly more terrible, than we imagined.

English author Frances Fyfield writes a series of dark Mysteries featuring Public Prosecutor Helen West and Police Superintendent Geoffrey Bailey, as well as Psychological Suspense under that name and under her real name, Frances Hegarty. Although her Mysteries are also a good crossover suggestion, her novels of Psychological Suspense are especially compelling. For example, *Blind Date* displays her skill at creating the dark and moody settings in which her often difficult heroines must battle to survive.[2] Fyfield fearlessly explores difficult topics—date rape, spousal abuse, battered women and children—but her books are never moral harangues. The characters and their obsessions always speak for themselves.

Twisted plots and layered stories also characterize Psychological Suspense. Although there is less physical action, there are no fewer twists of plot, and authors pride themselves on the levels of meaning they create. We as readers either add layer upon layer of information to discover the truth of the disturbing situation or peel these layers away, as we delve deeper and deeper into the story. Several titles by Thomas H. Cook exemplify this layering technique. He creates haunted protagonists, forced to explore lurid secrets that expose their own pasts as well as the mysteries they investigate. In *Instruments of Night,* popular Thriller writer Paul Graves investigates the unsolved murder of a young girl, but this task awakens memories of the torture and murder of his own sister.[3] More sympathetic than many protagonists of Psychological Suspense, Graves wrestles with mental as well as physical demons in this complicated, layered, and atmospheric story.

As in Literary Fiction, the endings of Psychological Suspense may be unresolved. This adds to the unease generated by the story: Authors raise troubling issues, create disturbed and disturbing characters, and then leave the reader to wonder at the outcome. J. P. Smith's *The Discovery of Light* exemplifies this unsettling strategy.[4] Protagonist David, an author of dark and intricate Thrillers, meets and marries Kate in London. She is a translator who happens also to be fascinated with Vermeer, and his paintings are discussed intermittently throughout the novel. When Kate is killed by a subway train, David investigates her last days and discovers, to his astonishment, that all was not what it appeared. However, the book is told from David's perspective. Can we believe his version of events? Densely written and intricately plotted with a film noir quality, this is a novel of obsessive love, fascinating on many levels. It leaves the reader wondering about characters as well as events.

Frame

The key to the unease inherent in books in this genre is found in the way the author creates the atmosphere. These are often stories of nightmares and madness. *Unsettling* is a term frequently used to describe them. The protagonist starts out in the normal world of everyday, but something goes awry, and we watch as he is trapped, mentally at least, in a nightmare world that may be inescapable. Madness, whether overt or undetected, often plays a role in Psychological Suspense. In his novel *Collectors* Paul Griner demonstrates this technique and its disturbing effect.[5] The collectors of the title seek out fountain pens, and this interest links Jean and Steven early on. Although Jean certainly seeks him out, her meetings with Steven are increasingly disturbing, and the level of violence he employs grows. But Jean is somehow hooked, seduced by her growing interest in him, until she and we, at the end of this chilling novel, similar in feel to John Fowles's classic *The Collector,* discover the depths of his depravity.[6]

Pacing

Pacing, the key element of both Suspense and Thrillers, is much slower, more measured here. Mental activity, rather than physical action, drives these stories, and, as a result, the plot may move more slowly, but the books remain compelling, engrossing reading. Classic writer Patricia Highsmith is a master of this style. In the much-imitated *Strangers on a Train,* two men meet by accident and, as strangers sometimes do in those circumstances, tell their darkest secrets.[7] Unluckily for the unsuspecting Guy, Bruno has a solution to Guy's problematic marriage: If each kills the person who is creating insuperable problems in the other's life, each will commit the perfect crime and never be caught. Unfortunately, such a scheme never works quite as planned, and here the murders create a spiraling nightmare in which Guy becomes trapped. Suspense, although slower paced than exemplars of that genre, figures prominently, but action is limited. What grips the reader is the sense of how out of control the story, started with so straightforward an act, quickly becomes. The dark, menacing atmosphere pervades the story, as does the sense that the outcome is inescapable. And unlike what we find in Suspense or Thrillers, here Guy fights more for his soul than his life. Highsmith's writing parallels the movies of Alfred Hitchcock and the classic stories of Edgar Allan Poe.

Characterization

Highsmith also underlines the reader's ambivalent feelings toward the protagonist, as well as their rather peculiar characters. In another classic title, *The Talented Mr. Ripley,* we feel uneasy with the protagonist from the very first, and by the last scene, when we realize both that he has escaped detection and that this amoral "hero" will continue in the path he has set for himself, we are aware of a terrible sense of foreboding.[8] We may not enter his consciousness, but we are certainly victims, mentally at least, of the nightmare he has created— one that lives on beyond the story and that we are powerless to stop.

Style

Finally, the writing style employed in Psychological Suspense is often more elegant and seldom pedestrian. As are writers of Literary Fiction, with which this genre overlaps, these authors are stylists, to whom words matter, and they carefully choose how the sentences are framed. In many cases, these are shorter books; the sense of menace is encased in a sparse, often poetic prose style. As in Literary Fiction, every word is important. In *Trick of the Eye* Jane Hitchcock uses trompe l'oeil, the medium in which heroine Faith Crowell excels, as a motif for her haunting story in which nothing is quite as it seems.[9] The elaborately constructed plot is filled with clues to be puzzled out, and the characters, whose true natures can only be discovered by the peeling away of layers (again, as with paint), are explored in this disturbing, stylish story, in which the heroine is drawn inexorably into a labyrinth of evil.

Key Authors

Ruth Rendell stands out as the benchmark of this genre. Although she has also written an award-winning Mystery series featuring Inspector Wexford, her Psychological Suspense, written in her own name and pseudonym Barbara Vine, sets the standard for the genre.

Claustrophobic, intimate glimpses into lives ruled by obsession and characters in crisis, these haunting stories remain with us long after we close the book. Her novels often feature two or three separate story lines, each with its own dysfunctional protagonist, and their convergence can only lead to disaster. *Sight for Sore Eyes* is a recent example of her skill.[10] Here fairy tale elements take on a distinctly sinister tone, as contrasting characters—the faded beauty; the mute but beautiful child; and the amoral, unnurtured young man—career through a frighteningly atmospheric London, headed surely for disaster—and murder. There is a fairy princess, ripe to be locked in the tower; a wicked stepmother, whose smothering love has created a young woman unfit for the world; and a murderous, amoral beast. Rendell's well-crafted stories create worlds of menace and danger where obsession reigns.

Although many of us classify her as a writer of Mysteries, Minette Walters also fits with writers of Psychological Suspense. Her powerful, atmospheric stories blend the puzzle of a Mystery with elements of Psychological Suspense: open endings, complex but unbalanced characters, psychological implications, and an elegant style that leaves the reader distanced, forced to play observer. In *The Scold's Bridle* the specter of the dead Mathilda Gillespie overshadows the characters and the action, yet we never see her alive and only learn of her through her diaries and the perceptions of others.[11] Unloved when she lived, she is mourned by few, least of all her daughter and granddaughter. But her death raises questions. Was it murder or suicide? Was the medieval scold's bridle meant to symbolize something? And why did she leave her fortune to her doctor, Sarah Blakeney? To remove suspicion from herself, Sarah must solve the crime, and in doing so, she uncovers many motives, some of which strike very close to home. Although Walters's books do feature a Mystery to be solved, they focus more on the psychological, and the Mystery is simply one of the elements that make up these unsettling novels.

Other popular authors worth exploring in this genre include Robert Goddard, Stephen Dobyns, and Patricia Carlon. In *Caught in the Light* Goddard writes of English freelance photographer Ian Jarrett, who, while on assignment in Vienna, photographs and then meets an Englishwoman who calls herself Marian Esguard.[12] They agree to meet on their return to England, but all Ian's attempts to contact her are in vain. Who is this woman and what is her connection to the nineteenth-century pioneer photographer of the same name? Goddard takes us on a twisted trail to discover the whereabouts and identity of this mystery woman and eventually reveals both Jarrett's obsession and the plot against him in this convoluted, layered, densely written tale.

In Dobyns's *Church of Dead Girls,* the first-person narration of a past crime pulls the reader into this claustrophobic tale of small-town life and murder.[13] Even though the story is related from the present, looking back at an event in the past, the tension is not lessened and builds as the story unfolds. Dobyns explores what happens in a small, isolated community when three young girls disappear, and how the close-knit, trusting community falls prey to paranoia and vigilantism.

Australian Carlon's understated and very disturbing novels have been published in the United States only within the last few years. Try *The Running Woman,* a richly layered and chilling tale of a young woman accused of murder.[14] As is often the case in this genre, there is a surprising twist at the end.

Preparing to Work with Readers

Readers of Psychological Suspense appreciate dark stories with psychological undertones. Although they may call them Psychological Novels or Psychological Suspense, they may also refer to them as Mysteries, Thrillers, Suspense, or Horror. When they talk about what they enjoy, however, we recognize the books they seek. They expect books that grip them with intense stories and elegant prose.

These are also readers who may read a range of books, across genres, to find the elements they seek. They are likely familiar with the psychological slant of titles in Mystery, Thrillers, Suspense, Horror, and Literary Fiction and, like readers of Literary Fiction, may be willing to experiment with new authors, as long as they meet their standards.

Fans appreciate well-drawn characters that they can observe from afar. Although they like details of their lives and predicaments, they do not expect to be drawn in, to sympathize or even empathize with them, as in some genres. These readers enjoy being observers of others' lives and obsessions. They expect to be distanced from the characters so that they might watch them, evaluate their strategies, and speculate on their success or failure, especially because so many of these novels are unresolved at the end.

Atmospheric stories also appeal to these readers. They anticipate a carefully drawn, detailed setting that also hints at a darker mood. Books in this genre are often more leisurely paced, in part because the detailed setting and mood slow the action, which itself is often interior.

Although twisted plots are often a characteristic of these story lines, readers also look for the intensity that underlines the mood and action. These are not fast paced, but they do exert a tremendous pull on readers. Seldom graphically violent, they more often suggest gruesome ends than show them. Readers look for the building of tension and the layers of meaning that make these such powerful and gripping stories. *See* Figure 9.2 for authors of Psychological Suspense who might appeal to fans of other genres.

FIGURE 9.2

An Introduction to Psychological Suspense Fiction

Psychological Suspense Fiction Writers to Try, If You Enjoy . . .

Fantasy	Jonathan Carroll
Historical	Thomas H. Cook
Horror	Jonathan Carroll
	Stephen King (Misery and Gerald's Game)[15]
Literary	Ruth Rendell
Mystery	Minette Walters
	Anna Gilbert
Suspense	Thomas William Simpson (The Caretaker)[16]
	Rosamund Smith
Women's Lives	Nicci French (Beneath the Skin)[17]
	Philippa Gregory (The Little House)[18]

Readers' Advisory Interview

When we work with readers, we always ask them to describe books they have enjoyed and listen for clues in preparing to suggest possible titles. In Psychological Suspense especially, we can listen for particular words that suggest that this is what readers are looking for. Do they describe disturbing books that deal with obsessions? Do they mention layers of meaning? Do they allude to a haunting quality? If so, titles in this genre would be a good choice.

As we look at books we are not necessarily familiar with, we can tell by flipping through the pages that a book is more densely written if there is less white space on the page. (White space suggests dialogue, and because this emphasizes description more than conversation, there is likely less dialogue.) Readers appreciate this kind of information, as it helps them make their own selections when faced with a variety of titles. Here, too, book jacket descriptions are often fairly clear about the psychological impact of the titles, although they may also veer into related genres, such as Horror.

Sure Bets

In this, as in all genres, there are authors who appeal consistently to fans and are good suggestions for others whom we suspect may also enjoy the genre. Scott Smith's *A Simple Plan* is one of these.[19] When two brothers and a friend discover a vast amount of money in the wreckage of a small airplane, they take the money, deciding to hide it until the search for the plane—and the money—is over. This turns out to be a fateful decision, however, which demands other choices from among increasingly poor options, and their lives spiral downward, as doubts lead to murder. This is a compulsively readable nightmare tale, which, although it does not involve the more obvious madness of some other titles in the genre, produces the same mood in the story and the same feeling in readers.

Minette Walters and Stephen Dobyns, described above, also make excellent suggestions for general readers who might enjoy the elements of books in this genre. And even though many of her books were written in the '50s, Patricia Highsmith proves an excellent choice, as her writing remains undated and very accessible.

Expanding Readers' Horizons

Every reader in every genre reaches the point when that genre does not offer enough of interest. They are ready for a change, but they may not want to range too far afield. That is when we examine the genre and think about ways that it links to other genres and to authors within those genres.

As is clear from the previous discussion, there is extensive crossover appeal to other genres for fans. Readers of Psychological Suspense find numerous writers of Mysteries who meet their requirements. Suggest Caleb Carr's murky tales set in turn-of-the-century New York City (*The Alienist*) or Elizabeth George (*A Great Deliverance*) and P. D. James (especially *Original Sin*) with their dark, psychological stories of detection.[20]

There is a range of Thrillers that might interest these readers as well, from the classic, interior stories of Graham Greene and John le Carré to those of someone like William Bayer, who writes fast-paced, action-centered, but quite violent Thrillers. The link with the first two may be more obvious in their pacing and themes, but Bayer, despite the increased action and violence writes, in stories such as *Blind Side,* twisted tales with a haunting quality that stays with readers.[21] Evan Hunter (*Criminal Conversation*) writes dark Crime Thrillers that might also appeal to readers of Psychological Suspense.[22]

Literary Fiction, with its elegantly written, often provocative plots offers other possibilities. Timothy Findley, with his disturbing tales of dreams and reality, is a good choice. Try *Headhunter,* which looses Kurtz and Joseph Conrad's *The Heart of Darkness* on a futuristic Toronto, to appreciate his chilling effect.[23] Joyce Carol Oates, D. M. Thomas (particularly, *The White Hotel*),[24] and John Fowles would also be good suggestions. Some of the Science Fiction written by the provocative philosophical writers—Roger Zelazny, Robert Silverberg, and Gene Wolfe, for example—also provide the psychological emphasis, the elegant prose, and the open endings fans of this genre prize. And certainly Horror writer Anne Rice would be a possibility, with her interior glimpses into the minds and lives of vampires and other ghouls, as would some of Stephen King's novels (*Misery,* for example).

Suspense offers a range of writers that might appeal to the Psychological Suspense reader looking for a change of pace. Marilyn

Wallace, in novels such as *Lost Angel* and *The Seduction,* offers claustrophobic stories of obsession.[25] Gary Devon is another name to know. *Wedding Night* owes a debt to Highsmith's subtle, obsessive characters and Mary Higgins Clark's softer Suspense, but it is a chilling story.[26] *Bad Desire* is a more disturbing and violent story of a murder-for-hire gone wrong.[27]

Serial killer novels, Hard-Edged Suspense, often cross over with Psychological Suspense, even though the pacing is usually at odds. Dean R. Koontz's *Intensity* is not to be missed by these fans.[28] This harrowing, atmospheric tale of a psychopathic killer offers all the elements fans of Psychological Suspense appreciate, even though it moves at a faster pace. And there is no denying that Thomas Harris's *Hannibal,* discussed in depth in chapter 13, "Suspense," would be of Interest to readers of Psychological Suspense.[29] Hannibal Lecter, the looming menace whose presence pervades *The Silence of the Lambs,* is the hero here (or, more appropriately, the antihero), and the manner in which Harris manipulates us readers, pulling us into the story so that we sympathize with the man we know we should despise, will fascinate fans of Psychological Suspense.[30] *See* Figure 9.3 for additional authors to suggest to take readers beyond the genre.

Reference Sources

If there were any doubts about the fact that Psychological Suspense overlaps with a wide range of genres, they will be dispelled in examining reference sources. We find references to this genre in a variety of other genre reference books, from the more general ones to specific titles for Horror and Mystery. As a result, no one source stands out as the best. In looking for these authors, we are best served by keeping our own lists. However, some of the general resources, examined in more detail in appendix 2, serve as excellent starting points.

I find *NoveList* particularly good for this kind of search that does not follow established genre lines. Typing "Psychological" in the Describe a Plot search yields hundreds of possibilities of different types of "Psychological Fiction." However, using the Browse Subject function, we can see what subheadings we might choose to narrow the search.

FIGURE 9.3

Expanding Readers' Horizons

Authors to Take Readers beyond the Psychological Suspense Genre

Fantasy	Stephen King (Dark Tower series)
Horror	Anne Rice
Literary	Joyce Carol Oates
	Timothy Findley
Mystery	Caleb Carr
	Elizabeth George
	Carol O'Connell
Science Fiction	Roger Zelazny
	Gene Wolfe
Suspense	Marilyn Wallace
	Dean R. Koontz (*Intensity*)
	Thomas Harris (*Hannibal*)
Thriller	Graham Greene
	William Bayer
	Evan Hunter

Where to Find . . .

INFORMATION ABOUT THE AUTHOR

Contemporary Authors, that standard literary reference source described in appendix 2, should be our first stop in seeking information about the authors. Again, because of genreblending, and also because some of the authors write in more than one genre, the St. James Press series should also be consulted, especially *St. James Guide to Horror, Ghost, and Gothic Writers,* described in chapter 6, and *St. James Guide to Crime and Mystery Writers,* described in chapter 8. *Killer Books,* by Jean Swanson and Dean James, described in detail in chapter 8, also has a chapter on authors who write "Suspense/Pyschological Mysteries," and their descriptions are often very useful in identifying an author's appeal and possible read-alikes.

PLOT SUMMARIES

Many of the general sources described in appendix 2 have annotations for the titles they include. *Fiction Catalog* uses the subject heading "Psychological" to access these titles, as does *What Do I Read Next? NoveList*, as mentioned above, is a good source. The variety of index terms used by reference sources requires us to be more inventive in our pursuit of these books.

SUBGENRES AND THEMES

Although no source identifies subgenres or even themes, they differ widely in what they call these novels and thus in how they place these books within other genres or subgenres. *Hooked on Horror,* described in chapter 6, makes a strong case for Psychological Suspense as a subgenre of Horror; Scribner's *Mystery and Suspense Writers* has an essay on Psychological Suspense; *What Do I Read Next?* makes it a category of the Thriller theme; in *Genreflecting,* we can find examples under both Horror and Suspense. Clearly, this is a genre that overlaps at many points, and this fact provides even more opportunities for us to help readers explore related areas.

GENRE DESCRIPTION, BACKGROUND, AND HISTORY

Both the essays in Scribner's *Mystery and Suspense Writers* and *Hooked on Horror* provide background on this rather nebulous genre.

Fans of Psychological Suspense value these carefully crafted stories for the spare, elegant prose. Not a word or image is ever wasted. As in the best short stories, every piece is important and adds a layer of knowledge and tension for the reader. And although style is certainly important to readers, they relish the twist at the end even more. Much is not really as it appears in novels of Psychological Suspense, and its many fans enjoy both the presentation and the unraveling of the puzzle.

NOTES

1. Henry James, "The Turn of the Screw" (New York: Heritage Press, 1949).

2. Frances Fyfield, *Blind Date* (New York: Viking, 1998).

3. Thomas H. Cook, *Instruments of Night* (New York: Bantam, 1998).

4. J. P. Smith, *The Discovery of Light* (New York: Viking, 1992).

5. Paul Griner, *Collectors* (New York: Random House, 1999).

6. John Fowles, *The Collector* (New York: Little, Brown, 1963).

7. Patricia Highsmith, *Strangers on a Train* (New York: Harper & Brothers, 1950).

8. ———, *The Talented Mr. Ripley* (New York: Vintage Books, 1992). Originally published in New York by Coward-McCann, 1955.

9. Jane Hitchcock, *Trick of the Eye* (New York: E. P. Dutton, 1992).

10. Ruth A. Rendell, *Sight for Sore Eyes* (New York: Crown, 1999, © 1998).

11. Minette Walters, *The Scold's Bridle* (New York: St. Martin's, 1994).

12. Robert Goddard, *Caught in the Light* (New York: Holt, 1999).

13. Stephen Dobyns, *Church of Dead Girls* (New York: Metropolitan Books, 1997).

14. Patricia Carlon, *The Running Woman* (New York: Soho Press, 1998).

15. Stephen King, *Misery* (New York: Viking, 1987); ———, *Gerald's Game* (New York: Viking, 1992).

16. Thomas William Simpson, *The Caretaker* (New York: Bantam, 1998).

17. Nicci French, *Beneath the Skin* (New York: Mysterious Press, 2000).

18. Philippa Gregory, *The Little House* (New York: HarperCollins, 1996).

19. Scott Smith, *A Simple Plan* (New York: Knopf, 1993).

20. Caleb Carr, *The Alienist* (New York: Random House, 1994); Elizabeth George, *A Great Deliverance* (Toronto, New York: Bantam, 1988); P. D. James, *Original Sin* (New York: Knopf, 1994).

21. William Bayer, *Blind Side* (New York: Villard, 1989).

22. Evan Hunter, *Criminal Conversation* (New York: Warner Books, 1994).

23. Timothy Findley, *Headhunter* (New York: Crown, 1994).

24. D. M. Thomas, *The White Hotel* (New York: Viking, 1981).

25. Marilyn Wallace, *Lost Angel* (New York: Doubleday, 1996); ———, *The Seduction* (New York: Doubleday, 1993).

26. Gary Devon, *Wedding Night* (New York: Avon, 1997).

27. ———, *Bad Desire* (New York: Random House, 1990).

28. Dean R. Koontz, *Intensity* (New York: Knopf, 1995).

29. Thomas Harris, *Hannibal* (New York: Delacorte, 1999).

30. ———, *The Silence of the Lambs* (New York: St. Martin's, 1988).

10

Romance

Imagine the following familiar scenario. On one side of the service desk we have a Romance reader, who is looking for a new book by her favorite author. Or perhaps she has read everything by that author, and she needs some readers' advisory assistance, perhaps some suggestions of new authors. She is a little wary of approaching library staff, because many people, and perhaps especially the librarians she has encountered, seem to deplore her reading taste. She knows, in a general way, what she likes about Romances: the independent heroines, the happy ending, and, especially, the feeling of satisfaction she gets from the Romances she reads. However, she may not be able to put these emotional responses into words. She may be embarrassed to ask about Romances and describe the kind of Romances she likes— perhaps the ones with explicit sex—and is certainly uneasy about asking for assistance.

On the other side of the desk, we have the librarian. Unless we librarians are Romance readers as well, what we feel when faced with a fan of the genre has been put succinctly by one of my staff: genuine fear. Most of us are terrified when a Romance reader asks for assistance. Every time we seek to assist readers in genres in which we are not well read, we feel uncomfortable and inadequate. How on earth can we help readers if we know little or nothing about the genre they love?

Unfortunately, a patron's embarrassment plus a librarian's fear do not produce a satisfactory readers' advisory interview. All too often, this scenario reflects reality, although an increasing number of librarians have discovered the appeal of this vast genre and have more success working with readers. However, in any genre in which the appeal is primarily to the emotions and thus difficult to verbalize, readers and librarians have more difficulty working together, and Romance is no exception.

A Definition

Every Romance reader, whether she has actually formulated it or not, has her own definition of the genre, based on the books she has read and enjoyed. How that affects the readers' advisory interview with Romance readers is discussed later in this chapter.

Defining a genre so large and diverse that it accounts for approximately 50 percent of all paperback fiction sales is not an easy task. This immense genre covers a wide range of books—from contemporary to historical, racy to gentle, realistic to paranormal, and much in between. Still, definitions help us focus our energies, come to terms with the genre, and better understand its fans.

In *Romance Fiction: A Guide to the Genre*, Kristin Ramsdell defines Romance as "a love story in which the central focus is on the development and satisfactory resolution of the love relationship between the two main characters, written in such a way as to provide the reader with some degree of vicarious emotional participation in the courtship process."[1] These are the two keys to Romance fiction. First, in Romances, the plot revolves around the love relationship and its inevitable happy ending; all else that happens is secondary. Other genres certainly rely on romantic themes, and we talk later about the appeal of these stories to Romance readers. In books that fall within the Romance genre, however, the romantic relationships in the story are the focus.

Secondly, these stories are told in such a way that the reader is involved in the outcome of the Romance; the reader participates on an emotional level and experiences genuine satisfaction at the inevitable happy ending. Although it is true that we may feel an emotional involvement with the characters in books in other genres, here it is the focus of the reader's participation in the story. We experience the story on an emotional level, and this makes our satisfaction in its outcome hard to explain to someone unfamiliar with the genre. In school we are neither taught nor expected to appreciate stories on this emotional level, and the fact that satisfaction with this genre depends so heavily on this element makes the appeal of the genre hard to explain to nonfans and difficult even for fans to understand and acknowledge.

Characteristics and the Genre's Appeal

Five elements characterize the Romance genre. Readers experience additional appeal elements in the different subgenres, but the five elements listed in Figure 10.1 should be discernable in all Romances.

Frame

As does Horror, Romance appeals first to our emotions. This is one of the reasons fans find the genre so difficult to talk about: It is almost impossible for them to characterize what it is that they enjoy. The key to the appeal of Romances is the evocative, romantic tone. Readers expect to be drawn in, to identify with the characters and their relationship, to experience these stories. It is the tone or atmosphere that prompts this vicarious emotional participation on the part of the reader. Through it, the author engages the reader's feelings to create an emotional involvement in the Romance. The tone may be upbeat throughout or may include darker moments, but the end always produces a satisfactory resolution.

This emotional pull forms one of the key factors of the success of Nora Roberts, for example, especially in her paperback series, which are more often pure Romance, without much secondary Suspense or Mystery. In the MacGregor series, featuring the curmudgeonly father-grandfather who engineers the romantic entanglements that occupy his children and grandchildren, this softer, involving, romantic tone pervades the novels.[2] We feel the power of love on all levels: parents

---

FIGURE 10.1

Characteristics of Romances

1. The evocative, emotional tone demands that readers be drawn in, that they experience this love story with its requisite happy ending.

2. The story features either a misunderstanding between the hero and heroine or outside circumstances that force them apart, followed by the ultimate resolution of their romantic relationship. Social and moral issues increasingly play a role in the story lines of Romances, although they are always secondary and do not interfere with the happy ending.

3. Characters are easily identifiable types. Men are handsome, strong, distant, and dangerous; women are strong, bright, independent, and often beautiful.

4. Although Romances usually can be read fairly quickly and are called fast paced by their fans, they can be stopped and started easily, without losing the story line.

5. Language plays an important role in setting the stage. The language of a Romance is instantly recognizable, with extensive use of descriptive adjectives to delineate characters, setting, and romantic or sexual interludes.

---

to children, among siblings and friends, with lovers. This tone may be difficult to define, but fans recognize it and respond to the atmosphere it creates.

Readers tell us they get a special feeling from reading Romances, and they read them to experience that emotional satisfaction of being part of a love story and its inevitable happy ending. That is why it is so hard even for those of us who read Romances to talk about what we enjoy and why—and for those who do not read Romances to recognize this attraction. It is a feeling the author creates. We expect it, and if we do not find it, the book simply is not as satisfying.

Certainly the tone in Romances may vary from book to book. Some are lighthearted, like Cathie Linz's Marriage Makers series, featuring an inept trio of fairy godmothers who accidentally distribute opposing virtues (for example, common sense together with sex appeal) with gusto and then help sort out the consequences.[3] Others, like Jennifer Crusie's laugh-out-loud *Crazy for You,* combine a light-hearted tone with more serious issues, including a crazed ex-boyfriend turned stalker.[4] Still others are darker, bleaker, even though the conclusion provides the requisite happy ending. Many of Mary Balogh's Historical Romances strike this tone; for example, *Tangled* is a Romance full of dark secrets among a trio of friends—and lovers—with the action set around the Crimean War.[5]

Story Line

The focus of the story line in the Romance is the romantic relationship and its resolution. All else that happens may be interesting, but it is secondary to the resolution of the relationship. By the way, we can always identify a Romance by that first kiss, which is like no other. The hero awakens passions in himself and the heroine that they have never experienced before. If you read Romances, you know what I mean.

Marriage between the hero and heroine does not always occur within the story itself; however, they must recognize and affirm their love, and the suggestion of marriage at some point is almost de rigueur. If this recognition and affirmation of love does not occur, the book is not a Romance—or certainly not a satisfying one. Robert James Waller's *The Bridges of Madison County* is a good example of a romantic book that is not a Romance.[6] Although critics and reviewers called this popular title a Romance, fans of the genre did not agree. In Romances the lovers are not separated at the conclusion of the novel, and that ending gives Waller's book a completely different feel.

This is not to say that many of us do not enjoy the added elements of Adventure, Intrigue, or Mystery found in authors such as Jayne Ann Krentz (for example, *Grand Passion,* with its mysterious legacy) or Nora Roberts (*Hidden Riches,* which combines antiques and intrigue), or the background on Regency customs and mores one finds in Marion Chesney (her House for a Season series provides an introduction to life above and below stairs; *The Miser of Mayfair* is the first), as well as extra details related to gems or antique books or paleontology that one also finds in many Romances, for example, those by Ann Maxwell (*The Ruby* features both the gemstone and Faberge eggs) and Amanda Quick (*Ravished* features fossils along with romance).[7] These are, however, pleasant extras. The point of the story line is the consummation of the romantic relationship. In the Romance, the hero and heroine will resolve their difficulties and discover their love. We read Romances because we find it so satisfying to participate in the courtship process. We read them for the emotional "high" they provide.

In her scholarly study of the Romance genre, *Dangerous Men and Adventurous Women*, Krentz writes in an essay with Linda Barlow that "her future happiness and his depend on her ability to teach him to love."[8] That is the key to the story line of Romances, and the plot is structured around this process. An example of this is Susan Carroll's *The Bride Finder.*[9] The hero, Anatole, rejected by his mother and ignored by his father, never learned to love. Now, brought the perfect bride by the eponymous bride finder, he must overcome his pride and admit his deficiency, his lack of understanding of the nature of love, before he and his wife can find happiness. Although Romances guarantee a happy ending, with the love relationship resolved, not all Romances are merely sweetness and light. Moral and social issues are often secondary themes in Romances. Kathleen Korbel's RITA Award–winning *A Soldier's Heart* deals with the very real problem of post-traumatic stress disorder among soldiers and nurses who served in Vietnam.[10] Several Regencies, including Mary Jo Putney's *The Rake* and Charlotte Louise Dolan's *The Unofficial Suitor,* address the social ills of that time (early nineteenth century), from alcoholism and other addictions to the problems of workers and factories.[11] In addition, countless Romances deal with the role of women in society and efforts throughout history to improve their plight. Social issues and taboos have long found a forum in the Romance genre.

Characterization

In a Romance the hero and heroine alike must come to terms with themselves and their relationships with each other. As readers, we see interior as well as exterior aspects of these characters, and we respond to them and their developing relationship. Although the characterization in Romance may, by necessity of the formula, be stereotypical, there is no question that in the best of the genre, the characters grow and change as they learn to love. In *Dream a Little Dream* Susan Elizabeth Phillips explores complex family relationships and the difficult concepts of guilt, forgiveness, and grief.[12] Although these affect the protagonists and force them to grow and mature, these themes do not detract from the power of the Romance. In fact, it is because of the environment the Romance creates, one in which the characters feel safe sharing their deepest emotions, that healing finally comes.

This growth, however, is not limited only to those Romances with a more serious side. In almost all, the characters are forced to change, to relinquish preconceptions about themselves (often their lack of self-worth) and the opposite sex before they are able to embrace the romantic union readers demand. For example, in Betina Krahn's *The Last Bachelor,* avenging widow Antonia Paxton makes a career of marrying off "surplus women" by setting them up in society and then forcing marriages when young rakes try to seduce them.[13] The unhappy gentlemen enlist the help of London's most outspoken bachelor, Remington Carr, the Earl of Landon, to stop her. Both Carr and Antonia come to recognize, understand, and accept each other's point of view before the story's satisfactory culmination.

That characters are stereotypes is important, too. The women are bright, independent, strong, and, perhaps surprisingly, not always beautiful but certainly interesting and articulate. The men must be strong, distant, and always dangerous, because the stronger the hero, the greater the victory when the heroine brings him to his senses and his knees. Conquering a gentle, affectionate, mild-mannered, sensible hero simply is not as satisfying, either for the heroine or for the reader.

The best also include well-developed, interesting, and often quirky secondary characters. For example, Patricia Veryan relies on a cast of characters in her various series of linked romances featuring Romance and Intrigue in Georgian England (start with *Practice to Deceive,* in the Golden Chronicles series, to get a good idea of Veryan's style).[14] Main characters from one volume reappear as secondary characters to enhance a later story.

One last important point about characterization is that we almost always get two points of view, that of both hero and heroine. This allows us to experience their inner dilemmas and follow their thoughts, as the characters work out their relationship. This is not just *her* story; it is his as well. Romances are almost never written first-person; the reader, and author, require the third-person perspective to create the full picture, to reveal easily the inner thoughts and struggles of both hero and heroine. For example, Carola Dunn's *His Lordship's Reward,* the sequel to *Miss Jacobson's Journey,* is more his story than hers.[15] The first novel tells of a dangerous trip across France and Spain with a British agent and a young woman transporting gold to Wellington's army. The sequel follows this agent after the war as he finds his own happiness in an unexpected quarter back in England.

Pacing

Fans tell us that Romances are fast reading, another endorsement of their appeal, because their primary readership is busy women, from housewives to executives, who may have little time for reading novels that move at a more leisurely pace. Because they are character centered, Romances rely more on dialogue than description, and they are seldom written in dense, more difficult prose. Romances are written to be accessible and easily read. Although a variety of events may take place, the stories are constructed so they can be put down, when a reader is interrupted. When that reader picks it up again, she falls right back into the story. This, again, is a big part of the appeal. In fact, readers tell us this is one of the reasons they enjoy them. Although the books may move quickly and can be read quickly, the reading can also be stopped and started frequently without losing the story line.

Style

Finally, writers use language to create the romantic tone and emotional attraction readers seek. One can identify a Romance in the first few pages, just by observing the way the story is constructed and language used. Romances are descriptive, and writers rely on adjectives to describe characters and places, as well as to set the mood. The vocabulary sets the tone and the stage for the Romance. In fact, writers such as Tami Hoag and Sandra Brown, who now write harder-edged Romantic Suspense instead of the Romances that established their reputations, have kept much of their Romance-reading audience, in part because they have retained the language of the Romance, even though their more suspenseful books do not fit within the Romance genre. The descriptions of character and place pull the readers into the story, allowing them to "see" the action, to participate more fully in the Romantic Suspense story. The books feel and read like Romances, even though the focus is different and the action more violent.

Key Authors and Subgenres

Although Romance, like every genre, is always changing, *New York Times* best-selling author Nora Roberts is certainly the first name most readers mention when they talk of Romance. A publishing phenomenon, Roberts has written more than 100 novels and continues to write about 10 a year. Interestingly she still writes category Romances (for Silhouette) and paperback single-title Romances. (Many authors, when they make the transition to hardcover, leave the paperback publishers—and audiences—behind.) Roberts also writes hardcover Romantic Suspense and a paperback futuristic series, the latter under the pseudonym J. D. Robb. No wonder she is an almost continual presence on best-sellers lists!

Roberts's category Romances remain the truest to the Romance genre, but recent trilogies—the Concannon Trilogy,[16] set in Ireland and featuring two sisters and their unknown half sister; the Dream Trilogy,[17] which follows three close women friends, their lives, their loves, and their search for a legendary treasure; and the Quinn Brothers Trilogy,[18] the story of four "bad boys," adopted by a professor and his physician wife, and the secret of the youngest's true parentage—also all meet the requirements for the Romance genre, even though they are longer books that feature secondary themes. Her newer hardcover titles really fit more appropriately in chapter 11, "Romantic Suspense," but even in these, Romance is an important element, and her books remain popular with a wide range of readers. All her books are characterized by a clash between the resourceful, passionate heroine and the strong man who listens and protects but who also respects her independence. These are fast-paced stories with a full measure of sexual tension and often explicit sex. Relationships, between family members, friends, and lovers, form the core of her plots, with secrets and treasures often adding an interesting frame.

Subgenres of Romance

There are currently several popular subgenres of Romance. Here I consider Contemporary, Historical, and Alternative Reality (which includes futuristic, time travel, and paranormal). As in all other chapters, these are appeal-based subdivisions, because a very real appeal, often the deciding factor in whether to read a Romance or not, involves the time in which the novel is set. Most readers have a definite preference, and although they may be able to tolerate a wider range of sex or setting or type of characters, they are more likely to prefer one time period over the others. Examples of category Romances, generally smaller in size and scope and written to a more precise publisher's formula, are considered within the larger subgenres. Ethnic Romances and Inspirational Romances are becoming increasingly popular, and important authors are highlighted within the subgenres. Genres that overlap with Romance are addressed separately throughout this book. Novels of Women's Lives and Relationships are considered separately, in chapter 16. Romantic Suspense, another subgenre often linked with Romance, is considered in chapter 11.

CONTEMPORARY ROMANCES

Constituting more than 50 percent of Romances published today, Contemporary Romances take place generally during the time period in which they are written. Thus, classic Romances by Elizabeth Cadell or Grace Livingston Hill, which may seem Historical to readers today, really fall within this subgenre. They make no concerted attempt to define and elucidate a historical setting; they simply reflect the times, culture, and mores in which they were written. In addition to reflecting the characteristics of Romances in general, Contemporary Romances also share the traits shown in Figure 10.2.

Contemporary Romances written today assign greater emphasis to the heroine and her professional life than previously, reflecting the importance placed on this dual role for women by society today. Women pursue careers before and during marriage, as well as before and fre-

---

FIGURE 10.2

Characteristics of Contemporary Romances

1. There is more emphasis on the heroine and her fulfillment professionally as well as personally.
2. The heroine is less likely to be innocent or virginal. The books present modern, rather than conventional, values.

---

quently after having children. Romances clearly reflect changes in society in this regard. In the novels of award-winning author of contemporary romances Jennifer Greene, for example, the women are career women before their marriage, and they plan to continue with their careers afterward, adapting, along with their cooperative husbands, to the issues involved in creating a time for family as well as career. Fulfillment on all levels is important—emotional, intellectual, and familial.

Another characteristic of today's Contemporary Romances is that the heroine is less likely to be the innocent young girl of decades past. Not only might she be a high-powered career woman, she is also likely to have had some experience with men, and she is probably not a virgin. Not that the innocent, virginal Contemporary Romances do not exist, but they are more difficult to find, except among some of the category Romances (Harlequin Romances and Silhouette Romances) and especially among Inspirational Romance publishers such as Heartsong, Bethany House, Harvest House, Multnomah Publishers, Tyndale House Publishers, and Zondervan. This change again reflects a shift in contemporary society; most readers do not expect the virginal heroines, and few publishers seek books featuring such characters. Books that reflect "modern values" (sex before marriage, previous sexual partners) rather than "conventional values" (the heroine, and possibly the hero, are virgins, and there is no sex before the wedding night) are simply more accepted in today's marketplace.

Along with Roberts, Jayne Ann Krentz is one of the most recognized authors of Contemporary Romances. She also has the distinction of writing best-selling Historical (as Amanda Quick) and Alternative Reality (as Jayne Castle) Romances, a feat that makes her unique in the genre. Krentz's novels are generally characterized by humor, quirky secondary characters, well-developed social settings with extended families and friends, interesting frames (from art to catering to glass blowing and much in between), scintillating conversation, and explicit sex. Her Contemporary Romances feature strong-willed, articulate women, who successfully manage high-powered, interesting careers without losing touch with close family and friends, not to mention developing a strong attachment to the troublesome heroes, whom they whip into shape. *Wildest Hearts,* with its quirky characters, empathetic heroine and hero, and mix of humor with serious family and relationship issues, is typical of her style.[19]

Susan Elizabeth Phillips's growing popularity attests to her new prominence as one of the foremost writers of Contemporary Romance. A good introduction to her writing is *It Had to Be You,* first in a series of linked novels featuring players from the Chicago Stars football team.[20] Set in Chicago and its suburbs—many of her novels are set in the Midwest where she lives—this features supposed airhead Phoebe Somerville, who will inherit the football team if she can just win the league championship. Needless to say, sparks fly between Phoebe and coach Dan Calebow; in fact, each is everything the other despises—until they finally discover something in common: their very intense passion for each other. The journeys to the title championship and their own romantic resolution may be rocky, but they are also humorous and touching. Interesting heroines with more depth than may at first appear, unexpected heroes (often active men involved in sports with as much brain as brawn), sparkling dialogue, explicit sex, and a general lighthearted approach, even if controversial issues are introduced and resolved, characterize Phillips's writing.

Debbie Macomber's writing offers a change of pace from Phillips and Krentz. Generally more innocent, the heroines are involved in heartwarming adventures, with more emphasis placed on domestic, rather than exotic, settings. Try *Lonesome Cowboy,* first of her Hearts of Texas series, which are not explicitly Christian romances but stories of gentle inspiration that often appeal to readers of Christian fiction as well as others who like gentle, small-town romances.[21]

Although there are certainly examples with historical settings, most Ethnic or Multi-Cultural Romances published today seem to feature contemporary settings. For example, Sandra Kitt, Bette Ford, Eboni Snow, and Francis Ray write of the African American experiences in contemporary society. Ruth Wind examines Latino culture, or the mix of cultures, as in her RITA Award–winning *Meant to Be Married,* in which a family feud has kept lovers apart.[22]

HISTORICAL ROMANCES

These Romances, which comprise 31.5 percent of books published in the genre, all assign some importance to the details of the historical setting in which they are placed. Although they are not as demanding in their insistence on extensive historical details as the Historical novels, discussed in chapter 5, many, especially those set in the Regency period, do emphasize accuracy in the trappings, the backdrop against which the Romance is played out. Certainly capturing the feel of the times is of prime importance. Real historical personages who play roles must be portrayed as accurately as possible, and details of the time may be more or less extensive, but no less accurate. For example, in Elisabeth Fairchild's *Marriage a la Mode,* Melodey Bainbridge is a woman scorned by society because she seeks a divorce from her abusive husband.[23] Her story is played out against the background of Queen Caroline's marital problems with George IV, so that real historical personages and their stories feature prominently in this darker Romance. Susan Johnson, using a slightly different approach, makes extensive use of footnotes to underscore the accuracy of her historical details, as in *Sinful,* in which hoyden Chelsea Ferguson arranges to be deflowered by the handsome Duke of Seth, rather than be married off to a man she does not love.[24] Unfortunately, neither of the pair is able to admit to loving the other, and it takes a journey to Tunis and back, with both held captive for stealing horses, to bring them to their senses. *See* Figure 10.3 for characteristics of this subgenre.

Others may simply have a "timeless" quality of being set in the unidentified past. Elizabeth Lowell's medieval Romances, for example *Enchanted,* exemplify this feeling and technique.[25] Although they are generally set in medieval Britain, the minimal historical detail could be altered slightly to allow them to take place in any of several more primitive times and countries, and descriptive details do not necessarily ground these stories in specific times and places. The times themselves

---

FIGURE 10.3

Characteristics of Historical Romances

1. In many, the details of a specific historical setting and characters in that time are important, although others may simply have a "timeless" quality, as if the characters, and the reader, are simply dropped into an indefinite time in the past.
2. Elements of Adventure, Intrigue, and Mystery often enhance the story.

---

are not as important as the passion, the warrior lords, and the women strong enough to capture their hearts and share their strength.

Another characteristic of Historical Romances is that they more frequently include additional elements of Adventure, Espionage, or Mystery, without diverging into Romantic Suspense, as Contemporary Romances seem more likely to do. Mary Jo Putney is an excellent example. Her Fallen Angels series of linked novels, following the exploits of a group of university friends, includes Adventure and Espionage with satisfying Romance, and the characters from previous titles in the series frequently reappear as secondary characters so readers can continue to follow events in their lives. *Dancing on the Wind,* second in her Fallen Angels series, features Lucien, Lord Strathmore, who infiltrates the notorious Hellion's Club (based, according to the author's note, on the actual Hellfire Club) looking for a traitor.[26] There he encounters Kit, seeking her twin sister who has disappeared. He believes she is spying on him, and although the sexual spark between the two is evident from the first, actual love and trust come much later. Adventure, Intrigue, Romance, and the particular relationship between twins add to this Historical Romance.

Krentz's alter ego Amanda Quick serves as the benchmark for Historical Romances. Her racy Historicals reflect the same humor, quirky characters, explicit sex, and element of Adventure that readers find in her Contemporaries. To get a sense of her style, try *Mistress,* a racy Regency in which bluestocking Iphiginia Bright tries to save her aunt from a blackmailer by posing as the mistress of one of society's most imposing men, Marcus Cloud, the Earl of Masters, who seems to have disappeared.[27] Unfortunately for Iphiginia, he reappears just in time to catch her in this deception, although he ultimately helps her capture the villain.

Other popular writers in this subgenre are Julie Garwood, Jo Beverley, and Mary Balogh. Although best-selling author Julie Garwood began her writing career producing Medieval and English Historical Romances, today she writes primarily Historical Romances set in America. *For the Roses* tells the story of three homeless "brothers" who find a baby girl, whom they name Mary Rose, and whom they take to Montana to raise.[28] It exhibits Garwood's characteristic humor, passion, and family emphasis, with a little mystery—the secret of Mary Rose's birth—adding an extra dimension.

Beverley's award-winning Historical Romances cover several periods—Medieval, Georgian, and Regency—and offer sweet Regencies, as well as longer, more sensuous novels that deal with serious social issues and often add elements of Adventure and Intrigue. Like Putney and others, she writes series of linked Romances. One charts the adventures of the Company of Rogues and is set during the Regency period. The second, the Malloren series, follows that family in Georgian England. Despite the seriousness of issues she often addresses, from abusive husbands to forced marriages and rape, humor often fills her novels. In *Forbidden Magic,* a missing *sheelagh* (a mystical Irish statue that grants wishes—but not always in the way one hopes), an earl desperate to marry to keep his promise to his grandmother, and a penniless young woman, left with four siblings to raise and threatened by a lascivious landlord, combine in a plot that can only lead to happiness for all, but the trip through the story's events is full of potential disasters.[29] (This book also contains, to my mind at least, one of the greatest lines in Historical Romances, as the hero wryly comments, "We live to amuse. What else are nobility for?"[30] Fans of Regencies agree: What else, indeed.)

Balogh's titles run the gamut from mostly innocent and gently humorous Regency Romances to more serious and sensual Historical Romances, with much in between. Balogh's heartwarming and frequently lighthearted Romances have a wide-ranging appeal, but generally they are distinguished by her ability to create a story that intertwines strong romantic and family concerns with other social problems. Several linked Regencies trace the adventures of friends and family, beginning with *Courting Julia,* in which the heiress Julia must choose a husband from among expectant would-be heirs and fortune hunters.[31] Further adventures follow the exploits of other characters introduced here.

Balogh's non-Regency Romances frequently go further in addressing social issues and problems of the day. These books are often darker in tone, as would be expected because of the seriousness of the plotlines, and have a completely different "feel" than the lighter, humorous Regencies. In *Thief of Dreams* Balogh introduces heiress Cassandra, the Countess of Worthing, who, on her twenty-first birthday when she is independent at last, meets Nigel Wetherby, a man of many secrets.[32] When he marries her after a whirlwind courtship, and against the wishes of her friends and former guardian, the drama unfolds and secrets emerge, most of them unpleasant concerning his own mission and the character of her late father.

Regencies remain one of the most popular subgenres of Historical Romances. Publishers tend to downplay this subgenre, currently cutting back on the number of titles, but loyal fans, in my library at least, are demanding more. Regency novels are set in England around the turn of the nineteenth century, just before and during the Regency period, when the Prince of Wales, who later became George IV, served as regent for his mad father, George III. Regencies re-create this historical period, focusing on details of dress, food, and manners, which create a backdrop for the Romance. A current trend in the subgenre also emphasizes a strong family feeling, and children play an important role in many of the stories. Regency Romances have a broad appeal, with enough style and society for sophisticated readers, often not much sex, wonderful humor—usually a spirited heroine with lively verbal sparring between hero and heroine, not to mention quirky secondary characters and humorous, sometimes even bizarre, animals—and a satisfying Romance, as well as those historical details (of carriages, clothing, and battles and characters from the Napoleonic Wars) for readers who want a little more.

Georgette Heyer, who wrote from the '20s into the '70s, set the standard for these witty Historical Romances, complete with extensive details of fashion and society. (*Faro's Daughter*, which also introduces the social issues implicit with a heroine who assists her aunt in a gaming house, provides a good example of her novels.)[33] Then, in the '80s, Marion Chesney revived the subgenre with several series of humorous Regencies, often featuring the fates of nobility and servants alike, as well as single titles. (Her first series, The Six Sisters Saga, focuses on the fates of the six daughters of a profligate clergyman, who schemes to wed them all above their station.)[34] More recently, award-winner Carla Kelly embodies the gentler side of this subgenre. Gentle humor and Romance underscore her stories, which focus primarily on the fates of women and children during this period. (In the RITA Award–winning *The Lady's Companion,* the heroine makes a rather daring decision: to make her own way in the world rather than remain dependent on the men who continually fail her.)[35]

Many of the authors of larger English Historical Romances—Putney, Beverley, Balogh, Kasey Michaels, and Jane Feather—write Regencies as well. Others, like Chesney, have made their reputation writing these witty, amusing novels in the tradition of classic Regency author Heyer.

Historical Romances published by Christian publishers fit readily into the Historical Romance subgenre, where the virginity of their heroines and the gentleness of the plot do not feel out of place to fans. In fact, a greater number of readers who would not necessarily choose Inspirational or Christian Romances read those with historical settings, because these stories match their other requirements for Historical Romances. Janette Oke popularized the Inspirational Historical Romance with *Love Comes Softly,* published in 1979.[36] Set in the American West just after the Civil War, these gentle stories follow the lives of those who settled the West. Other popular writers include Gilbert Morris, Judith Pella and Michael Pella, Francine Rivers, and Lori Wick.

ALTERNATIVE REALITY ROMANCES

This is a diverse subgenre, covering the gamut from vampires and ghosts to futuristic settings and time travel. However, it represents only a small part (about 6 percent) of the Romance market and readership. Following the example of Kristin Ramsdell in her comprehensive overview of the Romance genre (*Romance Fiction: A Guide to the Genre*), I am combining the most recent trends in the Romance genre into a single subgenre, with all types linked by their Fantasy elements. Alternative Reality Romances include Futuristic (set in future times and most similar to Science Fiction), Paranormal (supernatural and magical elements, including vampires, ghosts, etc.), and Time Travel (protagonists travel to and from time periods, sometimes transporting other characters as well). *See* Figure 10.4 for a summary of the characteristics.

Although some tend to be darker in tone and others more light-hearted, all share a sense of otherness and offer a time and setting alternative to the more straightforward Historical and Contemporary Romances. And, as in the larger, more popular subgenres, the focus remains on the romantic relationships among the characters. To make the distinctions among types of Alternative Reality Romances more complex, authors frequently write more than one type of Alternative Reality (not to mention other types within the Romance genre); there is more variety among these authors than in either other subgenre discussed. As a result of this crossover and the combining of disparate subgenres, no clear benchmark emerges. Rather, it is helpful to consider each aspect separately and there discuss representative authors and titles.

Of the writers of Futuristic Romances, Roberts, under her pseudonym J. D. Robb, with her series featuring twenty-first-century police detective Eve Dallas (*Naked in Death* introduces this ongoing series), is the best known and most popular.[37] Similarities to Science

---

FIGURE 10.4

Characteristics of Alternative Reality Romances

1. Elements of Science Fiction, Fantasy, and Horror join the basic Romance plot, with story lines that focus on time travel, the supernatural, or futuristic elements.

2. Language and tone may evoke the otherness of the setting and characters, but they also help ground the story in the Romance genre.

Fiction are clear in the futuristic setting, but the series also appeals to readers of harder-edged crime fiction and even Romantic Suspense.

Krentz continues to write Futuristic Romances under her pseudonym Jayne Castle. These feature strong elements of Suspense and are set on the imaginary planet of St. Helens. Although they take place in the future on another world, Krentz's trademark humor and characters make these less alien. Among her futuristic romances, *Amaryllis*, first in the trilogy of stories set on St. Helens, reflects her style and translates her trademark humor, quirky characters, and racy romance to the near future, with additional elements of Romantic Suspense and psychic phenomena.[38]

Justine Davis, on the other hand, creates a futuristic world complete with space battles and futuristic technology and thus adds more traditional Science Fiction elements. In her RITA Award winning *Lord of the Storm*, fighter pilot Shaylah Graymist is forced to choose between her political future with the Coalition and her own feelings of justice and love for the captured prince from a ruined planet.[39]

Everything from angels, ghosts, fairies, and witches to werewolves and vampires populate Paranormal Romances. Disparate in subject matter, these also range widely in tone from the dark, sensual vampire Romances of Susan Krinard and Anne Stuart to Macomber's light-hearted angel Romances. Macomber is among the best-known authors writing in this subgenre. *A Season of Angels* introduces the bumbling angels-in-training trio—Shirley, Goodness, and Mercy—who must earn their wings.[40] Humorous, inspirational, gentle stories of human and angel foibles make these popular with readers outside the Romance genre as well.

Krinard's darker, sensual vampire and werewolf stories have a different appeal for readers. These evocative novels, more dreamy in tone and with explicit sexual situations, have the feel of dark Fantasy, although, again, the outcome of the romantic relationship is always the focus. *Prince of Dreams* pits brothers, the last of their race, against each other, as they battle for love and survival.[41] Much of the action takes place in a dream state, and only a dreamer as powerful as the heroine can effect their salvation.

The current popularity of Time Travel Romance owes much to Jude Deveraux's *A Knight in Shining Armor*, which unites a modern heroine, jilted by her lover, and a sixteenth-century knight who comes to her rescue.[42] The juxtaposition of characters from different times creates a great deal of humor and allows readers insight into customs from present and past, as seen through the eyes of characters unfamiliar with those times. Diana Gabaldon followed quickly with her Outlander series (*Outlander,* the first title, was named Best Book of the Year in 1991 by Romance Writers of America), which begins in Scotland in 1945 and quickly goes back to 1743, the time of the Battle of Culloden.[43] After *Outlander,* the series entries move, in subsequent installments, from France to America. Readers appreciate the historical detail as well as the love interest between the protagonists. This has become a popular subgenre, and many authors who have established their reputations writing in other subgenres—Johanna Lindsey, Constance O'Day-Flannery, Kristin Hannah, Sandra Heath, Linda Lael Miller, Kasey Michaels, and Susan Sizemore—have also written Time Travel Romances.

Preparing to Work with Readers

As in every genre, fans have their own expectations when they select a book by their favorite authors or try someone new. It is useful to understand more precisely what Romance readers are seeking, as we prepare to work with them.

First, Romance readers do not expect to be surprised by the outcome of a Romance novel. They know the outcome of the story from the start; that is one of the reasons they have chosen a book in this genre. Fans of all genres find a specific formula that satisfies them and choose books that fit that particular formula. Many readers choose books in which they expect exactly the same pattern and outcome. In a Mystery we expect the crime to be solved and justice to triumph. Here, in Romances, hero and heroine will resolve their difficulties and discover their love. Fans read Romances because they find participating in the courtship and Romance so satisfying. Although they may tolerate a few twists or surprises in the general formula, for the most part they are not looking for something new and different. They seek the simple satisfaction of having their expectations fulfilled through the Romance formula.

Secondly, as in other genres, readers want to read everything by authors they enjoy and all titles in a series. In the Romance genre, series do not exist in the same form as they do in many other genres. Because Romances end with the satisfactory resolution of the romantic entanglement between hero and heroine, their story has been told, and further chapters or a new book featuring these characters would hardly be a Romance. On the other hand, the author may choose a family or a group of friends and successfully match each set of characters. Then couples from previous Romances can appear in later titles to help further that story, and readers get a glimpse of their continued happiness and the growth of their families. These are usually referred to as "linked" Romances, and it behooves every librarian to keep track of these, as publishers are not always thoughtful or savvy enough to include series information—titles and the correct reading order—in all volumes of the series. I have also found it useful to stamp in the book itself or on the pocket the word "series" and then list all titles. If a reader comes upon "number three," she has the titles of the two previous entries; or if the book is only stamped "series," she knows to ask for further information.

Patrons read in many different ways. That is a characteristic shared by readers in all genres, and Romance is no exception. Some read by author and want everything an author wrote (from our collections and then on interlibrary loan, wherever we can find the titles). Then they want someone else who writes "just like" the author they love. Some fans follow publishers' series and read only Harlequin American or Silhouette's Montana Mavericks, and they want to find them all and read them in order. Some read just Romances and like to be introduced to Romance authors they have not discovered. Others will enjoy a range of books that feature strong romantic themes, even if they fall outside the genre. Possibilities for that third group are discussed in detail below, in the "Expanding Readers' Horizons" section of the "Readers' Advisory Interview."

There is another kind of reader we meet: one who has not admitted to herself, or to anyone else, that *Romance* describes the kind of book she enjoys. This genre-denial syndrome is especially common in a genre such as Romance, which has received such bad press from reviewers and librarians alike. All of us have been in a position of sensing a reader might enjoy exploring another genre, based on what he or she enjoys reading, but have been frustrated by genre labels. One patron, for whom I had suggested titles for years, was talking one day about Historical Fiction and Adventure. I suggested the novels of Patricia Veryan, knowing they combined the two, as well as some of the Mystery elements this reader had long enjoyed. She was converted, quickly read everything Veryan wrote, and now eagerly awaits new releases. Had I called these Romances, as they properly are, she would have never attempted one. I still would not call her a Romance reader, but I know she has explored the genre, discovering other authors similar to Veryan. Many of us, especially voracious readers, find ourselves exploring—and enjoying—genres we never thought we would read. With Romances, however, the stigma of being perceived as a fan seems to leave readers open to mockery. Or so they believe. Not all readers are ready to acknowledge they may read and enjoy Romances, and they should not be forced into that admission. We, as Readers' Advisors, need to know the range of books that might be classified as Romance, as well as those that appeal to fans of the genre, and to recognize this genre when readers describe it.

Understanding these characteristics of readers, we librarians need to take measures, as we prepare to work with fans of the Romance genre. Because of the stigma that seems to be attached to Romance readers and their impression, faulty we hope, that librarians, especially, do not respect their choice of leisure reading, it is important for us to become familiar with the genre. How do we do this? The first step to prepare to work better with fans is to read a few Romances, to discover why they are so popular with such a large and diverse population of readers. It is important to read Romances and then to talk, positively, about the appeal with other staff or fans. This is the best way to identify what it is that makes the books and the genre so popular. We will not all become fans of the genre. Although that would be a happy result, that is not really our goal. Our goal is to encourage an environment in which sensitive, knowledgeable staff become more comfortable helping Romance readers. This process is relatively painless, but it goes a very long way in preparing us to work better with readers.

Although this is an important step in working with fans of any genre, it is crucial with Romance readers, who have low expectations of the service and respect they will receive in libraries. In addition to the benchmarks and other authors described above, readers not familiar with the Romance genre may want to try Romances that contain elements of genres they more frequently read. Some suggestions are given in Figure 10.5.

FIGURE 10.5

An Introduction to the Romance Genre

Romance Writers to Try, If You Enjoy . . .

Adventure	Elizabeth Lowell (*Tell Me No Lies*)[45]
	Loretta Chase (*The Lion's Daughter*)[46]
Fantasy	Maggie Shayne (*Eternity*)[47]
	Barbara Freethy (*Daniel's Gift*)[48]
	Nora Roberts (*Enchanted*)[49]
Gentle	Debbie Macomber
Historical Fiction	J. Suzanne Frank (*Reflections in the Nile*)[50]
Horror	Susan Krinard
Humor	Jennifer Crusie
	Rachel Gibson
Inspirational	Robin Lee Hatcher (*Patterns of Love*)[51]
Mystery	Alice Chetwynd Ley
	Jennifer Crusie
Romantic Suspense	Nora Roberts
Science Fiction	Justine Davis
	J. D. Robb
Thriller	Judith A. Lansdowne (*A Season of Virtues*)[52]
	Patricia Veryan
Western	Rosanne Bittner (*Thunder on the Plains*)[53]
	Janet Dailey (*This Calder Sky*)[54]
	Kathleen Eagle (*The Last True Cowboy*)[55]
Women's Lives	Kathleen Gilles Seidel

The second activity I recommend is that we develop strategies to let readers know that we value them and the books they enjoy. This undertaking may involve a commitment of money as well as time. However, any group that purchases more than 50 percent of mass-market paperbacks is an audience of readers we cannot afford to ignore, and it is important that we demonstrate that we value Romances and Romance readers.

We begin by evaluating our collections, as well as our service philosophy and practices. Too many libraries rely solely on donations to stock some of their genre collections, especially Romance. Unfortunately, those are not the books readers are really seeking. They are not the "keepers," those special books fans keep to reread and would not think of giving up under any circumstances. They would certainly not donate the best Romances in their collections to the library. Patrons, however, will read these donations if nothing else is available.

Instead, as we would for any other popular and heavily circulating area, we must also make a commitment to building the collection, to investing money in the reading interests of this group of voracious readers. There are several ways to do this. Traditionally, librarians rely on reviews, but until recently, library reviewing journals have ignored Romances or have universally panned them. This trend has been changing. In recent years *Library Journal* and *Booklist* especially have made a concerted effort to increase their coverage of Romances, both hardcover and paperback. Specific Romance reviewing guides, such as *Romantic Times,* also provide relatively inexpensive access to reviews in the genre.[44]

As in all book selection we do need to be aware of quality. Readers do not want just any Romance; they are discriminating, too. Patrons provide a good source of valuable information regarding selection, if we listen to their comments. Whose books do they eagerly await? Which authors can we never find on the shelf? We might also monitor returned books and patron requests, filling in titles by really popular authors.

Format is a stumbling block for many libraries. Most Romances are published only in paperback, and paperbacks are notoriously difficult to handle in libraries. Fortunately, more and more Romances are being published in hardcover both originally, or as reprints, or in large type, and those are easier to deal with, to catalog, and to put on our shelves. However, the bulk of the market is still paperback. At the very least, we need to treat paperback Romances as we do other genre paperbacks. If we catalog Mystery, Science Fiction, and Fantasy paperbacks, we need to do the same for Romances. In Science Fiction and Fantasy, especially, the market is dominated by paperbacks. What makes the *Star Trek* series or Marion Zimmer Bradley's novels of Darkover more worthy of cataloging than popular paperback Romances?

Readers suffer from no doubts about the value of paperback in the Romance or any other genre. That is the format in which they are accustomed to finding their favorite authors. In fact, many of the best-selling authors in the genre and on the *New York Times* hardcover best-sellers list—Danielle Steel, LaVyrle Spencer, Jude Deveraux, Catherine Coulter, Sandra Brown, Jayne Ann Krentz, Jennifer Crusie, and Nora Roberts—were first discovered by the paperback audience. That is another reason to treat the paperback Romance with respect and to buy and catalog paperback copies of titles that are popular. The best of these paperback authors are the ones who will become hardcover best-sellers, and we will be clamoring to find copies of their paperbacks for their ravenous fans.

Should Romances, hardcover and paperback, be shelved together in a separate collection? Sharon K. Baker's research clearly indicates that almost all libraries have fiction collections that are too big to browse effectively and that readers are well served by segregated genre collections.[56] However, some genres are easier to separate than others, and in Romance, the hardcover titles seem particularly difficult to identify. Is it possible to recognize a hardcover Romance without reading the book? Because Roberts writes Romances, do all her hardcover titles belong in this separate hardcover Romance collection? Or do they also appeal to a large number of readers who would never consider themselves Romance readers or discover the books in a separate Romance section? Clearly there are difficulties and trade-offs. One suggestion is to create a paperback Romance collection, following the publisher's designations on the books' spines. (If Romance is the noun, the book goes in the paperback Romance collection. Hence, Historical Romances are with Romances, but Romantic Suspense is not.) This will satisfy a number of readers; it can be achieved fairly easily by staff with little training; and it underscores the library's interest in providing a collection for Romance readers.

In addition to cataloging Romances and creating separate paperback and hardcover collections, there are other strategies we can use
to let readers know that we value the genre. For example, we can mark
the spines of Romances with stickers so they can be easily found on
the shelf. We can indicate award winners with a note on the pocket
or a stamp on the title page. We can also mark series and linked-novel
information, on the pocket or title page, so patrons realize the adventures of these characters are continued, as mentioned above. If we are
fortunate enough to work in a library with an accommodating cata-
loger and versatile cataloging system, we can also provide all of this
information and more through the library's computer catalog. All these
strategies help us as we prepare to work with readers of Romance.

Readers' Advisory Interview

How then do we conduct the readers' advisory interview with Romance readers? Of what special information do we need to be aware?
What techniques do we need to implement to serve this audience
well? What do we need to know to help readers when they ask for
a Romance?

There are three vital pieces of information we need to discover.
What does this particular reader mean by *Romance*? Does the reader
want a book set in a particular time period or with Paranormal elements? And, finally, how much sex does the reader want—or will
she tolerate?

First, what does the reader mean when she talks about Romances?
Readers could come up with an almost infinite number of definitions
of Romance, and each is very personal to that reader. As was discussed above, every reader has a different sense of what kind of books
the term *Romance* includes. A major difficulty we often experience
with a reader is not knowing exactly what she is looking for when she
says she reads Romances. Does she mean a paperback Silhouette
Desire or something more like Danielle Steel writes? Romances or a
romantic novel? Although we librarians may need definitions to gain
an understanding of the genre, we learn to put those aside when we

work with readers. If a reader says Steel writes Romances, we need to identify other "Romance" writers who write just like her. (In this book, however, authors similar to Steel are discussed in chapter 16, "Women's Lives and Relationships.") Posing the traditional initial readers' advisory request, "Tell me about a book you have enjoyed," usually elicits a response that allows us to get a sense of this reader's definition of a Romance. Our familiarity with authors across the genre—or any lists we have created to assist us—then allows us to make appropriate suggestions.

The next factor to consider is the time frame. Does the reader prefer a contemporary or a historical setting? Some readers enjoy both, but most have preferences, often strong feelings about what they are in the mood to read. Obtaining this information is straightforward, at least. I simply ask, "Do you prefer a book set in the past or in the current day?" Another similar question might identify readers of Alternate Reality Romances, but that information will likely have come out when they described Romances they enjoy.

Finally, the crucial piece of information we need to discover when we talk to readers is the amount of sex they want in their Romances. By this, I do not simply mean whether they want a lot of sex or very little and how graphically it is described. Sometimes one very explicit interlude leaves readers feeling this is a very sexy book, even if that was an isolated occurrence. The real point is the intensity and frequency of the sexual encounters, and whether they occur at the beginning, before the reader really knows the heroine and hero, or further along in the story. Often if the sex comes later, it feels different than books in which there is graphic sex right from the first few pages. If the sex is later and between a couple seen by readers as "made for each other," it is less likely to offend or even really be noticed, almost regardless of how graphic. We are often surprised by readers who say they are looking for books without a lot of sex, like those by Nora Roberts or Jayne Ann Krentz, when we know that explicit sexual interludes figure prominently in novels by these authors. This is a phenomenon I am unable to explain, even though I have encountered it with regularity in speaking with readers. It may have something to do with the reader's perception of the heroine. If she engages in sexual activity too early in the story, before we know and care about her, we may be more likely to view her as promiscuous. That perception creates a different tone in the story, and for many readers, it is not as satisfying.

How much sex a reader expects in a Romance may be the hardest information to discover, the one thing readers are least likely to want to talk about. We cannot simply ask patrons about this directly; they do not have a vocabulary to answer us, even if we could discover just how to phrase the question. Queries of this sort are simply too embarrassing, and because readers cannot come up with words for what they want, we have to provide them with a vocabulary and alternative choices as we suggest a range of authors.

I listen for clues when the reader describes books or authors she enjoys. If I am unsure, I offer a variety of titles. I might talk about "gentler" or "more innocent" Romances to indicate those without a lot of sex. Often Regencies fit the bill, early titles by Rosamunde Pilcher, or some of the paperback category Romances (Harlequin Romances and Silhouette Romances, for example), or romantic novels by authors such as Maeve Binchy or Eva Ibbotson.

To indicate the other end of the spectrum, I might talk about "racier Romances," by which I mean more risque Romances in which sex may be explicit and perhaps frequent. Many of these, especially those by Krentz and her alter ego Amanda Quick, also feature a sense of fun and a lighter touch, which readers who enjoy these authors expect. When I describe this kind of book, I might conclude by saying something like, "It's a little racier, the kind of book Jude Deveraux or Jayne Anne Krentz writes." I use a name I know the reader will recognize and thus understand. I like the term *racy* because it is not pejorative and can be used for authors with both contemporary and historical settings. This language allows me to provide information about the books and authors and then let the reader make choices from the range I have offered.

Having said this, I do want to add that I am sometimes surprised at the diversity of books people read. We need to be careful not to stereotype readers. A sweet, grandmotherly lady might "adore" Susan Johnson or other very explicit authors, and she may find the gentle Romances far too tame for her taste. Readers are really looking for that satisfaction Romances give them, and for some, sex too soon or too much sex destroys that feeling. The atmosphere and when sex occurs can make all the difference.

We should keep in mind those elements that readers tell us they appreciate: the strong, bright, independent women pitted against powerful, distant, and dangerous men; the classic misunderstanding between the two, and the ultimate resolution of their differences, with the heroine always victorious (although both really win when she is triumphant); and, most importantly, the evocative, emotional tone that allows us to be drawn in and to experience this love story with its inevitable happy ending. This is what readers are seeking when they ask for Romances.

Now for the hard part of the readers' advisory interview: Judging from my personal experience, when we come face-to-face with a Romance reader, we have only about five seconds to make a connection with the reader. This may sound absurd, but I guarantee it is true. We have no more than about five seconds in which to let this reader know that we understand Romances and their appeal. This is not the time to be aloof. Romance readers are accustomed to being looked down upon, and we need to learn ways to indicate immediately that we have read in this genre, that we are someone they can talk with about their favorites. This kind of pressure can be a little intimidating.

The good news is that even having read just one or two Romances and having thought about their appeal, we have a basis on which to make that connection. Readers do not expect us to be fans; they expect us to be fellow readers and to appreciate what they enjoy, whatever that is. We are simply required to smile and invite the readers to share information about the kind of book they are seeking.

Often the most difficult step is making this initial contact. Romance readers tend to be elusive. After a lifetime of being put down for their reading tastes, what can we expect? We need to seek out readers and make contacts. If we have Romance readers coming to our service desk in droves, we are doing something right. However, we are also the exception. Because so many Romances are paperbacks, talking to readers browsing at the paperback racks is a good place to start. If I see someone holding a Romance and looking for more, I might go browsing in that area myself and strike up a conversation.

If I recognize the author of the book she is holding, I might ask her if she has read another title by that author, or offer a comment about the author or type of book. Although this approach may sound intimidating, especially for staff new to the genre, this is a good way to gain self-assurance and win the confidence of Romance readers. It helps if I can talk about a title that I have read by that same author. (Even if I have not read that particular author, however, I can open the conversation by asking what it is that the reader likes about that author—or any author.)

This situation has its advantages. First, I can ease into the readers' advisory interview; it truly becomes a conversation about books we both know and enjoy, and the reader discovers that staff at this library are interested in Romances and may really be able to help. I might ask if she is finding enough good books to read or whether I can help. I might also ask whether we have the authors or series she likes and reinforce that we are interested in building the collection.

Another benefit is that not only have I made a contact with one person who is likely to talk with me again (or with whoever is on the desk, as I always remind readers that anyone at the desk can help), but I have also established with anyone else browsing in the area that we value readers and their interests. Whether they are Romance readers or not, they are more likely to talk with me. I have helped them feel more comfortable talking with staff about their reading interests.

When someone asks me specifically for a Romance, perhaps for one like those Roberts writes, I ask her to tell me about the books, perhaps to name her favorite and then get her to talk further. Even if I have read the author, I encourage the reader to tell me why she enjoys them, especially with an author like Roberts, who writes so many types. I need to hear what this patron likes and go from there to make additional suggestions.

I use the same technique when a patron asks me simply to suggest a Romance. I ask her to tell me what she has enjoyed or has not. It is sometimes easier to describe what we do not like, and that information is just as valuable, as it indicates what not to suggest.

We need to remember to offer a range of titles and let the reader choose. I may mention authors who write Romances, as we have defined the genre in this chapter, as well as those who really write romantic novels in other genres or perhaps Women's Lives and Relationships. I listen to and watch how the reader responds as I offer titles that cover a range of books that might appeal. As in every readers' advisory interview, I encourage readers to take more than one book, as well as to come tell us at the desk what they liked or what they have not enjoyed.

As with readers in every genre, sometimes the only way to get a readers' advisory interview started or to make any headway with someone who reads Romances, or whom we think would enjoy them, is simply to talk about one or two Romances we have read. This takes us back to that five-second rule. We need to be prepared to initiate conversations at a moment's notice. Sometimes it seems appropriate simply to make contact by talking about a Romance I have read or the author of the book the reader has in hand or has asked about. I might use something from my mental "Sure Bets" list (described below) to demonstrate that I am familiar with the genre and popular authors. I also make comments along the lines of "Readers of Marion Chesney say they also like the quirky characters and humor in books by Jeanne Savery and Carola Dunn," or "Fans of Nora Roberts have told me how much they like Ann Maxwell and Jayne Ann Krentz, because they, too, add elements of mystery and adventure to their contemporary Romances."

If we are not fans of the genre, we need to be careful how we talk with readers. It is important to acknowledge the great satisfaction Romances give so many readers and suggest the best we know in the genre. That is a useful bit of universal readers' advisory advice: Whenever we do not read or particularly care for a genre, it helps to acknowledge the genre's popularity and demonstrate our knowledge of what is popular in our suggestions. Doing this allows us to speak about Romances (and any other genre) in nonjudgmental terms, focusing on the popularity of the genre and its appeal to readers.

Acknowledging that we have read Romances breaks the ice and allows us to continue a conversation with the reader. I find readers much more willing to talk to me if they know I have read in this genre they love. Even reading as few as two or three Romances, thinking about why they appeal, and talking with their fans stands us in good stead with a large number of readers at our libraries.

Once we start reading Romances and making contact with patrons, we find more and more Romance readers coming to us for assistance. We do a lot more indirect readers' advisory: We might suggest books for one patron, who does not take them, only to find them taken by someone else who was standing there, or have that third person join in the conversation. The more readers we help, the more we are inspired to read, because readers give us excellent suggestions of what is popular, and thus the more we learn about the genre.

In the Romance genre especially, however, we need to practice describing the books using nonjudgmental terms. As I said above, Romance is a genre that gives a lot of librarians problems, probably more than any other fiction genre. That is why it is so important to practice describing Romances with colleagues, using nonjudgmental terms, focusing on the popularity of the genre and its appeal.

Sure Bets

Jennifer Crusie is currently one of the hottest names in Contemporary Romances. Although she began, as all the popular authors did, by publishing paperback category Romances, her recent hardcover titles have jumped to the best-sellers lists. In addition to her trademark humor, Crusie supplies interesting, well-developed characters in complex and interesting relationships, quirky story lines, and elements of Mystery and Suspense along with satisfying Romance. Crusie has also attracted a large number of readers who do not see themselves as Romance readers, so she makes a good suggestion for readers whom you think might appreciate the genre.

To attract readers who appreciate historical settings, do not forget Georgette Heyer, whose classic Regency titles are being reissued in paperback. Even our well-worn hardcover copies circulate extensively, and as a fan of audio books, I can vouch for the pleasures provided by that format. *The Talisman Ring* is a Georgian romp featuring two couples (one young and romantic, the other more staid), Adventure, Mystery (the plot hinges on the discovery of a stolen ring), and a perfidious villain.[57] The delightful dialogue leaves readers laughing out loud, and more than one has told me this is not necessarily the best book to be reading on a commuter train, if one cares what fellow passengers think.

Expanding Readers' Horizons

Many books outside the strict confines of the Romance genre appeal to Romance readers. Those who seek the satisfying love relationships they find in Romances may also find this as a secondary theme in a range of genre and nongenre fiction, from Mystery and Science Fiction to award-winning Literary Fiction. Romantic stories in all genres appeal to Romance readers, and the readers may not consciously recognize the difference between these and those that fit within the stricter confines of the genre. They may like a range of books that include romantic relationships, and their reading tastes may cut across all genres. What appeals to them may be the successful resolution of the romantic entanglements, and some days they will choose Romances for this fulfillment; on others they may seek that satisfaction in titles from other genres.

Lois McMaster Bujold's *Shards of Honor,* for example, can be enjoyed as Romance or Science Fiction or both.[58] Some readers may relate to the fast-paced action of this Science Fiction adventure, set in a future time and on other worlds. Others may find the development of the romantic relationship between Betan Commander Cordelia Naismith and her Barayarran captor, Captain Aral Vorkosigan, the main attraction. Both appeals are legitimate, and thus this title proves an excellent suggestion for readers in both genres.

There are any number of Fantasy authors who also rely heavily on the romantic tone, if not actual Romance, in creating their stories. Melanie Rawn's *Dragon Prince* and others in the series have enough of the elements of Romance, in tone and actual relationships, to please a range of Romance readers, as well as Fantasy fans.[59] In addition, Laurell Hamilton's series, featuring vampire hunter Anita Blake and her would-be lover (and master vampire) Jean-Claude, demonstrates crossover from the Horror genre.

Novels of Women's Lives and Relationships offer other examples. These are not really a part of the Romance genre either, even though the most popular are written by authors who made their reputations as writers of Romances. These novels, instead of focusing on the romantic entanglements of the protagonists, cover a broader scope and concentrate on the details of women's lives and their relationships, romantic and otherwise. Although books by authors such as Barbara

Delinsky and Steel certainly appeal to some Romance readers, Romance is not at the center of these novels.

Some readers enjoy Mysteries with a strong romantic interest, such as those by Elizabeth Peters. (Her first Amelia Peabody mystery, *Crocodile on the Sandbank*, focuses on the romantic relationships of Amelia and her friend Evelyn with the Emerson brothers; the recent *He Shall Thunder in the Sky* features the romantic entanglements of Amelia's son Ramses.)[60] Others will be better pleased with a Romance in which there is a Mystery subplot, as is the case in many by Krentz. Readers' Advisors should be open to the possibility of exploring other genres in helping these readers. *See* Figure 10.6 for additional suggestions.

FIGURE 10.6

Expanding Readers' Horizons

Authors to Take Readers beyond the Romance Genre

Adventure	Dorothy Dunnett
Fantasy	Jennifer Roberson
	Melanie Rawn
Gentle	Rosamunde Pilcher
Historical	Rosalind Laker
Horror	Laurell K. Hamilton
Mystery	Elizabeth Peters
	Gillian Roberts
Romantic Suspense	Elizabeth Lowell (*Jade Island*)[61]
	Linda Howard
Science Fiction	Lois McMaster Bujold
	Catherine Asaro (*The Veiled Web*)[62]
Suspense	Mary Higgins Clark
Thriller	Gayle Lynds
Western	Cindy Bonner
Women's Lives	Barbara Delinsky
	Eva Ibbotson

Reference Sources

Unfortunately, there is no perfect source for all the information Romance readers and librarians request about this genre: complete series information, for both author and publisher's series, and coverage of favorite authors. Sources are often limited almost exclusively to hardcover writers in this genre where most are published in paperback. However, there are two excellent resources that should be in every library that has a readership for the genre—or that wants to explore the genre further.

The first, Kristin Ramsdell's *Romance Fiction: A Guide to the Genre*, is another in Libraries Unlimited's very practical Genreflecting Advisory series. This is currently *the* source for detailed information on the Romance genre. Following the general format of *Genreflecting* (*see* appendix 2), each of nine chapters highlights a particular subgenre. Each subgenre chapter includes a definition, appeal information, suggestions for advising readers, a brief history, and a selective, often annotated, list of authors and titles. In addition, there are chapters that introduce the genre—its definition, appeal, tips for working with readers, and building the collection. The book concludes with several chapters on research aids, including review sources, reference sources, organizations, awards, and sample core collections. Access is provided through an author/title index.

What makes Ramsdell's book so valuable are both the scope of the study—she covers paperback-only authors with the same care as hardcover best-selling authors and offers detailed information about series titles and the various subgenres—and also the depth. In each of the subgenre chapters she offers information about various aspects of that subgenre and extensive lists of authors and titles, many annotated.

The Romance Readers' Advisory: The Librarian's Guide to Love in the Stacks, by Ann Bouricius, offers a different approach.[63] Her book provides an overview of the genre and tips to make our libraries Romance reader friendly. Although she also offers lists of award winners, reference sources (including Internet sites), booklists, and more, her book is a guide to understand the genre and its fans, rather than a reference resource to be consulted to answer reader queries. If you have staff reluctant to read Romances, this is the book to share with them.

Where to Find...

INFORMATION ABOUT THE AUTHOR

Although *Twentieth-Century Romance and Historical Writers* is certainly the standard biographical source for this genre, it should be noted that selection of authors is decidedly slanted toward authors of hardcover titles and very well established authors of paperback Romances.[64] *Contemporary Authors* (*see* appendix 2) is not much better in this regard. Author home pages are one possible source of information, and the Romance Writers of America Web site <www.rwanational.com> has links to many author home pages.

PLOT SUMMARIES

As I mentioned above, Ramsdell's book has many short annotations. Longer plot summaries can be found in many of the general sources listed in appendix 2: *NoveList* includes reviews from *Booklist, Library Journal, Publisher's Weekly,* and *Rendezvous; Ramsdell* provides annotations for *What Do I Read Next? Fiction Catalog* includes some Romances, accessed through headings such as "Love Stories" and "Love Affairs"; and *To Be Continued* includes Romances that are series or linked novels.

SUBGENRES AND THEMES

Ramsdell's book is the most complete source of this type of information, although it is also available through subject searches of *NoveList* and *What Do I Read Next? Genreflecting* also provides an excellent outline of the genre and lists representative authors and titles, as well as descriptions of the subgenres and themes. Bouricius also offers a useful overview of the subgenres.

GENRE DESCRIPTION, BACKGROUND, AND HISTORY

Both Bouricius and Ramsdell's books provide excellent background for librarians and fans. There are two books of essays about the nature of the genre that are certainly worth reading. Jayne Ann Krentz's *Dangerous Men and Adventurous Women,* mentioned above in this chapter, has become a classic. Twenty essays, written by Romance authors, characterize the genre and its appeal. A more recent collection along the same lines, *North American Romance Writers,* provides twenty-five essays by Romance authors about why they write in this genre.[65] This book was compiled by Kay Mussell and Johanna Tuñon, and it also includes an extensive bibliography.

CORE LISTS AND BEST BOOKS

Bouricius and Ramsdell both give core lists that can be used in collection development and in familiarizing ourselves with the genre. *Genreflecting* and *NoveList* offer lists of award winners, and *Genreflecting* has a "Best" authors list as well.

Romance readers are an audience worth cultivating. They are voracious readers and often heavy library users. Because many Romances are quite short, fans read a lot. The typical Romance reader often has a wide range of interests, and this group includes some of our most sophisticated readers. It is not uncommon to see the same reader preparing to check out a handful of category Romances, P. D. James, some Science Fiction, and perhaps Anne Tyler or John Updike.

Romances are fantasies, and their readers recognize them as such, just as Mystery, Science Fiction, Western, Thriller, and other genre readers recognize their favorites as fantasies. In the particular fantasy explored in each Romance, the woman always wins—and perhaps that is what makes the Romance so subversive. These are stories of women who are defined by what they do, not just by what they are. Best-selling Romance author Patricia Gaffney summarizes the genre's appeal: "Dress it up with ghosts, angels, werewolves, leprechauns; mix it up with murder, kidnapping, comedy, time machines—it doesn't matter. If the core is a believable story about two people finding and committing to each other for life, if it touches our emotions, if it rings true and makes us laugh, cry, and celebrate the miracle of human intimacy, it's romance."[66]

NOTES

1. Kristin Ramsdell, *Romance Fiction: A Guide to the Genre* (Englewood, Colo.: Libraries Unlimited, 1999), 5.
2. Nora Roberts, *The MacGregor Brides* (New York: Silhouette Books, 1997).

3. Cathie Linz, *Too Sexy for Marriage* (Toronto and New York: Harlequin, 1998); ———, *Too Smart for Marriage* (Toronto and New York: Harlequin, 1998); ———, *Too Stubborn to Marry* (Toronto, New York: Harlequin, 1998).

4. Jennifer Crusie, *Crazy for You* (New York: St. Martin's, 1999).

5. Mary Balogh, *Tangled* (New York: Penguin, 1994).

6. Robert James Waller, *The Bridges of Madison County* (New York: Warner Books, 1992).

7. Jayne Ann Krentz, *Grand Passion* (New York: Pocket Books, 1994); Nora Roberts, *Hidden Riches* (New York: Putnam, 1994); Marion Chesney, *The Miser of Mayfair* (New York: St. Martin's, 1986); Ann Maxwell, *The Ruby* (New York: Harper-Paperbacks, 1995); Amanda Quick, *Ravished* (New York: Bantam, 1992).

8. Jayne Ann Krentz, ed., *Dangerous Men and Adventurous Women: Romance Writers on the Appeal of Romance* (Philadelphia: Univ. of Pennsylvania Pr., 1992), 17.

9. Susan Carroll, *The Bride Finder* (New York: Ballantine, 1998).

10. Kathleen Korbel, *A Soldier's Heart* (New York: Silhouette Books, 1994).

11. Mary Jo Putney, *The Rake* (New York: Topaz, 1998); Charlotte Louise Dolan, *The Unofficial Suitor* (New York: Signet, 1992).

12. Susan Elizabeth Phillips, *Dream a Little Dream* (New York: Avon, 1998).

13. Betina Krahn, *The Last Bachelor* (New York: Bantam, 1994).

14. Patricia Veryan, *Practice to Deceive* (New York: St. Martin's, 1985).

15. Carola Dunn, *His Lordship's Reward* (New York: Kensington, 1994); ———, *Miss Jacobson's Journey* (New York: Walker, 1992).

16. Roberts, *Born in Fire* (New York: Jove, 1994); ———, *Born in Ice* (New York: Jove, 1995); ———, *Born in Shame* (New York: Jove, 1996).

17. ———, *Daring to Dream* (New York: Jove, 1996); ———, *Holding the Dream* (New York: Jove, 1997); ———, *Finding the Dream* (New York: Jove, 1997).

18. ———, *Sea Swept* (New York: Jove, 1998); ———, *Rising Tides* (New York: Jove, 1998); ———, *Inner Harbor* (New York: Jove, 1999).

19. Krentz, *Wildest Hearts* (New York: Pocket Books, 1993).

20. Susan Elizabeth Phillips, *It Had to Be You* (New York: Avon, 1994).

21. Debbie Macomber, *Lonesome Cowboy* (Toronto, New York: Harlequin, 1998).

22. Ruth Wind, *Meant to Be Married* (New York: Silhouette Books, 1998).

23. Elisabeth Fairchild, *Marriage a la Mode* (New York: Signet, 1997).

24. Susan Johnson, *Sinful* (New York: Doubleday, 1992).

25. Elizabeth Lowell, *Enchanted* (New York: Avon, 1994).

26. Putney, *Dancing on the Wind* (New York: Penguin, 1994).

27. Quick, *Mistress* (New York: Bantam, 1994).

28. Julie Garwood, *For the Roses* (New York: Pocket Books, 1995).

ROMANCE

29. Jo Beverley, *Forbidden Magic* (New York: Topaz, 1998).

30. Ibid., 103.

31. Balogh, *Courting Julia* (New York: Signet, 1993).

32. Balogh, *Thief of Dreams* (New York: Jove, 1998).

33. Georgette Heyer, *Faro's Daughter* (New York: E. P. Dutton, 1942).

34. Chesney, The Six Sisters Saga (*Minerva*, 1982; *The Taming of Annabelle*, 1983; *Deirdre and Desire*, 1984; *Daphne*, 1984; *Diana the Huntress*, 1985; and *Frederica in Fashion*, 1985) (New York: St. Martin's).

35. Carla Kelly, *The Lady's Companion* (New York: Signet, 1996).

36. Janette Oke, *Love Comes Softly* (Minneapolis: Bethany Fellowship, 1979).

37. J. D. Robb, *Naked in Death* (New York: Berkley Books, 1995).

38. Jayne Castle, *Amaryllis* (New York: Pocket Star Books, 1996).

39. Justine Davis, *Lord of the Storm* (New York: Topaz, 1994).

40. Macomber, *A Season of Angels* (New York: Harper Paperbacks, 1993)

41. Susan Krinard, *Prince of Dreams* (New York: Bantam, 1995).

42. Jude Deveraux, *A Knight in Shining Armor* (New York: Pocket Books, 1989).

43. Diana Gabaldon, *Outlander* (New York: Delacorte, 1991).

44. *Romantic Times Magazine* (Brooklyn, N.Y.: Romantic Times, 1981–).

45. Lowell, *Tell Me No Lies* (Toronto and New York: Worldwide, 1986).

46. Loretta Chase, *The Lion's Daughter* (New York: Avon, 1992).

47. Maggie Shayne, *Eternity* (New York: Jove, 1998).

48. Barbara Freethy, *Daniel's Gift* (New York: Avon, 1996).

49. Roberts, *Enchanted* (New York: Silhouette Books, 1999).

50. J. Suzanne Frank, *Reflections in the Nile* (New York: Warner Books, 1997).

51. Robin Lee Hatcher, *Patterns of Love* (New York: HarperPaperbacks, 1998).

52. Judith A. Lansdowne, *A Season of Virtues* (New York: Kensington, 1999).

53. Rosanne Bittner, *Thunder on the Plains* (New York: Doubleday, 1992).

54. Janet Dailey, *This Calder Sky* (New York: Pocket Books, 1981).

55. Kathleen Eagle, *The Last True Cowboy* (New York: Avon, 1998).

56. Sharon K. Baker, *Responsive Public Library Collection: How to Develop and Market It* (Englewood, Colo.: Libraries Unlimited, 1993).

57. Heyer, *The Talisman Ring* (London and Toronto: Heinemann, 1936).

58. Lois McMaster Bujold, *Shards of Honor* (New York: Baen, 1986).

59. Melanie Rawn, *Dragon Prince: Book I* (New York: Daw Books, 1985).

60. Elizabeth Peters, *Crocodile on the Sandbank* (New York: Dodd, Mead, 1975); ———, *He Shall Thunder in the Sky* (New York: Morrow, 2000).

61. Lowell, *Jade Island* (New York: Avon, 1998).

62. Catherine Asaro, *The Veiled Web* (New York: Bantam, 1999).

63. Ann Bouricius, *The Romance Readers' Advisory: The Librarian's Guide to Love in the Stacks* (Chicago: American Library Assn., 2000).

64. Aruna Vasudevan and Lesley Henderson, eds., *Twentieth-Century Romance and Historical Writers*, 3d ed. (Detroit: St. James, 1994).

65. Kay Mussell and Johanna Tuñon, comps., *North American Romance Writers* (Lanham, Md.: Scarecrow, 1999).

66. Patricia Gaffney, "Coming Out of the Closet and Locking It Behind Us," in *North American Romance Writers,* ed. Kay Mussell and Johanna Tuñon, 92.

11

Romantic Suspense

Before the line "It was a dark and stormy night" became a cliché, it was the phrase that epitomized the Gothic novel, the forerunner of the Romantic Suspense genre. In these prototypes, the final scene often did take place on a dark and stormy night, with the innocent, young heroine on the battlements of the isolated, crumbling castle, forced, finally, to choose between the two men who have promised safety and, ultimately, happiness. Tension has built throughout the story, and it is only in this last, fateful encounter that she can distinguish between the two, one the hero and the other the villain. Although the trappings have changed, the essence of that story remains in today's novels of Romantic Suspense. The threatened heroine is placed in jeopardy, and although she now may save herself rather than relying on a hero to rescue her, she is still faced with a dilemma concerning the hero. Either she must choose between two men, one who turns out to be good and the other bad, or she must reconcile her feelings toward the traditional bad-boy hero and learn to trust him, appropriating a theme from the Romance genre.

A Definition

Romantic Suspense is a genre with roots in both the Romance and Suspense genres. Elements of Mystery, Espionage, and especially Suspense combine with Romance to create a story that does not fit comfortably in any of the genres it draws from. The best examples blend Romance and Suspense so completely that it is only possible to consider them as their own genre.

Traditionally, Romantic Suspense was a Romance with an element of danger introduced. There was rarely actual violence, just the underlying suggestion that violence was possible or that it had occurred sometime in the past. The language was gentle, the romantic interest asexual, and any true violence offstage. Today's Romantic Suspense often depicts explicit violence and strong sexual situations, making these books seem very similar to many titles discussed in chapter 13, "Suspense." The powerful romantic entanglement, however, with both explicit sex and romantic overtones, does not always appeal to Suspense fans, just as the more violent and suspenseful episodes may offend some readers of Romances.

Romantic Suspense novels combine key elements from both the Romance and Suspense genres to create a story, told from the point of view of the threatened heroine. She is placed in a dangerous situation from which she must extricate herself, sometimes with the help of the hero. In Traditional Romantic Suspense, there are usually two men vying for her affection—one truly the hero and the other the villain—but not until the end can she, and the reader, distinguish between the two. In Contemporary Romantic Suspense, the heroine is more independent, but there is always a man to whom she is attracted. Now, rather than choosing between two men, she must often come to terms with the true character of the man she has come to love, despite her concerns about him. The hero may even appear as a villain, and he certainly seems untrustworthy in some way. In the end, however, he always exhibits the traits of a true hero. *See* Figure 11.1 for a summary of the genre's characteristics.

Characteristics and the Genre's Appeal

Characterization

Point of view is key to the appeal of Romantic Suspense. Although readers appreciate the suspenseful and romantic story line, they also demand the reassurance that the heroine has survived. The story

---

FIGURE 11.1

Characteristics of the Romantic Suspense Genre

1. The story is told from the threatened heroine's point of view, so the reader is aware that she has survived. Heroines are increasingly resourceful and independent, and their survival usually depends on their own skill.

2. Although Traditional Romantic Suspense is softer-edged, generally leaving bodies offstage, Contemporary Romantic Suspense may present graphic details, as well as strong language and explicit sexual descriptions.

3. The development of a romantic relationship is crucial to the plot. There may be two suitors, and the heroine must decide which one is the hero and which the villain. Alternatively, the heroine must come to accept and trust the hero, who may appear originally as a blackguard.

4. Pacing is fast. The action often starts on the first page and continues relentlessly at a breakneck speed.

5. A sense of uneasiness, generated by the building Suspense, prevails even in quieter moments and affects the tone of these novels.

6. Romantic Suspense rarely features series characters.

---

needs to be told from, filtered through, her point of view. If it is not, fans may consider the story suspenseful but will also recognize that something is missing. And even though other points of view are often represented—the villain's, as in all good Suspense stories, and often the hero's as well—the heroine remains the central character. It is for her story, because they identify and sympathize with her, that readers flock to novels of Romantic Suspense.

The emphasis on the heroine and her story is particularly clear in more traditional examples of the genre. Victoria Holt's classic *Mistress of Mellyn* features Martha Leigh's first-person narration, as she recounts her suspicions of the sinister incidents at Mellyn Hall, where she works as a governess.[1] Because events are filtered through her consciousness, we see only what she sees, and our perception of other characters, as well as our growing fears for the fate of the eponymous Mistress, are her own. Thus, the reader feels the immediacy of her situation as well as the extent of her growing uneasiness.

Story Line

The most dramatic changes in the genre over the past few years have been in the increase in explicit sex and violence and the addition of strong language. In the hands of classic writers Daphne du Maurier, Mary Stewart, and even Elizabeth Peters, these were books one could hand "safely" to any reader concerned about that content. Today, the genre is dominated by Romance writers who have turned to Suspense writing, and, interestingly, it is their contribution that has altered the genre's tone from softer- to harder-edged. Although these authors— Sandra Brown, Karen Robards, Iris Johansen—made their names and reputations writing Romances, they have added so much Suspense to their novels, as well as violence and strong language, that they are no longer considered Romance writers by fans of that genre. Yet the romantic language, tone, and situations in their novels play too important a role for them to be considered writers of straightforward Suspense. In fact, many have drawn their Romance fans with them to this reimagined Romantic Suspense genre, and although the readers may not find the Romances they expect in current titles by their favorites, author loyalty and strong romantic elements have encouraged them to stay fans.

Meagan McKinney is another example of a Romance author who turned to Romantic Suspense. In *A Man to Slay Dragons* she places her heroine Claire in jeopardy from her sister's murderer, as Claire works with supposed mercenary (really an FBI agent) Liam Jameson to solve the crime.[2] The story, with the narrative switching among Liam, Claire, and the unknown killer, features a serial killer and graphic scenes of sex and violence. Still, any Romance reader would recognize the tone and direction of the plot, as Romance plays a strong role in addition to the Suspense.

Although Nora Roberts continues to write traditional Romances, many of her novels, especially the newer hardcover titles, are much more Romantic Suspense than Romance. *Carnal Innocence* is a classic example.[3] The sultry climate of the South blends with a steamy Romance as concert violinist Caroline Waverly comes home to recover from a grueling concert tour and a failed love affair. Instead of a peaceful small town, she finds dark secrets and a long-ago murder. Yet Roberts also establishes a vital romantic relationship, and the romantic elements remain as intense and important as the Suspense. A more recent title, *Carolina Moon*, follows a similar theme.[4]

Although it is the heroine's story, the hero—or in many cases hero and villain—must also be carefully portrayed for the romantic elements to come together. Even with the increase in explicit violence, sex, and language, the romantic tone and relationship remain crucial to the story. If there is not a strong romantic relationship, the book probably fits in the Suspense genre instead. Elizabeth Lowell's Romantic Suspense titles, *Jade Island* for example, clearly depend on the romantic relationship as well as the Adventure and Suspense elements.[5] The resolution of the romantic entanglement, in this case that Lianne and Kyle discover and acknowledge their love, is as vital to the success of the story as the resolution of the other plot issues, which revolve around a powerful Chinese trading family, an equally influential American family with links to the government, and the intricacies of the jade trade. In addition, there is often that frisson of sexual tension that epitomizes Romances and the stereotypical first kiss, which, as in Romances, awakens passions that have lain dormant in these characters.

In Suspense we usually can distinguish the hero from the villain; although we have the villain's point of view, he is usually a shadowy figure, not necessarily identified by the author or protagonist. This is often not the case in Romantic Suspense. Here, we have reason to suspect the motives of both men, hero and villain, and not until the end do we—and our heroine—discover which is really which. In Heather Graham's *Drop Dead Gorgeous*, Lori Kelly returns to Miami after more than ten years' absence to be near her dying grandfather.[6] She is immediately caught up in her old group of friends, some of whom stayed in Miami and others who have returned. However, they share the terrible secret of a friend's death as a teenager—or was it murder?—and now someone has started killing again to protect the secret. Lori is torn, not knowing which of her old friends (several of whom have shown a romantic interest in her) to trust.

In other Romantic Suspense novels, the heroine has difficulty accepting the hero in that role, even though we as readers know him to be one. Typically in Ann Maxwell's novels of Romantic Suspense and Adventure, the hero is a man with a shady past, not the stock straight-arrow hero, and the heroine must uncover his virtues as their relationship develops. Traditional Romantic Suspense and especially Gothics, with their brooding heroes, seemingly set apart from the heroine and her needs, also reflect this characterization.

Another characteristic the Romantic Suspense genre shares with Romance is that it rarely features series characters. The accidents and dangers that assail the heroine are often so dramatic that few sane readers would expect to find her in the same situation again. Occasionally secondary characters reappear in subsequent titles, or main characters from one novel may reappear as secondary characters later, as in linked novels by Lowell, for example. Others, such as Peters and Johansen, do, in fact, feature series characters in their novels, described below. In both cases, however, the heroine's profession allows her to be placed in jeopardy in more than just a single adventure.

Pacing

As in the Suspense genre, pacing here is crucial. Although a sense of uneasiness underlies the whole story, the action often starts at the first page and builds to the confrontation at the end. Brown's *The Witness* begins in medias res, with our heroine involved in a car accident, and the man she is with, the man who should be rescuing her, suffers from amnesia as a result of the accident.[7] She and we, the readers, know he is an FBI agent, trying to protect her from a vicious vigilante group. To keep him at her side, she claims he is her husband, and although he suspects this is not true, he plays along. Brown is particularly stingy in providing information about the plot. She strings us along, giving mere tidbits of information, while there is always so much more we feel we need to know. We read more and more quickly to discover the truth of the situation. Eventually, and long after we would like, we learn the truth of her plight—she is a successful public defender in a small southern town, but she has married into a nightmare. Her escape, the evolving romantic relationship between the heroine and her amnesiac savior, and the frustratingly meager clues Brown provides make for suspenseful reading.

As in many titles in both the Suspense and Romance genres, there is enough action, perhaps even Adventure, to move the story quickly. For the most part, these stories are not densely written. The identification with the protagonist and her plight, the action and Adventure elements, and the desire to unravel the Mystery, as well as the building Suspense, often make these page-turners.

Frame

In addition, a particular tone pervades titles within the Romantic Suspense genre. There is always a sense of uneasiness, even in quieter moments within the story. We as readers sense that not all is as it seems, that danger still awaits our heroine, and often even before she sees the actual danger, we have sensed it. As in much Suspense, we are kept on the edge of our chairs waiting for danger to intrude. This feeling of edginess and uneasiness, a direct link to the genre's roots in Suspense, intensifies the descriptions and actions in these novels, and novels without this feeling do not satisfy fans of the genre in the same way.

Key Authors and Subgenres

Benchmark

Although she is a benchmark in Romance (see chapter 10), Nora Roberts is also the most popular writer of Romantic Suspense today. While she continues to publish traditional Romances, her hardcover titles are Romantic Suspense, and it is likely that her success in helping the genre evolve has tempted other Romance writers to join her in writing Romantic Suspense. One of her most recent, *River's End*, tells the story of young Olivia MacBride, who has witnessed her mother's murder.[8] She is then whisked to the safety of Washington's Olympic Peninsula by her grandparents, but years later she finds herself in danger again when a writer begins to investigate the case. This novel exemplifies what is currently most popular in the genre. First, there is a heroine, haunted by dreams and the buried memory of the monster who killed her mother. There is also a strong hero, whom the heroine shuns at first, as he forces her to confront her past. However, it is to him that she later turns for protection and love. Finally, there is the murderous villain, whose identity neither we nor the heroine suspects until the end, even though we know that he must be someone close to her, stalking her now to remove the final witness to his crime. In her Romantic Suspense, Roberts portrays strong women in difficult situations, explicit violence, and strong sexual themes; her heroines are supported by caring family, lovers, and friends, who may also be put in danger but who ultimately help to resolve the problem.

Subgenres of Romantic Suspense

Although Traditional Romantic Suspense fell into two categories, Historical and Contemporary, the Romantic Suspense written today is set almost exclusively in the present day. Some Historical Romances include elements of Suspense with Adventure and Intrigue, notably by Patricia Veryan, Monique Ellis, and Judith A. Lansdowne, but their books can hardly be considered Historical Romantic Suspense in the tradition of Victoria Holt. Instead, the most obvious subgroups today fall out between Traditional and Contemporary Romantic Suspense, a distinction of style rather than time period, with the latter far more prevalent.

TRADITIONAL ROMANTIC SUSPENSE

Traditional Romantic Suspense, in the fashion of masters Daphne du Maurier, Mary Stewart, Holt, and Phyllis A. Whitney, has practically disappeared from the publishing scene, much to the disappointment of this subgenre's many fans. Many readers enjoy reading, and rereading, the classic authors, but others find the situations and characterizations dated. One of the best current practitioners is Caroline Llewellyn. Her *Life Blood* harkens back to the traditional aspects of the genre.[9] More leisurely paced, with the story unraveling unhurriedly, this novel features the elements of Traditional Romantic Suspense, as a writer of children's books returns to her family's cottage and discovers terrible secrets from the past. There are the two men who woo her, and one is, of course, the villain, while the other offers her true love and future happiness. The slower pacing lends itself to more elegant, descriptive prose, while the Suspense and the romantic entanglements pull the reader into the story. There may not be as much fast action, nor as many Adventure elements, but the identification with the heroine and her story—the desire to discover what will happen next—pulls the reader along at a brisk pace. *See* Figure 11.2 for a summary of the subgenre's elements.

Although most libraries, mine included, classify them as Mysteries, Elizabeth Peters's Vicky Bliss novels may appeal as much to fans of Romantic Suspense as of Cozy Mysteries, as they are more suspenseful extrications from danger than actual solving of mysteries. The intrepid heroine, an art historian in Munich, finds Adventure and Romance among Europe and Africa's artistic treasures. Humor, Adventure, Suspense, and Romance characterize these stories, a series, in which there is never a question of whether the heroine will

---

FIGURE 11.2

Characteristics of Traditional Romantic Suspense

1. The focus is on the female protagonist; the story is told from her point of view and is often first-person. The hero and villain's viewpoints are less important and less frequently present.

2. The threat of violence, rather than actual explicit violence, places the heroine in jeopardy, as she seeks to solve some mystery or unravel a secret from the past. The plot revolves around her extrication, either by the hero or through her own efforts.

3. The heroine must choose between two male protagonists, one the hero and the other the villain. Neither she, nor the reader, can make that distinction between the two until the end.

4. Pacing may be slower, as the action may be less physical and the plot offers fewer Adventure elements.

5. Settings may be present day or historical, and they are frequently exotic locales. There may also be a supernatural element.

---

survive, simply how she will extricate herself this time. Romance is also an important element, in the form of Vicky's ongoing romantic entanglements with the mysterious John Smythe. Here, however, the pattern follows that more popular in Contemporary Romantic Suspense, with Vicky, and the reader, always left uncertain about Sir John's true nature, not to mention his real identity.

Brenda Joyce's *The Third Heiress* adds Gothic elements to the classic plot line.[10] Dancer Jill Gallagher is responsible for the car accident that kills her fiancé, English nobleman Hal Sheldon. His dying words proclaim his love for "Kate." Her curiosity aroused, Jill accompanies his body back to England and in his room discovers a cherished antique picture of his grandmother with her great friend Kate Gallagher, who disappeared at age eighteen. Could Kate have been an ancestress of the orphaned Jill? Determined to uncover the details, Jill returns to England to pursue this secret, amidst very real danger to her own life. She is also courted by both Hal's brother and his cousin, and not until the very end can we tell which is friend and which foe.

Most Romantic Suspense with historical settings falls into the Traditional category, with less explicit violence and language. Holt, who died in 1993, set the standard for historical Romantic Suspense with her classic tales of young heroines in jeopardy, set against exotic locations and in past times. Her books exemplify the main difference between Romantic Suspense with historical and present-day settings, whether of the Traditional or Contemporary mode: the heroine's reliance on the hero for her rescue. In those with a historical setting, the heroine relies almost exclusively on the hero, while in those with present-day settings, she tends to be more independent.

CONTEMPORARY ROMANTIC SUSPENSE

As I suggested earlier in this chapter, Contemporary Romantic Suspense dominates current Romantic Suspense publication. *See* Figure 11.3.

Nora Roberts, the benchmark for the genre, sets the standard for Contemporary Romantic Suspense as well. Romance writers who have migrated to Romantic Suspense in her wake are Sandra Brown, Tami Hoag, and Karen Robards, among others. As has Roberts, they have retained the romantic feel of their books and the emphasis on the satisfactory development of the romantic relationship, but they have

---

FIGURE 11.3

Characteristics of Contemporary Romantic Suspense

1. More explicit sex and violence, as well as strong language, predominate. The danger to the heroine is explicit, rather than implicit, and graphically described.
2. Heroines are stronger, more independent, and usually extricate themselves from difficulties.
3. Pacing is brisk, as a heavy measure of Adventure or Intrigue, along with the Suspense, moves the plot quickly.
4. Settings are present day.
5. The romantic relationship, usually between the protagonist and the law enforcement officer working on the case, remains an important element and sets the tone for the novel. The heroine must come to know and trust the hero.

---

also added a dimension from the Hard-Edged Suspense subgenre: mounting tension underlined by violent threats and encounters.

In fact, Iris Johansen's Eve Duncan stories (*The Face of Deception* and *The Killing Game*) are increasingly hard-edged, although they are still sought by fans who remember her historical novels of Adventure and Romance.[11] In these more recent novels she features a forensic sculptor who lost her own child—she was abducted and murdered—and now seeks to identify the bones of other "lost children." Stalking, graphic violence, building of Suspense, and an undercurrent of Romance characterize these page-turners.

Kay Hooper, another former Romance writer, adds elements of the supernatural to her Contemporary Romantic Suspense stories, creating Contemporary Gothics of a sort. Striking coincidences, mistaken identities, secrets, and lovers from the past all converge to create romantic, atmospheric stories, with the Suspense heightened by the addition of a ghost or two. In *After Caroline* Joanna Flynn escapes a car accident, but then begins to dream of another accident, a young woman, and a cry for help.[12] When she is mistaken for the eponymous Caroline, she decides to investigate and travels from her home in Atlanta to Oregon, where, on the same day as her own accident, Caroline, a young woman who could be her twin, was killed in an accident. Why does she seem to be calling Joanna for help? And how could secrets in this coastal town put her own life in danger? Hooper continues to write gripping, ghostly stories of Contemporary Romantic Suspense.

Preparing to Work with Readers

Many fans of this genre grew up with the classic stories of Mary Stewart, Phyllis Whitney, and Victoria Holt. Now, they see changes in their genre that may send them to other types of books. Other readers may have been Romance readers who have followed their favorite authors as their writing has changed. Still others may generally read Suspense but have been attracted to Romantic Suspense by popular authors whose names they recognize from the best-sellers lists.

In all cases, readers clearly expect and demand that the story be told from the threatened heroine's point of view. The story may be narrated first-person or it may be told in third-person, but it is crucial that the reader be allowed to follow the heroine, her plight, and her point of view throughout the story. Otherwise, readers lose that emotional link with the heroine and the danger she confronts. As in Romances, there is an emotional response to the heroine and, in this genre, her predicament.

Many readers choose Romantic Suspense for the exotic settings in which these stories often take place. The atmosphere, intensified by the isolation or foreign setting, heightens the Suspense. The heroine must be isolated, either physically or emotionally, from those who might help her extricate herself from the dangerous situation into which she has fallen. Stewart sets her stories around Europe, Ann Maxwell/Elizabeth Lowell writes of East Asia and Australia, and Whitney sets her tales at locales across the United States. Wherever they set their stories, these authors can be counted on to provide the details that create an excellent sense of place.

Although some authors use the traditional Gothic trapping, the crumbling castle (Elizabeth Peters's Vicky Bliss adventure *Borrower of the Night* is a good example), others more simply isolate their heroines in more or less familiar places, where, as in Nora Roberts's *Sanctuary*, the familiar can prove as frightening as the exotic.[13] Emotional isolation, keeping the heroine away from family and friends who might support her, remains a crucial element. In Brenda Joyce's *The Third Heiress*, not only is Jill an orphan, already without family to support her, she is also on her own in England, foreign territory, in the midst of a family who blames her for her lover's death. No physical isolation could prove more menacing.

Readers of Romantic Suspense expect a satisfactory resolution to their stories. As fans are drawn from both Suspense and Romance genres, not to mention Mystery, this should not seem unusual. These stories are end oriented; readers know what will happen at the novel's conclusion. (The loose ends will, of course, be tied up and the heroine safe.) Fans seek a romantically written novel of a woman placed in a dangerous situation. No matter which type of Romantic Suspense or author they choose, they expect to feel the heroine's plight, and they anticipate experiencing a range of emotions from that tingle of menace to outright fear. They read to discover just how the author will save the heroine—or allow her to save herself.

As in every genre, it is important to become familiar with Romantic Suspense writers popular with our patrons. In addition to the benchmarks and representative authors described above, those on the list in Figure 11.4 provide an introduction for librarians—and other readers—who generally read in another genre.

Readers' Advisory Interview

If a reader requests this genre, she likely means the classic authors such as Phyllis Whitney and Victoria Holt. (Readers of the "new" Romantic Suspense are more likely to request specific authors—Nora Roberts or Tami Hoag—than the genre.) Although there are few recent examples of this style, it is always good to keep a list of names to offer, while continuing to watch reviews for new authors. The annotated booklist for Traditional Romantic Suspense at my library is always extremely popular, but readers despair that new titles appear so infrequently.

FIGURE 11.4

An Introduction to the Romantic Suspense Genre

Romantic Suspense Writers to Try, If You Enjoy . . .

Adventure	Sandra Brown (Witness)
	Ann Maxwell (The Ruby, The Diamond Tiger)[14]
Gentle	Victoria Holt
	Phyllis Whitney
	Barbara Michaels
	Mary Stewart
Historical Fiction	Victoria Holt (The Time of the Hunter's Moon)[15]
Horror	Barbara Michaels
	Kay Hooper
Humor	Karen Robards (Walking after Midnight)[16]
	Elizabeth Peters (Vicky Bliss series)
Literary Fiction	Francesca Stanfill (Wakefield Hall)[17]
Mystery	Elizabeth Peters (Trojan Gold)[18]
	Iris Johansen (Eve Duncan series)
Romance	Elizabeth Lowell
Suspense	Sandra Brown
Thriller	Mary Stewart (Airs above the Ground)[19]
Western	Elizabeth Lowell (Fire and Rain)[20]
Women's Lives	Linda Howard

One of the advantages of a library, however, is that we can keep popular titles, even if they are not recent, and make them available to readers. We reprint the lists of Traditional Romantic Suspense authors, because we know the books will still be in our collection or available through interlibrary loan. Our job is not to convince fans of Traditional Romantic Suspense that they must accept and read newer authors—although we should keep an eye out for new titles in the Traditional mode as well as those that fans of the Traditional might enjoy. We continue to put Mary Stewart, Daphne du Maurier, Holt, and others on our displays, and fans discover or rediscover these authors and read their books.

Because fans of the "new" Romantic Suspense are more likely to request authors by name, we must verify first whether they seek their Romances or Romantic Suspense titles. If they talk about a title, we can usually easily tell. Simply asking if it was suspenseful also achieves the desired result. Some of these authors now write Romantic Suspense exclusively, while others continue to write straight Romances. With the former group, we need to keep their Romance titles, cataloging them and adding to our collections when the author's newfound success prompts the reprinting of all her titles. Linda Howard is one of the exceptions who has continued to write paperback Romances, while her Romantic Suspense titles are published in hardcover. In a recent Romantic Suspense title, *Mr. Perfect*, a group of friends create a tongue-in-cheek list of the requirements for the perfect man.[21] The list spreads, is even featured in the media—and then one of the friends is murdered. Who would be so offended by the list of qualities that he would resort to murder? Howard combines strong romantic elements, and even humor early on, with heightened Suspense as the friends' lives are in danger. Howard is another author who has brought her Romance fans with her and attracted new fans by adding the element of danger to her books. This popularity in one genre is clearly a straightforward way to offer crossover into the other. We need to watch for authors who write in more than one genre, as that helps us understand better what readers say they enjoy about one type of book and opens the door to the other.

We should remember, too, that newer authors may be published only in paperback and that they, too, may write in more than one genre. RITA Award–winning authors Anne Stuart and Suzanne Brockmann continue to write in both genres. Stuart writes Contemporary and Historical Romances as well as Contemporary Romantic Suspense, and all are characterized by dangerous heroes, humor (with witty repartee between hero and heroine), and steamy sexual scenes. Try *Shadow Lover*, with its dark hero, claiming to be an old friend, while the heroine knows the real Alex is dead.[22] Brockmann writes Contemporary Romances as well as Contemporary Romantic Suspense.

Body Guard features a young woman hunted by the Mob and the agent detailed to protect her.[23]

Carla Neggers emigrated from the Romance genre to Romantic Suspense, and to date, her books are only published in paperback form. Try *Night Scents,* with its historical Cape Cod house, sold to a southern businessman, and the deadly secret that the owner's great niece vows to help her aunt uncover.[24] Typically, despite the Suspense elements, Neggers's books also contain elements of humor, along with the necessary components to create compelling Romantic Suspense. Other paperback authors to be aware of—before and after they make the transition into hardcover—include Meryl Sawyer *(Tempting Fate)* and Heather Graham Pozzessere *(If Looks Could Kill).*[25]

Sure Bets

Depending on what our readers are seeking, there are a number of Romantic Suspense authors who make Sure Bets. Du Maurier, Stewart, Holt, and Whitney have retained many of their loyal readers— and gained new fans—with their classic stories of women in jeopardy. Newer fans flock to Roberts, Hoag, Catherine Coulter, and Sandra Brown, all of whom attract readers by their presence on the best-sellers lists, and these can certainly be successfully suggested to readers who do not mind more sex and violence.

The range of Roberts's writing makes her the ultimate Sure Bet. Even her Romantic Suspense novels are available in both paper and hardcover formats. Some of her Romance series (the Born In titles, for example) have enough Suspense to please Romantic Suspense fans. And Romance readers who like Roberts often read the range of her titles in both genres.

Expanding Readers' Horizons

Whom else might readers of Romantic Suspense enjoy? Fans of the Traditional end of the genre might explore Cozy Mysteries with more Adventure than puzzle. Try authors such as Elizabeth Peters and Sharyn McCrumb (the Elizabeth MacPherson series of which *Sick of Shadows* is the first).[26] Romances with well-defined Suspense elements and little or no explicit sex might also be acceptable alternatives. (These will most likely be Historical Romances, such as those by Monique Ellis or Judith A. Lansdowne. Readers who will tolerate a greater sexual content might also try Contemporary Romances by Jayne Ann Krentz or Historical Romances by her alter ego Amanda Quick.) Writers of novels of Women's Lives and Relationships may also add engrossing layers of information, sometimes about lost treasures and always about dark secrets, to their novels. Diane Chamberlain (*The Escape Artist*) is a possible suggestion.[27] The more romantic thrillers of Evelyn Anthony and Helen MacInnes may also appeal, but few new titles of this type are currently being published.

The reader who mentions best-selling authors such as Roberts and Brown is looking for the newer version of the genre. If readers identify titles they enjoy, it is easier to determine whether they want the Romances by these authors or Romantic Suspense. If their current interest tends in the latter direction, they might enjoy other Romance writers who are now writing Romantic Suspense, such as Hoag, Kay Hooper, and Coulter. They may also enjoy titles of Harder-Edged Suspense, if they feature strong heroines, such as Thomas Perry's Jane Whitefield series, described in chapter 13, "Suspense." They may also find some of the Medical Thrillers by authors such as Robin Cook and Tess Gerritsen (described in chapter 14, "Thrillers") satisfying, as these also often feature strong women in dangerous situations from which they must extricate themselves.

Readers who consider Mary Higgins Clark to be Romantic Suspense are likely looking for more Suspense and less Romance. I usually steer them toward others who write the Softer-Edged Suspense (described in chapter 13). However, they may also be satisfied by the Traditional Romantic Suspense novels, in which there is ultimately a romantic relationship, but it does not overwhelm the suspenseful story. Again, as in all readers' advisory interviews, we need to remain open to the idea that Clark may simply be a name they have heard in connection with the genre and that a few probing questions or a capsule summary of the type of book she writes may send us in other directions. As always, we offer possibilities, and the readers make their own choices. *See* Figure 11.5 for suggestions of links to other genres.

FIGURE 11.5
Expanding Readers' Horizons

Authors to Take Readers beyond the Romantic Suspense Genre

Adventure	Carol Doumani (*Chinese Checkers*)[28]
Mystery	Sharyn McCrumb
Romance	Monique Ellis
	Judith A. Lansdowne
	Jayne Ann Krentz
Suspense	Mary Higgins Clark
Thriller	Evelyn Anthony
	Thomas Perry
	Gerald A. Browne
	Tess Gerritsen
Women's Lives	Diane Chamberlain

Reference Sources

Readers' Advisors can draw on reference sources related to both Suspense and Romance genres to find information about Romantic Suspense. Unfortunately, no single source provides all the information we need. In her study of the Romance genre, *Romance Fiction: A Guide to the Genre,* Kristin Ramsdell has a chapter on "Romantic Mysteries," which includes a section on "Romantic Suspense."[29] This overview of the genre and related topics provides an excellent introduction, history, and lists of authors. In *Genreflecting* (*see* appendix 2), Diana Tixier Herald also provides a concise description and author/title lists.

Where to Find . . .

INFORMATION ABOUT THE AUTHOR

Some authors will be included in *Twentieth-Century Romance and Historical Writers,* others in *Contemporary Authors* (*see* appendix 2).[30]

Writers who publish only in paperback will be more difficult to locate, but they may have home pages with pertinent information. Because *Killer Books: A Reader's Guide to Exploring the Popular World of Mystery and Suspense* includes a chapter on this genre, authors are profiled there as well.[31]

PLOT SUMMARIES

Standard readers' advisory reference tools from appendix 2—*Fiction Catalog, What Do I Read Next?* and *NoveList* provide annotations of titles in this genre.

GENRE DESCRIPTION, BACKGROUND, AND HISTORY

As I mentioned above, both *Romance Fiction* and *Genreflecting* provide descriptions or histories of the genre. *Mystery and Suspense Writers* also includes an essay on the genre.[32]

CORE LISTS AND BEST BOOKS

Ramsdell provides a list of current authors of Romantic Suspense in her Sample Core Collection.

Although many of us regret the demise of Traditional Romantic Suspense, readers have certainly managed to adjust to the genre's new image, and there are probably more novels of Romantic Suspense on the best-sellers lists than ever before. Readers, primarily women, remain true to this genre that reflects the importance of strong female characters, caught in dangerous situations, who rescue themselves, as well as those they love. Seemingly as long as the genre continues to emphasize strong and interesting romantic relationships, the increasing level of explicit violence does not deter fans.

NOTES

1. Victoria Holt, *Mistress of Mellyn* (Garden City, N.Y.: Doubleday, 1960).
2. Meagan McKinney, *A Man to Slay Dragons* (New York: Kensington, 1996).
3. Nora Roberts, *Carnal Innocence* (New York: Bantam, 1992).
4. ———, *Carolina Moon* (New York: Putnam, 2000).
5. Elizabeth Lowell, *Jade Island* (New York: Avon, 1998).

6. Heather Graham, *Drop Dead Gorgeous* (New York: Onyx, 1998).

7. Sandra Brown, *The Witness* (New York: Warner Books, 1995).

8. Roberts, *River's End* (New York: Putnam, 1999).

9. Caroline Llewellyn, *Life Blood* (New York: Scribner, 1993).

10. Brenda Joyce, *The Third Heiress* (New York: St. Martin's/Griffin, 1999).

11. Iris Johansen, *The Face of Deception* (New York: Bantam, 1998); ———, *The Killing Game* (New York: Bantam, 1999).

12. Kay Hooper, *After Caroline* (New York: Bantam, 1996).

13. Elizabeth Peters, *Borrower of the Night* (New York: Dodd, Mead, 1973); Roberts, *Sanctuary* (New York: Putnam, 1997).

14. Ann Maxwell, *The Ruby* (New York: HarperPaperbacks, 1995); ———, *The Diamond Tiger* (New York: HarperCollins, 1992).

15. Holt, *The Time of the Hunter's Moon* (Garden City, N.Y.: Doubleday, 1983).

16. Karen Robards, *Walking after Midnight* (New York: Delacorte, 1995).

17. Francesca Stanfill, *Wakefield Hall* (New York: Villard, 1993).

18. Peters, *Trojan Gold* (New York: Atheneum, 1987).

19. Mary Stewart, *Airs above the Ground* (New York: M. S. Mill, 1965).

20. Lowell, *Fire and Rain* (New York: Silhouette Books, 1990).

21. Linda Howard, *Mr. Perfect* (New York: Pocket Books, 2000).

22. Anne Stuart, *Shadow Lover* (New York: Onyx, 1999).

23. Suzanne Brockmann, *Body Guard* (New York: Fawcett Gold Medal, 1999).

24. Carla Neggers, *Night Scents* (New York: Pocket Books, 1997).

25. Meryl Sawyer, *Tempting Fate* (New York: Kensington, 1998); Heather Graham Pozzessere, *If Looks Could Kill* (Don Mills, Ont.: MIRA Books, 1997).

26. Sharyn McCrumb, *Sick of Shadows* (New York: Avon, 1984).

27. Diane Chamberlain, *The Escape Artist* (New York: HarperCollins, 1997).

28. Carol Doumani, *Chinese Checkers* (Venice, Calif.: Wave Pub., 1996).

29. Kristin Ramsdell, *Romance Fiction: A Guide to the Genre* (Englewood, Colo.: Libraries Unlimited, 1999).

30. Aruna Vasudevan and Lesley Henderson, eds., *Twentieth-Century Romance and Historical Writers,* 3d ed. (Detroit: St. James, 1994).

31. Jean Swanson and Dean James, *Killer Books: A Reader's Guide to Exploring the Popular World of Mystery and Suspense* (New York: Berkley Books, 1998).

32. *Mystery and Suspense Writers: The Literature of Crime, Detection, and Espionage* (New York: Scribner, 1998).

12

Science Fiction

Science Fiction is a genre that strikes fear in the hearts of many librarians. If we do not read it, it seems as strange as the beings that populate the pages of its books. And Science Fiction readers often seem an exclusive club, into which it is hard for a nonfan to gain admission.

Upon further exploration, however, we are likely to find this a genre rich in both physical and intellectual adventure, with something to offer a wide range of readers. This vast genre, with roots in the nineteenth century, is respected by fans and others for its intellectual underpinnings, and its diversity offers a variety of interesting directions for readers to pursue. From Romance to Mystery and beyond, Science Fiction is an unexpected treasure trove of crossover authors and titles.

A Definition

Although it seems that every genre overlaps other genres at some point, this problem is so pronounced with Science Fiction that even the experts disagree when they try to do something as basic as define it. When it comes to deciding whether or not a book fits within this genre (or Fantasy, the genre with which it most frequently overlaps), everything is up for grabs. One problem is that many of the genre's popular practitioners—Orson Scott Card, Roger Zelazny, Ursula LeGuin,

Robert Silverberg, to name a few—write both Science Fiction and Fantasy. Card suggests, facetiously, we might use cover art to differentiate between Science Fiction and Fantasy. If there are rivets on the cover, the book is Science Fiction. If there are trees on the cover, it is Fantasy.[1] An interesting approach, but it likely says more about publishers and their covers than about the genres. Another difference suggested by Science Fiction fans is that Science Fiction is the left brain reaching out to the right brain, logic reaching toward the artistic, while Fantasy is the opposite. Unfortunately, neither distinction is particularly helpful when we are working with patrons or cataloging books.

In her chapter on Science Fiction in *Genreflecting,* Diana Tixier Herald offers the following definition:

> Science fiction novels are those that deal with scientific topics, space travel, aliens, and recognizably Earth-variant worlds or life-forms that have not been touched by magic. Time travel, not occasioned by magic, is here, as are stories of distant civilizations (whether present-day or set many years in the future or in the past) that show some relationship to Earth or Earth life-forms.[2]

This is as good a place as any to start, and the explanations of the characteristics of the genre should clarify this definition. Of course, each reader, and especially in this genre in which readers are vocal and opinionated, will bring his or her own definition to any discussion of books that fall within the Science Fiction genre.

Characteristics and the Genre's Appeal

The Science Fiction genre is characterized by the basic elements listed in Figure 12.1. Subgenres, which are examined in more detail below, evince additional characteristics, but the following form the background of the genre as a whole.

Story Line

Science Fiction is speculative fiction. As Betty Rosenberg suggested in the first edition of *Genreflecting,* "Science fiction has been labeled a fiction of questions: What if . . .? If only . . .? If this goes on . . .?"[3]

FIGURE 12.1

Characteristics of Science Fiction

1. This is speculative fiction, usually set in the future, which explores moral, social, intellectual, philosophical, and ethical questions, against a setting outside of everyday reality.

2. Setting is crucial and invokes otherness of time, place, or reality. This relates to the physical setting of the story as well as to the tone, which often is constructed to disorient readers.

3. Technical and scientific details form an important part of the story.

4. Characters are generally secondary to issues and atmosphere. However, authors do use aliens and otherworldly creatures to emphasize the otherness of their stories.

5. Because of the complexity of creating another world, authors often write series that feature continuing characters or at least characters that inhabit the same world for more than one book.

6. Pacing depends on the focus of the book. If there is more physical action, the pacing is usually faster; if ideas are emphasized more, the book generally unfolds at a more leisurely pace.

Questions such as these characterize the premise behind these books. As speculative fiction, these are books that consider moral, social, and ethical issues while exploring philosophical, technical, and intellectual questions. Science Fiction is a fertile ground for the discussion of challenging and often controversial issues and ideas, and authors use it expressly for that purpose. Science Fiction introduces an almost overwhelming wealth of concepts and ideas. Other fiction genres may also raise difficult questions, but in Science Fiction, the authors take a precept, perception, or idea and explore it, often in a setting outside our own world or in a future time, but certainly out of everyday contexts. For example, on one level Orson Scott Card's *Ender's Game* is a coming-of-age story set in the future.[4] The reality of the story is much more, as Ender unknowingly plays a key role in the war to save the human race and the planet from invaders. A further level requires the reader to consider more philosophical issues, such as moral and social questions about society, as well as more general questions about power and authority. As is the case with much Science Fiction, this is a book to be appreciated and explored on many levels.

Removing readers from what is safe and known forces them to think differently when considering the available possibilities, to see things as they might be—to consider "what if," not just what is. This otherness of time, place, or reality is crucial to the appeal of Science Fiction. The reader is taken from the known world to the unknown, to another world or time. Frank Herbert's *Dune,* for example, is not just another Adventure novel, although that is certainly part of its enormous appeal.[5] The fact that it is set on another world, where the dangers, denizens, and politics all create an atmosphere foreign to our world and the strategies we might employ, makes it something more. The author, and we as readers, must relate to this world differently.

As a consequence of this speculative nature, Science Fiction also affirms the importance of story in our lives, the importance of imagination in the survival of the species. In *Great Sky River* Gregory Benford speculates that only "dreaming vertebrates" know life holds more than just existence.[6] We are part of that group, and these writers imagine our dreams and those of other species and validate their importance in our lives. Small wonder that much of Science Fiction deals with the idea of dreams and dreaming.

Frame

Science Fiction is consistently evocative and visual. It is not surprising that the Golden Age of Science Fiction, its first real flush of popularity, was also the age of radio, a time when listeners were accustomed to using their imagination to visualize settings, characters, and events. In Science Fiction authors create and populate new and alternative worlds, and they have to be able to describe the alien nature of the worlds they create and the beings that inhabit them to place us there. There is a wide range of tone in this otherness in which Science Fiction is set. At one end there is the wacky exuberance of Douglas Adams. His books feature slapstick trips through the universe after Earth is destroyed. In a clear demonstration of his rather off-kilter sense of humor, Adams has titled his series The Hitchhiker Trilogy, even though there are now five books in the series.[7] The books follow the adventures of Arthur Dent and his incognito alien friend, Ford Prefect, and take potshots at Science Fiction throughout.

At the other end of the spectrum in terms of tone are Ursula LeGuin's *Left Hand of Darkness* and Brian Aldiss's Helliconia Trilogy, in which bleak wintery landscapes underline the darker tone of the novels.[8] As a general rule in Science Fiction, the frame—that special atmosphere or setting—establishes the basis for the tone of the novels and provides a background for the ideas.

It goes without saying that technical and scientific details are also an important part of the genre's appeal. However, there is a great deal of current Science Fiction in which hard science, hardware, and technology, although important, do not dominate the novels as they did in the '50s, when technology was the key to most Science Fiction. It came as a surprise to me to realize that one need not have an extensive scientific background to understand and enjoy much of what is currently being written in the genre. Even writers of so-called Hard Science Fiction add enough plot and frame to make their novels understandable to the science challenged, following the tradition largely established by Isaac Asimov, who had a gift for integrating ideas into stories that could be appreciated on several levels. In the same vein, Piers Anthony relies heavily on scientific detail in his classic *Macroscope,* but the story—and its implications—are perfectly understandable, even to the science novice.[9]

Characterization

Science Fiction focuses on frame and story line. The moral, social, and philosophical questions considered in the genre are woven into the story line of the books and are pursued most often through the action, through situations and events, rather than through characters. Although attention is paid to characterizations in the more literary end of the genre, generally the issues, story, and frame are a more important focus. In his Book of the Long Sun series (*Nightside: The Long Sun* is the first), for example, Gene Wolfe certainly develops his cast of characters, but the focus is on the role these characters, citizens of Whorl (a hollow spaceship), play in the political process of colonization.[10]

Science Fiction is often series centered. Because of the complexity of the worlds they conceive, authors tend to use them more than just once, creating continuing characters that people this world, or at least setting further adventures within this unique environment. The special problems created for libraries in terms of retaining all within a series and keeping up on series are discussed below.

Pacing

Action in Science Fiction may be interior, more philosophical or psychological, or exterior, with more physical Adventure elements included. Pacing is usually determined by the amount of action. Titles in which there is more physical action are usually seen as fast paced by fans. Others may be described as "engrossing" or "compelling," but the emphasis on more interior action and speculation may mean that they are actually read at a slower pace. To get a sense of this distinction, compare the popular Honor Harrington series by David Weber, which moves at a brisk pace, with action spurring the reader on, with Dan Simmons's complex novels of Hyperion, where the philosophical emphasis makes the books engrossing but slows the reader's pace.

Key Authors and Subgenres

Benchmark

The identity of the benchmark author for the Science Fiction genre depends on what source or fan one consults. With the death in 1992 of the genre's most famous and prolific author, Isaac Asimov, the leading candidate was lost. Current lists of the "Best" tend to contain more "classic" than contemporary authors. Depending on the subgenre or thematic group one reads, there could be a wide variety of possibilities. For example, Robert A. Heinlein was the darling of an entire generation, and the masterful work of Philip K. Dick is increasingly known through motion picture translations of his novels. However, neither of these award-winning authors reaches "benchmark" status. Although it is certainly important for us to be familiar with these classic authors, whose writing still influences readers and writers alike, it is to current authors that we look for new directions in the genre. Of the newer authors, likely candidates with whom we should be familiar include Connie Willis, Kim Stanley Robinson, and Orson Scott Card. Willis, who has won multiple Hugo and Nebula Awards, is known for her finely drawn (usually female) characters, her use of language to create readable yet literary writing and to make complex ideas accessible, her wit (sometimes subtle, sometimes laugh-out-loud), her scholarship, and her complicated, well-researched story lines. *Doomsday Book* and *To Say Nothing of the Dog* are among her best-known works.[11]

Robinson, on the other hand, often focuses on ecological issues and employs more scientific detail and technology. Known for his rambling narratives, interesting characters, effective use of language, and distinct literary style, Robinson focuses more on issues than characters. He is best known for his award-winning Mars Trilogy (*Red Mars, Green Mars,* and *Blue Mars*), which plots the terra forming and civilization of the planet.[12] Both Robinson and Willis are also known for their short stories, a format that appeals to both fans and writers of the genre.

Prolific author Card explores the Fantasy and Horror genres as well as Science Fiction. His *Ender's Game* is a genre classic, but it is by no means his only contribution to the genre, as the popularity of his Homecoming series (beginning with *Memory of Earth*), among others, attests.[13] Well-told stories, strong characterizations, and plots with far-reaching philosophical and religious implications characterize his writing.

Subgenres of Science Fiction

Many thematic possibilities could be examined here to discuss and understand the genre, and the reference sources covered below explore these. Another way to view the genre, however, is to examine the two primary appeal-based subgenres, which fall at opposite poles of the Science Fiction genre. For lack of more distinctive terms, I call them the Storyteller focus at one end (*see* Figure 12.2) and the Philosophical focus at the other (*see* Figure 12.3, on page 271).

STORYTELLER FOCUS

Although telling a good story is clearly the aim of most books in all genres, here the authors emphasize creating inviting stories in which

---

FIGURE 12.2

Characteristics of the Storyteller Focus

1. Books are cinematic. Detailed descriptions make characters and settings come alive.

2. Moral, social, and ethical questions are raised, but characters, who are generally stereotypes, react within a prescribed course of behavior.

3. The story is important, and Adventure is usually a key plot feature, making pacing fast.

4. The ending is generally upbeat, optimistic.

---

to make the ideas they promote interesting and accessible. Their enthusiastic approach to the topics and the stories make their books immediately accessible to readers. Books in this subgenre are often referred to as "cinematic." Readers can readily imagine these books as movies or television series, as, in fact, some of them are. Detailed descriptions make characters and settings live.

When readers talk about titles in this subgenre, they usually talk first about the characters as part of the story, rather than about the ideas or issues. These books have casts of familiar characters to whom the readers relate and react. The characters are generally stereotypes, but I do not mean that in a derogatory sense. These are characters who are instantly recognizable and understandable. Readers are introduced to the cast of characters early in the books, and there are often multiple points of view. These books are not as often related first-person, so the reader has a better understanding of and feel for several characters. In these stories, authors often emphasize the relationships among characters as well, and these relationships play an important role in the plot and the issues being raised.

In Science Fiction novels with a Storyteller focus, moral, social, and philosophical questions are also considered. However, the reader is provided a moral framework in which it is usually clear what is right. The books raise questions of behavior or ethics, but they also often answer them. Although speculative, as Science Fiction is by its nature, these are also generally more didactic and often advocate a prescribed course of behavior for characters and the readers. In A. C. Crispin's StarBridge series (*Starbridge* is the first), students who attend a special academy to train diplomats to make first contacts with intelligent species learn specific, noninvasive techniques and face the consequences of failure to follow them.[14] Although there are always choices in their encounters, their training has provided specific responses and a circumscribed set of rules to follow in making contact. The *Star Trek* series' Prime Directive, which advocates noninterference in the development of less-advanced species, is another example.

Readers also comment on the author's ability as a storyteller in these novels, and telling an interesting story is clearly important. The point is to feature the characters in interesting, usually problematic, situations that rely on a scientific premise. There is also little doubt as to the outcome of these books; and the assurance that problems, issues, and plot complications will be resolved satisfactorily is part of their appeal. Look at Lois McMaster Bujold's series featuring Miles Vorkosigan, physically weak and deformed, who must continually prove his military prowess and acumen to keep his position as a rising military leader of Barryar. This ongoing series features Bujold's characteristic wit and even romantic touches, as we follow Miles's exploits, always confident that he will survive threats to his reputation, as well as his life. Books in this subgenre are generally upbeat, as should be clear from these examples. Because they are often series, it is important to the reader that favorite characters survive whatever ordeals they are subjected to in each episode.

Pacing in this type of Science Fiction is usually brisk. For the most part, books start fast and hook the reader in the first few pages. Because the books deal with relationships among characters, there is also more dialogue to move the story quickly. Adventure elements also figure prominently in these stories and that also speeds the pacing. The action is physical and moves the plot. There is not much interior dialogue, and the focus of the story is on action and in working out the problem, not just on intellectual speculation. Willis's award-winning *Doomsday Book* provides an excellent example. Ostensibly the story of Kivrin Engles, a twenty-first-century historian sent back in time to fourteenth-century England, this time-travel Adventure reveals a great deal of the history of the times—just at the outbreak of the Black Death—as well as the problems Kivrin faces as a time traveler with equipment problems and a curious inability to make contact with her own time. We, as readers, understand that plague is currently ravaging both time periods, and the suspense generated by this knowledge, our fears for Kivrin and her future, drives the pacing.

Benchmarks for this subgenre are Bujold and David Weber. Bujold's Vor series focuses on the political machinations of the militaristic Barryar and, more specifically, on the role of Miles Vorkosigan, heir to an important name in politics and deformed from birth (his mother was attacked shortly before his birth). His physical deformity belies his exceptional mental agility, and he proves himself a match for all opponents, human or alien. Action, elegant language, and wit characterize Bujold's series, which also provides interesting scientific detail and speculation.

Weber also employs a more militaristic frame for his entertaining series featuring Honor Harrington, who works her way up through the ranks of the space fleet of the Star Kingdom of Manticore. High-tech weaponry, more fighting, and an ingenious universe that features, among other things, sentient tree cats characterize this popular series.

The *Star Trek* and *Star Wars* series also fit into this subgenre, as does Crispin's StarBridge series. Although much of what I have said emphasizes the accessibility of titles in this subgenre, it should be noted that literary style is not absent from these books. Even the popular *Star Trek* series varies in quality, with titles by authors such as Peter David and Barbara Hambly as well conceived and executed as other examples of excellence in the genre. However, this subgenre boasts a wide range of interesting authors, from the more formulaic media series to the prizewinning novels of Willis, Card, and Bujold.

Within this subgenre there is also a group of authors who write bigger, generally more complex, but equally cinematic, Science Fiction with a slightly different tone. Novels by Asimov, Piers Anthony, and David Brin, for example, do not consistently offer a happy, or even necessarily a resolved, ending. In these, a note of pessimism may be introduced, and there may be some ambiguity about the best answer to the problems presented. In general, they raise more complex and less easily answered philosophical questions but are still enjoyed by readers who, for example, read *Star Trek* but who also enjoy a slightly bigger book. Characters here are also generally stereotypes, but because these are bigger books with a larger scope, the characters do have room to develop. They are sometimes placed in situations in which they are forced to alter their perceptions, to come to a greater understanding of the universe and themselves. Brin's *Startide Rising* is a good example, with its space mission staffed by dolphins and humans.[15] The intricate relationships between the two groups, with humans as the less advanced members, play a major role, as they face danger from galactic battles without as well as from mutiny within.

PHILOSOPHICAL FOCUS

One of the first things one notices is that authors in this group pay more attention to literary style. As is the case with Literary Fiction, there is a certain elegance to the writing; style is important. Writers such as Gene Wolfe, Octavia Butler, and Kate Wilhelm are noted for their graceful, eloquent prose. As one might expect, care and time are taken with the development of plot and character as well, hallmarks of literary style.

FIGURE 12.3

Characteristics of the Philosophical Focus

1. Attention is paid to literary style, and these are generally more elegantly written.

2. Characters are usually multi-dimensional and introspective; they, rather than action or Adventure, drive the plot.

3. There is a greater emphasis placed on ideas, rather than on adventure or science. Moral, social, and ethical issues are raised, but clear answers are not always given.

4. These are usually more densely written, with a more measured pace.

5. These are generally bleaker, less optimistic novels.

These books generally feature more insightful characterizations. Characters are multi-dimensional, not stereotypes; they surprise the reader by their actions and decisions, and they seem not to be bound to the plot or driven by it. Characters are often introspective, and the emphasis is on psychological rather than physical or social traits. Ideas may be manifested through characters, rather than primarily through plot, as they generally are in those with the Storyteller focus. An example is the award-winning Science Fiction novel *The Sparrow*, by Mary Doria Russell.[16] Scientists have identified sounds from another planet in another galaxy: music, a sure sign of sentient life. And because they have access to money and personnel, the Jesuits mount a mission to make first contact. Of the group sent, only one returns, horribly mutilated—physically, mentally, and emotionally. As the book opens we meet the damaged space traveler, and then, through a series of flashbacks interspersed with real time, we learn the terrible story of his mission. Layer upon layer the story builds, and we discover the harrowing truth of the group's experiences during their stay on the planet. Although the book includes all the elements one expects in Science Fiction, it is through the character of Father Emilio Sandoz that we see what happened, and, in our reaction to him and his plight, we explore the book on a deeper level. We see into his mind and share his anguish as the story unfolds and the truth emerges.

Moral and social issues are very important here again. In these, questions are raised, but there are seldom clear-cut answers to what is right and what is wrong. Ambiguity is the key. Even the ending may be uncertain, with issues and questions left unresolved. Characters face difficult, sometimes impossible, choices, as is certainly the case in *The Sparrow*. Another example is Roger Zelazny's *The Dream Master*, with its rather unnerving look at future psychology and a man who dreams the future.[17] Here Charles Render is a shaper, a special psychologist who helps patients experience shared mental images through a connection between their brains. Eileen Shallot, blind since birth, is a resident in psychology who wants to go into this field, so, through this dream process, he helps her see. Unfortunately, in this classical tragedy, it is Render who becomes obsessed, trapped by his need for these dream sessions, and the dreams that he originally directed are increasingly dominated by Eileen's psyche. This chilling fable, laden with literary references, charts his fall.

As a result, these books are often more densely written and the pace is more measured than in those with the Storyteller focus. Greg Bear's *Queen of Angels*, set in future Los Angeles, also uses the theme of dreams and dreaming to create a nightmare quality.[18] Complex style and story line, as well as interrelated characters, slow the pacing in the novel that raises questions involving a murder and the subsequent investigation.

Setting is especially important in the Philosophical focus. As in Horror and other genres in which setting is crucial to the success of the novel, carefully developed atmosphere and mood seem to permeate the books. There is a darker quality to these books, which often seem bleaker, less optimistic than those with the Storyteller focus. Sometimes it seems as if there is more interest in the mood and atmosphere than action. Frame or setting is an area in which the writers in the Philosophical subgenre excel. Ursula LeGuin and Brian Aldiss are known for the atmospheric nature of their novels. Another example is Sherri Tepper's *Grass*.[19] The palpably dark and atmospheric mood of this story, which investigates the immunity of the single planet Grass to the plague that is devastating the solar system, directs our reaction. The underlying menace is tangible as Marjorie Westriding, joining her diplomat husband on that planet, seeks to discover the secret of Grass.

In this subgenre LeGuin is the benchmark. For a taste of her work, try *The Lathe of Heaven,* a chilling moral fable of a man who can dream permanent changes to reality.[20] (The PBS television production of this story is the single most requested program in the PBS video library, a clear indication of its power and popularity.) In general, her books are characterized by an emphasis on people rather than technology. Common themes include explorations of cultural diversity and politics, especially the ability of power to corrupt.

Readers who read this kind of elegantly written, philosophical, character-driven Science Fiction will also appreciate, in addition to LeGuin, authors such as Aldiss and Russell, mentioned earlier, as well as Arthur C. Clarke, Philip K. Dick, and Dan Simmons. Classic Science Fiction writer Clarke typically melds technological realism with elements of mysticism and religious imagery. *Childhood's End,* which portrays mankind at the edge of disaster, is acknowledged as one the best examples of his work.[21]

Dick wrote layered, intelligent stories that focus more on ideas than technology. Often exhibiting a surreal, nightmare quality, Dick's novels also feature an ongoing examination of the ambiguity of reality as well as an ironic sense of humor. Try *Do Androids Dream of Electric Sheep?* (which was made into the motion picture *Blade Runner*) for an example of his provocative style.[22]

One of my personal favorites is Simmons's *Hyperion*, a futuristic *Canterbury Tales* with each pilgrim to the Time Tombs on Hyperion telling his or her story.[23] Our knowledge of the planet Hyperion and the characters unfolds slowly, as we add story by story, layer by layer, to the plot. Literary references and provocative moral and social questions make this a really satisfying read.

Just as the Storyteller focus has an extreme end with the cinematic media space travel series (*Star Trek* et al.), so does the Philosophical focus: Cyberpunk. This is one of the more recent trends in Science Fiction, and although these novels share the features of the Philosophical focus, they are also much more cynical. The protagonist is often an antihero, not usually admirable, strong, or noble. The books envision a negative high-tech future in which humans are not necessarily the highest life-forms, science may not be our salvation, and somehow the universe has gone awry. As readers we are often not clear which characters are good and which are bad, and frequently the expected roles are reversed. Although cynical, these books are not without humor; however, it is a very bleak, black humor, as we might expect. Language is important in these as well, but unlike the elegant writing of the Philosophical group, language here is idiomatic, jargon-filled, and often incomprehensible to the uninitiated at first glance. The otherness of the world or futures in which these books are set is underlined by the disorienting effect of the language. In fact, the use of language seems sometimes to create a kind of word game or word play, another aspect of Cyberpunk's appeal. We have to be in the know to understand and relate to the language.

For an example, try William Gibson's classic *Neuromancer*, a fast-paced story of computer hacking and double crosses, filled with action and multiple plotlines, often jumping quickly from one to another.[24] The story itself is purposefully bewildering; we are thrown into the middle of the action with almost no attempt to orient the reader in time and place. In fact, part of the appeal of this type is the reader's sense of disorientation. Recent movies such as *Terminator 2* and *The Matrix* have picked up this theme in accentuating the sense of dislocation and technology gone mad.[25]

Other examples include Neal Stephenson's *Snow Crash* and *Cryptonomicon* and Jeff Noon's *Vurt*. [26] The former novels feature computer hacking and code breaking and provide technological and mathematical detail with intellectual underpinnings, while the latter adds elements of pulp fiction and drug culture to a surreal exploration of Scribble, who discovers his ability to enter the world of virtual reality at will.

One particular theme in Science Fiction, not covered in either subgenre as it cuts across them, is Alternative History. Although some books that explore this topic are really Fantasy because they employ magic (Card's popular Alvin Maker series, considered in chapter 3, "Fantasy," is a prime example), most novels fit here, in recognition of their speculative nature. "What would have happened if . . ." is the question these authors direct. This popular theme has been explored by a range of authors from contributors to the *Star Trek* series, who often play with Earth's history on other worlds (John Vornholt's *Masks,* part of the *Star Trek, the Next Generation* series, is one example) to Dick's award-winning *The Man in the High Castle,* a searching story of America's prospects if Germany and Japan had won World War II and partitioned the country.[27] Another practitioner of this type of Science Fiction is Harry Turtledove, who popularized these stories among general readers with his novels of a victory by the South in the Civil War (*The Guns of the South: A Novel of the Civil War*).[28] *The Great War* is an excellent example of his style and use of history.[29] His recent World War II series, beginning with *Into the Darkness* and featuring dragons and magic, is Fantasy, not Science Fiction.[30]

Preparing to Work with Readers

Fans of Science Fiction are among the most elusive yet outspoken readers who use our libraries. Elusive, because they often spurn our offers of assistance and certainly our suggestions; outspoken, because they know what they are seeking, and they feel it is unlikely that we can offer them new directions—unless they see us as fellow fans (and only a few of us qualify in that role). If we are able to make contact, however, we find them voluble on this subject. They know what they like—the *good* Science Fiction—and ignore, or even reject, everything else. They expect us to have new titles by their favorite authors as soon as they learn about them (which may be long before they are even written) and demand that we have all in a series that they enjoy. *Out of print* and *unavailable* are terms that do not exist in their vocabulary. For example, there is a Web site devoted exclusively to the author Cyril Kornbluth, who died in the '50s and whose work has been out of print for years but who nevertheless commands an intensely devoted following.

This means that we librarians need to be diligent and persistent in seeking out and then keeping all titles in a series. Science Fiction book clubs and some publishers help by reprinting these volumes, but obtaining and retaining all titles in a series remain difficult. Because many early titles, and some titles in current series, have been published only in paperback, the issue of keeping copies becomes even more problematical, although Science Fiction paperbacks do tend to stay in print longer than their counterparts in the Romance genre.

Asked to share suggestions for what should be added to our collections, Science Fiction fans are always ready to provide long lists of titles, authors, and series every self-respecting library should own. If we ask for suggestions to develop our collection, we do so at our peril. This technique should not be risked unless we have a healthy budget and shelf space to support extensive additions to our collection!

Unless we are longtime fans of the genre or have a truly excellent source of prepublication information, we find it almost impossible to make suggestions to fans. Many have read for years and know more about the genre than we can ever hope to discover. In my library we pump readers shamelessly for information about the genre and favorite authors, so that we can use their suggestions to discover authors that might appeal to readers new to the genre or to fans of other genres. Fans like to be acknowledged but not necessarily assisted. On the other hand, if they have been away from the genre for a few years, they like to be made aware of new authors they may have missed. We occasionally have readers who come home from college with time to read again, and they like to be updated on trends in the genre. Some of the reference sources described below can help them—and us— keep up-to-date.

The shared worlds of the Science Fiction and Fantasy genres create another problem for libraries. Do we catalog additions to the endless *Star Trek* series under the names of individual authors or under the series? If you do the former, you must not have many readers asking for the newest book in the series or for a particular title by number. It only took us a few weeks one summer, working with teen after teen, ourselves new to the Science Fiction collection and exploring that series, to convince us that the only hope was to Cutter all series under the series name so they would be shelved together. Now read ers can easily find all within a series—and so can we!

Knowing something about Science Fiction, even if we have only read one or two books, makes us more comfortable talking to fans and them more comfortable relating to us. They see that we understand what it is that they love in this genre. As in every genre, we need to encourage fans to talk to us. We ask them about the authors they currently enjoy reading and of what other books or authors a particular title reminds them. Fans are usually effusive when asked about the authors they enjoy.

Although it may be difficult to suggest titles to fans, especially if we are not fans ourselves, in even a cursory exploration of the genre we discover titles and series that might be of interest to fans of other fiction genres. Many Science Fiction titles might appeal to readers of other genres who would never think of choosing Science Fiction on their own. (When we suggest them, however, we do better if we describe their appeal first and the ways in which they parallel a reader's taste before revealing that they are Science Fiction. Genre labels both attract and repel readers; connections made without the encumbrance of labels often help readers see beyond the genre classification to the appeal of the book.) Those librarians who are not Science Fiction fans might approach the task of becoming familiar with the genre this way as well. *See* Figure 12.4.

FIGURE 12.4

An Introduction to Science Fiction

Science Fiction Writers to Try, If You Enjoy . . .

Adventure	Orson Scott Card (*Ender's Game*)
	Peter David (*Star Trek*, etc.)
	Barbara Hambly (*Star Trek*, etc.)
	Frank Herbert (*Dune*)
	Larry Niven (*The Mote in God's Eye*)[31]
Fantasy	Anne McCaffrey (Dragonriders of Pern series)
	Marion Zimmer Bradley
Historical	Connie Willis (*Doomsday Book*)
	Kage Baker (*In the Garden of Iden*)[32]
Horror	Kate Wilhelm (*The Dark Door*)[33]
Humor	Douglas Adams (Hitchhiker series)
	Piers Anthony
Inspirational	C. S. Lewis
Literary	Roger Zelazny (*The Dream Master*)
	William Gibson (*Neuromancer*)
	Michael Swanwick (*Vacuum Flowers*)[34]
Mystery	Isaac Asimov (Robot books)[35]
Psychological	Stanislav Lem
	Jack Finney (*Invasion of the Body Snatchers*)[36]
Romance	Lois McMaster Bujold (*Shards of Honor*)[37]
	Anne McCaffrey (Dragonriders of Pern series)
	Catherine Asaro
Thriller	Gregory Benford
	Harry Harrison (*The Turing Option*)[38]
	Neal Stephenson (*Snow Crash*)[39]
Women's Lives	Octavia Butler
	Louise Marley (*The Terrorists of Irustan*)[40]
	Pamela Sargent (*The Shore of Women*)[41]

The Readers' Advisory Interview

Working with Science Fiction fans is a little different than in other genres. As I mentioned earlier, readers of Science Fiction tend to be among the most knowledgeable and opinionated readers I have encountered. They often have definite ideas about what they like and do not like, and although they may listen politely, they are not usually interested in our suggestions. (Admittedly, it is difficult to suggest to fans of any genre, unless we are also fans; they have always read more than we have. However, fans in most other genres seem not so adamant about their taste as these.) On the other hand, Science Fiction fans are always very happy to share suggestions of authors and titles every civilized reader should have read. Thus, the dialogue with these readers is slightly different from that with readers looking for suggestions and ideas. (Their attitude may have been fostered by their sometimes-too-clear evidence that we librarians really do not know and appreciate the authors they love. They may have reason to distrust our offer of assistance.)

As always when we talk with readers looking for suggestions, the key is to get them to tell us what they enjoy most in the books they have read. Readers who talk about characters and action are more likely to enjoy those authors in the first group with the Storyteller focus. I might suggest a range from the media series books (*Star Wars* and *Star Trek*) through the more complex novels of classic authors such as Frank Herbert and Isaac Asimov or newer writers such as David Weber, Connie Willis, and Kim Stanley Robinson. Those who describe Science Fiction more in terms of the ideas or the mood are more likely to enjoy the Philosophical focus: Ursula LeGuin, Greg Bear, Philip K. Dick, and Gene Wolfe.

Movies and television series also make a useful jumping-off point in exploring what someone is in the mood to read. Obviously the *Star Trek* television series, in all its manifestations, would lead us to the Storyteller subgenre, while newer movies such as *Alien* and *The Matrix* might lead us to those that emphasize the Philosophical but include enough action to tempt the reader.[42]

Fans of Science Fiction often appreciate short stories. This is a genre in which short stories are a popular form—among fans, critics, and authors. Short story collections also provide a good introduction to the genre for nonfans (librarians and readers alike), and award-winning or critically acclaimed anthologies are good purchases for libraries, especially those on a tight budget. Fans can then pursue single titles by authors they enjoy through interlibrary loan. Try *Nebula Award Stories* or *The Year's Best Science Fiction,* as well as others mentioned in the reference books below.[43]

Science Fiction is another genre that attracts teen readers. This may be because of the strong Adventure element in many novels or because many authors choose teen protagonists; as does the Horror genre, Science Fiction often features teenagers in control of their lives and their destinies. Unlike Horror, there is less graphic sex and violence here, and these may be "safer" reading in that sense—but not if parents are concerned that these younger readers might be led into new ways of thinking and seeing the world. Another important appeal may be that these stories also examine ideas—social, political, philosophical—in varying degrees of intensity. Readers appreciate the opportunity to probe the issues they see in the world, even if, in Science Fiction, they are set in a context outside their own. A. C. Crispin's StarBridge series and Orson Scott Card's Ender series, as well as several by Willis, including *Doomsday Book,* Herbert's classic, *Dune,* and most of Lois McMaster Bujold's Vor series, feature adolescent protagonists, but based on what appeals to the teen reader, any of the authors and titles already discussed might make good choices. There is one important caveat in dealing with Science Fiction readers. The abbreviated name of the genre is "SF," never "SciFi." Be careful, as fans find the latter offensive and tend to dismiss those who use it as uneducated and not to be trusted.

Sure Bets

As in all genres, there are Science Fiction titles that appeal to a wide range of readers, even those who read outside this genre. Two that come immediately to mind have already been described in this chapter: Card's *Ender's Game* and Mary Doria Russell's *The Sparrow.* In fact, we have used both very successfully in our book discussion group at the library. Despite its size, Herbert's *Dune* is surprisingly accessible and enjoyed by a wide range of readers who simply appreciate a good Adventure story—and can ignore the sandworms if they seem too preposterous. Ray Bradbury's chilling *Fahrenheit 451* reaches readers on other levels, beyond the Science Fiction themes, as does Walter M. Miller Jr.'s classic *A Canticle for Leibowitz,* which combines black humor with the details of a post-apocalyptic world.[44] And if humor is the universal language, Piers Anthony, Roger Zelazny, Douglas Adams, and Spider Robinson offer a range of possibilities.

Expanding Readers' Horizons

Just as there are many Science Fiction authors who might appeal to nonfans, so there are a number of interesting directions we might steer Science Fiction fans seeking to explore other genres. First, keep in mind that many Science Fiction writers also write in other genres. The greatest crossover is with Fantasy, where authors such as Zelazny, Card, and LeGuin have popular series and fans in both. Other authors—Anne McCaffrey and Marion Zimmer Bradley—sit on a fine line between Science Fiction and Fantasy. They say they write Science Fiction, but in my library at least, their books, with the almost magical dragons and laran, appeal more to Fantasy readers than to fans of Science Fiction. Still other authors, Chelsea Quinn Yarbro and Dan Simmons, for example, write Science Fiction and Horror.

There is much in Literary Fiction to appeal to Science Fiction aficionados. Anthony Burgess and William Burroughs are good suggestions for fans of Cyberpunk, as these authors also feature experiments with words and interesting, provocative language. The very nature of Literary Fiction, the provocative story lines, parallels much of Science Fiction, and many authors cross over easily.

Romance offers a surprising amount of crossover as well. Just as Romance readers read Science Fiction for the satisfying love interest as well as for the strong, well-developed female protagonists, Science Fiction readers who appreciate these elements will find authors they enjoy in the Romance genre. With the increased popularity of Alternate Reality Romance novels, this trend will likely grow. Suggest Jayne Castle's series, beginning with *Amaryllis,* J. D. Robb's futuristic detective stories (*Naked in Death* is the first), or Justine Davis's *Lord of the Storm.*[45]

In addition to crossover with appeal elements from Science Fiction to other genres, there is also crossover of themes. Militarism is one of the popular themes of Science Fiction that readers will find in many other genres, especially Thrillers. Weber fans will find much to appreciate in Techno-Thriller benchmark, Tom Clancy, for example. Time travel is a popular theme currently, with examples in both Romance and Science Fiction genres, as well as in others. Michael Crichton's *Timeline* is a good suggestion for fans of Willis's time travel Science Fiction, and Diana Gabaldon might also work for Science Fiction readers who appreciate detail (albeit primarily historical) and are not put off by a love interest and romantic tone.[46] *See* Figure 12.5 for more suggestions.

FIGURE 12.5

Expanding Readers' Horizons

Authors to Take Readers beyond the Science Fiction Genre

Adventure	Clive Cussler
Fantasy	Orson Scott Card
	Raymond E. Feist
	Robert Jordan
Humor	Kurt Vonnegut
Inspirational	Frank Peretti
Literary Fiction	Anthony Burgess
	William Burroughs
Romance	Dara Joy
	J. D. Robb
	Justine Davis
Thriller	Tom Clancy
	Michael Crichton
	Stephen Spruill
Women's Lives	Margaret Atwood (*The Handmaid's Tale*)[47]
	Marge Piercy (*Woman on the Edge of Time*)[48]

Reference Sources

Reference materials are almost as prevalent in the Science Fiction genre as they are in Mystery. Of those specifically devoted to this genre, Neil Barron's *Anatomy of Wonder 4: A Critical Guide to Science Fiction* is the classic guide.[49] Covering more than 3,000 titles, this survey provides information on the history of the genre, trends, subgenres, core lists, and more (awards, series, translations, organizations, conventions, and useful reference titles). Access to annotations is provided through author/subject, titles, and theme indexes. Annotations also appear on *NoveList*.

This is also a genre in which the *Genreflecting* coverage is particularly strong, and that title includes, along with lists of reference sources and award winners, a helpful list of short story anthologies to suggest to readers interested in the genre.[50]

Where to Find . . .

INFORMATION ABOUT THE AUTHOR

St. James Guide to Science Fiction Writers includes detailed biographical and bibliographical information, in addition to signed critical essays that characterize the author's style and tone and analyze several titles.[51] It is a useful source of information on classic and more recent authors. *Contemporary Authors* (*see* appendix 2) also provides author information for many Science Fiction writers.

PLOT SUMMARIES

In addition to *Anatomy of Wonder 4*, several titles from the general listing in appendix 2 supply this information. *Fiction Catalog, What Do I Read Next? Sequels, To Be Continued,* and *NoveList* all include annotated titles in the Science Fiction genre.

SUBGENRES AND THEMES

Anatomy of Wonder 4 is an excellent source for this information, as are *Genreflecting, What Do I Read Next?* and *NoveList* (*see* appendix 2). *Genreflecting* offers descriptions and lists of authors and titles, and one can find appropriate titles through subject and genre searches in the other two resources.

GENRE DESCRIPTION, BACKGROUND, AND HISTORY

Anatomy of Wonder 4 is the best source for information on the history of the genre and information on current trends. However, the annual volumes of *What Do I Read Next?* also include a section of developments within the past year, and this provides an easy way to keep up-to-date. Although *Genreflecting* does not include a great deal of this kind of information, Diana Tixier Herald has provided extensive references to other sources, if readers are interested in pursuing this aspect of the genre.

CORE LISTS AND BEST BOOKS

Again, *Anatomy of Wonder 4* is the best source for this information, but *Genreflecting* also includes several useful lists of award winners, as does *NoveList*.

Science Fiction offers an amazing range of appeal, from the Storyteller subgenre with its emphasis on adventure and relationships among characters facing Philosophical and ethical questions on one end to the Philosophical focus with its more elegant style, less stereotypical characters, and strong speculative bent on the other, and much in between. In general Science Fiction deals with "why," with philosophical speculation, as well as with "where," with a futuristic setting outside of the usual—with alien beings as well as alien and unorthodox concepts. It cherishes the unexpected, in terms of setting, characters, and plot, and it is generally provocative and prides itself in its ability to raise challenging questions. The most successful examples can challenge the reader to question his or her concept of reality.

NOTES

1. Orson Scott Card, untitled luncheon speech at Public Library Association Preconference, March 28, 2000.
2. Diana Tixier Herald, *Genreflecting: A Guide to Reading Interests in Genre Fiction*, 5th ed. (Englewood, Colo.: Libraries Unlimited, 2000), 269.

3. Betty Rosenberg, *Genreflecting* (Littleton, Colo.: Libraries Unlimited, 1982), 173.

4. Card, *Ender's Game* (New York: T. Doherty Associates, 1985).

5. Frank Herbert, *Dune* (Philadelphia: Chilton Books, 1965).

6. Gregory Benford, *Great Sky River* (Toronto and New York: Bantam, 1987).

7. Douglas Adams, *The Hitchhiker Trilogy* (*The Hitchhiker's Guide to the Galaxy*, 1979; *The Restaurant at the End of the Universe*, 1980; *Life, the Universe, and Everything*, 1982; *So Long and Thanks for all the Fish*, 1992; *Mostly Harmless*, 1992) (New York: Harmony Books, 1983).

8. Ursula K. LeGuin, *The Left Hand of Darkness* (New York: Walker, 1969); Brian Aldiss, *Helliconia Spring* (New York: Atheneum, 1982); ———, *Helliconia Summer* (New York: Atheneum, 1983); ———, *Helliconia Winter* (New York: Atheneum, 1985).

9. Piers Anthony, *Macroscope* (New York: Avon, 1969).

10. Gene Wolfe, *Nightside: The Long Sun* (New York: Tor, 1993).

11. Connie Willis, *Doomsday Book* (New York: Bantam, 1992); ———, *To Say Nothing of the Dog; or, How We Found the Bishop's Bird Stump at Last* (New York: Bantam, 1998).

12. Kim Stanley Robinson, *Red Mars* (New York: Bantam, 1993); ———, *Green Mars* (New York: Bantam, 1994); ———, *Blue Mars* (New York: Bantam, 1996).

13. Card, *Memory of Earth* (New York: Tor, 1992).

14. A. C. Crispin, *Starbridge—Book One* (New York: Ace Books; published by Berkley Books, 1989).

15. David Brin, *Startide Rising* (Toronto and New York: Bantam, 1983).

16. Mary Doria Russell, *The Sparrow* (New York: Villard, 1996).

17. Roger Zelazny, *The Dream Master* (Boston: Gregg Press, 1976).

18. Greg Bear, *Queen of Angels* (New York: Warner Books, 1990).

19. Sherri Tepper, *Grass* (New York: Foundation Books, 1989).

20. LeGuin, *The Lathe of Heaven* (New York: Scribner, 1971).

21. Arthur C. Clarke, *Childhood's End* (New York: Harcourt Brace, 1953).

22. Philip K. Dick, *Do Androids Dream of Electric Sheep?* (Garden City, N.Y.: Doubleday, 1968); *Blade Runner* (Warner Studios, 1982).

23. Dan Simmons, *Hyperion* (New York: Doubleday, 1989).

24. William Gibson, *Neuromancer* (New York: Berkley Books, 1984).

25. *Terminator 2: Judgment Day* (PacificWestern, 1991); *The Matrix* (Warner Studios, 1999).

26. Neal Stephenson, *Snow Crash* (New York: Bantam, 1992); ———, *Cryptonomicon* (New York: Avon, 1999); Jeff Noon, *Vurt* (New York: Crown, 1995).

27. John Vornholt, *Masks* (New York: Pocket Books, 1989); Dick, *The Man in the High Castle* (New York: Putnam, 1962).

28. Harry Turtledove, *The Guns of the South: A Novel of the Civil War* (New York: Ballantine, 1992).

29. ———, *The Great War: American Front* (New York: Ballantine, 1998).

30. ———, *Into the Darkness* (New York: Tor, 1999).

31. Larry Niven, *The Mote in God's Eye* (New York: Simon & Schuster, 1974).

32. Kage Baker, *In the Garden of Iden: A Novel of the Company* (New York: Harcourt Brace, 1998).

33. Kate Wilhelm, *The Dark Door* (New York: St. Martin's, 1988).

34. Michael Swanwick, *Vacuum Flowers* (New York: Arbor House, 1987).

35. Isaac Asimov, *I, Robot* (Garden City, N.Y.: Doubleday, 1950).

36. Jack Finney, *Invasion of the Body Snatchers* (New York: Universal-Award House, 1955).

37. Lois McMaster Bujold, *Shards of Honor* (Riverdale, N.Y.: Baen, 1986).

38. Harry Harrison, *The Turing Option* (New York: Warner Books, 1992).

39. Stephenson, *Snow Crash*.

40. Louise Marley, *The Terrorists of Irustan* (New York: Ace Books, 1999).

41. Pamela Sargent, *The Shore of Women* (New York: Crown, 1986).

42. *Alien* (20th Century Fox, 1979).

43. *Nebula Award Stories* (New York: Doubleday, 1966–); *The Year's Best Science Fiction* (New York: HarperPrism, 1996–).

44. Ray Bradbury, *Fahrenheit 451* (London: Hart-Davis, 1954); Walter M. Miller Jr., *A Canticle for Leibowitz* (Philadelphia: Lippincott, 1959).

45. Jayne Castle, *Amaryllis* (New York: Pocket Star Books, 1996); J. D. Robb, *Naked in Death* (New York: Berkley Books, 1995); Justine Davis, *Lord of the Storm* (New York: Topaz, 1994).

46. Michael Crichton, *Timeline* (New York: Knopf, 1999).

47. Margaret Atwood, *The Handmaid's Tale* (Boston: Houghton, 1986).

48. Marge Piercy, *Woman on the Edge of Time* (New York: Knopf, 1976).

49. Neil Barron, ed., *Anatomy of Wonder 4: A Critical Guide to Science Fiction*, 4th ed. (New Providence, N.J.: Bowker, 1995).

50. Libraries Unlimited expects to publish a Science Fiction title, coauthored by Diana Tixier Herald and Bonnie Kunzel, in its useful Genreflecting Advisory series in 2001.

51. J. P. Pederson, ed., *St. James Guide to Science Fiction Writers*, 4th ed. (Detroit: St. James, 1996).

13

Suspense

Suspense is a genre that suffers from a great deal of ambiguity. Neither publishers, reviewers, readers, nor librarians are ever quite certain what is meant when a book is labeled Suspense or books by that genre are sought. Yet when readers come to librarians looking for fast-paced books that they do not want to put down, often it is Suspense fiction we put in their hands. Just as Suspense movies draw a crowd of captivated viewers, their book counterparts encourage the burning of the midnight oil, simply to see the book to its satisfactory conclusion.

A Definition

Suspense is an important element in many fiction genes, and any number of books in other genres might be called "suspenseful." However, the key to identifying books that fit within the strict confines of this genre is that Suspense is the focus of the book. In Suspense novels, all else—Mystery, Espionage, Romance, Adventure—is secondary to this building of tension and uneasiness. As Andrew Klavan wrote in his article "The Uses of Suspense," "Suspense is not about the things that are happening; it's about the things that might happen, that threaten to happen."[1]

Titles that fit within the strict confines of the Suspense genre feature a story in which tension builds. We know that something is going to happen; there is danger lurking, as yet perhaps unseen. A sense of menace permeates the book from early on. (In fact, many authors use a prologue to reveal the dangerous situation, then go back and tell the story up to that point, with the reader kept on the edge of his chair, understanding all along what will happen soon, anticipating the danger awaiting the protagonist.) We know that the protagonist is in peril; and even though we readers know much of what is going on and sometimes even who is responsible, we feel the protagonist's plight and anticipate his discoveries as he seeks the sinister cause of this deadly threat. Although we readers are really a step ahead of the protagonist, we are still kept on edge. Like the protagonist, we want to find out what will happen next and why. We readers eagerly anticipate the twist with which the best authors end their stories. Apprehension, this building of tension, forces readers to read quickly to find out how the plot will be resolved.

Part of the ambiguity in defining the Suspense genre is that Suspense plays a key role in many genres. Thrillers, Mystery, Romantic Suspense, Horror, Adventure, and even Romance rely on suspenseful situations to intensify their stories. Yet in each of these, the central focus is on something other than Suspense. Mysteries, for example, create a puzzle, and it is important to offer clues, while withholding vital information from the reader. In Suspense the reader needs to know almost everything and certainly more than the protagonist. (This is the reason that almost all Suspense novels are told by a third-person, omniscient narrator.) In both Mystery and Suspense, there is a puzzle, but in a Mystery, the reader's (and detective's) goal is to get into the puzzle, to discover its workings, in order to solve it. In Suspense the protagonist must get out of a puzzle, generally a confusing set of sinister circumstances, to escape and survive. In a Mystery, something has happened, and we want to find out "who-dun-it." In Suspense, something is going to happen; there is a sense of menace, lurking danger, and we are held in delicious anticipation as we try to discover what and why.

The pattern of Suspense novels, as discussed in detail below, often parallels the pattern of Horror novels, with danger entering the sphere of someone's normal life. In Suspense, however, the danger is human, while in Horror the danger usually contains an element of the supernatural. In addition, in Horror, the protagonist does not always survive, while in Suspense the survival of the hero or heroine is generally guaranteed.

Adventure novels and Thrillers also feature the fast-paced chase sequences that appear frequently in the Suspense genre, but the distinguishing feature of these chases in Suspense novels is that the protagonist often does not know who is chasing him or her—or why. Along with the protagonist we must sort out the history of events that has led to this particular situation. In Adventure and Thrillers, on the other hand, the chase is part of the action emphasis of the story line and serves to move the plot.

Needless to say, Romantic Suspense, discussed in detail in chapter 11, offers a heavy measure of Suspense, but the Romance element is also very strong. Traditional Romances often add an element of Suspense to move the plot along quickly. Suspense introduces an element of danger and apprehension to enliven the plot. In these and all other suspenseful novels, however, the Suspense is secondary, a device for creating a more compelling story. In books that fall within the Suspense genre, the building of tension is one of the keys to the book's success and readers' appreciation. *See* Figure 13.1 for a list of characteristics.

Characteristics and the Genre's Appeal

Characterization

The unique point of view is the definitive feature of Suspense novels. In the best, readers know the thoughts of both main characters, the hero and the villain, and thus more than the protagonist. This technique heightens the feeling of uncertainty and builds tension, because we know the danger the character is walking into before he or she does. We identify with the protagonist and, recognizing the danger he faces, are drawn more completely into the story.

This reader identification is a powerful tool, and Thomas Harris uses it masterfully in his 1999 novel, *Hannibal*.[2] With chilling finesse Harris forces us as readers to sympathize with his archvillain, Hannibal

---

FIGURE 13.1

Characteristics of the Suspense Genre

1. The reader empathizes with the protagonist and feels the same sense of peril. However, the reader often follows the antagonist's thoughts and actions, too, and thus knows more than the protagonist.

2. The action usually takes place within a narrow time frame, often in only a few days, and the reader is made aware of the danger to the protagonist early on, generally in the first chapter or even in a prologue.

3. Stories follow a similar pattern, with unexpected danger from an unknown source intruding into the protagonist's normal life. The resolution is brought about through a confrontation between the hero/ine and villain, and the protagonist survives.

4. A dark, menacing atmosphere is essential and underscores the danger to the protagonist. As the story unfolds, tension grows, and the reader, because he knows the danger, feels a sense of uneasiness, uncertainty, even before the protagonist senses anything is amiss.

5. Settings are present day.

Lecter, the terror of his earlier Suspense classic, *The Silence of the Lambs*, because here it is Hannibal who is stalked by an even more wicked adversary.[3] The power of reader empathy in the hands of a truly skilled writer is a formidable tool. We may not want to sympathize with this amoral villain, but we are unable to help ourselves. And the knowledge that we are placed in this position makes the novel, and its effect on the reader, even more sinister.

If the reader does not feel this link with hero or heroine, the story may be suspenseful, but it will not be as successful. The degree to which the reader is pulled in is important: In the best we feel every threat to the protagonist and the shock of every revelation, whether we want to or not. The mood created by this device can be very intense, even chilling, and this is exactly what readers expect.

Like the protagonist we often cannot tell exactly who the villain is until it is almost too late. We may not even be surprised by the identity of the villain, because we have been following his "voice" since the beginning, sometimes in separate chapters, sometimes alerted by a different typeface. Although discovering who the villain is remains important, of even more interest is why the protagonist is in jeopardy. We have more clues than the protagonist, so it is often possible for us to guess the villain's identity. Why the deadly danger exists is often the more difficult question.

Pacing

There is also a characteristic pacing in Suspense novels. In most cases the action takes place within a narrow time frame, often only a matter of days. There may be flashbacks to previous events to fill in details, but the actual story moves quickly within a limited time frame. In addition, the action generally starts early in the book. For example, Jeffrey Deaver's *The Devil's Teardrop* takes place in fewer than twenty-four hours, and the story opens with the murder of dozens of innocent commuters in a Washington, D.C., metro station.[4] Suspense novels typically do not rely on the longer setup of events found in related genres, such as Mystery or even Espionage. The story unfolds quickly in the first few pages.

In fact, many authors use a prologue to introduce the villain and set up the atmosphere of danger and uncertainty before the story itself even begins. Steve Thayer employs this technique in *The Weatherman*.[5] Our masked murderer attacks and kills a young woman in a hot parking garage, and the act, as well as the descriptions of the approaching stormy weather and the atmosphere created by the combination of the two, set the mood for the story to follow.

Some books are even laid out in sections, day by day, or even with specific times throughout the day. Joseph R. Garber's *Vertical Run* literally takes place in a single day.[6] As he arrives early at the office, David Elliott expects a normal day—until his boss tries to kill him. The day goes downhill from there, as sharpshooters and commandos of every description are clearly trying to kill him. Why? Neither we nor our Everyman hero knows the answer. Luckily Dave has had enough combat experience himself to survive, not to mention to set off cleverly rigged charges in the stairwell of his New York City office building. Bit by bit, through flashbacks, we discover what has gone wrong in Dave's life, why he is so ruthlessly pursued, and how he can escape and survive.

This telescoping of events and relationships into exceptionally short time frames intensifies the action and sense of danger. This strategy tends to make Suspense books compelling reads. The books grip the reader; the complex and action-filled plots force us to keep reading; we cannot put the book down, and when we must, the story stays with us, drawing us back to finish the book.

Story Line

In all genres, as we have seen, the story line follows a prescribed pattern and Suspense is no exception. Readers of Suspense recognize the formulaic pattern immediately. A nightmare intrudes into the hero/ine's normal life. He or she works out how to overcome this threat. The ending brings the confrontation between good and evil, and the protagonist always survives (although bodies may be strewn along the way, and even characters we care about may die).

This pattern sets up the inevitable chase scene, usually at the end of the novel, but sometimes at intervals throughout. The protagonist and villain have been skirting each other, but in the end there is always a classic chase scene, with the protagonist in real physical jeopardy. This sets up the showdown. All previous action and atmosphere generate the tension that leads to this confrontation. The buildup to this final scene drives the pace of the novel.

If you are a reader of Mary Higgins Clark, this pattern will sound familiar. Remember *We'll Meet Again*?[7] Here Molly Carpenter Lasch, on parole after serving time for her husband's murder (a crime she did not, of course, commit), returns home to the house her grandmother left her and to her memories of the murder that took place there. What did happen that night she returned home to find her husband's body? What were the sounds she heard and what do they mean? Slowly her memory returns: Not only is it clear that she did not murder her husband, it is increasingly obvious that something is very much amiss at the hospital her father-in-law built and her husband ran. In the end, as she continues to work out the correct sequence of events, she comes face-to-face with her husband's murderer, a villain who knows that Molly must die. Everything in the novel leads up to this final encounter between heroine and villain, and her ultimate victory and survival.

This confrontation between hero and villain is important to the success of a Suspense novel. The closer matched the two, the more tension is created. The match does not have to be exact. There may be a physically strong antagonist pitted against a weaker but more intelligent protagonist, as in Clark's books. The woman may not be a physical match for the male threatening her, but she escapes because she outwits the villain. In Hard-Edged Suspense, the protagonist is often a law enforcement officer, who acts for the beleaguered victim. Although the dynamic may be different, the necessity of this confrontation and of its outcome remains the same.

Although the structure of the plot may be similar across the genre, there are still enough twists, enough unpredictability in the best of Suspense, to keep us guessing as well. The pattern may follow an expected course, and the reader may know a great deal about the danger, but the twists keep us turning pages. Keeping the reader guessing about the outcome is particularly difficult in the numerous series this genre seems to inspire. An excellent example is Thomas Perry's series featuring Native American Jane Whitefield, who constructs new identities for people on the run. In each episode readers follow Jane step-by-step as she creates, and sometimes abandons only to re-create, new identities for her clients, setting them up in safe situations, only to come to their rescue again as danger intrudes. Each case is characterized by an evocative, menacing atmosphere; an intelligent, inventive female protagonist; elegant prose; and dense writing that still quickly propels the reader to the denouement. Each also includes a variety of twists, double crosses, mistaken identities, and layers of plot that make each adventure fresh and interesting. In the first, *Vanishing Act,* the scrupulous Jane "rescues" an ex-policeman in trouble, only to have him turn on her and her neighbor, so the tension builds to a second peak as Jane's own life is in jeopardy.[8] All in the series are gripping stories, well told, and everything depends on how well Jane uses her own tracking skills, ancient and modern, to read the signs.

Frame

Suspense is also characterized by a special atmosphere, an uneasiness that is essential. The author often uses setting to create a heightened sense of danger, through an isolated physical setting or more simply and usually just through mood. In Suspense much of the action takes place at night or on rainy or cloudy days. There are not many cheery, sunny days in Suspense novels, and even the sunshine often takes on ominous overtones. If you have read David Lindsey's novels set in Houston and the South, you know what I mean. Take *Mercy*, for example, in which there is a particularly gory murder investigation.[9] The sunshine and daylight there offer no safety; instead, the murky heat and humidity underscore the repugnant nature of the murder investigation.

Authors mix these elements to underscore the danger to the protagonist, and the sinister atmosphere thus created is crucial to the readers' impression of the story. Sometimes there is almost a nightmare quality to this frame. The hero is caught up in a situation he cannot understand. He does not know why he is pursued or by whom. Alfred Hitchcock mastered this technique in his movies, with the sense of menace lurking just below the serene surface. However it is used, this menacing atmosphere is crucial to the readers' impression of the story.

Finally, settings for Suspense novels are contemporary. Although Suspense may be an element in books with historical settings, novels within the genre are set exclusively in the present day. The reason for this likely relates to both the necessity for immediacy in the stories and the pacing. Creating an effective historical setting takes time away from the Suspense, and such a setting may seem too foreign, too alien for the reader identification necessary to make these such compelling reading.

All of these characteristics are vital in the creation of Suspense, but the most important, and the key to the appeal of the genre, is the point of view from which the story is told and the way it draws the reader into the story. The reader knows of whom and what to be frightened, even though the protagonist does not. The reader is kept on edge, always anticipating the danger to come. Even if the hero thinks he is safe, the reader knows he is not. In Suspense, the author draws the reader into the protagonist's story and emotions. We feel and see the danger; we see it build but are powerless to act, to do anything but keep on reading.

Key Authors and Subgenres

Benchmark

Titles in the Suspense genre fall into two distinct categories, Hard-Edged and Softer-Edged. This polarity makes choosing a benchmark, an author who represents the genre as a whole, more difficult. Most of the important, popular authors write the Hard-Edged Suspense. Thomas Harris, James Patterson, and John Sandford always achieve best-seller status, but none of them has the sales and name recognition of Mary Higgins Clark, who stands as the benchmark, the most popular author in the genre, the one most closely identified with Suspense.

In many ways, Clark is a problematic benchmark author. Few other writers publish the Softer-Edged Suspense that Clark has honed to an art form. Yet her enormous popularity makes her the most recognized name in the genre and thus its benchmark. Her stories feature women in danger, but not the weak, clingy heroines of the Gothics, an eighteenth- and nineteenth-century predecessor of Romantic Suspense. (And although some readers may consider her writing generically "Mysteries," Clark clearly falls within the Suspense genre, with "puzzles" to be escaped, not solved.) Clark's heroines are career women, not passive victims. They play an active role in extricating themselves from dangerous situations. Clark also keeps her novels up-to-date by centering the plots around timely topics: health care and beauty issues, post-traumatic stress disorder, serial killers. Though women of substance (and the books often contain "rich-and-famous" elements), these heroines are always down-to-earth and nice; certainly they come across as very appealing to Clark's fans.

Subgenres of Suspense

Basically, Suspense falls into two subgenres that represent opposite ends of the spectrum: Hard-Edged Suspense and Softer-Edged Suspense. Needless to say, not every book fits neatly within one of these subgenres; in fact, there are many that fall in between, drawing characteristics from each side. In working with readers, however, it is useful to have an understanding of the range of the genre so that we can better describe books and thus identify ones that fall within the reader's interests.

SOFTER-EDGED SUSPENSE

Books in this subgenre have all the general characteristics of the Suspense genre, but this Softer-Edged Suspense, epitomized by the writing of Clark, has a group of separate qualities that set it apart from Hard-Edged Suspense (*see* Figure 13.2).

In these, there is seldom much blood and gore. Just as in a Cozy Mystery, here the bodies are usually offstage, dead or injured certainly,

---

FIGURE 13.2

Characteristics of Softer-Edged Suspense

1. The bodies of the victims are usually offstage, and they are not described in grisly, clinical detail.

2. Although the protagonist is stalked by the villain, there is more threatened danger, more atmosphere, more building of emotion and tension, than actual physical peril. The Suspense is generated more by atmosphere than action.

3. The protagonist is often a woman who is resourceful and who saves herself in the end. The police may be present, but they often play a less important role in the final confrontation and resolution.

4. Details are more likely to relate to descriptions of the characters than to the crimes or crime scene.

5. Roller-coaster pacing is typical. It builds and then eases up, only to build again.

---

but not described in graphic, clinical detail. In these books we do not see a lot of violence. In fact, the plot may revolve around a secret from the past. More frequently there are threats of violence or indications that violence has occurred, again offstage. The strong emotional pull remains, a reaction to the threat of violence rather than to actual descriptions of violent events, as the reader relates to the protagonist and her plight. Our fear is not lessened, because violence is always lurking. The powerful threat of danger pulls us into the story and the lives of the characters.

Suspense in these novels is more frequently generated by atmosphere, by this growing sense of danger, than by action. Jonellen Heckler's *Circumstances Unknown* is a good example.[10] The story takes place within one week, with each section one day. This technique pulls the reader along; the suspense builds quickly as we follow this young widow and her child. Her husband is dead; we know he was murdered, and although we know the murderer is one of her husband's childhood friends, we are not certain which one it is until the end. However, the heroine has no sense of the danger she is in as she investigates what she suspects is foul play, until she is captured by the killer at the very end. We have been holding our breath as readers, of course, because we have seen her associating with the two men, one of whom is the murderer, their "friendships" developing as the story progresses. The suspense builds throughout these interactions, even though, except for hints of her danger and a growing sense of unease for both protagonist and reader, she is not in physical danger until the very end of the novel.

In fact, the details we get as readers more likely describe the characters than the facts about the crimes. We know more physically about the protagonist, usually a woman, and her lifestyle than in Hard-Edged Suspense. In addition, we have more information about the villain, who is often portrayed more sympathetically, almost pitiably, with hints that childhood abuse or something similar may be responsible for his behavior. His power over the heroine and the danger in which she is placed should not be underestimated, however, despite the possible justification for his character and behavior.

The characters in Softer-Edged Suspense are usually ordinary people whose lives are suddenly invaded by someone very dangerous, and they often do not know why. This creates a nightmare quality. A typical Suspense novel by Joy Fielding demonstrates this technique. In *Don't Cry Now* Bonnie Wheeler receives a call from her husband's ex-wife, warning her that her own life is in danger.[11] Then the woman is found dead, and Bonnie is the main suspect. Tension mounts as she investigates on her own, almost always in real danger, because the police refuse to believe that her life is in jeopardy. Who is the killer on the loose, and why has he chosen these two women as his victims?

Thus, in contrast to the Hard-Edged Suspense, these novels exhibit a more romantic worldview, in the sense that we see less violence and more details of the characters' ordinary lives. Although the worldview may be more "romantic," these are not to be confused with Romantic Suspense, covered in depth in chapter 11, in which Romance genre characteristics play a more important role and a romantic relationship involving the heroine is a necessity. There may be relationships between characters of the opposite sex, but romantic interests are very low on the scale of what is important in these novels.

The lack of much police presence in the Softer-Edged Suspense is another characteristic of this subgenre. The police are generally absent or arrive too late to be of much assistance. Whether the danger is over before the police can be called or they simply do not take the threats to the heroine's life seriously, the heroine saves herself, or is at least instrumental in effecting her own escape, almost always without police support. Reasons for not involving the police vary from story to story, but keeping them out of the case is important to the plot, as the heroine must be allowed to rescue herself, and sometimes her loved ones as well. In Patricia J. MacDonald's *Lost Innocents*, for example, young and unhappy wife and mother Maddy Blake believes early on that she has come across the kidnapped child in the news, but she fears calling the police because her own husband is a suspect in that case.[12] Whatever the excuse, authors must find a way to keep police to the periphery of the story.

Lastly, Softer-Edged Suspense often exhibits a rather unique pacing pattern. Clark typifies this with the roller-coaster pacing she employs to build the feeling of dreaded anticipation. Each chapter starts afresh, usually from a different character's point of view, so the chapters begin with Suspense at a low ebb and build to climax, a mini-cliffhanger. Then the new chapter, from another character's point of view, drops the reader down to that initial level again. It is this flow that keeps us reading; we want to know what will happen, but we also get some respite from potentially dangerous situations. In Softer-Edged Suspense, the reader is not kept continuously on edge, as we often are in Hard-Edged Suspense. Yet we read quickly to return to the story line that was left hanging at the end of the previous chapter.

Clark is the master of this Softer-Edged Suspense, and the benchmark for this subgenre, just as she is for the genre as a whole. Readers seek her popular best-sellers, knowing they will find the formula implemented by a master.

Unfortunately, it is increasingly difficult to find authors who consistently write this Softer-Edged Suspense. Many of our old standbys—Fielding, Heckler, Michael Allegretto—simply are no longer writing, or they are not writing this kind of book. Clark's ex-daughter-in-law, Mary Jane Clark, continues the tradition and follows the established pattern to some extent, although her stories contain a large measure of Mystery and not as much Suspense. Judith Kelman (for example, *More Than You Know*) also writes suspenseful, fast-paced stories of women and children in jeopardy, although some of her titles have more violent episodes than the traditional Clark novel.[15]

HARD-EDGED SUSPENSE

In these novels of Hard-Edged Suspense (*see* Figure 13.3), readers find countless details of both the crimes and police procedures, in part because the protagonist is usually a law enforcement officer. This is in sharp contrast to the ordinary individuals who are the protagonists of the novels of Softer-Edged Suspense. You can see the difference this kind of protagonist makes. If the hero is a law enforcement officer whose role is to stop the violent antagonist before more people are hurt or killed, he may not actually be in physical danger himself until the very end. Thus, the chase scene is prefaced by a duel of wits rather than the stalking of the hero. However, it still leads to the final confrontation between the two. The protagonist may not be in as much physical peril until the end, but throughout the novel he is engaged in an intricately developed cat-and-mouse game with the villain. In *Along Came a Spider*, the first of the Alex Cross novels,

---

FIGURE 13.3

Characteristics of Hard-Edged Suspense

1. The protagonist is often a detective, who may or may not be in immediate danger himself but may be working against time to protect someone else. Details of the crimes and of the police procedures play an important role because of the protagonist's occupation.

2. Descriptions are more graphic, and these books often include sexual situations, physical violence, and strong language.

3. The Suspense is generated more through action than atmosphere.

4. The pacing feels relentless. The novel seems to stay in high gear throughout, as tension builds the Suspense.

Patterson displays his ability to manipulate our fears, as a Washington, D.C., police detective–psychologist is called in to investigate the kidnapping of two famous children.[14] His job is to retrieve them safely, but he is hindered by the kidnapper's skill at the game he is playing with Cross. All along we sense the building danger, but Patterson holds off the chilling denouement until the end.

In these, the protagonist is more likely a man, and as we learn more about him, we relate to him and his situation. He is a strong character who engages our sympathy. On the other hand, villains in these Hard-Edged novels of Suspense are often more mad, more violent, and more dangerous than in Softer-Edged Suspense. The classic example is, of course, Hannibal Lecter of Harris's series, beginning with *The Red Dragon*.[15] A serial killer who not only toys with his victims, devising the most exquisite and always apt tortures, he also eats them on occasion. He has become the prototype for the wave of serial killers who were created in the wake of Harris's success.

There is also more violence, frequently sexual violence or other sexual situations, and more strong language in these Hard-Edged novels of Suspense. We see the underside of life, a much bleaker portrayal of the world than the more romantic view of the Softer-Edged novels. Crimes and criminals are more sordid at this end of the genre. Descriptions are also much more graphic. We see the bodies, rendered in intimate and gruesome detail, and the victims are often described during and after the killings. Characters are involved in intimately depicted life-and-death situations, well beyond the stalking and threats of the Softer-Edged Suspense, and the language used underlines the deadly nature of the situation portrayed. These are not for the weak of heart or stomach. On the other hand, many readers who abhor violence in novels have commented on how totally absorbed they have become in several of these novels of Hard-Edged Suspense. I find myself agreeing with these readers who acknowledge the frequent and graphic violence in Patterson and others—but who cannot stop turning the pages because the story is so engrossing and compelling.

Let me add, however, that there are not necessarily multiple and frequent graphically violent scenes in these books, although the impact of the scenes may leave the reader with that impression. The harder edge comes not only from violent episodes, but also from the reader's and the protagonist's perceptions that the situation and the villain are out of control. Even everyday activities take on a different perspective, become more sinister, when they become a part of this life-and-death game between hero and villain.

Suspense in these novels is also engendered by the action—that cat-and-mouse game and ultimately the chase. In most cases, the tension builds early and never lets up. Pacing in these novels seems relentless, with fewer breaks, building inexorably to the final confrontation between hero and villain. Once the scene is set, we are seldom allowed to return to normalcy until all is resolved, as the tension and the knowledge that the situation is so dangerous sustain the mood. These novels are reminiscent of the movie *The Fugitive*, in which the viewer is kept on the edge of the chair until the last scene.[16] There is a sense of continuous movement, of action, as the reader is engrossed in the plot and the building suspense. Twist following twist and unfolding layers of Suspense propel the reader through the book.

Because protagonists are often involved in law enforcement, there is an opportunity for multiple cases, for sequels, and novels in this subgenre are more often parts of series than are Softer-Edged Suspense.

Thomas Perry (Jane Whitefield), Sandford (Lucas Davenport), Patterson (Alex Cross), Harris (Jack Crawford and Clarice Starling), David Wiltse (John Becker), and Jeffery Deaver (Lincoln Rhyme) have all developed series characters, although they may also continue to write nonseries novels.

The classic writer of Hard-Edged Suspense is Harris, who popularized the serial killer motif that sustains this subgenre. Much imitated, Harris has only three Suspense genre titles to his name to date: *The Red Dragon, The Silence of the Lambs,* and *Hannibal.*

Sandford stands out as a consistently good practitioner in this subgenre. His series, more than ten books, all with *Prey* in the title, feature Minneapolis detective Lucas Davenport. In addition, he has several nonseries Suspense titles. His books are popular with readers and critics alike. They offer a consistently high degree of Suspense, and, of course, the concomitant satisfactions of an ongoing character whom readers know and to whom they relate. His melancholy hero must conquer his own self-doubts in each adventure, as he uses his sharp deductive skills to fight corruption (both within the police and among criminals) and to nab serial killers before they can kill again. Elegant writing, strong characterizations, and fast-paced Suspense characterize his series and nonseries titles.

Preparing to Work with Readers

Fans of the Suspense genre often read a wide range of suspenseful books. What they primarily seek are fast-paced books, in which they identify with the protagonist and share his or her rocky ride to the satisfactory resolution of the story. They read Suspense to find the elements described below.

First, they expect to follow the point of view of the protagonist but also to know what is happening with the antagonist as well. They expect to have some inkling of what will happen, and they derive pleasure and satisfaction from knowing more than the protagonist. However, they also expect a final twist at the end, a twist consistent with the plot, but one that catches them off guard and underlines the fact that even they have not anticipated all of the author's stratagems.

Closely related is the fact that the reader knows that the protagonist will survive. Whether this book is a part of a series or not, readers understand that the hero/ine will not be one of the victims. Even if the ending is not always precisely upbeat, there is resolution and the hero is among those left alive.

Third, readers choose Suspense because of the pacing of these books. They expect to be hooked in the first few pages and pulled quickly into the story and the fate of its protagonist. If the story does not grab them immediately or pull them in totally, they do not consider it a good, or typical, representative of the genre. They also expect the story and the growing apprehension to pull them along. Even if the story is not truly fast-paced, it is engrossing and readers turn pages quickly to find out how the story will be resolved.

Finally, readers may seek particular themes in the Suspense titles they read. They may want novels about serial killers or ones that feature a forensic pathologist, rather than a detective. Reference sources, discussed below, can be useful in identifying these. Remember, too, that patrons asking for these themes may also enjoy suspenseful titles in other genres.

Readers (and librarians) who are fans of other genres but are interested in exploring the Suspense genre might sample titles from the list in Figure 13.4 of Suspense authors and titles that share similarities with books in other genres with which they might be more familiar.

Readers' Advisory Interview

Probably the most important factor to consider in working with readers is the amount of violence they will tolerate in the novels of Suspense they seek. Many fans have strong feelings about the amount of violence in the titles they read. Some, as we discussed above, demand the Softer-Edged, while others tolerate more violence. It is important to have a mental list of authors in mind to suggest, to help us establish an acceptable level, just as it is vital to suggest a range of authors and let readers choose.

Note that it is more difficult to offer the Hard-Edged Suspense titles to patrons. It is awkward to inquire whether they like a lot of

---

FIGURE 13.4

An Introduction to the Suspense Genre

Suspense Writers to Try, If You Enjoy . . .

Adventure	Craig Holden
Gentle	Mary Higgins Clark
Literary	Thomas Harris
Mystery	Mary Jane Clark
	John Sandford
Romantic Suspense	Patricia J. MacDonald
	Bonnie MacDougal
	Lisa Gardner
Thriller	Greg Iles (*Mortal Fear*)[17]
	Philip Shelby (*Days of Drums*)[18]
	Andrew Klavan
	David Lindsey
	Joseph R. Garber (*Vertical Run*)
	Thomas Perry
Women's Lives	Judy Mercer

---

violence in the books they read; formulating a question so as not to offend on some level is not an easy task. We might ask, "Do you mind a book that has vivid descriptions of violence?" *Mind* seems to be a key word, replacing *like* or *enjoy* to put a different slant on the issue. When I know, and certainly if a patron inquires, I will try to indicate the level of violence or strong language.

If I have someone who wants to read Suspense, I ask the reader to name an author he or she has enjoyed or is in the mood to read. If the reader mentions Mary Higgins Clark, verify the appeal characteristics: "You like normal, ordinary people put in jeopardy; the body and violence offstage, but a real sense of danger as the villain stalks the hero or heroine." Readers of Clark may also enjoy Amateur Detective Mysteries, if there are a female protagonist, enough Suspense, and not too much violence (perhaps Dana Stabenow, Nevada Barr, or Gillian Roberts), and Romantic Suspense (Iris Johansen or Diane Chamberlain), if there is not too much Romance or violence.

If the reader mentions John Sandford or another writer of Hard-Edged Suspense, verify the desire for details of the crime, perhaps more violently presented, and the relentless pacing. Readers of the Hard-Edged Suspense may also like nonfiction true crime books, because they appreciate details of the crime and characters involved, and they are not interested in figuring out the identity of the murderer. They may also read hard-edged crime novels, such as those by Andrew Vachss, Elmore Leonard, and Eugene Izzi, as these portray strong protagonists caught up in dangerous situations. In these, however, the bleak atmosphere may be the link to the Suspense genre, rather than a similar plotline and the building of Suspense that characterize books that fall more strictly within the genre.

Although the focus of this chapter has been on the ends of the Suspense genre spectrum, there are many authors that fall in the middle, or authors that may write both types of Suspense, as well as books in between. If we understand the popular extremes, we can also make good use of the middle ground in working with readers, both those who are fans of Suspense and others, whom we believe might enjoy reading this genre. For example, Andrew Klavan has written Hard-Edged Suspense *(Don't Say a Word)*, Softer-Edged Suspense *(The Scarred Man)*, and, in 1999, a Suspense story that falls between the two, *Hunting Down Amanda*.[19] His versatility reminds us how important it is to suggest a specific title when we mention authors to readers, unless that author's books are all of a kind.

Among the authors who fall into this middle ground are Thomas Perry (discussed above), Craig Holden, and Philip Shelby. Holden has written several gripping novels of Suspense, but the complex plots force them to unfold more slowly than we might expect in this genre. *The Last Sanctuary* features Joe Curtis, traveling to Seattle to pull his brother out of yet another scrape.[20] Along the way he becomes involved with members of a cult, is drawn into a murder, and then is on the run from the cult, as well as the government. Plot twists, violence, atmosphere, revenge, and a strong sense of place make this a memorable novel for Suspense fans.

Shelby, in *Days of Drums,* includes elements of Political Thrillers as he creates a compelling story of a secret service agent who discovers a dangerous conspiracy involving the upper echelons of the government.[21] Short chapters and alternating points of view move the story quickly as we follow rookie agent Holland Tylo, trying to uncover the roots of the conspiracy and save her own life.

Remember also if comments from the reader during any readers' advisory interview lead you to suspect Suspense may be a good suggestion, describe examples from the range of the genre and give the reader choices. Readers who talk generally about fast-paced books or page-turners often appreciate Suspense. We need to remember that our role is not to slot titles into specific genre places but to see how they might appeal to a range of readers. Most readers do not choose books solely by genre classification. They enjoy certain elements in books and seek to find those characteristics in others. Suspense titles make good crossover reading for fans of other genres (*see* Figure 13.4), and Suspense readers often find books that appeal to them in other, related genres, as indicated in Figure 13.5.

Sometimes when readers find it difficult to talk about books they have enjoyed, they describe movies instead. As I mentioned above, a reference to *The Fugitive* may lead to the suggestion of other Hard-Edged Suspense titles. On the other hand, someone who enjoyed *Sleeping with the Enemy* may be more comfortable with Softer-Edged Suspense.[22] A fan of Alfred Hitchcock's classic movies of Suspense may enjoy a range of Suspense novels, from Hard- to Softer-Edged, as well as Psychological Suspense, discussed in chapter 9. The link here would be to find those with that particular twist so prized by Hitchcock's many fans, as well as the unraveling of the layered plot.

As in all genres, there is a range of what readers read and do not read, and we cannot always understand or anticipate their reactions. It is not uncommon to hear readers state they will not read any books in which children are placed in jeopardy, but Clark is one of their favorite authors. Because Clark has frequently employed the child-in-jeopardy theme, especially in her earlier books, it is clear that there is something in the way she handles the subject that is not offensive to the reader. We need to remember also that books affect us in dif-

---

FIGURE 13.5

Expanding Readers' Horizons

Authors to Take Readers beyond the Suspense Genre

Adventure	Alistair MacLean
	Jack Higgins
Fantasy	Robert Jordan
	Raymond E. Feist
Mystery	T. Jefferson Parker
	Dana Stabenow
	Gillian Roberts
Psychological	Scott Smith
Romantic Suspense	Iris Johansen
	Diane Chamberlain
Science Fiction	Frank Herbert
Thriller	Andrew Vachss
	John Grisham

---

ferent ways at different times, and we should be open to what patrons say they are seeking in the books they read.

Unlike some other genres, in Suspense the setting is usually less important to readers. If patrons request particular locations or settings, reference books often lead us to suggestions. Generally, however, fans are seeking a particular feel generated in fast-paced books that spiral to a satisfying conclusion.

Sure Bets

Suspense is a very popular genre at my library, and in addition to those authors who appear regularly on the best-sellers lists (especially Clark, James Patterson, and John Sandford), we have reserve queues for Perry, Greg Iles, and Jeffrey Deaver. Part of Iles's appeal, and what makes him a good Sure Bet, is that he crosses genre boundaries, adding Thriller, Historical, and Crime elements to many of his stories. Fast-paced, violent, and compulsively readable, Iles's elegant Suspense novels offer the action, building tension, and layers of story that fans appreciate.

A popular writer with a softer edge is Judy Mercer, whose continuing character, investigative reporter and later television producer Ariel Gold, first appeared in *Fast Forward*.[23] Gold awakens one morning, battered and with no memory of who or where she is. Not to mention the fact that she is pursued by a deadly killer. Why? Each title presents new adventures and dangers, as she struggles to sort out who she is. Mystery elements make this a series with broad appeal.

Expanding Readers' Horizons

Faced with Suspense readers who have read all their favorite authors or are interested in ranging further afield, we have a variety of directions to pursue, because so many genres rely on elements of Suspense to move the plot. They do not necessarily provide the two points of view—both of protagonist and antagonist—which is key to the Suspense genre.

Adventure offers stories of missions fraught with danger, and suspense builds along with the danger as the participants reach their goal. Try Alistair MacLean's titles or Jack Higgins, especially *The Eagle Has Landed*.[24]

Fantasy quests also offer possibilities for Suspense readers, as they share much of the same appeal of Adventure. Raymond E. Feist (*The Magician*) and Robert Jordan (*The Eye of the World*) offer the mix of Adventure and Intrigue that create Suspense.[25] In Science Fiction, on the other hand, the Suspense may be part of the unknown and unexpected intervening in the story. Frank Herbert's *Dune* and its sequels certainly build to suspenseful episodes that move the story.[26]

Mystery provides perhaps the greatest scope for crossover across the spectrum of the genre. As I mentioned above, Amateur Detectives are good suggestions for readers who prefer Softer-Edged Suspense, and Private Investigators and Police Detectives often work for readers of Hard-Edged Suspense. Of particular interest for this latter group is T. Jefferson Parker, a hard-edged investigator who explores venues similar to those found in Suspense with the same building tension. Try *The Blue Hour* to explore this relationship.[27]

Although Psychological Suspense lacks the faster pace of the Suspense genre, it creates a similar chill. This is not necessarily the crossover genre for readers of Clark and the Softer-Edged Suspense, as there is generally a very dark cast to the books. Scott Smith's *A Simple Plan* would be a possible suggestion.[28]

The Thriller genre offers similarly fast-paced books, usually building tension as they reach the denouement. In addition, there is often a chase involved, and the protagonist is involved in ferreting out "Why?" rather than "Who?" Certainly John Grisham's stories are suspenseful, as are Robin Cook's. Crime Thrillers seem also to link well with Suspense. Try Izzi, Vachss, and Leonard, and *see* Figure 13.5 for names of other authors to suggest.

Reference Sources

The Suspense genre is not currently well covered by any single source.[29] Some material can be found in general readers' advisory reference sources, as well as in a number directed to the Mystery genre, as a detective is often the hero of Suspense novels.

Where to Find . . .

INFORMATION ABOUT THE AUTHOR

In addition to the general resource, *Contemporary Authors* (*see* appendix 2), *St. James Guide to Crime and Mystery Writers,* and *Mystery and Suspense Writers* cover some of the authors classified here in the Suspense genre.[30] *Killer Books* also provides excellent information on the Suspense authors it includes.[31]

PLOT SUMMARIES

Fiction Catalog and *NoveList* (*see* appendix 2) provide easy access to annotated titles of Suspense.

SUBGENRES AND THEMES

None of the reference sources seem to identify subgenres of Suspense. Resources with extensive indexing—*What Do I Read Next? NoveList,* and some of the Mystery sources covered in chapter 8—help answer reader requests for stories featuring certain types of investigators or ones located in particular areas. *Genreflecting* includes Suspense in chapter 3, "Crime," and Diana Tixier Herald provides lists of general Suspense authors and those who write about serial killers.

CORE LISTS AND BEST BOOKS

Such lists are not readily available for this genre, although online bookseller Amazon.com does provide a list of best-selling Suspense titles, which may be useful. *Mystery and Suspense Writers* also gives a selected list of authors who write in this genre.

Although the Suspense genre may be hard to define precisely, there is no question that it has a broad appeal for a wide range of readers who look for stories of characters placed in jeopardy, who must work their way out of a bad situation. Readers who enjoy page-turners, those fast-paced, tension-filled stories that generally end with issues satisfactorily resolved, often choose Suspense. However, in the real world of readers and librarians, whether a novel truly falls within the confines of the Suspense genre or not is not the issue. If we have explored this genre and others, we have a good idea of the range of books that might appeal to readers who enjoy both Suspense and suspenseful stories.

NOTES

1. Andrew Klavan, "The Uses of Suspense," in *The Writer's Handbook,* ed. Sylvia K. Burack (Boston: Writer, 1996), 213.
2. Thomas Harris, *Hannibal* (New York: Delacorte, 1999).
3. ———, *The Silence of the Lambs* (New York: St. Martin's, 1988).
4. Jeffrey Deaver, *The Devil's Teardrop: A Novel of the Last Night of the Century* (New York: Simon & Schuster, 1999).
5. Steve Thayer, *The Weatherman* (New York: Viking, 1995).
6. Joseph R. Garber, *Vertical Run* (New York: Bantam, 1995).
7. Mary Higgins Clark, *We'll Meet Again* (New York: Simon & Schuster, 1999).

8. Thomas Perry, *Vanishing Act* (New York: Random House, 1995).

9. David Lindsey, *Mercy* (New York: Doubleday, 1990).

10. Jonellen Heckler, *Circumstances Unknown* (New York: Pocket Books, 1993).

11. Joy Fielding, *Don't Cry Now* (New York: Morrow, 1995).

12. Patricia J. MacDonald, *Lost Innocents* (New York: Warner Books, 1998).

13. Judith Kelman, *More Than You Know* (New York: Bantam, 1996).

14. James Patterson, *Along Came a Spider* (Boston: Little, Brown, 1993).

15. Harris, *The Red Dragon* (New York: Putnam, 1981).

16. *The Fugitive* (Warner Brothers, 1993).

17. Greg Iles, *Mortal Fear* (New York: Dutton, © 1997).

18. Philip Shelby, *Days of Drums* (New York: Simon & Schuster, 1996).

19. Klavan, *Don't Say a Word* (New York: Pocket Books, 1991); ———, *The Scarred Man* (New York: Doubleday, 1990); ———, *Hunting Down Amanda* (New York: Morrow, 1999).

20. Craig Holden, *The Last Sanctuary* (New York: Delacorte, 1996).

21. Shelby, *Days of Drums.*

22. *Sleeping with the Enemy* (20th Century Fox, 1991).

23. Judy Mercer, *Fast Forward* (New York: Pocket Books, 1995).

24. Jack Higgins, *The Eagle Has Landed* (New York: Holt, 1975).

25. Raymond E. Feist, *The Magician* (New York: Doubleday, 1992); Robert Jordan, *The Eye of the World* (New York: T. Doherty Associates, 1990).

26. Frank Herbert, *Dune* (Philadelphia: Chilton Books, 1965).

27. T. Jefferson Parker, *The Blue Hour* (New York: Hyperion, 1999).

28. Scott B. Smith, *A Simple Plan* (New York: Knopf, 1993).

29. Michael Gannon's forthcoming study of Adventure and Suspense, part of Libraries Unlimited's Genreflecting Advisory series, will fill a gap by providing solid reference information on this genre.

30. Jay P. Pederson, ed., *St. James Guide to Crime and Mystery Writers,* 4th ed. (Detroit: St. James, 1996); *Mystery and Suspense Writers: The Literature of Crime, Detection, and Espionage* (New York: Scribner, 1998).

31. Jean Swanson and Dean James, *Killer Books: A Reader's Guide to Exploring the Popular World of Mystery and Suspense* (New York: Berkley Books, 1998).

14

Thrillers

For many readers, and librarians, the genre classification Thriller is synonymous with the Espionage stories so popular in the '70s and '80s. Many types of books share similar characteristics and fit under the Thriller umbrella, however, as they combine fast-paced action and adventure with traditional heroes and an abundance of technical details. For example, Robert Ludlum, John Grisham, and Michael Crichton are linked for fans by their pacing, as well as the nature of their heroes and the obstacles they face, even though their stories focus on disparate subjects. This chapter will explore six types of Thrillers—Legal, Medical/Scientific, Political/Corporate/Financial, Crime/Caper, Espionage, and Techno-Thriller. Each type offers an insider's look into a profession, a field of expertise, and addresses the perennial question posed by titles in the genre: Whom can the hero trust?

A Definition

The size and diversity of the Thriller genre make it difficult to define in a straightforward fashion. Basically this genre focuses on a particular profession—espionage, medical, or legal, for example—and tells an action-packed story that reveals the intricacies of that profession and the potential dangers faced by those involved in it. The details supplied, their authenticity and their scope, provide the primary satisfaction for readers. Although important to a good story, the character of the hero is generally secondary to the action and detail. Readers can easily distinguish the good from the bad among these stereotypical characters.

The Thriller genre shares elements with the Suspense, Adventure, and Mystery genres. As in Suspense, the role of the readers of Thrillers is to watch, to follow the action step-by-step, and, in the best, to participate intellectually and emotionally in the unraveling of the plot complications. Here, however, the physical, emotional, and mental dangers faced by the hero are not ubiquitous and constant. Thrillers demand an element of Suspense, but it is not the focus of the book. Action, the primary element of the Adventure genre, plays a major role, but again it is not the most important aspect. Intrigue and the solving of a puzzle from the Mystery genre figure prominently as well. All these elements from other genres play a role in the Thriller genre, but here the focus is on the frame of the story, the details of the profession, and the way in which the hero uses his skill and knowledge within that profession to extricate himself from a dangerous situation. For example, in a Legal Thriller, it is the hero's knowledge of the law that allows him to succeed and escape the dangerous situation in which he finds himself, and it is the presentation of these often arcane details from the legal profession that enthrall readers.

What, then, is a Thriller? It is a gripping, plot-centered story, set in the detailed framework of a particular profession, that places heroes or heroines in dangerous situations from which they must extricate themselves. The general characteristics in Figure 14.1, as well as the specific features of each subgenre, will amplify this bare-bones definition.

Characteristics and the Genre's Appeal

Frame

As will be underscored in the discussion of each subgenre below, the details and the jargon of the subgenre, of each occupation, are vital. These must be profuse and accurate. Readers anticipate being immersed

---

FIGURE 14.1

Characteristics of the Thriller Genre

1. Extensive details and technical language related to each sub-genre (and occupation) are vital, and they are woven into the story in a way that does not detract from the pacing.

2. Stories center on the plot and the action generated by the intricately involved narrative. There is often a political focus with either national or international ramifications.

3. To achieve their goal, protagonists must pass through frightening perils, which may be physical or emotional. Violence or the threat of violence is often present.

4. Readers generally call these fast-paced, even though some are densely written, and readers may only feel that the story moves quickly because it is so compelling. The sense of action or movement increases the pace, but the action may be more cerebral than physical.

5. Protagonists are usually strong, sympathetic characters who sometimes operate under their own personal codes. Secondary characters are less well developed and may even be caricatures. Protagonists often operate alone, as they can never be certain, in their worlds of betrayal and deception, whom they can trust.

---

in the legal or medical professions, for example, and they expect their lawyers and doctors to sound just like the ones they know—or see on television. In fact, if the details are good enough, it does not matter for some readers how exciting, or even plausible, the plot or how realistic the characterizations. Although some readers may skim the technical details in Tom Clancy's Techno-Thrillers, for example, the most fervent fans of this subgenre see these as the core of the book.

Story Line

Story lines in Thrillers tend to be complicated, with frequent plot twists that surprise protagonist and reader alike. Power is often at the heart of the action: The antagonist plots to gain power for his own ends, and the hero is out to stop him or her. There is violence or the threat of violence, and a sense of constantly changing action and movement, thus increasing the pace of the story. The emphasis of the story line is on action and conflict, the prevention of the power-hungry villain from gaining control. Ultimately, the hero triumphs over evil and survives—although there may be a price to pay.

Pacing

Pacing in Thrillers sometimes seems problematical to the nonfans. How can one possibly allege that an 850-page book, full of carefully researched details about military hardware, is fast-paced? Yet the fans do. The answer seems to be that the books are compelling reads; they pull the reader in with the sympathetic portrayal of the hero and his plight, and the action as well as the detail keeps the reader turning the pages. Readers know that key plot elements can depend on these intricacies and details. Thrillers by other authors, such as the more cerebral Espionage Thrillers of a literary stylist such as John le Carré, seem equally compelling because the reader is pulled into the hero's moral dilemmas, as well as into interpreting the shades of gray that pervade his stories. *Engrossing* is a term often applied to this genre, and the books are often what readers want when they request page-turners.

Characterization

One of the essential features of the Thriller genre is the character of the protagonist, whether hero or antihero. The character of these primarily male protagonists pervades the novels. As do most Adventure heroes and Private Investigators in the Mystery genre, these characters often seem to operate under their own personal moral codes, which may be at odds with the law or common practice. Any reader of the genre also recognizes that these heroes are faced with a serious dilemma: Whom of the characters who surround them—and often appeal to them for assistance—can they really trust? This dilemma creates moral questions and drives the plot, often even turning the hero away from the police or anyone in authority as a possible betrayer, and forcing him to use his own skills and knowledge to overcome all obstacles in his way.

Secondary characters and villains fare less well, except in Crime Thrillers, where the villain is frequently the protagonist. Often characterizations are black and white, with the hero portrayed as very good and the antagonist very bad. Readers generally have no doubt which are the good guys and which the bad, although, as will be seen below, in some (especially in Espionage Thrillers) there are more shades of gray among the characterizations, and the threats to the hero may come from inside his organization or profession as well as from without.

Key Authors and Subgenres

Benchmark

Is there a benchmark who represents the appeal of the Thriller genre as a whole? Probably not. However, popular Thriller writers such as John Grisham, Stuart Woods, and Michael Crichton certainly exemplify the characteristics above, and they likely share more characteristics, more similarities, than a cursory look at the plots of their books would suggest. All write fast-paced, entertaining, detail-laden novels in the Thriller mode. Only the arenas in which the stories are set vary. In fact, they can often be suggested to the same reader, someone who likes this type of book, as long as he or she is not too particular about the background in which the story is set.

Subgenres of Thrillers

LEGAL THRILLERS

Premiere among the Thriller subgenres today, Legal Thrillers ride the wave of the enormous popularity of the two authors who represent the opposite ends of this subgenre. Just as Robert Ludlum and John le Carré drove the popularity of Espionage Thrillers in the '70s and '80s with myriad imitators, now the reading public follows Grisham and Scott Turow and their counterparts. As did the benchmarks in the Espionage Thriller subgenre writing two decades earlier, each represents an opposite trend and appeal—Grisham and similar writers of the fast-paced, easy-reading story versus Turow and his followers, with their more measured pacing and intricately developed psychological studies. *See* Figure 14.2.

One key to the popularity of the Legal Thriller, as it is in all Thrillers, is the character of the hero/ine. Although in their early life as Erle Stanley Gardner's Perry Mason stories and television episodes, Legal Thrillers focused more on the cases (despite the interest in series characters Mason, his faithful assistants Della Street and Paul Drake, and eternal underdog Hamilton Burger). Today, the emphasis of the story line is on the characters, their lives, and how these cases affect them. A range of characters connected with the legal professions might fill the role of hero, but the key is that readers need to relate to the character; they must identify with him and the battles he faces. These are likable characters, whether the naive heroes of Grisham's early novels, fighting against corruption both inside and outside the profession, for example in *The Pelican Brief;* damaged heroes, as the recovering alcoholic Charley Sloan of William J. Coughlin's satisfying Detroit-based stories, of which *Shadow of a Doubt* is the first; or strong women looking to make their mark in the profession, as in Lisa Scottoline's

---

FIGURE 14.2

Characteristics of Legal Thrillers

1. Heroes and heroines are portrayed sympathetically. Readers care about them and their fate.

2. The typical Legal Thriller story line finds the hero/ine caught in an intricate web of corruption and greed, forced to make a difficult decision that will have far-reaching implications both for himself and others connected to the case. Moral and social issues often figure prominently. Justice is served in the end.

3. Stories are often called "fast-paced" or "page-turners." Characters and story lines are compelling and pull readers into the story so that they seem to move quickly, even if they are more densely written.

4. Legal details and technical language are required by fans.

---

popular novels set in Philadelphia.[1] (*Everywhere That Mary Went* is the first.)[2] Whatever his or her character or background, it is vital that we readers intimately experience the character's involvement in the law, whether personal, as in Turow's *Presumed Innocent*, which follows lawyer Rusty Sabich's own harrowing trial for murder, or simply as a lawyer representing a client.[3] Our involvement with these characters draws us to these stories and keeps us reading to discover the outcome, the fate of the characters we have embraced.

Although in Legal Thrillers readers certainly identify with and care about the protagonist (usually a lawyer), the legal profession does not necessarily come off well. These are books that are enjoyed by lawyers and their fans, as well as by those who claim to dislike lawyers and the legal profession. The appeal of the story is that the corruption and greed the lawyer fights are as often within the profession as without. The protagonist is the white knight, strong enough to wage a battle against the corruption, wherever he encounters it, within the law or without. This story line opens up endless variations on questions of moral and social issues, and no venue—from the White House to the Supreme Court—is safe from the investigative talents of our knight on his quest.

Classic Legal Thrillers—Gardner's Perry Mason and Robert Traver's *Anatomy of a Murder* for example—may highlight the courtroom action, but today's most popular titles focus on the investigation.[4] An example is Grisham's first best-seller, *The Firm,* which features new lawyer Mitch McDeere on the trail of corruption within his own law firm.[5]

These books are cinematic, a blend of Adventure, Intrigue, and Suspense. Although characters may not be in life-and-death situations, they always face danger of some kind, certainly from a conspiracy if not a physical antagonist. Twists of plot play a major role and keep the reader guessing, not necessarily about the outcome, but about exactly how the triumph will be effected. And although justice is the end result, the means of achieving this may not always be strictly by the letter of the law. These are satisfying reads, with the good guys—usually the underdogs—victorious and the bad guys punished, although the victory never comes without cost and pain. In some cases, as in William Diehl's *Primal Fear,* for example, the cost may be too great, as our hero Martin Vail discovers, in an incredible twist at the end of the story, that he may have made a fatal error of judgment.[6]

No knowledgeable reader of this subgenre would say that titles are equally fast-paced. The works of Grisham and similar authors would certainly fit that description, but to call Turow fast-paced is like saying the same thing about titles by Fyodor Dostoyevsky, to whom Turow has been compared. Yet fans find Legal Thrillers to be compelling reading. If not exactly page-turners, they are gripping stories that hook readers early on and keep them satisfied as the story unfolds. We keep reading to find out what will happen next. These books have the feel of fast pacing, even though they may not actually read quickly.

Finally, as in all Thrillers, the frame, here the legal details, features prominently among reasons fans flock to this subgenre. The fine points of law, courtroom procedures, and reversals prove interesting fodder for writers to explore in these novels. Technical language should be fluent but not too abstruse for lay readers.

The tone of these books is also important. Although there is ultimately a satisfactory resolution, with the good guys triumphing over evil, the tone is often darker, bleaker than might be expected in books with this outcome. As mentioned above, these victories are often not without cost, and no satisfactory ending is completely without loss. This subgenre offers a range of violence and strong language, although details and language are usually not as graphic as in other genres, such as Suspense, for example.

As they have for a decade, the benchmarks (and opposite ends of the spectrum in terms of style, perspective, and pacing) remain Turow and Grisham. Although his newer titles feature larger social concerns and thus may engender a slightly different "feel," Grisham's titles typically focus on the cinematic story of the lawyer fighting for the little guy or the lawyer as little guy fighting against corruption, whether in a law firm or other corporation with a legal arm. Suspenseful, with a sense of danger pervading, these also contain the requisite chase scene, as well as the ultimate resolution, with David always triumphing over the evil Goliath. Interestingly, Grisham has never created a series character, although many who write in his style have done so. Grisham fans would likely enjoy Steve Martini's series featuring Paul Madriani and associates, with their complex plots, appealing characters, and effective resolutions. (*Compelling Evidence* is the first in the series.)[7] Although now, sadly, deceased, Coughlin wrote a strong series of Legal Thrillers featuring recovering alcoholic Charley Sloan, who was always ready to represent the underdog in any case against corruption. (The series begins with *Shadow of a Doubt*.)

Turow, on the other hand, has made his name and established his best-seller status with complex, literary, layered novels that deal with legal issues but are certainly Thrillers on a more cerebral level. As do others in the subgenre, Turow explores the nature of truth and corruption, the role of the law and justice, but he does so in more depth, philosophically and psychologically. Issues and characters are not often black and white, but more frequently shaded gray areas, in which the answers are not as clear. Turow also examines other issues in the lives and relationships of his characters—love, friendship, and family—as he explores the lives of his characters on a deeper level. All this is also done at a more measured pace, as befits the complexity of his approach. Unlike Grisham, Turow often pulls secondary characters from one novel and features them in a later story.

Although there is overlap in the appeal of these major writers, and certainly there are any number of fans who read both, readers often choose one type or the other to reflect their current mood. Turow fans might also enjoy Richard North Patterson, whose more densely written and intense stories unfold slowly, adding layers of details, story line, and characters. (*The Dark Lady* is a recent example.)[8] Robert K. Tanenbaum's popular series featuring Butch Karp and Marlene Ciampi, lawyers employed sometimes privately and sometimes officially in police and district attorney departments in New York City, offers similar depth of characterization and plot with the addition of strong series characters and their involved family life. (*No Lesser Plea* is the first.)[9]

MEDICAL/SCIENTIFIC THRILLERS

Second in popularity among fans of the Thriller genre are those that feature medical or scientific backgrounds and details, with suspenseful stories of experiments gone awry and maniacal doctors, not to mention Big Medicine as a danger to doctors and patients alike. *See* Figure 14.3 for characteristics of Medical/Scientific Thrillers.

FIGURE 14.3

Characteristics of Medical/Scientific Thrillers

1. Stories are plot driven, and story lines focus on newsworthy medical and science themes and play upon the fears of the readers.

2. Stories are fast-paced, with dangerous situations moving them along quickly.

3. The hero/ine is usually a good doctor or researcher caught up in a dangerous situation. Characters are often black and white, rather than fully developed.

4. Medical and scientific details are important. They are presented in such a way that the reader feels he receives an inside look at the profession or research topic.

Although the standard Thriller hero/ine is an important part of the appeal of this subgenre, even more important here may be the topical nature of the story lines and the way the authors make readers believe they too could be caught up in this kind of situation. It seems all too real—and frightening. Although the hero/ine is the maverick doctor or researcher who uncovers this terrifying abuse or conspiracy, we readers see ourselves intuitively as potential victims. The authors skillfully manipulate the plot and characterizations to play on our worst fears. Issues in Legal and Political Thrillers may affect us as well, but none do so as intimately as the possibilities raised in Medical Thrillers. Any one of us could be in a hospital with a mad doctor conducting secret tests or exposed to a deadly virus while riding in an airplane. These plots strike very close to home and thus pull the reader deftly into the story.

At the heart of the plot may be a conspiracy, with people as the villains; or there may be a virus, a natural disaster, or a catastrophe, often caused by a human villain. Whatever the case, Medical/Scientific Thrillers seem to produce higher body counts than many Thriller subgenres, certainly more than Legal Thrillers.

Because they often deal with topical issues—the Ebola virus or insensitive and even evil health maintenance organizations—Medical/Scientific Thrillers may date more quickly than other plots not tied to items in the news. On the other hand, well-crafted plots transcend time, and certainly until the threats are totally removed—or the diseases cured—these stories in the news today parallel those of yesteryear and consistently provide grist for these storytellers.

There seem to be more female protagonists or at least strong female characters in Medical/Scientific Thrillers than in any of the other subgenres. As usual, the heroine is fighting against corruption, conspiracy, or a deadly virus or disease. She is almost always alone in this crusade, sometimes the only character who sees the truth and realizes all the ramifications, and thus, as the protagonist, is frequently put in danger. Although the heroine may be a skilled doctor or researcher, she still possesses the naïveté that places her own life in jeopardy as she tries to fight the wrongs within her profession.

The jeopardy in which the protagonist is placed moves the plot quickly. For the most part, Medical/Scientific Thrillers unfold swiftly, gripping the reader in the first few pages. The danger persists, suffusing the story, with the protagonist frequently in mortal danger. This situation keeps the plot moving and the reader turning pages.

Medical and Scientific details remain of prime importance. Readers relish this inside look at the profession. Although they expect details about the operations of the hospital or research lab, medical procedures, and the nature of the disease or virus, they want them to be presented in an understandable fashion, rather than as dry, and perhaps overwhelmingly incomprehensible, facts.

Robin Cook remains the premiere author of this popular subgenre; his is the name readers mention most frequently when they come to the library seeking more titles. His fast-paced, crusading stories raise questions of medical ethics as they offer details of the profession. In Cook's Thrillers, the doctors are usually the good guys (and gals), pitted against the soulless, greed-driven health maintenance organizations, the hospitals, and the drug companies. Try *Toxin* for a recent example of his best-selling style.[10]

Michael Palmer is a good choice for Cook's many fans. His stories are also fast-paced, featuring good doctors and bad, with the good battling the conspiracy of Medicine as Big Business. In *Critical Judgment*, for example, emergency room physician Abby Dolan wages her own battle against a chemical weapons plant polluting the area where she lives and works.[11]

Steven Spruill is another author popular with Cook's fans at my library. His stories follow the typical Cook plan, with a fast-paced tale of medical skulduggery, uncovered by the crusading woman physician. *My Soul to Take* involves resident Suzanne Lord who assisted in a research project that implanted microchips in the brains of patients with visual problems.[12] Unfortunately, the side effects of the procedure turn out to be more harrowing than anyone expected.

Eileen Dreyer offers suspenseful tales of nurses championing the fight against medical corruption or conspiracy or both. Medical detail, tough language, and strong heroines characterize her stories, for example, *Brain Dead*, in which forensic nurse Timmie Leary moves to a small town in Missouri to be near her ailing father, only to discover a disconcerting number of deaths among the elderly patients at the hospital and attached nursing home.[13] And, of course, when she begins to investigate, the lives of her father and son, as well as her own, are placed in danger.

Related to Medical Thrillers are those that feature plots revolving around Scientific research. Crichton is the master of these, with both *The Andromeda Strain* and *Jurassic Park* reflecting the obligatory characteristics: crusading hero, story lines out of the news or certainly within the realm of scientific possibility, and fast pacing, not to mention copious scientific details.[14]

William Boyd also pursues scientific themes in *Brazzaville Beach*.[15] Here anthropologist Hope Clearwater, researching chimpanzees in Africa, comes upon an unexpected behavior, but before she can document and report it, her research is destroyed. Undeterred, she continues, only to find her life, as well as her research, in jeopardy.

In *The Third Twin* Ken Follett, a very popular writer who refuses to be confined to a single genre, has also written a Scientific Thriller featuring clones, genetic research, and an experiment gone awry, with scientist Jeannie Ferrami left to clear up the debris from this government attempt to breed the perfect soldier.[16]

Along the lines of Crichton's popular *Jurassic Park* is Steve Alten's *Meg*, in which a prehistoric shark is resurrected from a deep ocean trough to terrorize the innocent, and hero Jonas Taylor, whom *Booklist* terms in their review a "sort of paleo-ichthyological Indiana Jones," must conquer this modern-day monster.[17] Again, plausible scientific detail overcomes the implausibility of the reappearance of *Carcharodon megalodon,* supposedly extinct for 100 million years.

Although his other popular Thrillers deal with airplanes and conspiracies, not medical issues, John Nance's *Pandora's Clock* is a title worth knowing for readers who enjoy this subgenre.[18] In this novel, a man exposed to a genetically engineered virus (a plot perpetrated by those evil Soviets) dies aboard an airplane, exposing all aboard to the danger of the virus as well as keeping them from landing anywhere, as no airport will accept them.

Tess Gerritsen, who usually features a sympathetic female protagonist, as well as graphic medical detail and more far-fetched plots, crosses between strictly Medical and more Scientific plot emphases. *Harvest* brings the Russian Mafia to U.S. shores, and surgical resident Abbey DiMatteo discovers the skulduggery in this gripping organ-transplant conspiracy.[19]

POLITICAL/CORPORATE/FINANCIAL THRILLERS

Although this grouping may seem like the goulash of the Thriller genre—every topic not covered elsewhere—there are characteristics that link Thrillers on these topics and distinguish them from others in the genre (*see* Figure 14.4).

The newsworthy nature of the story lines remains a consistent thread, running through the Thriller genre, in this subgenre as in the others. Here readers find the political terrorists, the conspiracies to overthrow governments, the nonespionage assassination attempts, and frequently revenge, as well as financial schemes and machinations within corporations and governments.

The character of the protagonist follows the patterns established in the genre (either the naive innocent caught in a tale of corruption or the jaded veteran struggling to overcome his own doubts to support right over the bad guys). Likable protagonists remain key, and here, as in Legal and Medical/Scientific Thrillers, these are frequently women. For example, in both *A Nest of Vipers* and *A Wilderness of Mirrors,* Linda Davies relies on her knowledge of English financial

---

FIGURE 14.4

Characteristics of Political/Corporate/Financial Thrillers

1. Typical themes reflect current issues in the news: conspiracy, computer manipulation, corruption. Danger abounds, and it might have personal, national, or international implications.
2. Protagonists have backgrounds in government, finance, and/or management. The hero operates according to his or her own moral code, which may or may not reflect the laws of the land.
3. Plot twists, intricate story lines, and action drive the pacing.
4. Realistic details relating to corporate life, finance, politics, or government provide added insight into the story line and complications.

---

markets to weave tales of manipulation and financial espionage, with female characters on both sides.[20] In the former, insider trading on the foreign exchange market provides the setting for the story of Sarah Jenson's discovery of crooked traders—and then a much more nefarious and far-reaching plot involving top government officials.

Twists of plot drive the pacing, as they do in the other subgenres. And as in all the Thriller genres, it is the background frame—here the details of politics (and political chicanery), of financial machinations, and of power—that drive the plot and attract readers. Here, too, the frame may be more chillingly laid out, as in Frederick Forsyth's masterpiece, *The Day of the Jackal.*[21] Vivid details of the Jackal's preparations for his attempt to assassinate de Gaulle dominate the story and linger in the reader's mind. We remember these details—the breaking down and transporting of his weapon across borders, the elements of his disguise—almost more accurately than the story and the race to catch him. The wealth of details make the story more real—and all the more frightening.

David Baldacci makes a good benchmark for this hodgepodge. His plots focus on corporations (*Total Control*), financial manipulations (the lottery in *The Winner*), abuse of power in the office of the president (*Absolute Power*), and more.[22] High-tech and computer machinations make him a good crossover bet for Techno-Thriller readers as well, if they do not mind the lack of submarines or specialized aircraft.

The myriad novels of terrorists also fall here. Not spies, these agents seek the destruction of the government in action-packed, betrayal-fraught, and often revenge-motivated high-voltage dramas. Victor O'Reilly's series, beginning with *Games of the Hangman,* sets the standard for these intellectual Political Thrillers, which appeal to fans of Espionage as well.[23] Violent scenes mix with complex plotting and an intellectual and resourceful hero (Irishman Hugo Fitzduane, who works to fight terrorism) in these stories of revenge and passion, with political undertones.

Among those fighting the terrorists are also occasionally lone individuals, in the typical Grisham pattern of David against Goliath. Stephen Leather's *The Chinaman* is a classic example.[24] When his wife and daughter are killed in a random IRA bombing, Nguyen Minh leaves London to seek revenge on his own. He had left Vietnam when two other daughters were killed by terrorists, and the British government's assurances that in civilized England these men will be caught and punished are not enough. He then goes directly to the top of the IRA, but stonewalled there, he determines to use guerilla tactics to convince all involved that he is serious. Revenge and betrayal, as well as a multitude of details from bomb making to moral and social issues, make this a typical, fast-paced Political Thriller.

Not all Political Thrillers evoke such a dark mood. Newsman Jim Lehrer writes a series that features the one-eyed lieutenant governor of Oklahoma, a crusader against corruption on a slightly less global and dangerous level. Lehrer demonstrates that not all Thrillers have to be serious—although these clearly find a different audience or an audience that reads them for different reasons. The series opens with *Kick the Can* and throughout reflects both the characteristics of the Thriller genre and Lehrer's love of small-town life and people in Oklahoma and Kansas.[25]

Tim F. LaHaye and Jerry B. Jenkins's enormously popular series of the approaching Apocalypse, beginning with *Left Behind,* also fits roughly within the parameters of Political Thrillers.[26] Protagonists Ray and Buck face the return of the Antichrist and other perils of the forthcoming end of the world as predicted in biblical prophecy. Action and incidents from the pages of our newspapers drive events here, as they and the Saved battle evil.

Stephen Frey, known primarily for his Financial Thrillers (*The Vulture Fund, The Insider*), creates the sympathetic protagonist and topical story the genre demands and adds the financial and governmental details that flesh out the story of corruption and betrayal.[27] As always, the protagonist does not know as much as the reader, and certainly not as much as he needs to avoid the traps set by the sinister, and often unknown, villains. Whom can he trust? is a common theme in this example and throughout the genre. Conspiracy, whether political or economic, also plays an important role in Frey's fast-paced stories of Financial and Political subterfuge.

CRIME/CAPER THRILLERS

Neither a Mystery nor a Legal Thriller, these are Thrillers told from the criminal's point of view (Figure 14.5 lists additional characteristics of Crime/Caper Thrillers). They may be more humorous capers in the style of Donald Westlake, the black-comedic romps of Carl Hiaasen, or the noir escapades of Eugene Izzi's or George V. Higgins's Crime Thriller protagonists.

Crime/Caper Thrillers deal with the underworld, the underside of the Police Detective Mysteries discussed in "Mysteries," chapter 8. This is a world many of us readers know less about, but one that fascinates us. Just as many Mysteries go into intricate detail about the investigative process, these Thrillers provide the same level of detail about the planning and commission of the crime. A classic example is Lawrence Sanders's Edgar Award–winning first novel, *The Anderson Tapes*.[28] Here we follow ex-con Anderson, who attempts to make it big by robbing a luxury apartment building, unaware that both police and mob are eavesdropping on his every move. We follow the details of his preparations, aware all along that he is under surveillance. The layers of detail—the planning and the surveillance—heighten our enjoyment of the story and its denouement. Also, as is the case generally in Crime/Capers, even though there is an investigation into the

---

FIGURE 14.5

Characteristics of Crime/Caper Thrillers

1. Details of the criminal world—the crimes and those who commit them—dominate these stories. Although there may be an investigation, it is generally secondary to the activities of the criminals. Attention to small details of the crimes gives readers an insider's view of the preparations for and execution of the crime.

2. Complicated, intricately twisted plots are the hallmark. Double crosses are essential, and a final twist near the end often completes the story.

3. Protagonists are flawed, often even amoral. As criminals or part of the underworld, they are not always characters with whom we can comfortably sympathize.

4. Although action is important, the preparations for the crime and the aftermath drive the pacing. Although there are usually chase or other suspenseful scenes, much of the energy is mental, rather than physical.

5. Often graphically violent, these may also display an almost comic tone. The tone in titles in this subgenre runs the gamut from noir (Crime Thrillers) to more comedic (Capers).

---

crime, the focus of the story is on the criminals and their escape, not the investigative team.

In a more recent example, *Void Moon,* by Michael Connelly, heroine Cassie Black, an ex-con, hopes to put her life on the right track with just one more job that will give her enough money to take her daughter, born while she was in prison, and leave the country to start a new life.[29] Unfortunately, this last undertaking, set up to enable her to start a new life, takes her back to the scene of the end of her previous happiness, the Cleopatra Hotel and Casino in Las Vegas, where her lover died after a botched heist. Electronic surveillance as well as old-fashioned lock picking and much in between come into play as she sets up her part, only to discover much later that this was all part of a much bigger scam in which she was only a pawn. Our minds reel as each of the three main characters in turn reveals the labyrinth of twists and double crosses in which the others were forced to play.

This leads into the second characteristic, the complicated plots, including the requisite double cross and the final twist at the end. As with all Thrillers, the more complicated and coiled the plot, the more pleasure for the reader. Unlike in the Mystery genre, here in Crime/ Caper authors are not required to play fair and provide clues, and even though we expect a twist, its exact nature often comes as a surprise. Elmore Leonard's gritty but humorous novels of the seedy life of hapless crooks and the underworld provide extensive examples (*Get Shorty* is one).[30]

Story lines often feature the Mafia or other denizens of the criminal underworld. Dirty business dealings, rogue cops, and scams all figure prominently. Even enterprises that might seem legitimate are not, as in David Ramus's stories of the art world, *The Gravity of Shadows*, for example.[31] Although his art dealers seem legitimate, there is always a hidden underside to their work, and they get pulled in to a violent world not necessarily of their own making.

Here it is also the criminals who become the protagonists, and this switch creates a different kind of book. Unlike our reaction to most "heroes" and "heroines" in genre fiction, we may find that we do not always like these flawed characters. In fact, they may surprise us with their amorality and casual acceptance of illegal activities. Lawrence Block's compilation of noir short stories, *Hit Man*, features the day-to-day activities of the title character, as he completes assignments and deals with the everyday annoyances of his life.[32] However, the "hero's" chilling amorality creates an extraordinarily disturbing and compulsively readable collection.

There are even novels in this subgenre with no likable characters. An example that comes immediately to mind is Evan Hunter's *Criminal Conversation*.[33] Michael Welles is a lawyer who is obsessed with bringing down the Mafia. However, his world is turned upside down when he discovers that the Mafia head's new mistress is his bored wife. What he must do to extricate Sarah and himself from this situation demands a new morality, one no better than that of the man he wants to put in jail.

On the other hand, many of these protagonists have a genuine allure. Who can resist the wacko creations of Hiaasen and Laurence Shames or Leonard's appealing low-life characters? Authors at both ends of the spectrum from noir to comic offer a range of irresistible bad guys. From Westlake's hapless Dortmunder gang, which has bungled more operations than anyone deserves, to Mario Puzo's sinister Mafia family, protagonists run the gamut in this subgenre.

Pacing in these Crime/Caper Thrillers is less easily delineated. The extensive details in the planning and carrying out of the crime might tend to make the pacing slower, but the engrossing nature of these details pulls the reader along. Then, in the inevitable postcrime aftermath, there may be chases that make readers turn pages even faster. Suffice it to say that fans of this subgenre find these to be stories that pull them in and keep them turning pages, despite the wealth of details. In *A Calculated Risk,* Katherine Neville pits computer security expert Verity Banks against the bank that refused to acknowledge her contributions to their safety in a caper that involves diverting enormous amounts of money from the bank's "secure" system.[34] Imagine Grisham's typical protagonist, played with broad humor and inspired by a strong dose of revenge, in this intricately plotted yet fast-paced romp.

Just as the characters run the gamut from noir to comedic, so does the tone of Crime/Caper Thrillers. Capers are characterized by a more lighthearted tone. These are the stories of Hiaasen, Shames, Leonard, and Westlake. They are peopled by characters who delight readers with their outrageous disregard for law and practically all other conventions.

Characters in Crime Thrillers project a quite different tone. Puzo's Mafia novels or Higgins's stories of unglamorous small-time crooks, characters drawn with more dark shadows than glints of humor, typify these. The late Izzi was a master of this type of Crime Thriller, both on paper and perhaps in his real life as well. Try the posthumously released *Safe Harbor,* which pits an ex-Mafia thief, now in the Witness Protection Program, against his former comrades.[35]

Hiaasen, with his over-the-top skewerings of life in south Florida, typifies the Crime/Caper subgenre today. His enormous popularity has inspired imitators, and the south Florida scene is well covered by him, along with authors such as Leonard, Shames, and Tim Dorsey.

The typical Hiaasen Crime/Caper Thriller features murder and black humor, over-the-top secondary characters and situations, an antihero protagonist, corruption promulgated by those in authority, and labyrinthine plots. His venal and often loopy characters seem destined to turn south Florida simultaneously into an environmental disaster and a madhouse. Try *Native Tongue* to sample his work.[36] Here ecoterrorists threaten a sleazy Disney-style theme park.

Although they may lack the south Florida setting, others writing in this vein—Thomas Perry's earlier titles (*The Island*) and Pete Hautman (*Ring Game*)—provide the same black humor.[37] Many of these authors harken back to skilled satirist Damon Runyan and his stories of the less-than-prominent New Yorkers.

ESPIONAGE THRILLERS

In their heyday in the '70s and '80s, the genre designation Thrillers meant only one thing: Espionage. At the height of the cold war, these dramas of spies and intrigue dominated the genre and headed the best-sellers lists. Then, with the end of the cold war and the loss of an evil empire as villain, their popularity was superseded by other forms of Thrillers. However, authors and fans sought solutions to the loss of a forum for these action stories, and the subsequent rise in the adventures of terrorists and mercenaries can likely be attributed to the demise of the Espionage Thriller. After all, what else would a self-respecting spy do with these finely honed skills?

When my department did our first genre study in the mid-1980s, we chose Espionage Thrillers, and it was a fortunate selection, as this was an enormously popular genre, the characteristics of which lay out in a satisfactory, orderly fashion (*see* Figure 14.6 for characteristics of Espionage Thrillers). Now, unfortunately, these Thrillers are not so popular, neither with writers nor readers, and the information we discovered then and found so useful in working with patrons has lost its impact in a world that has left behind the arena of international spies for the boardroom, autopsy room, and courtroom. Of the subgenres of Espionage Thrillers that we identified then—Action (Ludlum), Superhero (Ian Fleming's James Bond), Cynical Realism (le Carré), Amateur Agent/Adventure (Helen MacInnes), and Technology (Tom Clancy)—only the latter remains an active subgenre,

---

FIGURE 14.6

Characteristics of Espionage *Thrillers*

1. The resourceful protagonist may or may not be trained as an actual spy, but he always has skills that serve this purpose. He operates under a personal code, and this may not always correspond with that of the government he represents.

2. The intricate and involved plot relies heavily on twists and puzzles within puzzles. Betrayals, secrets, conspiracies, and revenge make up many story lines.

3. The political focus and implications emphasize Espionage and the gaining of information, rather than actual politics. Story lines have international, not merely national, implications.

4. There is violence or the threat of violence or both. The protagonist passes through frightening perils, both physical and mental. Those stories that emphasize action move more quickly than those that focus on the cerebral deliberations of the hero.

5. The tone and mood are often dark, reflecting the senses of alienation and paranoia that plague these agents.

---

and it is considered separately below. As the nature of Techno-Thrillers has changed, and Clancy and others continue to write and expand the boundaries of that subgenre, their books depend less on the Espionage aspect and more simply on the technical details of weaponry and politics.

Again here, the character of the hero—and historically these are male protagonists, although there are more female protagonists among current series—sets the tone for the story. This hero, like the protagonists of hard-boiled Detective stories, operates under his own personal moral code. He may be a highly trained intelligence agent, or he may as likely be an intelligent amateur, caught up in the game of spies. In fact, within this broad definition, the character of the hero ranges widely from the straight-arrow agent of Ludlum's classic tales, to the complex, flawed heroes of le Carré and John E. Gardner, to the parody heroes of Marc Lovell's Appleton Porter series, begun with *Spy Game* in 1980.[38] (These feature the hapless Apple, who bumbles his way through the Espionage arena in a series of entertaining spoofs.)

Although they are often part of an established Espionage network, these heroes operate primarily alone, drawing on assistance from time to time, but generally acting independently as they carry out their assigned missions. As in all Thrillers, the protagonist never knows, until the die is cast, whom he can trust. In many of these, the characters, especially the "villains," are less black and white. Good and bad, among characters and governments, is not always clear-cut. In fact, in many of these, the danger to and betrayal of the hero are as likely to come from within as without. In Bryan Forbes's *Quicksand*, for example, defector Alex Hillsden, framed for a murder he did not commit and living quietly in exile in Russia, is given a chance to return, with his wife and daughter, to Great Britain and safety.[39] He agrees, but from the beginning something seems not quite right in the scheme to uncover the ring of neo-Nazis. There seem to be threads harkening back to Alex's own past as well as to episodes in Britain's history during World War II. The labyrinthine plot, double agents, revenge, and betrayal make this a compelling story.

Many Espionage Thrillers are series, with the reader following the character through years of adventures. Unlike series in other genres, however, here we learn almost nothing about the characters' private lives: They are defined and described through their jobs, a technique that underlines the insular, intensely private nature of their lives— and their lack of any life outside their work. Adam Hall's *Quiller* provides an appropriate example.[40] Not only do we not know his first name, this man also works for a division so secret it does not even have a name or exist officially. Quiller is described only in terms of the knowledge and skills required to complete his increasingly dangerous missions; it is as if he has no emotional, or even intellectual, life outside his work. Even for a character such as Len Deighton's Bernard Samson, we find that although we know details of his life, their importance is still obscured by his devotion to "the job," even when his wife defects to the East after *Berlin Game*.[41]

In contrast to this depiction of the antihero protagonist of Espionage Thrillers emerges the work of a small group who confound that designation. Within the rather bleak world created by most authors in this subgenre, there are a few authors who have defied convention and created the quirky, sometimes hapless, spies who add a measure of levity in the darkness. Brian Freemantle and Lovell, mentioned above, are among the first that come to mind. Freemantle, in his depiction of superspy Charlie (not Charles) Muffin, has raised humor to a fine art. Charlie is a rumpled holdover of the good old days of the British Secret Service and a master at misleading friends and foe into believing he is no more—and likely less—than he appears. The lighthearted tone obscures the fraudulent world beneath the exterior, and the deceptively simple story is revealed in all its complexity only as Charlie unravels all the threads at the end. *Charlie M* is the first in this series.[42]

Finally, there is no denying that the Mrs. Pollifax series (*The Unexpected Mrs. Pollifax* is the first) by Dorothy Gilman features spies and technically falls within the Espionage Thriller subgenre.[43] Yet it is not fans of the Thriller genre but rather fans of Cozy Mysteries who follow this humorous series portraying a retired homemaker who always wanted to work for the Central Intelligence Agency (CIA) and falls into her new career through serendipity and a series of misunderstandings. Still, this is a woman born to the profession, and these stories do feature Espionage situations in exotic locales.

Espionage Thrillers take place in worlds of international spies and intrigue, with the action set against a background of looming international catastrophe that only the hero can avert. Although they are often suspenseful, it is not the Suspense, but rather the complexity of the plot, with its unexpected twists and turns, that attracts readers. Readers of Espionage Thrillers expect the unexpected, the out of the ordinary, the situations that change frequently and in unanticipated directions. These are layered puzzles, and for many readers, the more complex and intricate the puzzle and the execution of the solution, the more satisfying the story. *Labyrinthine* frequently describes these mazelike plots. And although the plots are complicated, these convolutions relate not simply to the action or intrigue but rather to the underlying power struggle. Double crosses abound. Gardner's Herbie Kruger is a British agent of German birth. In *The Confessor*, for example, Herbie must come out of retirement to investigate the murder of one of his old colleagues, Gus Keene, the department's confessor, who once could elicit confessions from anyone and even interrogated Kruger.[44] Keene was Kruger's friend, and now Herbie seeks revenge, as well as the identity of the murderer. Thus begins his trip back through his friend's possessions and files to see who might have wanted revenge. In this complex story with multiple plotlines, nothing is as it seems, and the comparisons between magic and espionage (and by inference between magicians and spies) seem particularly apt and revealing.

That Espionage Thrillers are international in scope sets them apart from the Political Thrillers described above. This distinction likely derives from their cold war roots, but even Rudyard Kipling's classic novel of the Great Game, *Kim,* pits erstwhile super powers England and Russia on the battlefield of India.[45] Yet this is part of their great appeal for readers. One of the features that made MacInnes's Espionage Thrillers so popular with a wide range of readers was their settings around the world. India, France, Germany, Greece, Italy, and her native Great Britain were just a selection of the locales to which she took her readers. Travel details as well as clever Espionage plots, not to mention Romance, fueled enthusiasm for her stories.

Espionage Thrillers seem fast-paced to readers. The sense that the situation is so uncertain and that it might change in an unknown direction at any point makes the books read quickly. There is a sense of movement, whether the books are the more physical and action-oriented titles by Ludlum or the more cerebral of Gardner and le Carré. In fact, these may be densely written, certainly longer books. Yet they are compelling reading for their fans, who read anticipating the unforeseen and thus turn the pages at a faster pace.

Although details of the world of Espionage figure prominently in these Thrillers, the best also capture that claustrophobic mood of alienation and loneliness, the paranoia of the amateur who has not yet learned whom to trust and of the jaded professional who knows he can trust no one. For the most part, this is a world of one man or woman, operating alone, and with only a government bureau, not a family, as backup. These are not bright and happy books, and even though these characters are successful on their missions—and they have saved the free world once again—the mood is generally uncompromisingly bleak. Especially in this world without a "real" villain, the outlook for these heroes is dark. A sense of doom pervades many of these. Le Carré provides the classic examples of this type of characterization and the mood of bleak melancholy thus created. No one can read *The Spy Who Came In from the Cold,* for example, without a deep sense of tragedy created by betrayal and double cross.[46]

Espionage or Spy Thrillers have fallen into a decline in the years following the fall of the "evil Soviet Empire." Without a strong, familiar antagonist, Espionage writers seemed stumped, unable to discover a replacement enemy. With Ludlum deceased and le Carré writing fewer or other types of books, the genre has become less popular. In fact, many authors have turned to historical settings, particularly World War II and the cold war years immediately following, and are writing "historical" Espionage Thrillers. Alan Furst sets the standard for this offshoot. In *Red Gold* he re-creates the mood and atmosphere of World War II Paris under German occupation, as his antihero Jules Cassom fights for the Resistance.[47]

Because of the decline in the popularity and publishing of this subgenre, it is difficult to identify a benchmark. Certainly in previous decades those would have been Ludlum and le Carré. One of the few writing Espionage Thrillers today is newsman Lehrer, mentioned previously for his series of Political Thrillers. He also writes a seriocomic series that stars ex-CIA agent Charles Avenue Henderson, who now, accompanied by his charming wife, runs a pricey bed-and-breakfast in Virginia. In *Blue Hearts,* the first in what one can only hope will be a long-lived series, Henderson is drawn back into "the Game" after two attempts on his life.[48] The puzzle involves the Kennedy assassination and the possibility of a Soviet mole in a high position in the CIA.

Another master of the genre, Robert Littell, continues to produce high-quality Espionage Thrillers but at far too slow a pace to satisfy fans. *Walking Back the Cat* offers a full measure of twists and betrayals, as two unlikely partners—a disillusioned Gulf War veteran and a recently activated Russian spy, planted years earlier in the United States—track back a double cross that has put one's life in danger and exposed a leak in the other's network.[49] Littell's books are atmospheric, convoluted, and satisfying in the tradition of Espionage Thrillers at their best.

Interestingly, two other writers currently publishing series within the subgenre are women: Janice Weber and Maureen Tan. Weber's protagonist, Leslie Frost, world-renowned violinist, is part of a team of female agents (reminiscent of television's *Charlie's Angels*), all with alternative careers that would place them in the center of the action around the world. These are Espionage Thrillers in the James Bond vein, featuring a heroine of superhuman skills and strength and a range of exotic weaponry, not to mention sex and violence. Here, unlike many Bond stories, the emphasis is on Espionage, not Adventure.

Tan's series, on the other hand, presents in Jane Nichols a more human secret agent. A successful career as a mystery writer provides her cover, as Jane travels on missions for the British Secret Service. Unlike many of her male predecessors in the genre, this is a character who also carries emotional baggage from the murder of her lover and the deaths of friends in a terrorist incident. In this series, exotic weaponry, violence, and even sexual details mix with excellent spy craft, strong characterizations, and emotional details beyond the expected in the genre.

TECHNO-THRILLERS

Once these might have been considered a part of Espionage Thrillers, but as the technology and gadgetry have increased in these stories, and the emphasis on Espionage missions decreased, they seem better as a separate category (Figure 14.7 details the characteristics of the Techno-Thriller). It is no longer the Espionage aspect that is important to readers but the gadgetry and intricate details, primarily of a military nature. (The emphasis on military is important; computer gadgetry, in business use, for example, does not have the same appeal for readers. Here, as in Espionage Thrillers, the fate of the Free World is often at stake.)

Benchmark Clancy and his followers provide trained military men as heroes. These are men who operate within a community of other men; they are men who may not be in a position of authority but who, like Clive Cussler's Adventure heroes, save their comrades and their country through wit and ingenuity, not to mention the wide array of weaponry they handle with such skill and finesse.

As in Westerns, there are almost no women in Techno-Thrillers. The ones who do make an appearance are either very good (the little

---

FIGURE 14.7

Characteristics of Techno-Thrillers

1. Protagonists are almost exclusively male, often part of a community or team of men. Stereotypical characterizations are more often the rule than the exception.

2. This resourceful protagonist uses ingenuity and problem-solving techniques, not to mention exotic weaponry and military gadgets, to extricate himself and others from dangerous situations.

3. Story lines focus on military activities, and they have an international scope.

4. Technical expertise is important, because this story hinges on the technical details in the plot. Accuracy, not just plausibility, of these details is vital.

5. Political affiliation is distinctly right wing.

---

wife, waiting patiently at home) or very bad (the siren, trying to lure the hero from his mission). The men are also stereotypes: courageous, moral heroes, driven to fight for their country, to succeed in whatever mission to which they aspire or are sent.

There is a political undertone to these books; they promote a hawkish stance against foreign dangers, and the politics of the heroes and their companions fall fairly far to the Right. These characters are always prepared to respond to any threat against the government, even though the government often remains oblivious to the danger toward which it moves. For example, in Dale Brown's adventures of the fighter plane, the Old Dog (*Flight of the Old Dog* and sequels), the men are as likely to exceed orders as not, because they know better than the president and those in charge what really needs to be done and how to do it.[50]

These are stories that prey on cold war paranoia and, more recently, fear of terrorists. The villains are always evil, in contrast to the more personable heroes. Pacing is fast, as the action-filled plots, along with the clear-cut war between good and evil, pull readers into the story and keep them turning pages.

And although there may be interesting characters, it is the technology and the detail that are really the stars of the story. The more interesting and arcane, the better. In fact, it is rumored that David Poyer's Techno-Thrillers (*The Gulf,* for example) are required reading at the U.S. Naval Academy.[51] These novels also often feature maps and illustrations (as an example, *see Nimitz Class,* by Patrick Robinson) that add greatly to the sense of authentic detail that drives these stories.[52]

Clancy remains the benchmark. He created the Techno-Thriller subgenre with the appearance of Jack Ryan in *The Hunt for Red October* in 1984.[53] Now that Clancy has placed Ryan in the White House, he may be concentrating his action-demanding adventures on John Clark, ex-SEAL, who exhibits slightly more violent tendencies than Ryan and thus becomes the darker side of that heroic personality. Try *Rainbow Six* for an example of Clark's exploits.[54]

Stephen Coonts (whose series featuring Navy pilot Jake Grafton, beginning with *The Flight of the Intruder,* is set during the Vietnam War) and Craig Thomas (*Firefox* and sequels, featuring pilot Michael Gant) continue to provide satisfaction to the fans of this subgenre.[55]

Preparing to Work with Readers

What do we know about the fans of the Thriller genre, with its diverse subgenres? What do these readers expect when they request a "Thriller"? Having thought about the genre, we understand that most are not looking for novels with complex characters. They expect the plots, with their twists and unexpected turns, not the characters, to generate surprises. For the most part, they expect their characters to be stereotypes, heroes they can relate to and emphasize with, and villains they love to hate. Although characters, especially villains, may be caricatures, many characters, good and bad, are drawn from real life. Although they may be exaggerated, they are easily recognizable from television and the news.

Pacing is generally fast in Thrillers, and that is another element readers expect. When they request "page-turners," these are among those books we suggest. As observers, and perhaps even fans, we know intellectually that all Thrillers are not equally fast-paced. However, we also know that they may seem that way to their fans, as the writers pull the readers into the stories and keep them turning pages.

Plots in this genre should be complex. The more convoluted and surprising the better. These are also stories in which the good guys win, despite the odds and the dangers. Readers do not usually like an author to play with this formula, and we, in exploring the genre, should make note of those who overstep the boundaries of the formula, so that we can warn fans. Within this formula, readers expect the unexpected. They are looking for frequent plot twists and rapidly changing situations—the out-of-the-ordinary books in which things never go according to plan, for the hero at least. They want to see how the author—and the hero—will handle the problems that inevitably arise.

As we explore the Thriller genre—talking with fans and reading books and reviews—we should also be aware of the range of violence in the books included in this genre. As I have mentioned throughout this book, readers often have a level of violence beyond which they are reluctant to go. If I am aware of a particularly violent scene or that a title tends to be more (or less) violent, I try to make a mental note so that I can share that information with readers for whom it may be an issue.

Readers also seek the frame, those details that form the basis of each of the subgenres. They demand both jargon and procedures related to the professions. Maps, illustrations, and intricate descriptions add to the appeal of these stories. Detractors may complain about the melodramatic, soap opera elements sometimes found in these stories, but fans appreciate characters they care about, clear distinctions between good and evil, and cases in which justice, although not always the law, is served in the end.

Becoming familiar with subgenre benchmarks is a place to start in preparing to work with readers. But reading almost anything typical of the genre, or a specific subgenre, helps in making contact with readers. Fans of other genres might try authors listed in Figure 14.8, who include aspects of other genres in their writing, to gain firsthand experience of the Thriller genre.

FIGURE 14.8

An Introduction to the Thriller Genre

Thriller Writers to Read, If You Enjoy . . .

Adventure	Lionel Davidson (*Kolymsky Heights*)[56]
	Howard Coyle
Gentle	Ellis Peters (*Horn of Roland*)[57]
	Helen MacInnes
Historical	Nicholas Guild
	Martin Cruz Smith (*Stallion Gate*)[58]
Horror	Stephen Spruill
	John Saul
Humor	Donald Westlake
	Edward Abbey (*The Monkey Wrench Gang*)[59]
Inspirational	Tim F. LaHaye and Jerry B. Jenkins
	Frank Peretti
Literary	Scott Turow
	John le Carré
Mystery	Dorothy Gilman (Mrs. Pollifax)
Psychological	John le Carré
Romance	Evelyn Anthony
Romantic Suspense	Helen MacInnes
Suspense	John Grisham
	David Lindsey

Readers' Advisory Interview

Discovering what readers enjoy about a particular author or genre is always difficult, but because Thrillers, like Adventure, are so cinematic and have often been made into movies, sometimes we can more easily explore that format with fans. If they are unable to describe titles or authors they enjoy, they can often tell us about movies and we can readily discover what Thriller elements they appreciated. These may simply be subject elements—details of the legal or medical professions—but fans also describe movies in the same way they describe books—by pacing, characterizations, story line, and frame. We simply listen for those elements and offer a selection of Thrillers that might meet that reader's interests and mood today.

And when we are standing at the book stacks with a reader, and nothing comes to mind, or a reader asks us about a Thriller that we never remember seeing before in life, we should also remember that this is that occasion when we can ignore the old adage: Never judge a book by its cover. Because the covers of books in the Thriller genre often reveal a great deal about the content, we should certainly make the most of covers—and titles—in sorting books into subgenres. As Thriller/Adventure/Suspense expert librarian Michael Gannon suggests, we do not even need much imagination to be successful. A syringe indicates a Medical Thriller; a jet or submarine, a Techno-Thriller; a swastika, likely a World War II Espionage Thriller; and the words *indictment, justice,* and *evidence* all suggest Legal Thrillers. What could be easier?

Sure Bets

Sometimes a good strategy is simply to describe popular writers who fit generally within the Thriller genre, those Sure Bets that appeal to a wide range of fans within the genre and without. Stuart Woods is one possibility. Enormously popular, his books are almost impossible to slot within a genre designation, yet he probably appeals more to Thriller readers than any others. In addition to two series (those featuring ex-cop Stone Barrington, an increasingly amoral investigator who has a lot of appeal for readers of Crime/Capers, and the set begun with *Chiefs* and continued with *Run before the Wind, Grass Roots,* and *The Run,* which features political themes), his single-title Thrillers appeal to a wide range of readers who enjoy fast-paced, interesting stories.[60]

Gerald A. Browne, another author difficult to describe in terms of any particular genre, fits well with authors in several Thriller subgenres. His protagonists, however, are generally likable, if felonious, heroes. These characters are real people, interesting men caught in unusual situations. There is less violence, and it is usually not graphically described. Women characters also fare better in Browne's books than they do in many in this genre. One of my personal favorites is *Hot Siberian,* overflowing with spies, the diamond industry in Russia, and Faberge animal figures.[61]

Expanding Readers' Horizons

Faced with readers who have read "everything" by an author or in a subgenre they love, we need to remember that the Thriller genre offers extensive crossover, both within the genre and without (*see* Figure 14.9). Readers who choose Thrillers for their pacing might enjoy any number of fast-paced titles from Thriller subgenres as well as from other genres, especially Adventure and Suspense. *The Big Picture,* by Douglas Kennedy, with its roller-coaster pacing or Joseph R. Garber's *Vertical Run,* described in chapter 13, "Suspense," would make good suggestions.[62]

FIGURE 14.9

Expanding Readers' Horizons

Authors to Take Readers beyond the Thriller Genre

Adventure	Alistair MacLean
	Clive Cussler
Horror	Douglas Preston and Lincoln Child
Mystery	Kathy Reichs
	Paul Levine
	Carol O'Connell (Mallory series)
Romance	Patricia Veryan
Romantic Suspense	Nora Roberts
	Sidney Sheldon
Science Fiction	John Varley (*The Golden Globe*)[66]
	Neal Stephenson
Suspense	Joseph R. Garber

Medical/Scientific Thrillers contain elements of Suspense, Adventure, Mystery, and even Horror, and thus those genres also offer titles that appeal. For example, Mystery writers Patricia Cornwell and Kathy Reichs offer extensive forensic details that these Thriller fans may appreciate. If they simply like details and do not care particularly if they are medical or scientific, these readers may also enjoy Techno-Thrillers, as the details in this subgenre are more specific and often esoteric. They may also find titles of interest among novels dealing with environmental issues and biological or chemical warfare, such as Greg Iles's *Black Cross,* the gripping account of an attempt to sabotage one of Hitler's chemical weapons plants.[63]

Crime/Caper readers may find a number of titles by Romance and Romantic Suspense author Nora Roberts to their liking, if they are not put off by the additional romantic themes. In *Sweet Revenge* an actress and socialite seeks to avenge her mother's death by stealing the fabled necklace her father treasures.[64] Sidney Sheldon's titles also offer complicated capers for fans of this subgenre.

Fans of Techno-Thrillers also enjoy many authors in the Adventure genre (chapter 2). Adventure novels of Clive Cussler and the Military Adventures of a fast-paced writer such as Alistair MacLean or, more recently, Joe Weber would also make good crossover suggestions. Watch for the aircraft or submarine on the cover to identify possibilities more easily.

And readers of Legal Thrillers also read true crime and nonfiction accounts of actual trials. Mysteries also appeal to fans of Legal Thrillers. Although there may be less emphasis on the actual practice of law, the investigation figures prominently in both. Private Investigators who also happen to be lawyers or provide extensive legal details are good choices for Legal Thriller fans. (For example, Paul Levine's Jake Lassiter series, beginning with *To Speak for the Dead,* appeals to readers who appreciate a good mystery with abundant legal details.)[65]

Because of the character of most Private Investigators—the white knight hero who operates under his own moral code and solves cases, restoring order and justice to the world—many Mysteries featuring P.I.s appeal to a wide range of Thriller readers, from Legal to Espionage. Thriller readers may also appreciate any story in which the underdog wins against the giant corporation (or other unfeeling, powerful entity), whatever the genre.

Reference Sources

Despite the size and range of this genre, there are no reference sources that specifically cover it.[67] *Genreflecting* (*see* appendix 2) provides information on several aspects in the chapters on "Crime" and "Adventure."

Where to Find . . .

INFORMATION ABOUT THE AUTHOR

Contemporary Authors (*see* appendix 2) includes many of these best-selling authors, as does *St. James Guide to Crime and Mystery Writers*, an acknowledgement of the crossover with that genre.[68] *Killer Books: A Reader's Guide to Exploring the Popular World of Mystery and Suspense* also includes a chapter on "Legal Thrillers," and *Mystery and Suspense Writers* includes some of the authors discussed in this chapter.[69]

PLOT SUMMARIES

Thrillers and the various subgenres are included in a number of sources that offer plot summaries: *Fiction Catalog, What Do I Read Next?, NoveList, Sequels,* and *To Be Continued* (*see* appendix 2).

SUBGENRES AND THEMES

Lists of authors and titles who write in the subgenres are easy to find in many of the resources already mentioned: *Fiction Catalog, What Do I Read Next? NoveList, Sequels,* and *To Be Continued,* as well as in *Killer Books* and *Genreflecting. Mystery and Suspense Writers* includes essays on Legal, Medical, and Spy Thrillers.

GENRE DESCRIPTION, BACKGROUND, AND HISTORY

No single source covers the entire thriller genre, although *Genreflecting, Mystery and Suspense Writers,* and *Killer Books* provide background on some aspects.

Combining elements of Suspense, Adventure, and intriguing puzzles with professional expertise and jargon, these tales of lawyers, spies, doctors, and others are the books readers often seek when they ask for page-turners, those fast-paced novels that demand we read them at a rapid rate. These books appear with regularity on best-sellers lists; small wonder they are so popular with readers, for they feature the thrill of the chase as beleaguered heroes and heroines fight both to stay alive and to solve the puzzle that has put their lives in danger.

NOTES

1. John Grisham, *The Pelican Brief* (New York: Doubleday, 1992); William J. Coughlin, *Shadow of a Doubt* (New York: St. Martin's, 1991).

2. Lisa Scottoline, *Everywhere That Mary Went* (New York: HarperPaperbacks, 1993).

3. Scott Turow, *Presumed Innocent* (New York: Farrar, Straus & Giroux, 1987).

4. Robert Traver, *Anatomy of a Murder* (New York: St. Martin's, 1958).

5. Grisham, *The Firm* (New York: Doubleday, 1991).

6. William Diehl, *Primal Fear* (New York: Villard, 1993).

7. Steve Martini, *Compelling Evidence* (New York: Putnam, 1992).

8. Richard North Patterson, *The Dark Lady* (New York: Knopf, 1999).

9. Robert K. Tanenbaum, *No Lesser Plea* (New York: Franklin Watts, 1987).

10. Robin Cook, *Toxin* (New York: Putnam, 1998).

11. Michael Palmer, *Critical Judgment* (New York: Bantam, 1996).

12. Steven Spruill, *My Soul to Take* (New York: St. Martin's, 1994).

13. Eileen Dreyer, *Brain Dead* (New York: HarperCollins, 1997).

14. Michael Crichton, *The Andromeda Strain* (New York: Knopf, 1969); ———, *Jurassic Park* (New York: Knopf, 1990).

15. William Boyd, *Brazzaville Beach* (New York: Morrow, 1990).

16. Ken Follett, *The Third Twin* (New York: Crown, 1996).

17. Steve Alten, *Meg: A Novel of Deep Terror* (New York: Doubleday, 1997); Ray Olson, review of *Meg,* by Steve Alten, *Booklist* 93 (April 15, 1997): 1364.

18. John J. Nance, *Pandora's Clock* (New York: Doubleday, 1995).

19. Tess Gerritsen, *Harvest* (New York: Pocket Books, 1996).

20. Linda Davies, *A Nest of Vipers* (New York: Doubleday, 1994); ———, *A Wilderness of Mirrors* (New York: Doubleday, 1996).

21. Frederick Forsyth, *The Day of the Jackal* (New York: Viking, 1971).

22. David Baldacci, *Total Control* (New York: Warner Books, 1997); ———, *The Winner* (New York: Warner Books, 1997); ———, *Absolute Power* (New York: Warner Books, 1996).

23. Victor O'Reilly, *Games of the Hangman* (New York: Grove Weidenfeld, 1991).

24. Stephen Leather, *The Chinaman* (New York: Pocket Books, 1992).

25. Jim Lehrer, *Kick the Can* (New York: Putnam, 1988).

26. Tim F. LaHaye and Jerry B. Jenkins, *Left Behind: A Novel of the Earth's Last Days* (Wheaton, Ill.: Tyndale House, 1995).

27. Stephen Frey, *The Vulture Fund* (New York: Dutton, 1996); _____, *The Insider* (New York: Ballantine, 1999).

28. Lawrence Sanders, *The Anderson Tapes* (New York: Putnam, 1970).

29. Michael Connelly, *Void Moon* (Boston: Little, Brown, 2000).

30. Elmore Leonard, *Get Shorty* (New York: Delacorte, 1990).

31. David Ramus, *The Gravity of Shadows* (New York: HarperCollins, 1998).

32. Lawrence Block, *Hit Man* (New York: Morrow, 1998).

33. Evan Hunter, *Criminal Conversation* (New York: Warner Books, 1994).

34. Katherine Neville, *A Calculated Risk* (New York: Ballantine, 1992).

35. Eugene Izzi, *Safe Harbor* (New York: Avon, 1999).

36. Carl Hiaasen, *Native Tongue* (New York: Knopf, 1991).

37. Thomas Perry, *The Island* (New York: Putnam, 1987); Pete Hautman, *Ring Game* (New York: Simon & Schuster, 1997).

38. Marc Lovell, *Spy Game* (New York: Doubleday, 1980).

39. Bryan Forbes, *Quicksand* (London: Heinemann, 1996).

40. Adam Hall, *Quiller* (New York: Berkley Books, 1985).

41. Len Deighton, *Berlin Game* (New York: Knopf, 1984).

42. Brian Freemantle, *Charlie M* (Garden City, N.Y.: Doubleday, 1977).

43. Dorothy Gilman, *The Unexpected Mrs. Pollifax* (Garden City, N.Y.: Doubleday, 1996).

44. John E. Gardner, *The Confessor* (New York: Otto Penzler Books, 1995).

45. Rudyard Kipling, *Kim* (New York: Modern Library, 1928).

46. John le Carré, *The Spy Who Came In from the Cold* (New York: Coward-McCann, 1963).

47. Alan Furst, *Red Gold* (New York: Random House, 1999).

48. Lehrer, *Blue Hearts* (New York: Random House, 1993).

49. Robert Littell, *Walking Back the Cat* (Woodstock, N.Y.: Overlook Press, 1997).

50. Dale Brown, *Flight of the Old Dog* (New York: Berkley Books, 1988). Originally published by D. I. Fine, 1987.

51. David Poyer, *The Gulf* (New York: St. Martin's, 1990).

52. Patrick Robinson, *Nimitz Class* (New York: HarperCollins, 1997).

53. Tom Clancy, *The Hunt for Red October* (Annapolis, Md.: Naval Institute Press, 1984).

54. ———, *Rainbow Six* (New York: Putnam, 1998).

THRILLERS

55. Stephen Coonts, *The Flight of the Intruder* (Annapolis, Md.: Naval Institute Press, 1986); Craig Thomas, *Firefox* (New York: Holt, 1977).

56. Lionel Davidson, *Kolymsky Heights* (New York: St. Martin's, 1994).

57. Ellis Peters, *Horn of Roland* (New York: Morrow, 1974).

58. Martin Cruz Smith, *Stallion Gate* (New York: Random House, 1986).

59. Edward Abbey, *The Monkey Wrench Gang* (Philadelphia: Lippincott, 1975).

60. Stuart Woods, *Chiefs* (New York: Norton, 1981); ————, *Run before the Wind* (New York: Norton, 1983); ————, *Grass Roots* (New York: Simon & Schuster, 1989); ————, *The Run* (New York: HarperCollins, 2000).

61. Gerald A. Browne, *Hot Siberian* (New York: Arbor House, 1989).

62. Douglas Kennedy, *The Big Picture* (New York: Hyperion, 1997); Joseph R. Garber, *Vertical Run* (New York: Bantam, 1995).

63. Greg Iles, *Black Cross* (New York: E. P. Dutton, 1995).

64. Nora Roberts, *Sweet Revenge* (New York: Bantam, 1996).

65. Paul Levine, *To Speak for the Dead* (New York: Bantam, 1990).

66. John Varley, *The Golden Globe* (New York: Ace Books, 1998).

67. Some aspects of Thrillers will certainly be included in Libraries Unlimited's forthcoming volume on Adventure and Suspense, written by Michael Gannon and part of the Genreflecting Advisory series.

68. Jay P. Pederson, ed., *St. James Guide to Crime and Mystery Writers,* 4th ed. (Detroit: St. James, 1996).

69. Jean Swanson and Dean James, *Killer Books: A Reader's Guide to Exploring the Popular World of Mystery and Suspense* (New York: Berkley Books, 1998); *Mystery and Suspense Writers: The Literature of Crime, Detection, and Espionage* (New York: Scribner, 1998).

15

Westerns

Many librarians dismiss Westerns as a dying genre. At one time, I did too, stickering the several hundred books we categorized as Westerns and intershelving them throughout the fiction, where they were almost impossible to find by all but the most desperate. My excuse was that we were out of space, however, as readers came to complain week in and week out, I began promising a separate Western section again, if we expanded the library. The Western section, an active and growing part of our fiction collection, now thrives, as we tackle that universal question faced in every genre: What is a Western? And what should be cataloged in this section?

A Definition

Although one would expect Westerns to be an easy genre to identify and define, this turns out not to be the case. What is a Western and what is a Historical Novel about the Western Expansion, often called a Novel of the West? It used to be easy to differentiate between the two just by the size of the book. As were Mysteries earlier, Westerns were smaller books, easily distinguished from the longer Novels of the West. In Westerns we traditionally expect cowboys, cattle drives, gunslingers, adventure, and gunplay. What we find are novels that cover these, as well as explore the clash between civilization and anarchy. We discover stories that fit our expectations of a Western Adventure and that go beyond to create mythic stories of men and the land.

There is, unfortunately, no clear division between Novels of the West and Westerns. The former accurately depicts the western expansion, and many of us categorize them as Historical Fiction and shelve them with Fiction, not Westerns. (They are discussed in more detail in chapter 5, "Historical Fiction.") These titles may feature explorers or, more likely, settlers, those who stayed on to civilize the West. True Westerns often portray a more mythical time in the West and the men who brought order to the new territory. They feature the conflict between the civilizing influences of the East and the wild, uncivilized West. The West, in the world of Westerns, is a land of opportunity that offers the possibility of redemption for those who have escaped the confines of civilization. Novels of the West, on the other hand, deal more with the civilizing of that wild area of the country. They often include strong women characters, as it is usually the women who bring civilization. Novels of the West are about the people who came and stayed, while Westerns more frequently depict the lone man riding into a community and then leaving once his job is complete, the loner who makes his way through the rugged terrain. Western writer Elmer Kelton makes the distinction succinctly: "Whenever you see a milk cow, it's time for the cowboys to make room."[1] That is the attitude that epitomizes the characters in the Western.

However, as those lines are increasingly blurring in terms of the novels written and read by fans of both Westerns and Historical Fiction, the distinction between the two becomes harder to make. The Western Writers of America acknowledges this difference by bestowing two Spur Awards each year, one for Best Western Novel (Short Novel), which is for the traditional Western, and Best Novel of the West (Long Novel), for those that fall outside of these narrow confines. Yet even their categories are unclear, as is confirmed by Larry McMurtry's having won a Spur Award for Best Western Novel (thus, short) for *Lonesome Dove,* published at 843 pages![2] If the "experts" cannot easily distinguish between Westerns and Novels of the West, we poor librarians are out of luck!

Without a doubt, Westerns feature more romanticized representations of the West and the problems faced there, although even within the genre there is a range in how the West is depicted, from the more romantic to the more realistic. In Westerns it is important to create the feel of the Old West, a sense of time and place; historical accuracy, in terms of events at least, is not necessarily required by fans. I do want to acknowledge that readers of Westerns do expect realistic detail in firearms and accoutrement; they are, however, not as fussy about dates. Westerns speak to basic, deep-seated feelings about the land and the men who brought justice to the wild, uninhabited country and thus helped make it safe for those who civilized it. Novels of the West go beyond this bare framework, bringing more historical detail and exploring more of the community created and the issues arising in the civilizing of the West. Realistic historical detail, as is always required in Historical Fiction, is demanded in Novels of the West.

Westerns, then, are novels set in the western United States, primarily from the end of the Civil War to the beginning of the twentieth century. They feature the adventures of cowboys, scouts, Indians, and lawmen, and although they may accurately represent the time and place in which they are set, the mythic feel of the West and of those times, as well as the struggle to survive against myriad perils, takes precedence over history. Figure 15.1 summarizes the characteristics of the Western.

Characteristics and the Genre's Appeal

Characterization

Even though one might believe action to be the most important element of Westerns, a large part of their appeal for fans is the character of the hero, whose similarities to the medieval knight-errant as a champion of justice raise these stories from tales of cows and cowboys to almost mythic proportions. The classic hero is a loner, a kind of paladin (as in the television hero, played by Richard Boone, on *Have Gun, Will Travel*, in the late '50s), who rides throughout the land, righting wrongs and administering justice. Then, when his mission is completed, he moves on, rather than staying to settle down and start a

---

FIGURE 15.1

Characteristics of the Western

1. The hero, a likable protagonist, is often a loner, who arrives to right wrongs and then moves on. Heroes use strategy before guns to win arguments, although they are often forced to use violence in the end.

2. The exterior descriptions of the landscape and terrain frame the books. There is a romantic, nostalgic tone. These are often set in unidentified places (simply the West) and in an unspecified past time, adding to the feeling of timelessness.

3. Plots may be complex or more straightforward. Common themes include the redemptive power of the West, the difficulties surviving in a harsh landscape, revenge, and the lack of law along with the necessity of creating good laws.

4. The pacing is not necessarily fast. These are short books but not always page-turners, although books with more action certainly move at a faster pace.

---

family. He is a wanderer, the imparter of justice (surely one of the touchstones of civilization) but unwilling to stay to become too civilized himself. Jack Schaefer's classic, *Shane,* exemplifies this kind of character.[3] Shane, the knight-errant, arrives, mysteriously, into a community torn apart by disputes between farmers and cattlemen. He is the strong, silent type, yet his presence creates fear only among those who have something to fear. The Starret family with whom he stays all come to love, not fear, this menacing gunfighter. And even when he is faced with violence, he tries reason first to achieve resolution, before resorting to guns to solve the problem. He gains the respect of all and leaves his mark on the community when he rides away.

Although the hero is often the more mythic loner, sometimes the Western hero is a young man, a knight in training, and the Western provides the setting for a Bildungsroman, as the young cowboy learns the role he is to play. In these cases there is a mentor, an established knight, who teaches him the ropes, literally and figuratively. Elmer

Kelton's *The Pumpkin Rollers,* quoted above, provides an example of this. Young Trey McLean leaves home to make his own way as a cattleman. Along the way, he meets evil in the form of a man who steals his small herd but finds his mentor in drover Ivan Kerbow. He also discovers love with a rancher's daughter. Together the two try to create their future on Kerbow's isolated ranch, faced with dangers from ruthless ranchers and bad guys alike, not to mention the heartless landscape. There is even the good-guy-gone-wrong who finds redemption in the infinite healing landscape of the West. Trey and Sarah mature in this refining fire, facing their difficulties, aided by their innate strength and the help of friends, and the book closes as civilization comes to west Texas. The cowboys are off again, rounding up herds to drive to the railroads in Kansas, but Trey and Sarah stay to make their own way.

The character of the Western hero is reminiscent in many ways of the hard-boiled Private Investigator (chapter 8, "Mysteries"), another loner, with few close companions. And if he does have comrades, they are likely unexpected—like the pairing of the Lone Ranger and his Indian partner, Tonto. Like the P.I., the Western hero may sometimes operate outside the law to administer justice, "frontier justice," rather than the more traditional legal justice. Both operate under the aegis of a strict moral code, which supports their actions but does not always follow the letter of the law.

More recent representations of the Western hero have moved slightly from the mythic to the more realistic. When he talks of the Western genre, Spur Award–winning author Don Coldsmith likes to joke that early heroes were 6'4" and invincible; Kelton's heroes, on the other hand, are 5'8" and decidedly nervous in emergencies, as is clearly evident throughout *The Pumpkin Rollers.* Traditional Western heroes are men of iron; writers like Kelton and Larry McMurtry have given them human frailties. Still, despite their weaknesses, they suggest the qualities of the idealized hero who brings justice to the uncivilized West.

Some authors introduce real historical figures, primarily lawmen or outlaws, into their novels. These stories run the gamut, presenting a range from the idealized to the more accurate versions of the lives of famous men. Loren D. Estleman often takes historical incidents—the trial of the killer of Wild Bill Hickok (*Aces and Eights*), the gunfight at the OK corral (*Bloody Season*), the lives of Buffalo Bill Cody (*This Old Bill*) and Pat Garrett, who killed Billy the Kid (*Journey of the Dead*)—as the basis for his Westerns, an approach for which he has twice won Spur Awards.[4] Other authors rely solely on fictional characters. The crucial point is that in most Westerns, except for the most literary, characters are generally stereotypes, good or bad. Readers appreciate the clear distinctions.

Secondary characters also play a role in Westerns. Occasionally the hero has a sidekick, as in Terry C. Johnston's series beginning with *Carry the Wind*.[5] Mountain man and trapper Titus Bass takes on Josiah Paddock, fresh out of St. Louis, as his partner on adventures that lead them through the western mountains to New Mexico. Women and Indians often play important roles, and in much of the genre they are surprisingly well drawn. Racism and sexism, although present especially in titles from the first half of the century, do not run rampant in the genre. This is not to say that these portrayals are not stereotypical. Women are usually either fallen women, who turn out to have hearts of gold, or very good women, who stand by their men and work to make a home in the wilderness. Only occasionally do bad women appear in Westerns. Indians may be the force against whom the hero battles, but many novelists are nonjudgmental in their portrayal as well. In fact, many of the characters have spent time with the Indians—sometimes raised by, or rescued by, or simply friends and fellow hunters. Recent writers, and many classic authors, know enough history to play fair with a group that has been lied to and cheated but who can also be disturbingly brutal in their encounters with those who try to take their game or their land. In fact, both women and Indians have become "heroes" in award-winning Westerns in the past years. Ellen Recknor's *Leaving Missouri*, Spur winner in 1997, tells the story of Chrysanthemum "Clutie Mae" Chestnut and her transformation into the "Duchess" of Dollar Creek.[6] Johnston's *Carry the Wind* won a Spur in 1982, an acknowledgement of the positive role of Indians in the Western.

Frame

Although the character of the hero dominates the Western, the nature of the land runs a close second. Here again, the mythic nature of the

Western is evident. The landscape, almost a character itself in many Westerns, consists of treacherous terrain, where survival may be difficult for men and animals. The landscape is often portrayed as bigger than life, more rugged, more merciless, yet more open to possibilities than the confined landscapes of cities or civilized areas. For those who can survive in the landscape, the West offers limitless possibilities, as well as transforming powers.

Another feature of Westerns is the imprecise time and place in which stories are often placed. We know the time to be generally the twenty to thirty years after the Civil War, and the place is certainly this mythic West, but beyond that we are often at a loss. The point these writers make, of course, is that this kind of precision is not necessarily important for the story or for the reader. Dates and place-names add an inflexibility, a forced reality, that is often at odds with these vague times and places found in the mythic Western. Max Brand, for example, sets his myriad adventures in the High Mountain Desert, which becomes a familiar, but unidentifiable, location to fans of his stories. Creating a place outside of specific geography and a time outside of time adds to the mythic dimension of these stories and their more universal message and appeal.

That they are not necessarily set in particular times or places does not mean that these are not descriptive. The Western landscape is often so carefully drawn that it is a character itself. Westerns take readers back to another time and to a place where life is dangerous but also beautiful. Landscapes are carefully described, but it is also the openness and the infinite possibilities this virgin landscape offers that set the tone for these stories. Nature is larger than life, and to survive in this kind of landscape, the men here must also be larger than life, adding another element to the mythic dimension of the stories and the heroes.

Another aspect of the frame of these stories is the tone, which is often nostalgic, with the author forcing the reader to look back on a time when this kind of story was possible. Like the knights of old, heroes of Westerns cannot easily exist in today's world. Westerns take us back to a time when, in fiction at least, it was possible for a moral man to make a big difference in the world. This characteristic is especially easy to recognize in a book such as I, Tom Horn, by Will Henry, in which the protagonist and the reader look back longingly to that time when the West was a more open territory.[7] This story takes place after the turn of the century, when civilization has all but wiped out the last of the true West, and poor Tom Horn, having lived too long, finds the modern West no place for someone seeking the personal freedom, honor, and dignity he once found there. Henry creates a nostalgic, introspective account of a cowboy who has outlived his time.

Story Line

Morality plays a role in the story lines as well. Westerns are stories in which justice restores order to a community. The character of the hero, as discussed above, demands that wrongs be righted and order restored. His moral code pervades the story and directs the story line.

Survival in this harsh landscape is another common theme in Westerns. This is a dangerous world, and the perils come from the terrain and animals as well as from other people. Westerns are frequently stories of lives lived at the edge of death. Death permeates these books from the harshness of the landscape, sometimes so rugged that nothing can survive there, and only the strong can pass through to the life and death confrontations between good and evil that characterize the stories. Although gunfights may not be as frequent and graphic as one might expect, the image of the gunfight, that ultimate showdown, runs through the novels and defines this sense of ritual: the good man facing death at the hands of his opponent, whether human or nature. Westerns are, in many ways, the ultimate adventure/survival novel and definitely project an elegiac tone.

Damaged characters come to the West both to escape and to find healing or redemption there. It is a place where one could start over, begin afresh with a clean slate. Something about the landscape and the perils in which characters are placed initiates healing, as well as sense of purpose and well-being in the hero. That is one of the primary themes. Even "bad guys" occasionally find redemption here. In Owen Wister's classic, *The Virginian,* our hero brings justice and peace to a Wyoming community and offers the possibility of redemption to bad-boy Trampas, only to have to fight him in a gun duel at the end.[8] Other characters, such as Chris in Schaefer's *Shane,* accept the proffered olive branch and reform.

Revenge, a common theme in genre fiction, finds a place in the Western genre as well. Betrayal and the consequent revenge are themes that fit easily into the mythic nature of the West and are often played out against this background. Brand's *Destry Rides Again* is a classic example.[9] Destry, a favorite in town until he is convicted of robbing the stage, serves his term in jail and returns, supposedly a broken man but actually to exact revenge against the real thief. Charles Hackenberry updates this theme in his more recent Western, *Friends*.[10] Here, Willie Goodwin, deputy sheriff in Dakota Territory in the 1870s, seeks the man who shot his friend the sheriff and killed two other friends by burning their cabin. Is it revenge or justice when he takes the law into his own hands? Who better to do this than a sworn lawman? This questioning of the rectitude of frontier justice would never have arisen in the earlier title, and it reflects a change in tone from classic to newer titles in the genre.

Resolution is key to the end of the Western story. This resolution may not parallel that of other genres, but it is a resolution nonetheless. The hero may ride off into the sunset but not until his mission is accomplished. In fact, the hero may even die at the end of the story. This seldom happens in novels in other genres, but here it serves another purpose and is the natural result of the action. The point of the conclusion is that justice is brought to the Wild West, whether conventional legal justice or frontier justice, and lives are sometimes lost in bringing about this end. Elmore Leonard's *Hombre*[11] features a man who, like Tom Horn, has outlived his time. In a story narrated by an anonymous friend to set Jack Russell's story straight, we learn that Russell, the Hombre, was on a stage with a government employee who was escaping with embezzled funds. The stage was held up and all aboard escaped to a mining shack from which there seemed no rescue. Russell must then decide whether to help this motley group, who had scorned him earlier on their journey. There are, of course, no good choices: Either they die in the shack from lack of food or water or Russell must sacrifice his own life to allow the others freedom. We know the choice he has made from the beginning of the novel, but the evocative, nostalgic tone imbues this story of a man who no longer fits in his world. Now, death seems his only future. This is a fast-paced story of survival that highlights the most enduring themes in the genre.

Pacing

Although Traditional Westerns are smaller books, they are not necessarily fast-paced. The creation of mythic elements in character, description, and plotline may slow the pacing, while action certainly increases the speed at which we read the novels. For example, while the almost nonstop action drives the pacing of Louis L'Amour's Westerns, novels such as Wister's *The Virginian* and Schaefer's *Shane* move at a more leisurely pace, as details and atmosphere slow the action.

Key Authors

Benchmark

If you are new to the Western genre, it is useful to know that the classic authors are probably as popular now as they were when they were originally published. In fact, titles of many popular Western authors are being reprinted for a new audience. Although newer authors are interesting and useful to know, we can go a long way with Western fans if we are familiar with a few basic authors. Louis L'Amour, even though he died in 1988, remains the benchmark, the most popular Western writer, with good reason: His Adventure-filled Westerns still thrill readers. Action plays a role in every chapter, and he pulls readers into the stories with his inviting characters and detailed descriptions of the terrain. Although the early entries in his saga of the Sacketts read more as Historical Fiction than Westerns, later additions attest to his place as the most popular writer in the genre, with stories set in the Wild West, featuring action and adventure as the progeny of the original Sackett travel across the United States. Try *Hondo*, which, although not one of the Sackett series, boasts all the trademark elements of the traditional Western: the murderous landscape, an Apache uprising, the lone hero, and a woman in distress.[12]

Almost as famous and prolific as benchmark L'Amour, Zane Grey wrote more than eighty books between 1903 and 1939. Of these, *Rangers of the Lone Star* may be a better introduction to his work than the classic *Riders of the Purple Sage,* with its pejorative comments about Mormons.[13] Like L'Amour, Grey tells an action-filled story of the search for justice in the West. Here Texas Rangers hope to justify their continued existence—and funding—by cleaning up one of the worst towns in Texas.

Others, like Jack Schaefer and Owen Wister, are primarily known for only one title each, but Schaefer's *Shane* and Wister's *The Virginian* helped form the genre and establish its popularity. A more prolific writer, Will Henry often depicts a disappearing West, a landscape that provides difficult living for those like the eponymous Tom Horn (*I, Tom Horn*), who were born a generation too late for the real West and find it impossible to cope with its current form. (The audiotape version published by Recorded Books, with Frank Muller reading, is a particularly haunting rendition.)

In his Spanish Bit series, Don Coldsmith, another popular practitioner, follows the cultural development of the Plains Indians from the arrival of the Spanish Conquistadors in the sixteenth century to the early eighteenth century. In the first, *The Trail of the Spanish Bit*, a young Spanish soldier falls injured on a scouting foray, and he is nursed back to health by the Indians.[14] Eventually he becomes part of the tribe and helps initiate the change in Indian culture from the more peaceful nomadic existence, concerned primarily with hunting, to the warrior life, aided by horses in battle as well as in day-to-day existence. Coldsmith's treatment of the Plains Indians as protagonists sets the standard for the genre. Like his Tallgrass series, these books also appeal to readers of Historical novels, but this Spur Award–winning author captures the spirit of the West and the Western with his evocative settings, characters, and themes, and the primary appeal of his books is to the fans of Westerns.[15]

The Western genre boasts some unexpected practitioners. Not only do writers such as Larry McMurtry qualify as writers of Literary Fiction as much as of Westerns, others have made a name and reputation in another genre, sometimes while still writing Westerns. Loren D. Estleman, although better known for his Mysteries, continues to write provocative, rather melancholy Westerns, sometimes featuring real characters from the past, and in which it is often difficult to make a clear distinction between the good guys and the bad. Elmore Leonard wrote Westerns before he turned to Crime Thrillers, and his *Hombre*, both in book and film versions, remains a classic in the genre.

As Traditional Westerns became less profitable in the late '60s and '70s, another type of Western emerged from publishing houses—the "Adult" Western, featuring explicit sexual situations and descriptions. Jake Logan's Sheriff John Slocum series, Tabor Evans's Marshall Longarm stories, and Jon Sharpe's Skye Fargo series (with more than 200 titles in print!) are examples of these publishers' series, often written by several writers to a particular formula. Although they may appeal to some Western readers and others, these are often not what fans of classic Westerns are seeking.

Preparing to Work with Readers

Western fans appreciate a good story, set in the West during the nineteenth century and featuring the knight-errant hero who searches out injustice and brings his own form of frontier justice to the wilderness. Readers have had to make adjustments over the years, as fewer Westerns have been published and many reflect different mores than they might expect. (Even Charles Hackenberry's *Friends*, described above, contains more sex than the Traditional Western, and the Adult Westerns are another matter altogether.) Because story, character, and sense of place are the primary attractions for them, they enjoy a range of books set in that specific geographic location.

Although they may tolerate and even enjoy a range of books, the patrons asking for a "Western" are likely seeking a shorter book about cowboys and the Wild West. These are probably readers who are not interested in technology in their stories. They likely seek what we might call a "Gentle Read," a safe book without graphic or excessive violence (or sex and strong language). Western readers want Adventure in their stories; they seek escapism, but not stories full of technological details, as in Techno-Thrillers or Clive Cussler's Adventures. They may or may not appreciate the ambiguity of character by writers such as Loren D. Estleman and Elmore Leonard. Many read for the black-and-white characters, the clear-cut distinctions between good and evil. They like to know where they stand.

Although we often use the masculine pronoun in discussing these readers, I would be remiss not to point out that the genre has many female fans, myself included. I came late to appreciate the pleasures of this genre, but I confess to find these extraordinarily satisfying and affirming reads. Fans of the Western might also appreciate Jane Tompkins's *West of Everything: The Inner Life of Westerns*.[16] This is a classic study of major authors, books, and films, as well as an accessible look at the genre for fans and students alike, from an author who writes lovingly and evocatively about the Western genre. *See* Figure 15.2 for authors whose works also exhibit elements of other genres and thus might provide a good introduction.

Readers' Advisory Interview

When a reader asks for a Western in a readers' advisory interview, he is likely not looking for classic stories of the Old West by authors such as Bret Harte, Mark Twain, or Jack London. Readers seeking Westerns want the traditional stories of Louis L'Amour and Zane Grey or their

---

FIGURE 15.2

An Introduction to the Western Genre

Western Writers to Try, If You Enjoy . . .

Adventure	Louis L'Amour Max Brand (*Donnegan*)[17]
Fantasy	Louis L'Amour (*The Haunted Mesa*)[18]
Gentle	Judy Alter
Historical	Will Henry Don Coldsmith
Inspirational	Stephen Bly
Literary	Larry McMurtry
Mystery	Loren D. Estleman (Page Murdock) A. B. Guthrie Jr. (Chick Charleston and Jason Beard)
Romance	Cindy Bonner (*Lily*)[19]
Women's Lives	Elizabeth Fackler

more modern and perhaps bleaker versions by authors such as Larry McMurtry and Loren D. Estleman. Traditional Westerns by classic authors of the genre remain in print and make good choices for fans.

Some readers ask for novels that deal with historical figures—the lives of gunfighters and lawmen, for example. Many of the reference sources listed below will help with this, but it is also useful to know that there are authors who write primarily about real characters from the Wild West. For example, any number of writers have delved into the life of Wyatt Earp, from Matthew Braun (*Tombstone* and *Wyatt Earp*)[20] and Estleman (*Bloody Season*) to Richard Parry, with his series featuring Wyatt Earp at the end of his life, living in Alaska, and hunted by his son. (*The Winter Wolf* is the first.)[21]

Other readers may also enjoy contemporary Westerns, a phrase that seems almost an oxymoron, because we are so accustomed to thinking of Westerns and Novels of the West as set in the nineteenth century. Novels set on twentieth-century Texas or Montana ranches (McMurtry's *Horseman Pass By* or Ivan Doig's *Ride with Me, Mariah Montana*) and featuring the loner-hero may work for these readers.[22] It is sometimes more difficult in these Westerns set in modern day to find the same kind of hero, who lives only on the edge of civilization, but usually fans are prepared to be generous in the interpretation of the Western appeal characteristics.

Women authors are also coming to the fore in the genre and offer inviting stories for this kind of reader. Try Cynthia Haseloff's Spur-winning *The Kiowa Verdict* or its prequel, *Santanta's Woman*, with their sensitive portrayal of women and Indians, in addition to traditional Western themes.[23] Elizabeth Fackler's series features ex-gunfighter Seth Strummar (*Badlands* is the first), who, although he tries to settle down, seemingly cannot escape his past.[24]

Looking at the books themselves, as in every genre, provides clues about the nature of the Western in hand. Maps imply an adventurous journey over an area, and they certainly suggest more adherence to a specific place and perhaps time. The size of the book may be indicative, as Westerns, traditionally at least, are smaller books. Flipping through the pages, we might notice more white space, implying more dialogue and a faster pace. Denser writing, less white space, likely means the book is more descriptive, with more emphasis placed on creating the evocative mood that characterizes many titles in the genre.

Sure Bets

As I mentioned above, L'Amour is an author who still has enormous appeal for readers. Anyone who enjoys action finds great satisfaction in his fast-paced novels of strong heroes fighting for justice in a Western landscape. These are books that I hand sell. (Even though the popularity of the genre has increased, Westerns do not necessarily fly off our displays.) Readers return to tell me of the pleasure they found in L'Amour's books.

Elmer Kelton also writes the kind of Westerns that make him a sure bet. Unlike L'Amour's, Kelton's tend to be more character centered, often featuring young men in difficult situations. Kelton has won multiple Spur Awards for these historically accurate novels, set in his native Texas, which rely less on action and more on characters placed in realistic, believable situations.

Expanding Readers' Horizons

Books that appeal to fans of Westerns run the gamut from the more limited traditional Western to the more historical, broadly interpreted Novel of the West, and much in between. Although some readers look for these more mythic Westerns, others seek the more realistic portrayals found in the Historical novels set in the West. They want multidimensional characters, strong and feisty women, historical details. For readers who talk of these characteristics or mention writers such as McMurtry or Don Coldsmith, other newer writers may be appropriate suggestions. Offer Richard S. Wheeler, whose character-centered stories of frontier life present both Indians and white men (and women) equally in a detail-rich historical perspective. (His first Barnaby Skye Western is *Rendezvous*).[25]

Traditional themes with wider implications make a good bridge from the Traditional Western to the larger Novel of the West. Doig might be a good choice. His series, set in Montana from the late nineteenth through the twentieth centuries, features the problems and uncertainties of the Old West as well as the New. *Dancing at the Rascal Fair* is the first chronologically.[26]

Fans of both Westerns and Novels of the West are often pleased with books in other genres that feature the elements they enjoy in these books. For example, readers who talk about the character of the hero may be interested in other genres with that loner-as-hero character. Mysteries featuring Private Investigators, for example, may be a good choice, especially those by authors who also write Westerns. Tony Hillerman's Mysteries, set in the modern Southwest and featuring Native American detectives, offer the landscape and tone of the Western, but with a different time period. Michael McGarrity's contemporary Western setting and introspective, loner detective might also appeal to these readers. Robert B. Parker is another possible suggestion, as the character of Spenser, his Private Investigator, has much in common with the Western hero. Or they may enjoy Historical Fiction featuring an adventurer-hero. Dorothy Dunnett's series featuring Francis Crawford of Lymond (described in chapter 2, "Adventure") might be a good suggestion, as well as L'Amour's historical Adventure novel, *The Walking Drum,* with its medieval setting and young hero, and Bernard Cornwell's series featuring the exploits of Sharpe, as he moves up through the ranks of Wellington's army. (*Sharpe's Triumph* is the first chronologically.)[27] These readers might also enjoy Thrillers that feature action and adventure, although the technology of some may be a drawback. Still, these are areas worth exploring, and even L'Amour wrote an Espionage Thriller (*Last of the Breed*), which might provide an entrée into that genre.[28]

Readers who read for the mythic landscape may be more interested in Historical Fiction set in the West, or Novels of the West, with bigger stories but no less emphasis on the location. They may also appreciate stories with mythic settings and characters, such as the *Star Wars* series and Quest Fantasies through mythic landscapes. This is not a suggestion for every Western fan, as space and the addition of magic, not to mention the nature of the nonhuman characters in these genres, put some of these stories well outside the interest of Western readers. More adventurous readers, however, might be interested in trying them.

In working with fans of Westerns, I have discovered a number of writers of Historical Romances set in the West that appeal to these readers. Rosanne Bittner's Western Romances provide the proper setting, as well as action and adventure for those readers who do not mind the added element of a strong romantic interest. (Try *Mystic Dreamers,* first in a planned series about the Lakota Nation.)[29] Janet Dailey's Calder series (*This Calder Sky* is the first) follows the lives of the Calder family and their Montana ranch.[30] Jeanne Williams's novels have strong Western settings and less Romance, which make them a good suggestion for fans of Novels of the West as well (for example, *No Roof but Heaven,* set on the Kansas frontier just after the Civil War).[31] Kathleen Eagle writes sensitively about Native Americans in many of her Contemporary Romances, and one of her most recent might also appeal to Western fans. *The Last True Cowboy* features city-girl Julia Weslin, who enlists the help of cowboy K. C. Houston to help her save her family's ranch from the grasp of developers.[32] Modern ranching issues, the traditional Western mythos, and a strong love story propel this novel.

Mainstream novels also feature themes and characters "borrowed" from the Western. For example, who could miss the parallels to the Western hero in Nicholas Evans's popular *The Horse Whisperer?*[33] Cowboy Tom Booker may be able to heal and communicate with horses, but this loner's foray into love and a relationship only lead to tragedy. Figure 15.3 lists other authors outside the genre that Western fans might enjoy.

Reference Sources

At one point we had a number of fairly recent reference sources that explored the Western genre. We still have the books, but one could hardly call them new now. This is a genre that has been passed by; many newer sources omit it completely.

Luckily for those of us who still have fans at our libraries, *Genreflecting, NoveList,* and *What Do I Read Next?* (*see* appendix 2) have continued to include them. Some of the new guides to the Historical Fiction genre also offer useful indexes to names and places that are of interest to our Western fans. Even if they do not have reference resources limited to the Western genre, many libraries already have tools that are useful in providing access to information on Westerns.

FIGURE 15.3

Expanding Readers' Horizons

Authors to Take Readers beyond the Western Genre

Adventure	Dorothy Dunnett
	Louis L'Amour (*The Walking Drum*)[34]
Fantasy	Stephen King (Dark Tower series)
Gentle	Jeanette Oke
Historical	Douglas C. Jones
	Glendon Swarthout
	Norman Zollinger
Inspirational	Brock Thoene and Bodie Thoene
Literary	Cormac McCarthy
Mystery	Tony Hillerman
	Michael McGarrity
Romance	Rosanne Bittner
	Janet Dailey
Science Fiction	*Star Wars* series
Thriller	Louis L'Amour (*Last of the Breed*)
Women's Lives	Kate Lehrer (*Out of Eden*)[35]
	Jane Smiley (*The All-True Travels and Adventures of Liddie Newton*)[36]

Where to Find . . .

INFORMATION ABOUT THE AUTHOR

If you still own *Twentieth-Century Western Writers,* you will find it continues to be useful in providing biographical information about the authors—up to 1991, when it was published, that is.[37] Bibliographies of their writing are also up-to-date to that point. The genre has not attracted that many new writers, so many favorites can be found there. *Contemporary Authors* (*see* appendix 2) is also useful for new and older writers alike.

PLOT SUMMARIES

Many Westerns are covered in Historical Fiction sources, and thus plot summaries are available. Three titles discussed in more detail in chapter 5, "Historical Fiction," provide extensive index access to useful plot summaries: *Historical Figures in Fiction, American Historical Fiction: An Annotated Guide to Novels for Adults and Young Adults,* and *What Historical Novel Do I Read Next?* [38] The last title is kept up-to-date in the multi-genre annual book volumes and Web version of *What Do I Read Next?* (*see* appendix 2). Coverage of Westerns in *NoveList* is also extensive, and many entries have plot summaries. Westerns are also a separate section in the annual volumes of *What Do I Read Next?* and thus incorporated into the Web version.

SUBGENRES AND THEMES

Access to these is provided through the three Historical Fiction sources listed above, as well as *Genreflecting,* which identifies thirty-two themes in the Western genre, and *What Do I Read Next?*

GENRE DESCRIPTION, BACKGROUND, AND HISTORY

Twentieth-Century Western Writers offers background information on the genre, in addition to biographical information on the authors. *Genreflecting* also offers a brief overview of the genre. *What Do I Read Next?* offers an annual summary of titles and themes.

CORE LISTS AND BEST BOOKS

NoveList provides both a list of "Best Westerns"—one can do a subject search with those words—and a feature article on the top ten Westerns published in 1998. As does *Genreflecting, NoveList* also offers an updated list of award winners in the genre. *What Do I Read Next?* offers an annual summary of titles and themes.

Although readers accept and expect that Westerns are genre titles fraught with stereotypes and clichés, some read them for reasons beyond the logical. In the interviews with readers that form the backbone of his readers' advisory training, Duncan Smith talked with one reader, a North Carolina native, who reads Westerns for the pleasure they bring as they take him to a place he has never been. They take him outside the context of his everyday life; they take him away.[39] Jane Tompkins, in *West of Everything,* writes of another reader who chooses them for the way they take him back to his roots, to an area, a landscape, he has known and is now distant from. They take him back, and the stories allow him to relive his memories.[40] We read for the basic pleasure these stories bring, whatever the reason they affect us.

NOTES

1. Elmer Kelton, *The Pumpkin Rollers* (New York: Forge, 1996), 301.

2. Larry McMurtry, *Lonesome Dove* (New York: Simon & Schuster, 1985).

3. Jack Schaefer, *Shane* (Boston: Houghton, 1949).

4. Loren D. Estleman, *Aces and Eights* (Garden City, N.Y.: Doubleday, 1981); ———, *Bloody Season* (Toronto, New York: Bantam, 1987); ———, *This Old Bill* (Garden City, N.Y.: Doubleday, 1984); ———, *Journey of the Dead* (New York: Forge, 1998).

5. Terry C. Johnston, *Carry the Wind* (Aurora, Ill.: Green Hill: Caroline House, 1982).

6. Ellen Recknor, *Leaving Missouri* (New York: Berkley Books, 1997).

7. Will Henry, *I, Tom Horn* (New York: Bantam, 1975).

8. Owen Wister, *The Virginian* (New York: Macmillan, 1902).

9. Max Brand, *Destry Rides Again* (New York: Mead, 1930).

10. Charles Hackenberry, *Friends* (New York: M. Evans, 1993).

11. Elmore Leonard, *Hombre* (New York: Ballantine, 1961).

12. Louis L'Amour, *Hondo* (New York: Fawcett, 1953).

13. Zane Grey, *Rangers of the Lone Star* (Unity, Maine: Five Star, 1999); ———, *Riders of the Purple Sage* (New York: Harper, 1912).

14. Don Coldsmith, *The Trail of the Spanish Bit* (Garden City, N.Y.: Doubleday, 1980).

15. ———, *Tallgrass* (New York: Bantam, 1997); ———, *South Wind* (New York: Bantam, 1998).

16. Jane Tompkins, *West of Everything: The Inner Life of Westerns* (New York: Oxford Univ. Pr., 1992).

17. Brand, *Donnegan* (New York: Chelsea House, 1923).

18. L'Amour, *The Haunted Mesa* (Toronto, New York: Bantam, 1987).

19. Cindy Bonner, *Lily* (Chapel Hill, N.C.: Algonquin Books, 1992).

20. Matthew Braun, *Tombstone* (New York: Pocket Books, 1981); ———, *Wyatt Earp* (New York: St. Martin's, 1994).

21. Richard Parry, *The Winter Wolf: Wyatt Earp in Alaska* (New York: Forge, 1996).

22. Larry McMurtry, *Horseman Pass By* (New York: Harper, 1961); Ivan Doig, *Ride with Me, Mariah Montana* (New York: Atheneum, 1990).

23. Cynthia Haseloff, *The Kiowa Verdict: A Western Story* (Unity, Maine: Five Star, 1997); ———, *Santanta's Woman: A Western Story* (Unity, Maine: Five Star, 1998).

24. Elizabeth Fackler, *Badlands* (New York: Forge, 1996).

25. Richard S. Wheeler, *Rendezvous* (New York: Forge, 1998).

26. Ivan Doig, *Dancing at the Rascal Fair* (New York: Atheneum, 1987).

27. Bernard Cornwell, *Sharpe's Triumph: Richard Sharpe and the Battle of Assaye, September 1803* (New York: HarperCollins, 1998).

28. L'Amour, *Last of the Breed* (Toronto, New York: Bantam, 1987).

29. Rosanne Bittner, *Mystic Dreamers* (New York: Forge, 1999).

30. Janet Dailey, *This Calder Sky* (New York: Pocket Books, 1981).

31. Jeanne Williams, *No Roof but Heaven* (New York: St. Martin's, 1990).

32. Kathleen Eagle, *The Last True Cowboy* (New York: Avon, 1998).

33. Nicholas Evans, *The Horse Whisperer* (New York: Delacorte, 1995).

34. L'Amour, *The Walking Drum* (New York: Bantam, 1984).

35. Kate Lehrer, *Out of Eden* (New York: Harmony Books, 1996).

36. Jane Smiley, *The All-True Travels and Adventures of Liddie Newton* (New York: Knopf, 1998).

37. Geoff Sadler, ed., *Twentieth-Century Western Writers*, 2d ed. (Detroit: St. James, 1991).

38. Donald K. Hartman and Gregg Sapp, *Historical Figures in Fiction* (Phoenix: Oryx, 1994); Lynda G. Adamson, *American Historical Fiction: An Annotated Guide to Novels for Adults and Young Adults* (Phoenix: Oryx, 1999); Daniel S. Burt, *What Historical Novel Do I Read Next?* (Detroit: Gale, 1997).

39. Duncan Smith, Readers' Advisory Workshop, Joliet, Illinois, November 1999.

40. Tompkins, *West of Everything*, 221–23.

16

Women's Lives
and Relationships

One of the most popular annotated booklists at my library is one devoted to books about women and their lives, written by women authors. If the popularity of our booklists is any indication of what women read, we know that many women, in my library at least, are requesting books that generally deal with Women's Lives and Relationships. These are books that do not fall easily into a genre, books that explore concerns faced by women of their age group or by women in general. Sometimes readers seek a lighthearted book in this vein; at other times they look for a title that deals more seriously with an issue; at times a "soap opera" approach satisfies their need to escape the reality of their lives; and at other times they seek something more provocative. Fortunately for librarians and readers alike, this is a market publishers have recognized and worked to meet, providing books that reflect Women's Lives and Relationships for readers who want books that deal with the concerns and joys found in women's lives.

A Definition

Although some call this genre Women's Fiction, I do not intend to use that term here. I find it too limiting, as it could suggest to the uninitiated that this is all women read. Or that this is what women should read. Or what we should suggest to any woman who asks for assistance. We know that just as there is no single type of fiction all men read, no comparable Men's Fiction, there is no one genre all women read. Therefore, this genre, Women's Lives and Relationships, is shortened in this chapter to Women's Lives instead.

These are books that explore the reaches of women's lives; that deal with the dynamics of relationships with family, friends, and lovers; that may or may not end happily (although they do end with issues resolved or the resolution suggested); that examine the issues women confront in their lives (at home and at work) and the distinctive way in which women deal with these concerns. Written almost exclusively by women for a primarily female audience, these are stories that chart the courses of their lives. They deal with real problems and real solutions. They provide their readers a glimpse into the way others have confronted dilemmas similar to those they face themselves, as well as into lifestyles and problems very different from their own.

Novels of Women's Lives and Relationships, then, delineate the stories of women, and they focus on issues, domestic and professional, related to women's lives. Although questions are raised, solutions are generally found or at least mapped out, and these books usually suggest upbeat, or at least resolved, endings. They overlap with books in other genres, with titles that feature strong women and emphasize the same kinds of relationships and struggles with issues; this crossover and how to use it to help readers find more of the types of books they enjoy are discussed below in the "Expanding Readers' Horizons" section of the "Readers' Advisory Interview." *See* Figure 16.1 for characteristics of the genre.

Characteristics and the Genre's Appeal

Characterization

These are novels written by women, and they explore the lives of female protagonists while they focus on the protagonist's relationships with family, friends, and lovers. Occasionally male authors write successfully in this genre, as Richard Peck did in his popular *London Holiday*,

---

FIGURE 16.1

Characteristics of the Women's Lives and Relationships Genre

1. The protagonist is female, as is the author. Secondary characters, especially women, are also important. Protagonists may have a support group composed of female family members and friends.

2. Story lines reflect the issues affecting women's lives, and they usually focus on a single issue, thus portraying women facing difficult situations. Although there may be elements of Romance or Suspense, that is not the focus of the stories. Story lines reflect universal female themes—family conflicts, family relationships, work versus family, friendships—and how the protagonists react to these issues. Endings are resolved satisfactorily (or solutions are put in place), rather than left open.

3. The setting is usually contemporary. These are books about today's women and the problems they face.

4. These books adopt a familiar, intimate tone. The writing style may range from elegantly poetic to more prosaic and conversational to humorous, and differences in tone, from more soap opera or melodramatic to realistic or provocative, distinguish the story lines of these novels.

5. Pacing runs the gamut from leisurely unfolding to faster-paced. Fans talk of these as compelling reads that pull readers in and involve them with the protagonist's story.

---

the story of three friends who escape to London, leaving behind rather dreary lives and problems with husbands, families, and work.[1] Together these women recover their lives and their friendships. However, it is usually other women who write these stories that touch the hearts and minds of fellow females. These novels may follow a single character and examine the ways in which she relates to others and attempts to make sense of her life, or they may explore a group of women, usually friends, and the interrelated issues of their lives and friendships.

These books are character centered, and although the protagonists are the primary focus, secondary female characters are also important. Even though these books may deal with a group of friends, there is generally one woman who stands out as the protagonist or the focus. Although the lives of the secondary characters may also be examined, all plotlines and characters finally converge on the protagonist and her story. Rebecca Wells's *The Divine Secrets of the Ya-Ya Sisterhood* stands out as a popular example.[2] In addition to revealing the history of a group of friends, their coming of age, and their lives now, this is also more specifically the story of one mother-daughter pair who attempt to resolve their personal relationship, with the help, of course, of the other Ya-Yas.

In others, more frequently written by more established authors in the genre, there is clearly a single protagonist who fights her way out of her difficulties and makes her own way, with more or less help from her friends. In novels by Danielle Steel, Fern Michaels, LaVyrle Spencer, and Barbara Delinsky, the protagonist is more frequently on her own, only occasionally finding succor in female friends or relatives. Kristin Hannah, known primarily for her writing in the Romance genre, seems to be moving toward Women's Lives with her recent titles. In *On Mystic Lake* Annie Colwater sends her daughter off to college and is ready to start the second half of her life, when she is devastated by her husband's announcement that he wants a divorce.[3] She returns to her hometown of Mystic Lake, where she seeks to rediscover herself. Romantic elements are important, but more important are her realization and the creation of her own future.

Story Line

Unlike much other genre fiction, part of the appeal of this genre is the currency of the issues. Themes in these books reflect problems women face today. Although some Historical Fiction may also reflect women's issues, as in Catherine Cookson's studies of the plight of nineteenth-century women in rural England, these do not have the same impact and feel for fans as contemporary titles. Readers may read and enjoy both, but they look to these contemporary stories of Women's Lives and Relationships for different reassurances and satisfactions.

On the other hand, some authors successfully employ story lines in past and present to reflect universal themes that affect women's lives. *Hanna's Daughters,* by Swedish author Marianne Fredriksson, tells the stories of Hanna, who was born in the nineteenth century; her daughter Johanna, born at the end of that century; and her granddaughter Anna, the narrator, who has two daughters of her own.[4] Anna charts her mother's and grandmother's lives, seeking to understand her mother, who is approaching death, and thus she reveals the similarities and differences of character as well as of milieu and opportunity. And through this examination of a specific situation, she illuminates universal truths about these relationships.

Although these stories may contain elements of Romance, Suspense, and Mystery, the basic story deals with problems and issues affecting women's lives. The additional elements serve only to enhance, rather than overwhelm, the basic story. Popular themes examine generations of families, family relationships and friendships, issues with health and career, and women triumphing over adversity and reconstructing their lives. Although some verge on the melodramatic, novels in this genre revolve around healing and discovering solutions to problems many women share. (In fact, the prospect of a solution is an important aspect of their appeal. If the story is left open-ended, with a satisfactory resolution not ensured, the story probably belongs with titles in another genre, Literary Fiction, perhaps, rather than here.) Contrast the novels of Spencer and Barbara Kingsolver to understand the range of this genre. Spencer's novels of Women's Lives generally feature a female protagonist on her own, and in her books, the love interest is consistently of more importance than it is in much of this genre. (Her last novel, *Then Came Heaven,* exhibits this emphasis, as a nun must choose between her profession and her feelings for a widower and his daughters.)[5] Kingsolver, on the other hand, features a community of men and women, and the women seek solutions together. Her first novel, *Bean Trees,* exemplifies this story line.[6] Traveling cross-country to escape her dead-end life in Kentucky, Taylor Greer's car breaks down in Oklahoma, and she finds she has "inherited" an abused three-year-old Indian girl. In Tucson, Taylor acquires an unusual group of friends who help teach her what it is to be a mother and to create a family that transcends the traditional definition. An elegantly told but accessible story of a young woman's journey to discovery, this novel appeals to fans of Literary Fiction as well.

"Family" in the broadest sense pervades these stories. Children, siblings, spouses, parents, and the extended family of friends people these novels. These are stories of relationships and of coping with problems and issues. At one end of the spectrum is the earthy tone of Terry McMillan's *Waiting to Exhale,* the story of four African American women who deal with a range of traumas from a parent with Alzheimer's to love gone awry.[7] At the other are the gentle Irish settings of Maeve Binchy. In books such as *Circle of Friends,* the choices faced by her characters are no less difficult, despite the softer tone.[8] Here, the story of young women and their prospects is cast against the social and religious strictures that also play an important role in their lives.

Although primarily domestic, these stories are as noncompartmentalized as the lives of the women they describe. Family, friends, work, and home must all fit together into a woman's life, and the focus of the novel may be on the way the protagonist must juggle all to avoid disaster. Delinsky's aptly titled *A Woman's Place* puts Claire Raphael, successful businesswoman (who has created her own company out of her home), wife, and mother, in an impossible situation as her husband sues for divorce and custody of their two children.[9] She battles back from this nightmare, and, with the help of her business partner (who later becomes her lover), succeeds in regaining her life. The conflicts arising from juggling work and home responsibilities are at the heart of many of these stories, and compromise is the key to the resolution. Novels of Women's Lives and Relationships reflect universal themes that highlight the strength and resilience of the heroine but often also set up conflicts that demand thoughtful reconciliation and resolution.

Tone

Many factors distinguish these stories, one from another, and a key element is tone: the atmosphere created by the author in the kind of story she is telling and the desired effect of this tone on readers. For example, books may deal with the same topic—facing the death of a friend or family member—but handle it in different ways and create a distinct and identifiable tone in each case. Patricia Gaffney's consideration of the death of a friend in *The Saving Graces* differs in tone from Anna Quindlen's *One True Thing*.[10] The former is told through the voices of four friends, and although they confront the death of one of their group, this is also a story of friendships, of their intertwining lives, of the healing power of their friendship even in the face of death. Quindlen, in contrast, employs a single narrator, daughter Ellen Gulden, who is forced home by her father so that she can nurse her dying mother. Thus, the story is more focused, emphasizing mother-daughter and father-daughter relationships and the impact of the mother's dying on both husband and daughter. It is also more intense, told solely through Ellen's eyes, rather than diffused through alternating narrators.

This is not to say that one is "better" than the other, simply that each has a different tone and possibly readership. Both treat the same topic but on different levels and to different purposes. Fans recognize the distinction, and although they may read and appreciate both books, they do not see them as the same kind of book. That rather ephemeral distinction clouds much of our consideration of genre fiction, but in this genre, which approaches basic truths in women's lives, it becomes clearer that authors, by their intention and direction, create a range of books that deal with similar, always difficult and emotional topics. Some readers may never want to go beyond a more superficial look at an issue or circumstance, and they choose particular books, because they know they can count on authors to meet their expectations. Others are disappointed if authors do not delve deeply into issues, reflecting, often poetically, on the possibilities. Tone is a vital consideration in this genre.

However, this tone, as I suggested earlier, also runs the gamut. Elinor Lipman and Susan Sussman tell their stories with large measures of wit and humor. Steel and Michaels rely on more sentimental devices. Readers would not choose Helen Fielding's *Bridget Jones's Diary* and expect to find the style and tone similar to fellow Englishwoman Erica James, whose quiet, gentle stories portray quite different characters and situations.[11] While Fielding concentrates only on her title character, James, in novels such as *Airs and Graces,* develops a cast of characters and enlivens her stories with a quieter, more gentle humor.[12] Each author has her fans, and readers may read both at different times to meet different needs.

Writing style is an issue in all genres. Here, the writing styles range from Kaye Gibbons's poetic prose to the more conversational style of Michaels. Although some readers choose authors based on writing style, for others, language is but the means to tell the story of women and their lives. Readers choose among a range of styles, sometimes indiscriminately, or so it seems, just as they do in all genres (except perhaps Literary Fiction, in which style is often of primary importance), finding the story and the characters that resonate with them, that suit their mood. Many of these authors (Steel, Rosamunde Pilcher, Delinsky, to name a few) previously wrote paperback Romances, and as a result, their books are characterized by a romantic tone. Others, for example Kingsolver and Alice Hoffman, are appreciated equally by fans of Literary Fiction as consummate stylists who deal with provocative issues. Every genre has a range of writing styles and here it may be even more extreme than in most.

Pacing

Finally, the pacing of these novels tends more toward the leisurely unfolding, generally lacking the elements of Suspense or Adventure that might move the story more quickly. Still, readers speak of them as compelling reading, books that pull them in and keep them engaged. The sense of the pacing, of moving forward through the problems faced by the protagonist and her friends, likely feels brisker than the actual turning of pages reflects. Even though Barbara Chepaitis's first novel, the recent *Feeding Christine,* takes place in only two days—a telescoped time frame that in other genres suggests a fast-paced story—this rather quirky tale of food, families, and female friends unfolds at a comfortable, leisurely pace.[13] As Teresa DiRosa, assisted by her two friends and employees, prepares the annual holiday buffet for her catering clients, she must also deal with her niece, who attempts suicide. Teresa's immediate solution may raise some eyebrows, but as the women cook together and share their conversation, more than one problem is resolved.

Key Authors

Benchmark

This is a genre that is changing rapidly. In the '80s and early '90s, Danielle Steel was certainly the unrivaled benchmark. No one else wrote of women's lives in the way she did, and fans flocked to the library whenever she published a new title. We seemed never to have enough copies of her books. Steel remains popular at my library, although I now buy fewer copies of her books, and it is clear from conversations with readers that she is no longer universally liked and read. Still, her success and influence—not to mention the fact that she has been so prolific—are enough to ensure her the position of benchmark, at least for now.

Steel's books feature strong female characters, timeless values (love for children, home, and family), a romantic and often sentimental tone, rich-and-famous elements (brand names, designer labels, etc.), and, as expected, the issues that women face in their lives, from divorce and breast cancer to problems with children. She writes stories, each focusing on a single issue, that are both touching and satisfying, about women who face tragedy and emerge stronger. Try *The Gift*, an unusually short novel but certainly a typical example of her style.[14] Fans of Steel should be familiar with the novels of LaVyrle Spencer, as well as Fern Michaels, as all three share similar tone, style, characters, and story line.

Key Authors

Identifying other important names in the genre opens a Pandora's box of possibilities. There are those who write a more conversational prose versus those with a more literary style, those who write more humorously versus those who take a more serious approach, the sentimental versus the realistic schools. Despite this range, this is a genre that seems to lack easily identifiable subgenres; writers write and fans read a range of titles that all reflect the same features to a greater or lesser degree. Some of the contrasts are considered below, as I discuss how we interact with readers.

Barbara Delinsky, an emigrant from the Romance genre, has enormous appeal for readers in both camps, with her leisurely paced stories of women wronged who bring their lives together again. *Lake News* provides a recent example of her style and charm in this story of a victim of yellow journalism who builds a new life in her tiny hometown, to which she runs to escape publicity in Boston.[15] This is a story of a woman whose career is destroyed when she is unjustly accused by the press of having an affair with a cardinal, but it is also a book about healing and building trust. Although she is also a good suggestion for fans of Steel, she has attracted a wide audience of her own fans, who simply appreciate her style and the stories she tells.

Another strong rival to Steel's benchmark status is Irish writer Maeve Binchy. Often told as short stories braided together into a novel form, Binchy's character-centered books touch a chord that resonates across the Atlantic. Her Irish women face universal situations similar to those of their American counterparts, and they deal with them in similarly traditional ways. Binchy's stories are evocative, descriptive of both geography and character, and although they do not always produce happy endings, stories are resolved in a way that leave readers satisfied. That Oprah chose *Tara Road* as one of her Book Club selections is an indication of the appeal of these interwoven, layered stories.[16]

English author Barbara Whitnell (*A Clear Blue Sky*) is a good suggestion for Binchy's fans.[17] Although several of her titles have historical elements, all have a timeless quality, as do Binchy's, which makes them an excellent suggestion for readers who desire a quieter look at issues and relationships. Also popular with fans of these two are Sarah Woodhouse, Mary Sheepshanks, Joanna Trollope, and Mary Wesley. Family secrets and crises, set against generations of English class and civility, run through these stories. In fact, novels of Women's Lives and Relationships have, for the most part, replaced the popular family saga of earlier decades. Now the lives of the women supplant the generations of the family, even though much of the story remains the same and exerts the same pull for readers. Although they touch on serious issues, they are often gentle, evocative, soothing, and more elegantly written books, appealing to fans of stories of women as well as those who enjoy Gentle Reads and Literary Fiction. Of these writers, Woodhouse has a softer touch, while Sheepshanks, Trollope, and Wesley have more of an edge.

Woodhouse writes gentle, thoughtful stories of Women's Lives. Timeless settings in restful locales (even rather exotic—Italy and Greece), memory-laden tales, intertwined generations and family stories, and a cozy feel make her books inviting reading for fans of Gentle Reads, as well as Women's Lives. *My Summer with Julia* displays the charm and appeal of her books.[18]

Although she certainly deals with difficult issues—adultery plays a major role in *Facing the Music*—Sheepshanks employs a light touch, and her evocative, engaging family stories reveal light humor as well.[19] In *Picking Up the Pieces* widowed fiftysomething Kate Rendlesham literally picks up the pieces of her life, a year after her husband's death, creating a promising career and resolving relations with the three generations of women who encompass her world: her sympathetic mother-in-law (who knew more of the truth of Kate's awful marriage than she could reveal), her daughter who loved her father unconditionally, and her granddaughter, who is on her own quest to discover her birth father.[20] In the midst of these changes, Kate also struggles with the possibility of love, despite the dark secrets from the past that may shatter her chance for happiness.

Trollope, whose popularity has been boosted by several PBS renditions of her works, is another author frequently requested by readers. Her layered stories of English middle-class life—of love, friendship, family—consistently satisfy her fans. *Booklist* reviewer James Klise may have uncovered the key to Trollope and the genre's popularity in his review of *Other People's Children*.[21] He writes, "Reading Trollope's work is like spending an afternoon with a friend, sharing problems over a pot of tea, and provokes in the reader the ultimately satisfying response of, yes, I've felt that way, too."[22]

Wesley began her writing career at age seventy, but judging from the issues she confronts in her novels, she is not the stereotypical "little old lady." Her best may be *An Imaginative Experience*, in which recently widowed Julia Piper performs an impulsive act—rescuing a sheep stuck on the train tracks—that opens her up to recovery through friendship and eventually love.[23] Wesley's novels are often sexually explicit and do not shrink from addressing hard issues, from prostitution to rape, but the overall tone is far more gentle and the emphasis on discovery and resolution in women's lives make these interesting reading for all generations.

Although the English and Irish contingent is certainly popular in American libraries, there are American writers as well, in addition to Steel and Delinsky, who attract crowds of readers. Elizabeth Berg, another writer Oprah has selected for her Book Club, has broad appeal in many of our libraries—even before Oprah discovered her. It is her earlier titles that fans remember fondly and share with their friends, as these seem to have captured emotional depths and set the feelings and issues in lyrical prose. Try her first, *Durable Goods*, a thoughtful coming-of-age story, as an example of her style.[24]

Jodi Picoult writes intelligent, provocative novels of Women's Lives with far-reaching implications. Often emphasizing the spiritual and psychological aspects of characters and issues alike, Picoult writes serious, intriguing, and insightful dramas that raise difficult questions. *Plain Truth,* for example, provides insight into the life of a young, unmarried Amish woman, accused of murdering her child, as well as into the Amish culture.[25]

Diane Chamberlain is an author who brings elements of Romance and Suspense to her stories of Women's Lives. In novels such as *Breaking the Silence,* family secrets exposed bring resolution to damaged lives.[26]

Elinor Lipman adds humor to her glimpses of the fates of her female protagonists. For example, imagine that your birth mother finally reveals herself to you, and she is a cross between Oprah and Sally Jessie Raphael. That is what happens to April Epner in *Then She Found Me*.[27] How that discovery affects her job as a teacher (Latin, no less), her relationship with her adopted parents (Holocaust survivors), and her own budding romance, as she researches the several stories about her birth father, makes a diverting but thoughtful story. This is a novel of contrasting relationships, sophisticated and witty dialogue, and home truths about what it is to be a parent.

Preparing to Work with Readers

What do we know about fans of the genre? Readers are primarily women, and they may read a range of authors from benchmark Danielle Steel to the more literary Kaye Gibbons. These are readers who appreciate stories of women facing difficulties in their everyday lives and coming to terms with them, often with the help of friends, almost exclusively female. These readers seek stories that reflect the domestic aspects of women's lives, as well as the way in which women have always been required to juggle domestic and professional demands. Issues are usually resolved in these stories, which makes them immensely satisfying. Even though we know these are "just" books, the fact that solutions can be found offers hope to readers. Problems may not always be solved neatly, but possible solutions are presented and the characters begin on the path toward working out the difficulties. These are generally hopeful stories, featuring a range of women and situations that explore the dilemmas that often comprise women's lives. That is what readers expect.

Readers may be attracted to protagonists of roughly their own age, as those are characters who are facing issues similar to the ones readers themselves confront in their own lives. This breakdown provides a good place to start when exploring the range of authors in this genre, and it makes these authors and their books easier to describe to readers. However, I would be the last to advocate pigeonholing readers—or writers—in this fashion. The themes that direct these stories are timeless and ageless. The best appeal to readers of all ages, and all readers find, at some point, a similar interest in these authors and their characters, no matter what their own age or that of the protagonists.

Among those authors who often feature protagonists in their twenties and thirties are Sarah Bird, Mameve Medwed, Caroline Leavitt, Ann Hood, Helen Fielding, Katie Fforde, Elinor Lipman, Sara Lewis, Jane Heller, and Barbara Kingsolver. The younger protagonists might be sassy, feisty heroines or more contemplative, quiet observers of the world. Just out of school and beginning careers, these women face the problems arising from leaving one's family and living on one's own, resolving career obstacles, finding mates (or deciding not to), and generally sorting out their futures. Whether American or British, these authors often view the world with a humorous, sometimes irreverent, eye. In *The Boyfriend School,* Bird captures the sense of what it is to be a single female, satisfied with her work, yet yearning for the possibility of more—perhaps love—in her life.[28] Quirky characters fill all her stories, as do the traumas that afflict the twentysomething on her own, and the hope for the possibility of better days.

As the protagonists move into their thirties, their stories address issues of husbands and young families, along with careers and sustaining friendships, a slightly different focus and often a less frantic tone. Lewis is a good author to know for this age group. She explores the lives of her thirtysomething characters with both whimsy and sentiment. *Heart Conditions* plots the life of Alice Hammond, caught in a dead-end job, who discovers she is pregnant just as her lover tells her he is leaving.[29] She decides against abortion and turns instead to her grandmother, with whom she has never gotten along. Sympathetic, if somewhat eccentric, characters drive the plot of this charming story of relationships and family bonds.

Characters in their forties and fifties star in the novels of Elizabeth Berg, LaVyrle Spencer, Sarah Woodhouse, Mary Sheepshanks, and Anne Rivers Siddons. Although these protagonists may have children, they are usually older or grown and away. Regaining relationships with husband and friends and the specter of death (of parents, peers, or children) are the themes that dominate these stories. Many of Barbara Taylor Bradford's books feature women in this age group. She often adds "rich-and-famous" elements, as well as Romantic Suspense and Mystery, to her touching stories of women, their lives, their families, and their friendships. *Her Own Rules* exemplifies her style and themes.[30]

Older protagonists, in their sixties and above, also find their stories told in this genre. Nina Bawden, a British writer who has published novels since the '50s, writes in *Family Money* of the problems that accompany aging and concerns for independence.[31] Viqui Litman treats these issues with a lighter touch in *The Ladies Farm,* in which a group of older ladies with a history of friendship (in fact, the wife and mistresses of one man) join forces to create a spa, in order to pool resources and ensure their futures.[32]

Some authors who have written for several years—Steel, Maeve Binchy, Nancy Thayer—tend to place their heroines near their own current age. Margaret Drabble is a master of this. Many of us read of the lives of her younger protagonists in the '70s and later followed through the lives of the more mature women who people her titles of the '90s. (If you are interested in experimenting, start with an early novel from the '70s—the award-winning *The Millstone* perhaps, with its story of an unwed mother—and continue through the trilogy beginning with *The Radiant Way*, which charts the lives and friendship of three women in Britain in the '80s, as well as the role of women in society.)[33] This sense of following an author through similar periods in our lives is a real draw; we feel we know each other and face similar problems. Reading earlier titles brings back earlier days in our own lives, while later titles by those authors may be harbingers of our futures. That these authors seem to chart our own lives is part of their enormous, satisfying appeal.

One interesting aspect of books in this genre is that they tend to cross lines of age and ethnic background in ways that books in other genres may not do as easily. In my library, Terry McMillan's *Waiting to Exhale* was sought by a range of readers, from the young to senior citizens and of all ethnic backgrounds. Arthur Golden's *Memoirs of a Geisha*, unique in many respects, not the least of which is that this very personal story of a woman is written in first-person by a man, was embraced by women of all ages and by some men as well.[34] Amy Tan created a new standard for the exploration of mother-daughter relations in *The Joy Luck Club*, revealing the universality of these themes and their appeal.[35]

Readers of this genre also appreciate Multi-Cultural novels, both to see themselves (for example, in the universal themes of mothers and daughters in Tan) and to learn about how issues that affect women are played out differently in other cultures. *Breath, Eyes, Memory*, by Edwidge Danticat, provides a glimpse of Haitian women, from coming of age to their prospects as adults, while Susan Power presents a unique American culture, that of the Sioux Indians, in *Grass Dancer*, which follows generations of Indian women back in time.[36]

Fans of family stories will often find titles that appeal to them in this genre. Bradford first gained fame for her sagas (*A Woman of Substance*), and although later books have added other elements, the feel of the saga often remains.[37] Belva Plain tells stories both of generations of women and of the years in the life of one woman in other novels that have a definite appeal for those who like that sense of generations of a family. Another suggestion for these fans might be Lorna Landvik's *Patty Jane's House of Curl*, which features Minneapolis sisters, their lives as beauticians and their loves, all related by Patty Jane's daughter as she uncovers their stories.[38]

For readers of Literary Fiction, Gibbons appeals to both heart and mind in her poetic stories of women's lives. Jill McCorkle adds humor and quirky characters, as did the late Laurie Colwin, who is still much lamented and frequently read in my library. Jacqueline Mitchard and Anna Quindlen add the provocative problems of Literary Fiction to their stories of Women's Lives and Relationships.

It is clear from the previous descriptions of authors and titles that other genres overlap with Women's Lives and Relationships, and themes from those genres may play a role in these stories. On the other hand, if you are a fan of another genre but want to explore novels of Women's Lives and Relationships, it is useful to find authors that reflect the elements you enjoy in genres you currently read. Figure 16.2 offers suggestions of authors to try.

FIGURE 16.2

An Introduction to the Women's Lives and Relationships Genre

Women's Lives and Relationships Writers to Try, If You Enjoy . . .

Gentle	Maeve Binchy
Historical	Jean Stubbs (By Our Beginnings)[39]
	Sandra Dallas
Humor	Elinor Lipman
	Karen Karbo
Literary	Alice Hoffman
	Kaye Gibbons
Mystery	Susan Isaacs (After All These Years)[40]
Romance	Kristin Hannah
	LaVyrle Spencer
Romantic Suspense	Diane Chamberlain
Suspense	Jodi Picoult
Western	Molly Gloss

Readers' Advisory Interview

Women's Lives and Relationships is another genre that readers do not generally request by name. In fact, readers might be surprised to discover that we consider this a genre. They may come to the desk and offer the names of some of these authors as ones they have read and enjoyed, or they may describe a book about relationships and coping, and this seems a logical genre to explore with them. They may also talk about some of the genres listed in previous chapters, and the suggested links to writers of novels about Women's Lives and Relationships will give them new directions to explore. Or they may request titles from Oprah's Book Club, or other books like those, but perhaps not so "depressing." The key for us is, of course, to listen to which authors they enjoy and how they describe them. Are they looking for the more literary or "popular" authors? More serious treatment or less? And we must develop ways to pose these questions, or offer authors and titles, so that we do not offend this audience by denigrating their favorite authors and the themes that have touched them.

Oprah's choices seem as if they should fit here, as they are certainly books with female characters and the audience is primarily women. As I write, Oprah and her selections are probably the single greatest influence on what many women choose to read—or at least on the women who have not been readers recently but whom Oprah has enticed back into the fold. For the most part, her choices are books that reflect the themes of this genre. Unlike many mentioned above, however, Oprah's choices, for the most part, are fairly bleak—women as parts of dysfunctional families and placed in terrible and dangerous situations. Mainstays of her reading are authors like Toni Morrison, Jacqueline Mitchard, and Anita Shreve. These are more elegant, literary writers who focus on words and ideas, and their books certainly have a different feel, even though the underlying subject may be the same. However, many of the readers whom Oprah has inspired to read again come to us to ask for books on the same topics that are not quite so depressing. For these readers, authors who write about Women's Lives and Relationships are often an excellent suggestion.

Novels of a young woman's coming of age often fit in with novels of Women's Lives and Relationships. They, too, explore universal and timeless issues dealing with friends and family, love and loss. While helping younger readers to deal with these issues, they also take older readers back to that time in their own pasts and remind them of how they felt, producing satisfaction in a wide range of readers. Recent titles to consider include *The Romance Reader,* Pearl Abraham's first novel with its look at a young Hasidic girl coming of age in upstate New York in the 1950s; Gail Godwin's *Father Melancholy's Daughter,* with its powerful and far-reaching story of a clergyman's daughter who must care for her father, helping him in his bouts of depression, after her mother leaves; or Faith Sullivan's upbeat *The Cape Ann,* which features a mother and daughter during the depression and their dream of a house—and escape.[41]

Sure Bets

Katie Fforde's novels, set in England, attract a number of readers, in part because of her deftly humorous touch. In the lighthearted and romantic *Stately Pursuits,* twentysomething Hetty has just lost her boyfriend and her job.[42] So she takes up house-sitting in her uncle's neglected mansion. As she sorts out her future, she also falls in love, first with the house and then with the man who wants to destroy it. *Wild Designs* offers an older heroine in Althea, a divorced mother, confronting the problems of three teenagers, a difficult younger sister, and an impossible ex-husband.[43] Having lost her job, her only hope, winning a gardening competition, is dashed as the vacant greenhouse where she has been secretly growing plants has been purchased by the attractive and rich Patrick. Fans of Romances will have no difficulty envisioning the story to its happy conclusion, but Althea's dilemmas appeal to readers beyond the confines of that genre, as she addresses the family and personal issues that affect women of her age and position.

Susan Isaacs is another good choice, an author popular with many types of readers. Two contrasting titles, *Almost Paradise* and *After All these Years,* are among her most popular.[44] The former is a touching, more romantic story of the relationship that develops between two people from completely different worlds. The latter stars a woman who, just after her twenty-fifth anniversary celebration, learns that her husband is leaving her for another woman. That night she finds him dead on the kitchen floor, and she is, of course, the prime suspect. How she outwits the police and solves the crime while on the lam make amusing reading for readers who enjoy the added elements of Mystery and Romance.

Expanding Readers' Horizons

Readers of novels of Women's Lives and Relationships find much they enjoy in related genres. As is clear above, many titles in this genre have Romantic themes; others fit closely with Literary Fiction or Gentle Reads. But there are also authors in other genres, Mysteries for example, that deal with many of the same issues, adding Mystery trappings to the story. Gail Bowen is such an author. Her Mysteries feature Canadian professor and widow Joanne Kilbourn. Although these focus on serious, often very disturbing, crimes, they also highlight Jo and her family—two daughters (the younger one, an artistic prodigy, adopted after her mother, a close friend, is murdered) and two sons—and her difficult but intensifying relationship with Alex, an Ojibwa police inspector. The sense of motherhood and family pervades these stories so completely that I have yet to give them to another mother who has not found them intensely satisfying. (Not that one has to be a mother to enjoy these, but that link is especially strong.) This is also a clear case when it is better not to start with the first title, which is not the strongest. *Love and Murder* provides a good introduction to the characters and the family.[45]

Although closely related to many in the Romance genre, novels of Women's Lives and Relationships have a broader emphasis than the romantic entanglements of their characters. Romance may be an element in these books, but the focus is on the bigger picture of women's lives and the problems they face, how they meet crises and resolve them. However, readers may find the elements they seek in Romance authors such as Kathleen Gilles Seidel, whose strong sense of family relations and women's roles without an overpowering Romance should provide them with the satisfactions they seek in Women's Lives. A good place to start is her recent *Summer's End*, with its story of a blended family, including adult children, and a strong emphasis on sibling relationships.[46]

Literary Fiction authors Shreve and Anne Tyler also address issues of interest to readers of this genre. In fact, many of the authors in this

---

FIGURE 16.3

Expanding Readers' Horizons

Authors to Take Readers beyond the Women's Lives and Relationships *Genre*

Gentle	Rosamunde Pilcher
Historical	Jeanne Williams
Literary	Anita Shreve
	Anne Tyler
Mystery	Gail Bowen
	Marianne Macdonald
Romance	Kathleen Gilles Seidel
Western	Judy Alter
	Elizabeth Fackler

---

genre are extremely difficult to "slot" into specific genres. Shreve, Tyler, and Sue Miller probably fit better as Literary Fiction authors, because their provocative novels explore beyond women's issues. On the other hand, elegant stylists such as Alice Hoffman and Kaye Gibbons certainly meet the literary criteria, but their stories seem to place them more comfortably here than in Literary Fiction. Luckily, patrons are not hindered by our attempts to group authors by genre. They read the ones they enjoy, whether their books seem to fall into one genre or another. Our task is to help them discover those similar authors, no matter what genre we find them in. *See* Figure 16.3 for suggestions.

Reference Resources

When we venture beyond the standard fiction genres, we find it more and more difficult to discover reference sources that support that genre. In the case of Women's Lives and Relationships, there are academic sources that support Women's Studies programs at universities, but those are not the kinds of useful tools we seek for readers' advisory work in public libraries. As with all genres, however, it is important to keep an eye out for reviews of new sources that might fill the gaps we find—and then share that information with the rest of us. In the case of Women's Lives and Relationships, we rely heavily on standard literary resources to provide access to the information we seek.

Where to Find . . .

INFORMATION ABOUT THE AUTHOR

Contemporary Authors (*see* appendix 2) provides biographic and bibliographic information on many of the popular authors who write in this genre.

PLOT SUMMARIES

Standard readers' advisory sources—*Fiction Catalog* and *NoveList* especially—provide plot summaries of many of these books, because they are considered mainstream fiction, for the most part. Titles in series are also included in *Sequels* and *To Be Continued*. (All these titles are described in detail in appendix 2.)

SUBGENRES AND THEMES

One problem is that the term *women* is almost too broad to search successfully. On *NoveList* even in the Browse Subject function, which allows us to select which subheadings to search, we bring up more than 1,400 headings that include the word *women*. Choosing themes, such as coming-of-age stories, produces a long but more manageable list.

Because the themes of these novels potentially touch more than 50 percent of our readers, novels of Women's Lives and Relationships have a broad appeal. Although readers may not read these exclusively, they often like to sample them when they come to the library. These authors, in their various guises, are often good suggestions for readers looking for something new. Depending on how the reader describes what she enjoys—or what she is looking for today—a variety of these authors may be satisfying.

Novels of Women's Lives and Relationships strike a chord with a range of female readers, whether they read extensively in this particular genre or not. These are books that are often passed by word of mouth, hand to hand, from one reader to another. They meant something to one reader going through a difficult time and are offered to another in similar circumstances. Like Gentle Reads and Romances (not to mention Horror and many Mysteries), there is a strong emotional element to these books, and the ways in which the protagonists cope often offer a pattern to follow—and hope—that obstacles can be overcome.

NOTES

1. Richard Peck, *London Holiday* (New York: Viking, 1998).
2. Rebecca Wells, *The Divine Secrets of the Ya-Ya Sisterhood* (New York: HarperCollins, 1996).
3. Kristin Hannah, *On Mystic Lake* (New York: Crown, 1999).
4. Marianne Fredriksson, *Hanna's Daughters* (New York: Ballantine, 1998).
5. LaVyrle Spencer, *Then Came Heaven* (New York: Putnam, 1997).
6. Barbara Kingsolver, *Bean Trees* (New York: Harper & Row, 1988).
7. Terry McMillan, *Waiting to Exhale* (New York: Viking, 1992).
8. Maeve Binchy, *Circle of Friends* (New York: McGraw-Hill, 1967).
9. Barbara Delinksy, *A Woman's Place* (New York: HarperCollins, 1997).
10. Patricia Gaffney, *The Saving Graces* (New York: HarperCollins, 1997); Anna Quindlen, *One True Thing* (New York: Random House, 1994).
11. Helen Fielding, *Bridget Jones's Diary* (New York: Viking, 1998).
12. Erica James, *Airs and Graces* (London: Orion, 1997).
13. Barbara Chepaitis, *Feeding Christine* (New York: Bantam, 2000).
14. Danielle Steel, *The Gift* (New York: Delacorte, 1994).
15. Delinksy, *Lake News* (New York: Simon & Schuster, 1999).
16. Binchy, *Tara Road* (New York: Delacorte, 1999, © 1998).
17. Barbara Whitnell, *A Clear Blue Sky* (New York: St. Martin's, 1995).
18. Sarah Woodhouse, *My Summer with Julia* (New York: St. Martin's, 2000).
19. Mary Sheepshanks, *Facing the Music* (New York: St. Martin's, 1997).
20. ———, *Picking Up the Pieces* (New York: St. Martin's, 1999).
21. Joanna Trollope, *Other People's Children* (New York: Viking, 1999).
22. James Klise, review of *Other People's Children*, by Joanna Trollope, *Booklist* 95 (April 1, 1999): 1387.
23. Mary Wesley, *An Imaginative Experience* (New York: Viking, 1995).

24. Elizabeth Berg, *Durable Goods* (New York: Random House, 1998).

25. Jodi Picoult, *Plain Truth* (New York: Pocket Books, 2000).

26. Diane Chamberlain, *Breaking the Silence* (Don Mills, Ont.: MIRA Books, 1999).

27. Elinor Lipman, *Then She Found Me* (New York: Pocket Books, 1990).

28. Sarah Bird, *The Boyfriend School* (New York: Doubleday, 1989).

29. Sara Lewis, *Heart Conditions* (New York: Harcourt Brace, 1994).

30. Barbara Taylor Bradford, *Her Own Rules* (New York: HarperCollins, 1996).

31. Nina Bawden, *Family Money* (New York: St. Martin's, 1991).

32. Viqui Litman, *The Ladies Farm* (New York: Crown, 1999).

33. Margaret Drabble, *The Millstone* (New York: Morrow, 1965); ———, *The Radiant Way* (New York: Knopf, 1987).

34. Arthur Golden, *Memoirs of a Geisha* (New York: Knopf, 1997).

35. Amy Tan, *The Joy Luck Club* (New York: Putnam, 1989).

36. Edwidge Danticat, *Breath, Eyes, Memory* (New York: Soho Press, 1994); Susan Power, *Grass Dancer* (New York: Putnam, 1994).

37. Bradford, *A Woman of Substance* (Garden City, N.Y.: Doubleday, 1979).

38. Lorna Landvik, *Patty Jane's House of Curl* (Bridgehampton, N.Y.: Bridge Works, 1995).

39. Jean Stubbs, *By Our Beginnings* (New York: St. Martin's, 1979).

40. Susan Isaacs, *After All These Years* (New York: HarperCollins, 1993).

41. Pearl Abraham, *The Romance Reader* (New York: Riverhead Books, 1995); Gail Godwin, *Father Melancholy's Daughter* (New York: Morrow, 1991); Faith Sullivan, *The Cape Ann* (New York: Crown, 1988).

42. Katie Fforde, *Stately Pursuits* (New York: St. Martin's, 1998).

43. ———, *Wild Designs* (New York: St. Martin's, 1997).

44. Isaacs, *Almost Paradise* (New York: Harper & Row, 1984).

45. Gail Bowen, *Love and Murder* (New York: St. Martin's, 1993). Originally published as *Murder at the Mendel*, 1991.

46. Kathleen Gilles Seidel, *Summer's End* (New York: HarperPaperbacks, 1999).

Tips for the
Readers' Advisory Interview

Firstst, let the patrons talk about what type they like or do not like. This is similar to a reference interview, and we should verify our understanding of their comments. For example, saying "It sounds as if you like a book with a lot of adventure" or "a novel that explores the life of a real person" confirms the readers' preferences. Now it is their turn, in the course of this conversation, to correct or corroborate our observation. Then we should ask the important follow-up query, "Are you in the mood for this kind of book today? Or something different?"

Second, as in any readers' advisory interaction, we offer a range of suggestions from what we know or discover in reference sources. Patrons love to learn about reference sources, too, so we should remember to let them participate in the process of discovering suggestions in book and electronic sources. This also validates the fact that they have asked a *real* question and allows them to see how they can explore further on their own, if they are interested.

Third, if we do not come up with book suggestions on the spot, we take the patron's name and note the question, treating it like any other reference question, and call him when we have suggestions. Then we talk with other staff members, who may be fans of the genre; we pursue ideas in reference sources; we post the question on a readers' advisory maillist like Fiction_L[1]. As with many reference queries, not all readers' advisory questions need to be answered that minute.

TIPS FOR THE READERS' ADVISORY INTERVIEW

Readers appreciate our efforts, and taking time with a question helps set up a relationship with the reader. This also allows us the time to think through a question without the pressure of a waiting reader.

Fourth, we *always* encourage readers to come back and tell whoever is on the desk whether they enjoyed the books or not. I like to remind readers that there are many I could suggest, and I may not have discovered the best choices this time. If they let us know which ones they enjoyed and which they did not, we can move forward from there.

Finally, remember to pump fans for their favorites. Encourage them to talk about why they enjoy them. This is the kind of information we can share with other readers and use to expand our own knowledge, whether we actually have time to read the books or not. We also set up relationships with readers; we let them know it is okay to talk about books and that we appreciate their opinions, too. Many fans will return for repeat readers' advisory interactions once we have communicated our interest and excitement in helping them find books they enjoy.

NOTE

1. Fiction_L [Online], (Morton Grove, Ill.: Morton Grove Public Library, 1995 [cited February 26, 2001]); available at <http://fiction_l@maillist.webrary.org>.

Readers' Advisory Reference Tools

Why Reference Sources Are Important

I love reference sources, and if it were not for budget constraints we would have every genre reference book published! I believe they are important because they provide us with added memory. No matter how good we are at remembering authors and titles, there are times every day when our minds go blank. Consulting a reference source jogs our memory or introduces us and readers to new possibilities. There is a magic trapped deep within reference tools, within all books. They know when we are desperate, and by consulting them, we often get our minds jump-started and remember useful authors to pursue with readers. On a more mundane level, there is simply something about consulting a reference book, browsing through the names of authors and descriptions of their books, that really does start us thinking. Our minds are opened to the possibilities, and we are more likely to remember authors that might work for the patron standing by us. And, of course, good reference tools are essential if we are trying to discover information about a genre or subgenre with which we are unfamiliar.

Reference sources are also valuable because using them to answer a question validates a reader's query. If we can go to a reference source, book or electronic, and look up information for a reader, we have reinforced that this reader has asked a "real" question. Readers looking for the next book in a series do not always feel sure that they have asked a legitimate question. Consulting a reference tool validates their request. Reference sources confirm that this is a serious query and that there are places to look for an answer. This can make a real difference with readers and staff.

In every library there seems to be an invisible line drawn between requests for information about fiction and nonfiction. Nonfiction requests are always taken seriously, as they generally require the librarian to look up a fact or piece of information in a reference source. Fiction requests, especially the request for "a good book," fall in a gray area. If one cannot look up an answer, if one has to discover the answer simply based on an interview and one's knowledge of fiction, interpreting the patron's request and suggesting the possibilities one thinks might work, can this truly be reference? Those of us who help patrons daily with their fiction requests know the answer to this question, but convincing others is sometimes more difficult. A collection of reference tools that we use with readers helps us legitimize our own service, as well as the questions themselves in the eyes of those who ask them. Even though much of the work requires intelligent recall and understanding of what we have read, much also depends on sources we can employ to increase or jog our memories.

Although the focus of my comments in this appendix is on commercially produced readers' advisory reference tools, I would remind readers that every list we create becomes a reference source that we should cherish and keep for future retrieval. Annotated booklists, bookmarks, lists of authors who write similarly, and much more qualify as resource tools that we can and do use and reuse to help our readers.

What to Look for in
Commercially Produced Reference Sources

When I browse through reference sources, I try to ascertain the point of view from which the material is written. For the most part, genre fans are not looking for critical evaluations of a favorite genre or authors whom they enjoy. We can usually find that kind of material in book reviews. What makes a reference source valuable to Readers' Advisors and readers is that it be written from the fan's point of view.

We want to know the best things about the writers and genre. What makes this author or genre so popular? Why do fans consistently read this type of fiction? A reference source written with that tone conveys the pleasure readers find in the genre and the authors who write that kind of fiction. This kind of tool may also mention an author's best book or the best place to start a reader. That tone is invaluable for Readers' Advisors, and the books in which we find it should be treasured.

Secondly, I look for access points, indexes. I confess I am an index junkie. The more points of access, the better I like a reference tool. In my defense, I would argue that I am more likely to be able to answer a variety of questions or use a book to develop booklists and other tools if there are more, rather than fewer, access points.

Plot summaries are another valuable feature to note in reference sources. Again, if they are written by and for fans, rather than as critical evaluations, they help readers decide whether they might want to read the book. Readers also use them to help them recall whether they have already read a title.

Finally, I look for useful material about the books and authors. What are an author's best or most representative titles? Where should I start a reader new to this author? Books that provide this kind of information prove invaluable reference sources.

General Readers' Advisory Reference Tools

A word about the Internet: Although it is becoming one of the most useful reference tools available to librarians and patrons alike, I have not made a conscious attempt to include specific Web sites. Many of the reference sources listed here and in individual genre chapters provide more detailed information about Internet sites. Unfortunately, the addresses change rather quickly, and any list is quickly out of date. Any librarian who must check links from a library's home page on a regular basis would agree. If you are interested in the best sites on a particular genre at any given time, post the question on Fiction_L, the superb readers' advisory maillist described below. Within hours you will have more addresses than you have time to try.

Below is an annotated list of readers' advisory reference tools that cover more than one genre. Titles that are specific to a genre are included in the genre chapter.

Fiction Catalog.[1]

This is the grande dame of readers' advisory resources, a standard reference source for fiction with extensive subject and geographic indexing. Classic and popular titles, chosen through a voting list, are included. Entries are organized by author, then title, and include publishing information, pagination, and occasionally sequel info. A quoted, descriptive review serves as plot summary. There is a combined title and subject index, which includes names, places, and often genres.

Wilson is finally indicating that this source will be available electronically, although as of March 2001, the projected date for online access (August 2000) has come and gone. This once standard resource has been surpassed by excellent coverage and indexing in many newer titles, but perhaps the electronic version will be more useful. Simply providing a list of the subject headings assigned to each title in the body of the annotation would greatly increase its value.

Diana Tixier Herald. *Genreflecting: A Guide to Reading Interests in Genre Fiction.*[2]

This is the book that freed many of us librarians to admit our pleasure in genre fiction. Herald has done an admirable job following in the tradition established by Betty Rosenberg, who wrote the first two editions. This newest edition also includes a chapter on Historical Fiction, in addition to the traditional chapters on Westerns, Crime (including "Detective Story and Detectives," "Suspense," "Crime/Caper," "Legal Thriller"), Adventure (including "Spy/Espionage," "Techno-thrillers," "Biothrillers," "Financial Intrigue/Espionage," "Political Intrigue and Terrorism," "Survival," "Male Romance," "Military and Naval Adventure," "Male–Action/Adventure Series"), Science Fiction, Fantasy, Horror, and Romance. Herald defines these various genres, analyzes their characteristics by grouping authors according to type or subject matter, discusses subject content, and provides a selective annotated bibliography of history and criticism of each genre. Chapters also include a list of award winners, useful reference sources, and addresses for online resources. Author/title, subject, and series characters indexes provide excellent access.

The "Themes and Types" section under each genre is invaluable if we are looking for a list of Mysteries that feature cooking or parodies of the Science Fiction genre. Herald has expanded her genre definitions in the latest edition, and she has also added information on the appeal of the genre and tips for working with readers.

Janet Husband and Jonathan F. Husband. *Sequels: An Annotated Guide to Novels in Series.*[3]

Organized alphabetically by author, each entry includes an introduction to the author; it may cover style, relation to other authors, and similar authors. Novels are annotated briefly. The third edition has expanded coverage of genre titles, especially in Science Fiction/Fantasy. Subject and title indexes provide access to entries. The subject index includes geographic locations, character types (e.g., amateur detective), and names.

This is the book I hand to someone who is reading a series but is not quite certain what she has read and what comes next. The one-line descriptions allow readers to see readily whether or not they have read a book. These authors are also among the very best at encapsulating an author's style and appeal. If staff want to know how to describe books and authors, have them browse here.

What's Next? A List of Books in Series.[4]

Available in book form annually for a nominal fee, the Web version is free and is an easy way to check for series information, as it is updated continuously. Searching can be done by author, titles, or series name. There are no annotations and no information about publishers, but this is still the perfect source to use to print up a quick list of series titles in order for a waiting reader.

Merle Jacob and Hope Apple. *To Be Continued: An Annotated Guide to Sequels.*[5]

This source covers sequels in nineteenth- and twentieth-century mainstream and genre fiction with nearly 2,000 entries in the new edition.

The book is organized alphabetically by author and includes title, genre, subject, literary forms, and time/place indexes. Each entry lists the index terms, so one can gain a better understanding of the series from the entry and more easily discover matching points. Mysteries and series written by many authors, such as *Star Trek,* are excluded. Data from this volume are included on *NoveList,* described below.

The extensive indexes are invaluable in exploring a genre or subject, and the annotations are inviting and informative. That the material is also searchable electronically on *NoveList* increases the usefulness of this tool. Although the scope and coverage are amazing, the lack of Mystery coverage is a drawback.

Barron et al., eds. *What Do I Read Next? A Reader's Guide to Current Genre Fiction.*[6] Also available on Galenet and in some cumulative volumes organized by genre.

The most recent version of this popular tool covers Popular Fiction, Mystery, Romance, Western, Fantasy, Horror, Historical, Inspirational, Multi-Cultural, and Science Fiction. Each section, compiled by experts in the genre, includes entries for books published during the year. Entries give author, title, series information, story type, names of major characters, time period, locale, plot summary, review citations, additional titles by author, and "other books you might like." There are also essays describing "The Year" in each genre (available in the book version only), lists of award winners, and numerous useful indexes, including series, time period, geographic, genre, subject, character name, character description, author, and title. Although the same information is available on the Web version, the search strategies work differently. Web searches include specific search screens for Author, Title, and Custom (where you can select from genre/story type, subject, location, time period, character descriptor, and character name) and Browse searches (Help me find a book, Genre Search, Award Winners and Top Picks, Who? What? Where? When? which allows searching with those pieces of information). New in the 2000 version, the Popular Fiction section includes more literary authors.

We have both the annual volumes and the Web version of this useful tool. Although the original book volumes were more limited in scope, covering only Romance, Westerns, Mystery, Science Fiction,

Fantasy, and Horror, the newer books and Web version cover a broader range of genre and popular fiction. By manipulating the indexes or pull-down menus on the Web version, one can locate genres related to those covered, such as Adventure and Psychological Suspense.

NoveList[7]

Created and managed by Readers' Advisor Duncan Smith, *NoveList*, a Web-based resource, provides access to almost 100,000 adult, young adult, and children's fiction titles, many annotated. (Annotations come primarily from *Booklist, Library Journal, School Library Journal, Rendezvous,* and *Publisher's Weekly.*) The menu offers searches by Author, Title, and Subject (either by entering words that describe a plot or by typing in a more general term and selecting from that and related headings). There are other features of particular interest to Readers' Advisors: Explore Fiction provides the information from *Genreflecting* and links to full records in the database; Best Fiction includes lists of awards and winners, again with links to the full entry in the database; Feature Articles are written on a theme and include an annotated list of authors and titles; Book Discussion Guides; Book Talks; and For Staff Only, which provides professional continuing education materials for Readers' Advisors.

Although this tool provides valuable access to popular and classic fiction and easy search strategies, what sets it apart is that it is also the only one of the tools that offers ongoing readers' advisory training. Smith's commitment to continuing education, in addition to continually improving coverage and ease of access, make this a valuable resource on several levels.

Fiction_L[8]

This Readers' Advisors' maillist, created by Roberta Johnson and maintained at the Morton Grove Public Library, Illinois, is the place to post any questions regarding fiction, genres, authors, or readers' advisory in general. If you are interested in Internet resources specific to a genre, post a query on this maillist to receive up-to-the-minute information on sites. Archives are fully searchable and provide access to all topical lists created by members, as well as to messages on all subjects discussed. This excellent maillist links Readers' Advisors to a worldwide network. To subscribe to the regular version of the list or to the digest version, send mail to requests@maillist.webrary.org, with one of the following commands in the body of message: subscribe fiction_l (to subscribe to the regular list) or subscribe digest fiction_l (to subscribe to the digest).

Contemporary Authors.[9]

This is a standard reference source of value to Readers' Advisors, as the extensive coverage of popular authors includes many described in this book. In addition to a complete bibliography for each author, the "Sidelights" section features a useful description of the author and his works, as well as occasional author interviews.

Read-Alikes

The second hardest question posed to Readers' Advisors (after "Can you help me find a good book?") is, "Who else writes just like X?" then fill in the blank with the patron's favorite author. Be wary of tools that claim to provide this information. How can one know who writes like that author if one does not know what it is about the author that the reader enjoys? We help readers find this information by listening to what they like about an author and suggesting possibilities that may provide the same satisfactions. When we make lists at my library, we try to be careful and open about what characteristics we are matching. For example, our list of read-alikes for Rosamunde Pilcher, when everyone was clamoring for her books after the publication of *Winter Solstice,* defined the authors we listed as writing similarly "heartwarming and family-centered" books.[10]

NoveList provides similar authors through subject matching, allowing readers to match all subjects or to view a list of possible subjects and choose the ones they are particularly interested in. *What Do I Read Next?* also offers lists of "other books you might like" but offers no explanation for the matches, although they seem also to be subject based.

All of us who work with readers know that subject matches are not enough, and we hope that these tools will become sophisticated enough to allow us to go beyond that. Until then, the lists generated by these sources are a place to start in our own searches or for patrons who are looking for read-alikes. We can evaluate the names listed, pursue additional clues, and often find useful names to suggest.

NOTES

1. *Fiction Catalog,* 13th ed. (New York: Wilson, 1996).

2. Diana Tixier Herald, *Genreflecting: A Guide to Reading Interests in Genre Fiction,* 5th ed. (Englewood, Colo.: Libraries Unlimited, 2000).

3. Janet Husband and Jonathan F. Husband, *Sequels: An Annotated Guide to Novels in Series,* 3d ed. (Chicago: American Library Assn., 1997).

4. *What's Next? A List of Books in Series* [Online], (Grand Rapids, Mich.: Kent District Library, 2000 [cited February 26, 2001]); available at <http://www.kentlibrary.lib.mi.us/whats_next.htm>.

5. Merle Jacob and Hope Apple, *To Be Continued: An Annotated Guide to Sequels,* 2d ed. (Phoenix: Oryx, 2000).

6. Barron et al., eds. *What Do I Read Next? A Reader's Guide to Current Genre Fiction* (Detroit: Gale, 1990–); available at <http://www.galenet.com>.

7. *NoveList:* Web-based resource [Online], (Ipswich, Mass.: EBSCO, 1994 [cited March 28, 2001]); available at <http://novelist.epnet.com>.

8. Fiction_L [Online], (Morton Grove, Ill.: Morton Grove Public Library, 1995 [cited March 28, 2001]); available at <http://fiction_l@maillist.webrary.org>.

9. *Contemporary Authors* (Detroit: Gale, 1962–).

10. Rosamunde Pilcher, *Winter Solstice* (New York: St. Martin's, 2000).

The Five-Book Challenge

In her excellent introduction to the Romance genre, *The Romance Readers' Advisory: The Librarian's Guide to Love in the Stacks,* author Ann Bouricius issues her "Five-Book Challenge": Read five books in a new genre every year to gain an understanding of that genre.[1] In the spirit of that challenge, I offer five authors and titles in each of the fifteen genres covered in this guide. These are suggestions, culled from the titles mentioned in each chapter. However, I have made an attempt to acknowledge the range of each genre's appeal, to name popular authors and titles that will stand you in good stead with fans if you read them. I hope these will provide a starting place for your exploration of a genre and its appeal and, more importantly, that you will enjoy what you discover.

Adventure

Clive Cussler. Each action-filled novel in Cussler's series pits quintessential contemporary Adventure hero Dirk Pitt, an inventive and resourceful protagonist, against terrible odds and nefarious villains in satisfying, over-the-top tales of derring-do on the high seas and beyond. *Atlantis Found* finds Pitt up against an evil plot to flood the world.[2]

Dorothy Dunnett.   Many of us became Dunnett's loyal fans after discovering Francis Crawford of Lymond, second son of a Scottish lord, who seeks the truth of his background and his future as he travels across Europe, the Middle East, and even Russia in a series of six novels set during the sixteenth century. *The Game of Kings* is the first.[3]

W. E. B. Griffin.   In his recent *In Danger's Path,* Griffin returns to his popular hero Fleming Pickering of the Marine Corps and his ongoing adventures, this time on a rescue mission in the Gobi Desert during World War II, in this typical, action-filled military Adventure.[4]

Patrick O'Brian.   *Master and Commander* sets the stage for this popular series of historical Military Adventure, set during the Napoleonic Wars and featuring Captain Jack Aubrey and his friend, surgeon (and spy) Stephen Maturin.[5]

Wilbur Smith.   First identified to me by a patron who called him "the English Robert Ludlum," Smith, a native of South Africa, sets most of his novels on that continent. Frames vary widely but often feature Military Adventure as well as historical details. *Birds of Prey* chronicles the escapades of seventeenth-century pirate Sir Francis Courtney.[6]

Fantasy

Terry Brooks.   With novels that cover many popular Fantasy subgenres, from the Shannara epic quest series to the humorous Magic Kingdom novels and the darker Demon series, Brooks remains one of the genre's mainstay authors. *Magic Kingdom for Sale—Sold!* sends the reader to the Landover, where lawyer Ben Holiday finds old problems and new in his alternative reality.[7]

Robert Jordan.   A direct descendant of the Tolkien tradition but with more military details and political infighting, Jordan is known for his massive, epic quest, the Wheel of Time series, which continues to attract fans. Start with *The Eye of the World,* in which a young shepherd gathers his comrades for the battle against the growing evil.[8]

Terry Pratchett.   Novels set in the Discworld exemplify the satirical side of the Fantasy genre. In Pratchett's long-running series nothing escapes the humorous barbs of his parody. Try *Carpe Jugulum* as an example.[9]

J. K. Rowling.   Begin the adventures of Harry Potter with the first volume, *Harry Potter and the Sorcerer's Stone,* but you may want to continue following his coming of age at Hogwarts School of Witchcraft and Wizardry.[10] By book 4, *Harry Potter and the Goblet of Fire,* the classic themes of the genre have been unveiled, and the series proves not just for children but for all readers who appreciate the genre's magic.

J. R. R. Tolkien.   A classic author whose influence dominates much late-twentieth-century Fantasy, Tolkien is best known for his Lord of the Rings Trilogy, beginning with *The Fellowship of the Ring.*[11] A seemingly impossible quest, the age-old battle between good and evil, and a variety of lovable and horrible characters make this wonderful reading for a wide age range.

Gentle Reads

Eva Ibbotson.   Not prolific enough for her fans, Ibbotson sets her gentle domestic dramas in Europe, often in Austria. *A Song for Summer* is typical of her heartwarming stories with characters we love.[12]

Jan Karon.   Readers, even fans of Gentle Reads, either love or hate Karon. Her cheerful stories follow the adventures of Episcopal priest Father Timothy Kavanagh and his flock in Mitford, North Carolina. *At Home in Mitford* is the first.[13]

Terry Kay.   *To Dance with the White Dog* is a classic example of Kay's books, which are generally lyrical, although often bittersweet, stories of friendship and love.[14]

Rosamunde Pilcher.   She started as a writer of romantic novels, but Pilcher's later titles are quintessential Gentle Reads. Charming stories, interesting characters, and beautifully drawn settings add to the appeal of her books. *Winter Solstice* is a recent title.[15]

Nicholas Sparks. Like Karon, Sparks writes of small-town life, and like Kay, of friendship and love. *A Walk to Remember,* which looks back on an unlikely high school romance, captures his style.[16]

Historical Fiction

Bernard Cornwell. Considered in greater detail in chapter 2, "Adventure," Cornwell also provides a good introduction to Historical Fiction, as his series are praised for their accurate historical detail and the historical notes that set each book in the context of a particular military battle. *Rebel,* the first of the Starbuck Chronicles and set in the U.S. Civil War, is a good starting point.[17]

Cecelia Holland. With novels set in the United States and around the world, Holland covers more territory than most writers of the genre with her well-researched stories, peopled with fascinating characters, both real and fictional. The recent *Lily Nevada* explores late-nineteenth-century San Francisco and a traveling theater troupe.[18]

Edith Pargeter. Known primarily now for her Brother Cadfael series of Historical Mysteries under the pseudonym Ellis Peters, Pargeter is also an acclaimed author of more straightforward Historical Fiction. Try the Heaven Tree Trilogy, which displays her excellent storytelling skills and eye for historical detail.[19]

Sharon Kay Penman. Skilled at weaving historical events, biography, and period details, Penman offers elegantly written and richly told stories. Try *The Sunne in Splendour,* which chronicles the life and times of Richard III.[20] (Penman also writes a series of Historical Mysteries, set in the time of Henry II and Eleanor of Aquitaine.)

Michael Shaara. Shaara won a Pulitzer Prize for *The Killer Angels,* an emotional, evocative examination of the Battle of Gettysburg, told through the eyes of the men who fought there.[21] Son Jeff, in three additional novels, has expanded the stories before and after that event, creating a poignant and inspiring view of mid–nineteenth century U.S. military history.

Horror

Laurell K. Hamilton. Vampires are a popular Horror theme, and Hamilton places her popular vampire hunter, Anita Blake, along with her human and supernatural companions, in St. Louis in a near-future time when even the Undead have rights. *Guilty Pleasures* is the first installment.[22]

Shirley Jackson. This classic writer of Horror tales provides an excellent introduction to the haunting, psychological stories that comprise another aspect of the genre's appeal for Horror fans, as well as readers of Literary Fiction and Psychological Suspense. In her stories one can feel and sense the evil, sometimes even before one sees it, as in Jackson's classic psychological ghost story, *The Haunting of Hill House.*[23]

Stephen King. King's books are generally characterized by sympathetic, although certainly haunted, protagonists, a "normal" environment into which the Horror intrudes, and a long buildup to the horrific situation. In *The Shining,* young Danny battles evil in a mountaintop hotel where his father has taken a job as a winter caretaker.[24]

Dean R. Koontz. In his classic Horror tale *Watchers,* the Horror builds as we follow the fates of two animals who escape from a genetic engineering laboratory.[25] One has near-human intelligence and adopts a family, but he and they are in danger as the other, a beast bred to kill, stalks them.

Anne Rice. In sharp contrast to the novels of King and Koontz, Rice tells her stories from the evil's point of view, creating a more disturbing feel. Try *Interview with the Vampire* to explore this intense atmosphere.[26]

Literary Fiction

Isabel Allende. A prominent voice among Latin American writers, Allende reflects on issues, past and present, in her native Chile and beyond. *Daughter of Fortune* relates a rich story of love and family set in nineteenth-century Chile and California.[27]

Margaret Atwood.   Elegant, layered novels focusing on serious topics (but not without a strong measure of wit and often humor), Atwood's award-winning fiction generally features topics related to women and their lives. *The Blind Assassin* is a recent example.[28]

John Irving.   Irving, whose success was firmly established with *The World according to Garp,* in 1978, exhibits an unmistakable style that attracts readers, and although there are always darker moments in his novels, the upbeat, optimistic tone is another draw.[29]

Anne Tyler.   Known for her quirky, yet familiar characters and accessible, satisfying stories, all Tyler's books display her unique characters and style. In the Pulitzer Prize–winning *Breathing Lessons,* a journey to a funeral brings resolution and a rebirth of affection to Maggie and Ira Moran.[30]

John Updike.   With his quartet of novels plotting the state of America as seen through the life of Harry Angstrom (*Rabbit, Run* is the first of this series of four titles, each published a decade apart), Updike has secured his reputation as one of the premiere writers of this genre.[31]

Mysteries

Janet Evanovich.   Evanovich playfully parodies the hard-boiled genre, releasing a Lucille Ball–Ethel Mertz-type team on the bail-bond jumpers of New Jersey. Humor, from bounty-hunter-in-training Stephanie Plum to her eccentric grandmother, and a range of villains, from deadly to inept, abounds, but a measure of sex and violence takes these beyond the confines of the Cozy Mystery. Start with *One for the Money.*[32]

P. D. James.   James writes complex, layered novels of detection, following the exploits of Scotland Yard Commander Adam Dalgleish. Critically acclaimed best-sellers, these are read by fans of Mysteries as well as those who appreciate character-driven Literary Fiction. *A Certain Justice* is a recent example.[33]

Jonathan Kellerman.   Kellerman's popular series features complex plots, building tension, and interesting characters in his protagonist, child psychologist–amateur detective Alex Delaware, and his friend Milo Sturgis, a policeman on the Los Angeles force. The recent *Monster,* although more violent than many of his Mysteries, is a good example.[34]

Robert B. Parker. Parker refined and updated the hard-boiled detective formula, creating Spenser, a detective with '90s sensibilities but the muscle demanded by the formula. Descriptive scenes of Boston and the Northeast, witty dialogue, strong and sympathetic characters, action and building tension, and stories that pull readers into the characters and the problems they face characterize his books. Try *Double Deuce* as an example of his style.[35]

Anne Perry. Perry sets her two popular Historical Mystery series in nineteenth-century England. The first, generally lighter in tone, features Inspector Pitt and his aristocratic wife, Charlotte. *The Cater Street Hangman* is the first.[36] The second, set later in the century and beginning with *The Face of a Stranger,* follows William Monk, a policeman who has lost his memory in an accident.[37] These are bleaker, evocative, more atmospheric Mysteries.

Psychological Suspense

Thomas H. Cook. An author of disturbing stories set in past and present, Cook creates haunted protagonists, forced to explore their own pasts as well as the cases they investigate in the present. *Instruments of Night* is an example of the complicated, layered, and atmospheric story that results.[38]

Stephen Dobyns. Known also for his humorous horse-racing Mystery series, Dobyns writes compelling, paranoiac novels of Psychological Suspense. *The Church of Dead Girls* relates the details of a past crime in a claustrophobic tale of small-town life and murder.[39]

Patricia Highsmith. Classic author of Psychological Suspense, Highsmith builds Suspense as her protagonists flail helplessly out of control in a nightmare world. *Strangers on a Train* exemplifies her style, with the story pervaded by the dark, menacing atmosphere and the sense that the outcome is inescapable.[40]

Ruth Rendell/Barbara Vine.   Under both names English novelist Rendell writes elegant, gripping stories of psychological obsession. *Sight for Sore Eyes* is a recent example.[41] (Be aware that as Rendell she also writes a series of English Police Detective Mysteries featuring Chief Inspector Wexford.)

Minette Walters.   Often cataloged in the Mystery section, Walters's writing exemplifies elements of both genres with its atmospheric puzzles, open endings, complex but unbalanced characters, psychological implications, and elegant style. *The Scold's Bridle* provides a good introduction.[42]

Romance

Jennifer Crusie.   A recent addition to the Romance hierarchy, best-seller Crusie offers humor; interesting, well-developed characters in complex relationships; quirky story lines; and elements of Mystery and Suspense along with satisfying Romance. Try her recent *Welcome to Temptation*.[43]

Julie Garwood.   Humor, passion, and family ties feature prominently in Garwood's Historical Romances, most recently set in the United States. *For the Roses* exemplifies her style and introduces the Clayborne family, featured in subsequent novels.[44]

Jayne Ann Krentz/Amanda Quick/Jayne Castle.   Like Nora Roberts, Krentz is a publishing phenomenon, and her writing covers all Romance subgenres. Witty dialogue, humorous situations, explicit sex, and elements of Adventure and Suspense characterize her best-selling novels. Try *Mistress* (historical), *Wildest Hearts* (contemporary), or *Amaryllis* (futuristic) to sample her writing style.[45]

Debbie Macomber.   Popular writer Macomber's gentle, domestic Romances are favored by readers who prefer conventional to modern values and innocent heroines in heartwarming stories of love and family. *Lonesome Cowboy*, first in her Hearts of Texas series, is a good starting point.[46]

Nora Roberts. For many readers, Roberts and her books define the Romance genre. Try her recent Irish trilogy, starting with *Jewels of the Sun*, for a feel of her books with their passionate, resourceful heroines; strong, empathetic heroes; and family emphasis.[47]

Romantic Suspense

Sandra Brown. Many Romance fans have followed Brown as she has crossed genres and established herself firmly as a writer of Romantic Suspense. *The Witness* is a classic title, with Romance and fairly Hard-Edged Suspense carefully intertwined to create a fast-paced story.[48]

Linda Howard. Like Nora Roberts, Howard continues to publish category Romances, but her hardcover novels of Romantic Suspense have found their place on best-sellers lists and an audience among Romance and Suspense fans. The recent *Mr. Perfect* combines strong romantic elements, and even humor early on, with heightened Suspense.[49]

Iris Johansen. Formerly a writer of Historical Romances, Johansen now creates page-turning novels of Hard-Edged Romantic Suspense. Stalking, graphic violence, building of Suspense, and an undercurrent of Romance characterize her recent titles, such as *The Killing Game*.[50]

Elizabeth Lowell. Strong romantic relationships form the basis of Lowell's novels, which also feature explicit violence, sex, and language, as well as Adventure and Suspense elements and interesting frames. *Jade Island*, one of the series featuring the Donovan family, displays her best-selling form.[51]

Nora Roberts. In her novels of Romantic Suspense, Roberts portrays strong women in difficult situations, explicit violence, and strong sexual themes. Her heroines are supported by caring family, lovers, and friends, who may also be put in danger but who ultimately help to resolve the problem and escape danger. *River's End* exemplifies what is currently most popular in the genre.[52]

Science Fiction

Lois McMaster Bujold. With her characteristic wit and romantic touches, Bujold leads readers through political machinations and military adventures on the planet Barryar and beyond in her popular Vor series. Action and elegant language, as well as interesting scientific detail and speculation, characterize this series, which begins with *Shards of Honor.*[53]

Orson Scott Card. If you have time to read only one Science Fiction novel, make it Card's *Ender's Game,* a coming-of-age story set in the future, featuring moral, social, and philosophical issues.[54] This is a book to be appreciated and explored on many levels.

Kim Stanley Robinson. Robinson's issue-oriented novels provide copious scientific detail and technology. Interesting characters, effective use of language, and a distinct literary style characterize his work. He is best known for his award-winning Mars Trilogy (*Red Mars, Green Mars,* and *Blue Mars*), which describes the terra forming and civilization of that planet.[55]

Mary Doria Russell. Russell made her mark on the Science Fiction genre with her first novel, *The Sparrow,* an elegantly and densely written, idea-centered, philosophical novel, peopled with multi-dimensional characters.[56] This classic title transcends genre boundaries and appeals to a wide range of readers, especially fans of Literary Fiction.

Connie Willis. Winner of multiple Hugo and Nebula Awards, Willis writes novels and short stories known for their finely drawn (usually female) characters, effective use of language, wit (sometimes subtle, sometimes laugh-out-loud), scholarship, and complicated, well-researched story lines. *Doomsday Book,* a story of a time-travel experiment gone awry, is one of her best-known works.[57]

Suspense

Mary Higgins Clark. The traditional Clark formula features roller-coaster pacing; appealing heroines placed in dangerous situations from which they try to extricate themselves; and plots that center around timely topics. While the body and violence are kept offstage, there is a real sense of danger created as the villain stalks the heroine. *We'll Meet Again* provides a good introduction to her writing.[58]

Jeffrey Deaver. Although it does not feature Deaver's series character Lincoln Rhyme (he only makes a token appearance), Deaver's *The Devil's Teardrop* demonstrates the genre's frantic pacing, as the story takes place in fewer than twenty-four hours.[59]

James Patterson. Alex Cross, Patterson's detective-psychologist hero, pulls readers into these fast-paced, violent, and compulsively readable novels of Hard-Edged Suspense, with details of the crime and the criminal, as well as the police procedures. Start with *Along Came a Spider.*[60]

Thomas Perry. Perry's excellent series featuring Native American Jane Whitefield, who constructs new identities for people on the run, exemplifies some of the best Suspense writing. *Vanishing Act,* the first adventure, is characterized by an evocative, menacing atmosphere; an intelligent, inventive female protagonist; elegant prose; and dense writing that nevertheless propels the reader to the denouement.[61]

John Sandford. Author of the Prey series, featuring Minneapolis detective Lucas Davenport, in addition to several nonseries Suspense titles, Sandford writes elegant novels that offer strong characterizations and fast-paced, often-violent, Suspense. *Rules of Prey* is the first in the series.[62]

Thriller

David Baldacci. With plots that focus on topics such as corporate corruption, financial manipulation, and abuse of power in the presidency, Baldacci appeals to a wide range of readers who look for intricately plotted, fast-paced stories of conspiracy and corruption. *Absolute Power* makes a good introduction to his work.[63]

Tom Clancy. Clancy's trademark Techno-Thrillers offer a community of men, seldom invaded by women, and trained military men as heroes. These men save their comrades and their country through wit and ingenuity, not to mention the wide array of weaponry they handle with such skill and finesse. *The Hunt for Red October* introduced hero Jack Ryan and created this subgenre.[64]

Robin Cook. Cook remains the preeminent writer of Medical Thrillers, and his fast-paced, crusading stories raise questions of medical ethics as they offer details of the profession. *Toxin* represents a recent example of his style.[65]

Michael Crichton. Scientific Thrillers by the popular Crichton continue to top the best-sellers lists. Copious scientific details, a crusading hero, story lines out of the news or certainly within the realm of scientific possibility, and fast pacing characterize Crichton's novels. *Jurassic Park* is a genre classic.[66]

John Grisham. If Legal Thrillers are currently the most popular type of Thriller, Grisham certainly tops the growing list of writers in the subgenre. His first, *The Firm,* remains an excellent example of his cinematic style, which blends Adventure, Intrigue, and Suspense, with convoluted plots that feature a good-guy lawyer fighting corruption.[67]

Westerns

Don Coldsmith. One of the top Western authors, Coldsmith is best known for his Spanish Bit series, which follows the cultural development of the Plains Indians from the arrival of the Spanish Conquistadors to the early eighteenth century. The first is *The Trail of the Spanish Bit*.[68] His novels capture the spirit of the West and the Western with his evocative settings, characters, and themes.

Will Henry. Prolific writer of Westerns, Henry often depicts a disappearing West, a landscape that provides difficult living for those like the eponymous Tom Horn (*I, Tom Horn*), who were born a generation too late for the real West and find it impossible to cope with its current form.[69] Nostalgia for a lost time and landscape often characterizes his books, which accurately describe Indians as well as white men in the West.

Elmer Kelton. Preeminent among contemporary Western writers, Kelton offers less-than-mythic heroes in detail-rich Western landscapes. His character-centered novels, which often feature young men in difficult situations, rely less on action and more on characters placed in realistic, believable situations. *The Pumpkin Rollers* is a good introduction to his work.[70]

Louis L'Amour. L'Amour stands as proof that, in the Western genre at least, classic authors remain popular; his Adventure-filled Westerns still thrill readers. Action plays a role in every chapter, and he pulls readers into the stories with his inviting characters and detailed descriptions of the terrain. Try *Hondo,* which boasts all the trademark elements of the traditional Western.[71]

Larry McMurtry. Although McMurtry may differ from other Western writers with his elegant style and expansive novels, his writing reflects the same passionate view that characterizes the genre: leisurely paced novels of a loner, set in an evocative and dangerous Western landscape. While *Lonesome Dove* depicts the quintessential cattle drive, among other things, *Horseman Pass By* reflects the modern West.[72]

Women's Lives and Relationships

Elizabeth Berg. Although Oprah also tapped her for her Book Club, Berg has been popular in libraries for a number of years. It is her earlier titles that fans remember fondly and share with their friends, as these seem to have captured emotional depths and set the feelings and issues in lyrical prose. Try her first, *Durable Goods,* a thoughtful coming-of-age story, as an example of her style.[73]

Maeve Binchy. Irish writer Binchy writes character-centered books that touch a chord that resonates across the Atlantic. Her stories are evocative, descriptive of both geography and character, and although they do not always produce happy endings, stories are resolved in a way that leave readers satisfied. *Tara Road* was also one of Oprah's Book Club selections.[74]

Barbara Delinsky. Popular for her leisurely paced stories of women wronged who bring their lives together again, Delinsky writes charming stories with inviting heroines. *Lake News,* the story of a woman whose career is destroyed when she is unjustly accused by the press of having an affair with a cardinal, also exhibits Delinsky's characteristic themes of healing and building trust.[75]

Danielle Steel. Steel continues to writes touching and satisfying stories that feature strong female characters, timeless values (love for children, home, and family), a romantic and often sentimental tone, rich-and-famous elements (brand names, designer labels, etc.), and the issues that women face in their lives, from divorce and breast cancer to problems with children. Although it is atypically short, *The Gift* offers an example of her style.[76]

Joanna Trollope. Trollope's popularity has been enhanced by several PBS renditions of her works. She writes comfortable, layered stories of English middle-class life—of love, friendship, family—that consistently satisfy her fans. *Other People's Children* is a recent example.[77]

NOTES

1. Ann Bouricius, *The Romance Readers' Advisory: The Librarian's Guide to Love in the Stacks* (Chicago: American Library Assn., 2000), p. 67.

2. Clive Cussler, *Atlantis Found* (New York: Putnam, 1999).

3. Dorothy Dunnett, *The Game of Kings* (New York: Putnam, 1961).

4. W. E. B. Griffin, *In Danger's Path* (New York: Putnam, 1998).

5. Patrick O'Brian, *Master and Commander* (Philadelphia: Lippincott, 1969).

6. Wilbur Smith, *Birds of Prey* (New York: St. Martin's, 1997).

7. Terry Brooks, *Magic Kingdom for Sale—Sold!* (New York: Ballantine, 1986).

8. Robert Jordan, *The Eye of the World* (New York: T. Doherty Associates, 1990).

9. Terry Pratchett, *Carpe Jugulum* (New York: HarperPrism, 1999).

10. J. K. Rowling, *Harry Potter and the Sorcerer's Stone* (New York: Arthur A. Levine Books, 1998).

11. J. R. R. Tolkien, *The Fellowship of the Ring: Being the First Part of the Lord of the Rings* (Boston: Houghton, 1965).

12. Eva Ibbotson, *A Song for Summer* (New York: St. Martin's, 1998, © 1997).

13. Jan Karon, *At Home in Mitford* (New York: Viking, 1998).

14. Terry Kay, *To Dance with the White Dog* (Atlanta: Peachtree Publishers, 1990).

15. Rosamunde Pilcher, *Winter Solstice* (New York: St. Martin's, 2000).

16. Nicholas Sparks, *A Walk to Remember* (New York: Warner Books, 1999).

17. Bernard Cornwell, *Rebel* (New York: HarperCollins, 1993).

18. Cecelia Holland, *Lily Nevada* (New York: Forge, 1999).

19. Edith Pargeter, *The Heaven Tree Trilogy* (New York: Warner Books, 1993).

20. Sharon Kay Penman, *The Sunne in Splendour* (New York: Holt, 1982).

21. Michael Shaara, *The Killer Angels* (New York: McKay, 1974).

22. Laurell K. Hamilton, *Guilty Pleasures* (New York: Ace Books, 1993).

23. Shirley Jackson, *The Haunting of Hill House* (New York: Viking, 1959).

24. Stephen King, *The Shining* (Garden City, N.Y.: Doubleday, 1977).

25. Dean R. Koontz, *Watchers* (New York: Putnam, 1987).

26. Anne Rice, *Interview with the Vampire* (New York: Knopf, 1976).

27. Isabel Allende, *Daughter of Fortune* (New York: HarperCollins, 1999).

28. Margaret Atwood, *The Blind Assassin* (New York: Doubleday, 2000).

29. John Irving, *The World according to Garp* (New York: E. P. Dutton, 1978).

30. Anne Tyler, *Breathing Lessons* (New York: Knopf, 1988).

31. John Updike, *Rabbit, Run* (New York: Knopf, 1960).

32. Janet Evanovich, *One for the Money* (New York: Scribner, 1994).

33. P. D. James, *A Certain Justice* (New York: Random House, 1997).

34. Jonathan Kellerman, *Monster* (New York: Random House, 1999).

35. Robert B. Parker, *Double Deuce* (New York: Putnam, 1992).

36. Anne Perry, *The Cater Street Hangman* (New York: Simon & Schuster, 1999).

37. ———, *The Face of a Stranger* (New York: Fawcett, 1990).

38. Thomas H. Cook, *Instruments of Night* (New York: Bantam, 1998).

39. Stephen Dobyns, *The Church of Dead Girls* (New York: Metropolitan Books, 1997).

40. Patricia Highsmith, *Strangers on a Train* (New York: Harper & Brothers, 1950).

41. Ruth A. Rendell, *Sight for Sore Eyes* (New York: Crown, 1999).

42. Minette Walters, *The Scold's Bridle* (New York: St. Martin's, 1994).

43. Jennifer Crusie, *Welcome to Temptation* (New York: St. Martin's, 2000).

44. Julie Garwood, *For the Roses* (New York: Pocket Books, 1995).

45. Amanda Quick, *Mistress* (New York: Bantam, 1994); Jayne Ann Krentz, *Wildest Hearts* (New York: Pocket Books, 1993); Jayne Castle, *Amaryllis* (New York: Pocket Star Books, 1996).

46. Debbie Macomber, *Lonesome Cowboy* (Toronto and New York: Harlequin, 1998).

47. Nora Roberts, *Jewels of the Sun* (New York: Jove, 1999).

THE FIVE-BOOK CHALLENGE

48. Sandra Brown, *The Witness* (New York: Warner Books, 1995).

49. Linda Howard, *Mr. Perfect* (New York: Pocket Books, 2000).

50. Iris Johansen, *The Killing Game* (New York: Bantam, 1999).

51. Elizabeth Lowell, *Jade Island* (New York: Avon, 1998).

52. Roberts, *River's End* (New York: Putnam, 1999).

53. Lois McMaster Bujold, *Shards of Honor* (Riverdale, N.Y.: Baen, 1986).

54. Orson Scott Card, *Ender's Game* (New York: T. Doherty Associates, 1985).

55. Kim Stanley Robinson, *Red Mars* (New York: Bantam, 1993);———, *Green Mars* (New York: Bantam, 1994); ———, *Blue Mars* (New York: Bantam, 1996).

56. Mary Doria Russell, *The Sparrow* (New York: Villard, 1996).

57. Connie Willis, *Doomsday Book* (New York: Bantam, 1992).

58. Mary Higgins Clark, *We'll Meet Again* (New York: Simon & Schuster, 1999).

59. Jeffrey Deaver, *The Devil's Teardrop: A Novel of the Last Night of the Century* (New York: Simon & Schuster, 1999).

60. James Patterson, *Along Came a Spider* (Boston: Little, Brown, 1993).

61. Thomas Perry, *Vanishing Act* (New York: Random House, 1995).

62. John Sandford, *Rules of Prey* (New York: Putnam, 1989).

63. David Baldacci, *Absolute Power* (New York: Warner Books, 1996).

64. Tom Clancy, *The Hunt for Red October* (Annapolis, Md.: Naval Institute Press, 1984).

65. Robin Cook, *Toxin* (New York: Putnam, 1998).

66. Michael Crichton, *Jurassic Park* (New York: Knopf, 1990).

67. John Grisham, *The Firm* (New York: Doubleday, 1991).

68. Don Coldsmith, *The Trail of the Spanish Bit* (Garden City, N.Y.: Doubleday, 1980).

69. Will Henry, *I, Tom Horn* (New York: Bantam, 1975).

70. Elmer Kelton, *The Pumpkin Rollers* (New York: Forge, 1996).

71. Louis L'Amour, *Hondo* (New York: Fawcett, 1953).

72. Larry McMurtry, *Lonesome Dove* (New York: Simon & Schuster, 1985); ———, *Horseman Pass By* (New York: Harper, 1961).

73. Elizabeth Berg, *Durable Goods* (New York: Random House, 1998).

74. Maeve Binchy, *Tara Road* (New York: Delacorte, 1999).

75. Barbara Delinksy, *Lake News* (New York: Simon & Schuster, 1999).

76. Danielle Steel, *The Gift* (New York: Delacorte, 1994).

77. Joanna Trollope, *Other People's Children* (New York: Viking, 1999).

Index

Authors, editors, titles, subjects, and series are interfiled in
one alphabet. Authors print in roman, titles in italics,
subjects in boldface, and series in quotation marks.

Psychological Suspense *(continued)*
characteristics, 188–91
five-book challenge, 410–11
key authors, 191–93
and literary fiction, 140
reader expectations, 193–94
and suspense, 309
Publishers Weekly, 11
Pullliam, June Michele. *See Hooked on Horror*
Pullman, Philip, 44
Pumpkin Rollers (Kelton), 353, 416
Purser, Ann, 69
Putney, Mary Jo, 206, 214
Puzo, Mario, 330
puzzles in mysteries, 147, 165, 173
Pym, Barbara, 70
Pynchon, Thomas, 100, 128

Queen of Angels (Bear), 273
Queen's Man (Penman), 138
Queen's War (Mackin), 91
quest
and adventure, 31, 55
fantasy, 40, 50
and suspense, 308
and westerns, 364
questions, "real," 395–96
Quick, Amanda. *See also* Castle, Jayne; Krentz, Jayne Ann
five-book challenge, 411
historical romance, 206, 211, 214–15, 257
sexual situations, 228
Quicksand (Forbes), 333
"Quiller" series (Hall), 333
Quilter's Apprentice (Chiaverini), 64
Quindlen, Anna, 376, 385
"Quinn Brothers" trilogy (Roberts, N.), 209

Rabbit, Run (Updike), 133, 409
"racier Romances," 228
Racing the Music (Sheepshanks), 380
Radian Way (Drabble), 383
Ragman's Memory (Mayor), 163

Rainbow Six (Clancy), 339
Raise the Titanic (Cussler), 21–22, 28
"Raisin, Agatha" mysteries (Beaton), 75, 170
"Raj Quartet" (Scott, P.), 93
Rake (Putney), 206
Ramsdell, Kristin. *See Romance Fiction*
Ramus, David, 179, 329
Ranganathan's laws, 13
Rangers of the Lone Star (Grey), 358–59
Rankins, Ian, 162
Raptor (Jennings), 20
Ravelstein (Bellow), 133
Raven Ring (Wrede), 39
Ravished (Quick), 206
"Rawlings, Easy" mysteries (Mosley), 176
Rawn, Melanie, 48, 52, 233, 234
Ray, Francis, 213
Read, Miss, 67–70
read-alikes, 9, 402–3
reader expectations
adventure, 27–28
fantasy, 48–51
gentle reads, 70–71
historical fiction, 88–91
horror, 116–18
of librarians, 201, 395–96
literary fiction, 133–35
mysteries, 171–73
psychological suspense, 193–94
romance, 220–26
romantic suspense, 252–53
science fiction, 275–78
suspense, 302–3
thrillers, 339–40
westerns, 360–61
women's lives, 381–85
readers, embarrassment of
genre-denial syndrome, 221–22
readers' advisory interview, 8, 393–94
adventure, 29–32
fantasy, 51–53
gentle reads, 72–74
historical fiction, 91–95
horror, 118–20

Joyce G. Saricks has worked as coordinator of the Literature and Audio Services Department at the Downers Grove Public Library since 1983. In addition to coauthoring *Readers' Advisory Service in the Public Library* (ALA), she has written several articles on readers' advisory, presented more than seventy workshops on that topic for public libraries and library systems, and spoken at state, regional, and national library conferences. In 1989 she won the Public Library Association's Allie Beth Martin Award, and in 2000 she was named Librarian of the Year by the Romance Writers of America.